CW01617492

Self and Future Generations

Self and Future Generations

an intercultural conversation

edited by

Tae-Chang Kim

and

Ross Harrison

The White Horse Press

Copyright © The Future Generations Alliance Foundation 1999

First published 1999 by The White Horse Press, 10 High Street, Knapwell, Cambridge CB3 8NR, UK

Set in 11 point Adobe Garamond
Printed in Great Britain by Biddles Ltd, Guildford and King's Lynn

All rights reserved. Except for the quotation of short passages for the purpose of criticism and review, no part of this book may be reprinted or reproduced or utilised in any form or by any electronic, mechanical or other means, including photocopying or recording, or in any information storage or retrieval system, without permission from the publishers.

A catalogue record for this book is available from the British Library

ISBN 1-874267-37-5 (cloth bound)
1-874267-38-3 (paper)

Contents

Contributors

Yoon-Jae Chung is Associate Professor, The Academy of Korean Studies, Seoul, Korea. He was a Visiting Scholar, Centre of International Studies, University of Cambridge at the time of the conference.

John Dunn is Professor of Political Theory at the University of Cambridge, and a Fellow of King's College, Cambridge.

Ross Harrison is Reader in Philosophy at the University of Cambridge and a Fellow of King's College, Cambridge.

Takatoshi Imada is Professor of Sociology, Graduate School of Decision Science and Technology, Tokyo Institute of Technology, Tokyo, Japan.

Tae-Chang Kim is President, Institute for the Integrated Study of Future Generations, Kyoto, Japan and member, Board of Directors, Future Generations Alliance Foundation, New York, USA.

Masaya Kobayashi is Associate Professor, Faculty of Law and Economics, Chiba University, Chiba, Japan. He was a Visiting Scholar in the Faculty of Social and Political Sciences and Visiting Bye-Fellow at Selwyn College, Cambridge, 1995/6-97 and September 1998.

John O'Neill is Profesor of Philosophy, Philosophy Department, Lancaster University.

Onora O'Neill is Principal, Newnham College, Cambridge.

Edward Page is a Research assistant in the Department of Politics, Southampton University.

Takeshi Sasaki is Professor and Dean, Faculty of Law, University of Tokyo, Tokyo, Japan.

1

Introduction

Ross Harrison

We are people, separate people, and it is as such that we confront our world. It is a world which we do not only confront but also change and some of this change is harmful: harmful to the world, to its environment, to the people who live in it. It seems clear that if we continue in our current practices, the environment in which future generations will have to live will not be as favourable for them as our present environment has been for us.

Let us assume that this is the case, that we are harming the environment in which we live. Things are getting worse. Therefore, as a result of our present actions, other people, future people, will suffer. The fates and fortunes of future generations are in our hands and at the moment it does not seem that we are treating them very well. They are in our power; they have done us no wrong; yet we are harming them.

These people we harm are not us. They are other people. Yet they are still people, people like us. They have done us no wrong; they are, as far as we are concerned, innocent. So in reducing the quality of the environment for future generations we are making innocent people suffer, innocent people who are unfortunate enough to be in our power.

When innocent people suffer as a result of our actions, we normally think that this is wrong. It is something which should not happen or be allowed. It is something which we should be able to show to be theoretically mistaken, and for which we should be able to devise a political prophylactic. Yet we in fact run into peculiar problems in showing that this harm is wrong and in working out how to prevent it. The purpose of this collection of papers, contributed equally from thinkers from the East and thinkers from the West, is to tease out answers to these problems and to attempt to resolve them.

We may think that this sort of harm to the unborn is wrong because it is unfair (we are harming people who have not harmed us) or because it is a harm (our actions are reducing people's welfare, or quality of life). So it might seem simple to say that it is wrong. However the reason why it poses peculiar problems is quite simply because future generations do not yet exist. These future people are not here to speak for themselves or defend their interests or rights. This means that they are likely to be overlooked politically: only current voters have power in a democracy.

However it also causes more theoretical problems of justification. Much currently made justification of the good (or of right conduct) starts with people's interests and the effects which possible actions have on these interests. Yet future generations, as yet unexisting, do not as yet have interests. They are merely possible people; as yet there are no actual interests. Indeed, to take a point which Derek Parfit has made familiar, it depends partly upon us which of these possible people become actual. Many future people cannot have an actual interest in our having made the world better: for if we had made it better, they would not have existed, and so it would not have been better for them.

However quite apart from this particular point of their actuality depending upon us, the whole idea of justice to future generations is difficult to sustain, at least from a characteristically Western perspective. This is because much justification in the Western tradition starts from the basis of people's self-interest, either in a narrow or in a more enlightened perspective. To show that something is good for someone, that is, is to give them a reason for action. Such justifications do not need to be restricted to obvious and narrow self-interest, in which someone has a reason for promoting their own good as the expense of someone else. This kind of reasoning may also be used to provide justification for apparently more altruistic behaviour, such as behaving fairly or keeping contracts. For it can be argued if these kind of practices become conventionally established, they are generally speaking in people's own individual interest.

Yet if justification (in the Western tradition) tends to start with self-interest, then it is hard to see how this can justify treating future generations well. For it is hard to see what self-interest, even of an enlightened kind, could be served by the present generation engaging in such treatment. The state of the world long after we are dead does not seem to be of any self-interested benefit to us.

Of course even in the Western world, with respect to the people with whom we live, we do not seem to behave in any obviously self-interested way. However, these people we care for and look after are usually ones with whom we have immediate contact and reciprocal relations. It is this reciprocity of concern which is analysed by some people in terms of enlightened self-interest: you care for me, and I will care for you. On this can be founded implicit or explicit contracts or conventions of social life, and some rough system of justice. Generally speaking, we play fair with the people with whom we have to live; or, otherwise put, there is a mutually advantageous bargain in playing fair. However none of this applies with people who will only live long after we are dead. There is here no reciprocity, no mutual advantage. There is no such basis for contract or rough principles of justice.

Of course mutually advantageous bargains do not always correspond to what we might independently think of as just division of resources. It all depends upon the antecedent strengths of the bargaining parties. If they are roughly equal, the result may be roughly fair, or just. However, if they are greatly unequal, the strong are likely to exploit the weak to gain more than their fair share. In the case of future generations (if we think of it as modelled by some kind of bargain or contract) there is complete inequality of power. We, the present, have the future totally in our power. Any putative bargain struck will be badly biased towards our present interests. So there would seem to be here no basis for justice to future generations.

These reflections follow from a particularly narrow starting point, of which considerable use has been made in the Western tradition, namely self-interest. However it may be thought that the source of the damage is deeper, and it is another idea which lies behind this which is principally to blame. This is the idea of the self as a separate, atomistic, individual, with its self-contained and wholly separate interests. Without such selves, there would be nothing on which self-interest could work. Yet this deeper conception also seems to be something distinctively Western. It is something which plays a part even in non-self-interested Western value systems such as Kantianism or (some forms of) Utilitarianism. For in them it is held that the interests of any one of such atomistically separate selves should count as equal to any other. Again it would not be possible to state or promote the value without the idea of a separate, atomistic, individual. Yet it may be felt that it is the individualistic atomism which in itself does the damage, rather than the particular way in which this atomism feeds into the calculus of reasons.

We may, that is, think of the problem of our concern for future generations as a characteristically Western problem. So we may think that it stems from a particular (and, by implication, mistaken) Western way of conceiving the self. It is only if we think of selves as separate, atomic, entities which live, die and are then no more, that we have this problem. And yet although we may classify these ideas as Western, nevertheless the central assumptions involved here are spread through the whole contemporary world. Throughout the whole contemporary world it is assumed that we are separate people with separate lives and thoughts; that separate people have separate individual interests; and that collective political decision should take account of such separate and partially competing interests. These are the assumptions which form the basis of the currently successful (or dominant) industrial and economic system as well as its habitual democratic political environment. This system and some form of its political environment are currently spread through both East and West. In both the Eastern and the Western world individuals make and destroy things; individuals make and waste money; and have their individual votes solicited by their political masters.

This dominant political system is in danger of not delivering the goods, either in the East or the West. Both in the East and the West we have a problem of how we should proceed faced with the possibility of harming future generations. We have the same problem, but we may have different, and complementary, intellectual resources with which to face it. The examination and criticism of such resources, both Eastern and Western, is the point of the present volume. It represents a conversation, or encounter, between Western and Eastern thinkers. The papers are drawn about equally from East and West and display the attempts of a group of philosophers and social scientists to illuminate and resolve these difficult problems.

They also represent a particular encounter, or occasion. They start from a conference in which a group of Western and Eastern thinkers met together for three days in Cambridge, England in November 1996 in order to read and discuss earlier versions of the papers which follow.

Not all the papers printed here were read at the conference, nor is everyone's presentation to the conference included here. We had at the conference, for example, the benefit of a presentation of Peter Laslett's important ideas in this area as well as an incisive analysis from Anthony Giddens. We had a speech by Kido Inoue, Zen Master of the Geishu Tadanoumi Shorinkutsu Seminary. However, a revised version of the great majority of the papers at the conference are given here, and the great majority of the papers here were given at the conference. I hope that they manage to give the flavour of a unique and stimulating encounter. In it, I think, the Western contributors managed to show how much more can be extracted from the resources of the Western tradition than might have been expected from the rapid account which I have just given of it, and the Eastern contributors managed to show the riches which are available in their alternative traditions. The conference also put in some hard work, which has been subsequently developed into the central section of this volume, into resolution of Derek Parfit's problem about how the identity of future people depends upon present practices.

This short introduction is followed by a longer presentation by Professor Kobayashi in which he gives an account of the history of significant contributions to the future generations problem by both Western and Eastern thinkers before the Cambridge conference. He also outlines the significant role played in this by The Future Generations Alliance Foundation, of Kyoto, Japan. It was this foundation which sponsored the conference from which these papers came and which made the whole fruitful encounter possible. The conference was opened with an address by Katsuhiko Yazaki, the chairman of the foundation. I am sure I speak on behalf of the other contributors in thanking him and the foundation for the interesting and intellectually stimulating conference which they mounted in Cambridge. We all learnt from it, more, I think, than we had antecedently expected. I hope, in presenting this collection of the papers to a wider world, other people will also be able to participate in some of that stimulation and interest, as well as being guided some way towards a resolution of what are probably the most important problems facing the contemporary world.

2

Atomistic Self and Future Generations: A Critical Review from an Eastern Perspective

Masaya Kobayashi

1. Introduction

§1. Self and Future Generations

Let me start by quoting the first sentences of a classic article, 'Man and Politics', written by the greatest political theorist in the post-war period in Japan.

> Thinkers who seriously confront the question of politics have always taken up the study of humankind, namely, anthropology. Plato, Aristotle, Machiavelli, Hobbes, Locke, Bentham, Rousseau, Hegel, Marx, and Nietzsche; all of these people posed their political thinking on the issue of human nature and humanity. There is a profound reason for this.[1]

The author, Masao Maruyama, had a remarkable influence on both intellectual and public opinion after the second world war. He died on 15th August, 1996 – the anniversary of Japan's defeat 51 years earlier – and has been the subject of many memorial articles and much recent discussion in Japan. His main concern is considered to be the modernisation of Japanese culture by serious reflection on the past 'thought and behaviour'[2] of Japan, in particular, on the defeat in the war: he is the representative political liberalist of the post-war generation. While I myself am a critical follower of his thought as a researcher in a successive generation, I am afraid that my own view on human beings, which I discuss in this book, diverges to some extent from that of Maruyama, the great predecessor of Japanese political theory. However, since being so impressed by this article in my student years, I have never doubted that 'Self' is one of the most important issues for political theory. I suppose that it is not too much to say that it has long been a way of thinking in Japanese political theory to consider seriously the relation between human nature and politics.[3]

Consequently, when I heard that the Future Generations Alliance Foundation proposed the theme 'Self' to start discussion between East and West for the benefit of Future Generations, this theme sounded very natural for me. However, it became clear in organising this seminar that some Cambridge participants entertained doubts over the fruitfulness of the theme of 'Self' for developing studies for Future Generations,[4] though they place just as much importance on inter-generational problems as the Foundation does. To take account of these considerations, we changed the subtitle of the theme from 'Towards a Multi-Dimensional Understanding of "Self"' to 'Multi-Dimensional Approaches from East and West'. However, I myself still consider the original theme to be one of the most important issues not only for Philosophy and Social Sciences on the whole, but also for studies of intergenerational problems, especially those on Future Generations. Accordingly, the discussion proceeds from a brief overview of the present Western arguments on intergenerational problems to their limits, and how these are related to the theme 'Self'.

First, five stages of Western theoretical development will be distinguished. Secondly, three common theoretical problems for these theories will be extracted. Philosophical reflection upon these theoretical obstacles will point to a fundamental character of modern Western sciences. Thirdly, as John Rawls' theory (from the second stage) is especially important amongst the first three stages, this will be critically examined, focusing on his responses to the theoretical problems extracted above. Fourthly, criticisms of the Rawls theory (the third stage) will be briefly reviewed.

The conclusion will be reached that atomism, in particular the assumption of the Atomistic Person, is the major source of the Western predicaments on the issue of Future Generations. The concept of the

Atomistic Person will be defined in terms of rationality, self-interest or egoism, as the principle of his/her everyday action, derived from the self-image of separative existence. Therefore, neither altruistic individuals such as ideal Christians nor existential or reflexive subjects are necessarily regarded as Atomistic Persons, and the following criticism of atomism does not necessarily apply to some Western theories such as non-egoistic individualism/liberalism, and some forms of existentialism or theories of subjectivity. The argument here will be confined to the first three of the five stages. Derek Parfit's argument (the fourth stage) will be scrutinised in my article in Chapter 8 while Peter Laslett's theory of 'Intergenerational Tricontract', at the fifth stage, will be only touched upon there. However, my argument in Chapter 8 will not change this conclusion, but be based upon it.

Finally, in contrast to the Western impasse, a recent Eastern attempt on Future Generations will be introduced for Western readers. Though Eastern approaches still remain in an early phase of rapid development, they may contribute to the solution of the Western predicament: it is hoped my attempt in Chapter 8 will offer one possible example. Our purpose in organising this conference is to develop studies on Future Generations globally through the academic interchange between East and West.

§2. Five Stages in the West

Peter Laslett and James Fishkin wrote in the editors' preface of their important book, *Justice Between Age Groups and Generations,* 'We discovered to our surprise, moreover, that in Western thought this theme of Justice Between Generations is of extremely recent origin.'[5] According to a section named 'Justice over Time in the History of Philosophy and Political Theory', this theme 'did not exist as a subject of analysis or discussion, or even as a concept, before the 1970s, or before the 1960s at the earliest'[6], apart from the brief mention by thinkers such as Edmund Burke in his *Reflection on the Revolution in France* or Henry Sidgwick in *The Methods of Ethics* (1874). This is considered to be an important or interesting discovery; but they give no clear explanation for it, though they refer to 'Obstacles to the Understanding and Analysis of Justice over

Time'.[7] This is an important point, to which we shall return later.

Setting aside this problem, I shall attempt to analyse briefly, from the perspective of one Eastern person, the admirable and serious efforts since the late 1960s that have been made to fill this theoretical vacuum.[8] Basically, five important stages can be chronologically discerned in the recent development of Western theories, in particular, Anglo-American theories.

The first stage is the phase of raising this issue by J. Narveson (1967, 1973) and M. Golding (1968, 1972)[9] in the late 1960s and early 1970s. These early articles already pointed to difficulties which we have to face in considering problems concerning Future Generations.

The second stage is the appearance of *A Theory of Justice* (1971)[10] by John Rawls. One section of this classic of today is titled 'The problem of Justice Between Generations' (Ch. 5, 44). This should be considered to be one of the indications of the author's great insights, on what issues are to be treated seriously, though his efforts were criticised later as being 'no more than gestures'.[11]

It is worth pointing out that theoretical attention to intergenerational problems was invoked as early as, by the Rawls theory, political philosophy was beginning to revive from the 'dead' state described by the first series of *Philosophy, Politics and Society*[12] (1956). This can be taken to be a sign that this theme is one of the most important issues in contemporary social and political philosophy.

Under the enormous influence of Rawls and the gradual recognition of serious global problems such as that of the environment, the importance of this theme was acknowledged widely, in particular by two collections of essays, namely *Obligations to Future Generations* (1978) and *Responsibilities to Future Generations* (1981).[13] This period, from the late 1970s to the early 1980s, can be called 'the third stage'. During this period, research from various standpoints was stimulated by Rawls' pioneering work. The understanding of theoretical difficulties regarding future generations was deepened, and a few basic patterns for overcoming the difficulties were proposed, which may be regarded as constituting the basis of present discussion on this issue. In particular, the works by J. Passmore (1974) and Brian Barry (1977) seem to be valuable, whilst David Gauthier's contractual theory published a little later (1986) seems to me to be less convincing than that of Rawls.[14]

However, studies on Future Generations did not proceed in a straight line. Most of this research was at least tacitly motivated by the assumption of humane goodwill, that our generations should take care of interests of Future Generations, who are unable to speak for themselves, now that we recognise the serious dangers of the future world, including environmental deterioration. The appearance of Derek Parfit's *Reasons and Persons* (1982)[15] made it impossible for us to maintain this tacit assumption without arguments, though even the author himself was reluctant to abandon it.

Although Parfit's book is less known in Japan than that of Rawls, it is so acclaimed in Britain that a few quotations will suffice to prove the value of the work for Japanese readers. According to Samuel Scheffler, this book 'may be the greatest work of substantive moral philosophy in the utilitarian tradition since Sidgwick's *The Methods of Ethics* published over a century ago';[16] according to Alan Ryan, this is 'something close to a work of genius'.[17] I myself follow their lead, though I wonder if Parfit's conclusion really supports the utilitarian tradition.

Therefore, it is particularly significant that Part Four of *Reasons and Persons* is titled 'Future Generations'. This means that roughly one-quarter of Parfit's book focuses on problems around Future Generations, while Rawls allotted only one or two out of 87 sections.[18] To be sure, Parfit did not propose a new theory to enable us to think for the benefit of Future Generations, but only illuminated the impasse of such efforts by showing peculiar conclusions and well-contrived paradoxes. However, his work can be considered to contribute to studies on Future Generations in an original, 'negative way' rather than in a 'positive way', as he himself acknowledged.[19] His impact is so great that it has been almost impossible to discuss this issue in Britain without referring to his work. The period after the publication of Parfit's book, that is from the middle of the 1980s onwards, then, may be distinguished as 'the fourth stage'. As the discussions around it have as yet not in the least faded, the present time can be also included in this stage: my article in Chapter 8 will concentrate on the problem raised by Parfit, in fact.

However, even the impact of Parfit was unable to prevent intergenerational studies from developing in a positive direction. The publication *Justice Between Age Groups and Generations* (1992) which I mentioned earlier, may be regarded as a *symbolic* event for this area, because this is presented to the world as a sixth series of the globally acclaimed *Philosophy, Politics and Society* edited by Peter Laslett and others. Although there was no particular theme in previous series, in this sixth collection, 'For the first time, a theme has been followed in choosing the contributions'.[20] This is a significant change for the series of established reputation, and this may reflect the editors' respectable judgement that intergenerational issues should be a central theme in contemporary social and political philosophy no less than other important themes such as distributional justice, much discussed following the lead of Rawls.

Indeed, from a Japanese point of view, this collection could be regarded as the culmination of Western developments on intergenerational problems since 1960s;[21] short articles at the first stage, one or two minor sections of a classic at the second stage, edited collections of articles at the third stage, one important part of a highly acclaimed book at the fourth stage, and finally, one volume of a series of international fame. This development can be summarised as follows: Western studies on intergenerational problems started with the revival of political philosophy itself, and reached the point where it can legitimately request the most serious attention by all of the social and political theories; we think that this is appropriate, because justice between generations should have as much weight as justice within one generation in contemporary political philosophy. Thus, this new present stage at the 1990s can be called 'the fifth stage'.

Of course, this collection not only symbolises the developments of the studies, but also embodies substantive advance. In particular, while Parfit with T. Cowen elaborated a relatively minor theme of his book,[22] the article of the senior editor himself, 'Is There a Generational Contact'? developed his basic ideas briefly described in 1972,[23] almost as early as Rawls' book, and proposes a new concept: 'Intergenerational Tricontract'. There is no doubt that whilst Parfit's work represents the development of a negative kind, Laslett accomplishes one of the highest positive attainments based on the Western tradition of contractual theories. Moreover, the positive turn has not been restricted to this collection, but can be recognised in several other attempts. In contrast to the fourth stage, the fifth stage can be characterised as the revival or proliferation of positive theories (see §10).[24]

Thus, it was a great honour and pleasure for us to have an opportunity for discussion with the editor, Peter Laslett himself, and his company in the gathering around him at Trinity College. As we think that this issue requires interdisciplinary approaches especially from philosophy, social theory and political theory, the conference was organised into these sessions and entitled 'Philosophy, Social Sciences and Future Generations – Multi-Dimensional Approaches from East and West'.[25] This structure of the conference closely corresponds to the name of the series *Philosophy, Politics and Society* in which Laslett and Fishkin's volume was published, though it was planned independently of this series. This unexpected correspondence may reflect the simple truth that it is really necessary for us to approach the new issue through various disciplines. Although the contributions including those both of Laslett and of Parfit in the sixth series of *Philosophy, Politics and Society* may be regarded as the present summit of Western theories,[26] it will be argued that these are still confined within the limit of Western, in particular Anglo-American, tradition. I hope that this encounter between East and West on 'Philosophy, Social Sciences and Future Generations' will open the way for the next stage of this field: the sixth, seen from the Western perspective.

2. Theoretical Obstacles concerning Future Generations

§3. The Theoretical Obstacles

Peter Laslett titled his pioneer article of 1972, which I mentioned above, 'The Conversation Between the Generations'.[27] This is an attractive metaphor even now, but it was left to subsequent theorists to discuss whether and how this metaphorical conversation can be achieved in reality.[28] Once the intergenerational problem was recognised to be a theoretical frontier, the natural attempts to solve it by Western scholars were either by contractual theory or by utilitarianism of one kind or another, which have been the stock-in trade of the Western tradition of social and political theory. However, no sooner had sincere efforts begun in these directions than serious obstacles were encountered.

On the one hand, contractual theory of any kind assumes that there are real persons who make the contract. However, we are unable to make a contract with future persons, because they have not yet been born and do not exist in the world: so far as future generations or future persons are defined like this,[29] they are unable to claim their rights, negotiate and agree.[30] Moreover, there is a fundamental asymmetry in the position between the present generation and future generations. That is, the former can affect the circumstances and destiny of the latter, while the latter can not influence those of the former at all. Presupposing this asymmetrical situation, there would be absolute inequality in the power or resources of both sides. So, if a contract between them were to be considered, a relevant contract would be inconceivable except that of a unilateral situation in which the present generation voluntarily declare their rights and obligations, and in which future generations can do nothing and are without redress. Speaking precisely, this absolute asymmetry of power might be discounted, because future generations can influence or decide posthumous reputations of the present generation. However, though this factor might influence actions of the present generation, few will believe that this influence is great enough completely to counteract the basic asymmetry, in that material self-interests can be presumed to be usually far stronger for the present generation than an interest in posthumous fame.[31]

On the other hand, it is also impossible in principle to apply classical, atemporal universal utilitarianism such as that of Sidgwick to problems of Future Generations, because of the indeterminacy or uncertainty of the future; in consequence of which, we are unable to calculate accurately the amount of total happiness or utilities.[32] Though it might be possible to estimate the appropriate amount for near future, we would be unable to foresee exactly that of the remote future. However, one of the most serious problems for the present world is the kind of danger which will not cause visible effects in the near future, but may result in a catastrophe or serious collapse in the remote future ('sleeping effect') like some forms of environmental deterioration. This is a starting point or an example of more complicated difficulties and paradoxes, first identified by Narveson, and later elaborated by Parfit.[33] Besides, even if it were possible to estimate total happiness or utility in some way, it has been countered that always to impose such a calculation on our present actions 'demands too much of us: we can not reasonably be expected to share our resources with our posterity'.[34]

Following the lead of B. M. Barry and Edward Page (whose paper appears in this volume), the obstacles to theorisation on Future Generations can be summarised as:

① Non-Existence (contingency of future generations),

② Indeterminacy (uncertainty about future generations and consequent ignorance of future generations by the present generation),

③ Asymmetry (inequality of power and resources between present generation and future generations).[35]

As was briefly explained, ① and ③ are the major obstacles to contractual construction, whilst ② is the principal obstacle for the application of classical utilitarianism, though the other obstacles are also associated with each theory in some way, as will be shown concerning the arguments of Rawls and Parfit. I shall refer to these obstacles as '(Western) Theoretical Obstacles concerning Future Generations' (abbreviated to TO in the following).

§4. Two Kinds of Responses

As it has been impossible for any serious researchers to ignore these obstacles, the possible responses were either to abandon the possibility of theorising for the benefit of future generations or to question the authenticity of the recognised obstacles, unless the theorist is able to propose a new theoretical construction to overcome these difficulties (see §5, 6).

One representative forerunner at the first stage, Martin Golding, could be said to have chosen the first negative way rather than to have searched for the other possibilities.[36] In brief, his logic can be summarised as follows: As it is impossible for future generations to make claims against the present generation (TO ① Non-Existence), 'obligations to future generations' (the title of his article) are only a consequence of the fact that future generations can be members of 'our moral community'.

Moreover, as future generations are unable to form a moral community with the present generation through an explicit contract or social agreement (TO ①, once again), the moral community can be constituted only by a common 'social ideal' amongst those generations. However, as our social ideal may not be relevant for future generations (TO ②), the more remote a future generation is, the more doubtful it is whether it belongs to our moral community and hence, whether we have any obligation toward it. Therefore, it would be better for us to confine our ethical concern to our immediate posterity: not to extend it to future generations beyond our own children.

Golding's logic can be formulated as:

Golding TO ① → no social contract (¬C)*
TO ② → uncertainty about common 'social ideal'
} → no obligation to future generations except our immediate posterity

*The sign ¬X will be intended to mean the irrelevancy of the argument of X to theorise for the benefit of future generations (C, the abbreviation of social contract, will be used in the following).

In brief,

Golding TO ① ∧ TO ② → little obligation

The conclusion of Golding was developed by Terrance Ball (1985). Citing the works of Golding and Michael Walzer,[37] he affirmed that the idea of intergenerational justice was itself incoherent: as concepts (like justice) 'constitutive of moral and political discourse have historically mutable meanings',[38] 'The more distant the generations, the greater the likelihood that their moral concepts and ours will be at least partially or even perhaps wholly incommensurable'[39] (the TO ②). Since he directly denies the use of the concept of intergenerational justice, his conclusion is more bold and negative than Golding's, though he practically reduces this negativity by an additional remark.[40] His logic is simpler than that of Golding:

Ball TO ② → incoherence of intergenerational justice

However, most of the theorists who are interested in the issue have been unwilling to follow these negative conclusions, because these are against their intuition for the benefit of future generations. Accordingly, some have turned to another way to overcome these Theoretical Obstacles: questioning the authenticity of the obstacles themselves. Nevertheless, it is difficult to doubt the existence of Theoretical Obstacle ① (Non-Existence) and ② (Indeterminacy). As far as I know, then, the most popular attempt has been to raise a question to the obstacle ③ (Asymmetry): Such theorists have insisted the asymmetry is offset because there exist *objective* posthumous harms (beyond that of subjective reputations) to the present generation by future generations[41].

Some theorists (for example, Edward Page) will call this 'the Symmetry View'; that is, the idea that 'while present persons have in their power to influence the identities and numbers of future persons, and what sort of world they are born into, future generations when they come into being will be able to affect not only the posthumous reputations of present persons but also the actual success of present persons' life's works, plans, projects, and goals'.[42]

However, as advocates themselves recognise, such a theory necessitates deep reflection on the philosophical background of the concept 'posthumous harms': If all worthwhile considerations for the sake of persons were what could be perceived during their lives, there would obviously be no objective posthumous harms, because people are unable to know subjective posthumous reputations. Thus, the concept 'posthumous harms' basically contradicts an empirical philosophy like utilitarianism, and so, the introduction of this concept requires a new philosophy which is unfamiliar to the present mainstream of Western academia.[43] This philosophical reflection, however, need not be confined to issues concerning Theoretical Obstacle ③, but might be applied to those of all obstacles. The generalisation of this line of argument is the purpose of the next section.

§5. The Philosophical Reflection

Some thinkers who clearly recognise the Theoretical Obstacles have concluded that we need a 'new ethic' (Brian Barry) or a 'new theory'

(Annette Baier)[44]; as they do not wish to succumb to a negative response like that of Golding, this is the only possible way for them. For example, Brian Barry explicitly mentioned the asymmetry of power (TO ③) and 'Determinism' (TO ②) as characteristic of this issue, and has denied the validity both of contractual theories including the ideal contractarian construction of Rawls and of universal or average utilitarianism. His argument is typical and has one of the most systematic logics.

TO ③[45] → (∧TO ①) →
- 1.¬ self protection theory (that of, from Hobbes, Hume to Hart, Warnock)
- 2.¬ community theory (M. Golding) (that of M. Walzer, T. Weldon)
- 3.¬ entitlement theory (that of R. Nozick)

TO ② → 4 .¬ universal utilitarianism (J. Passmore)[46]

TO ① ∧ TO ② → 5.¬ ideal contract theory[47] (that of Rawls, David Richard)

TO ① → 6.¬ average utilitarianism

(1–6) → no relevant theory → we need a 'new ethic'

In brief,

$$\text{TO ①} \wedge \text{TO ②} \wedge \text{TO ③} \rightarrow \left\{ \begin{matrix} \neg C \\ \\ \neg U \end{matrix} \right\} \rightarrow \text{need for a 'new ethic'}$$

(U means utilitarianism)

Hence, according to Barry, we have to search for a new theory or a new ethic to overcome these theoretical obstacles. Let me put this another way: the Theoretical Obstacles point to the reasons why existing Western theories fail to provide sufficient logic for the benefit of future generations. In this sense, the Theoretical Obstacles show the unusual characteristics of intergenerational problems, that is, different aspects from synchronic problems. Thus, the process of recognising the Theoretical Obstacles can be regarded also as that of extracting the critical features which prevent Western theories from coping with this new kind of problem.[48]

The first Theoretical Obstacle, Non-Existence, is associated with the empirical character of modern science. Modern Western theories such as contractual theories do not or can not cope with nonexistent or invisible entities like future persons. As they excluded the invisible God or spirits from the sphere of sciences, they now also refuse to take future nonexistent generations into consideration.

In this regard, an interesting argument is whether we should or can conceptualise 'possible persons' who will be actualised in the future.[49] If so, it may be possible or necessary to consider the rights or interests of the unborn future individuals. For example, classical or religious thinkers tend to think like this, for they believe in the existence of non-physical essence of humans, sometimes called 'Soul'. If we do not conceptualise possible persons, it is difficult to take the rights or interests of the unborn into account. This is actually the tacit assumption behind the 'Non-Identity Problem' discussed in Chapter 8 . This argument is critical not only for intergenerational problems, but also for other contemporary social issues such as abortion.

The second Theoretical Obstacle 'Indeterminacy', is of course the opposite of 'determinism', which is one of the central aspects of modern science under the enormous influence of classical physics. Under the arguments of a temporal and universal utilitarianism, there lies the deterministic assumption that we are able to count the amount of happiness or utility of future generations from the available information for the present generation.

The Third Theoretical Obstacle, asymmetry, can be considered to reflect 'causality'. Causality implies that a previous event can be the cause of a subsequent event, while the latter is unable to be the cause of the former. Absolute asymmetry of power between present and future generations is the natural consequence of this basic reality.

Thus, the three Theoretical Obstacles, namely, Non-Existence, Indeterminacy and Asymmetry can be regarded as derivatives of the fundamental characteristics of Western modern science: empiricism, determinism and causality. The source of the obstacles is indeed no other than these basic philosophical features of Western modern theories.

What, then, about the theories themselves? I would like to return to a basic insight of Masao Maruyama. He emphasised the historical importance of the transition from medieval political thought to modern political theories such as contractual theories by proposing a categorical dichotomy of 'the natural / the artificial'. As a representative of Japanese modernists, he valued highly the Western individualisation concomitant with this theoretical transformation, and rightly pointed out that these changes are associated with or are the consequences of the enormous impact of the emerging natural sciences. The basic philosophical character of modern orthodox Western, especially Anglo-American, theories is 'Individualism' in the social and political sphere, which, put in a broader context, corresponds to 'atomism' in general. It goes without saying that the essence of contractual theorists is the agreement of individuals to a contract, whilst the basis of utilitarianism is the happiness or utility of individuals. There is no room for doubt that both of them share somehow this fundamental characteristic of Western theories. I shall term these theories 'Atomistic Theories' hereafter.

3. The Impasse of Contemporarily Contractual Theories

§6. The Critical Interpretation of the Rawls Paradigm

As has already been mentioned, some have doubted the authenticity of the theoretical obstacles; others have denied the validity of any existing theories, including contractual theories, for this new field. Whichever course a theorist may adopt, these considerations lead to the same destination: the fundamental philosophical reflection on Western theories and their limitations.

However, regardless of these reflections, some theorists with creative talents dare to propose, within the Western tradition, original arguments that are intended to avoid or overcome the theoretical obstacles. Reflecting the strong tradition and the current revival of contractual theories, most of the new arguments share more or less the contractual construction. The first attempt was made by Rawls himself (the second stage mentioned at §2), and the representative subsequent thinkers may be David Gauthier and Peter Laslett (the fifth stage).

Notwithstanding the failure of classical contractual theories, how have these theorists hoped to surmount the Theoretical Obstacles? Rawls' theory, formulated in his *A Theory of Justice* (1971), provides a prototype or even a paradigm in this respect. He discussed 'The problem of Justice Between Generations' (§44) in the context of finding a 'just savings principle' [50] in the original position. This principle is supported to enable each generation to contribute to 'the process of accumulation' of real capital for 'the good of all subsequent generations' up to a certain 'just state of things beyond which no further net saving is required'.[51] As 'the life of a people is considered as a scheme of co-operation spread out in historical time',[52] 'the just savings principle can be regarded as an understanding between generations to carry their fair share of the burden of realising and preserving a just society'.[53] Notice that, in the concept of 'real capital', he incorporates not only 'factories and machines' but also 'the knowledge and culture as well as the technology and skills, that make possible just institutions and fair value of liberty'.[54]

His well-known concept of the 'Veil of Ignorance' means that 'the persons in the original position have no information as to which generation they belong'[55] in the context of intergenerational justice. This hypothetical situation can be considered to function as a contrived logic which enables us to overcome the second Theoretical Obstacle, 'Indeterminacy'. No one knows what generation the person belongs to (and, of course, the various historical and personal conditions around the person, according to the general principle of 'veils of ignorance'): this is indeed equivalent to a completely indeterminate situation. Therefore, a contract agreed under the 'veil of ignorance' should be relevant to any possibility of indeterminacy. Thus, the sub-assumption which can be named the 'Veil of Ignorance of One's Generation' gives an ingenious solution to the second Theoretical Obstacle: 'the veil of ignorance' succeeds in the problem of intergenerational redistribution.

However, the other two Theoretical Obstacles still stand despite this success. With regard to the first obstacle 'Non-Existence', there is an interesting theoretical possibility that Rawls himself denied. He wrote as follows:

> These remarks show that the original position is not to be thought of as a general assembly which includes at one moment everyone who will live at some time; or, much less, as an assembly of everyone who could live at some time. It is not a *gathering of all actual or possible persons.* To conceive of the original position in either of these ways is to stretch *fantasy too far:* the conception would cease to be a natural guide to intuition.[56] (italics mine)

In spite of the proponent's opposition, the idea of a gathering of 'all actual and possible persons' can be considered to be plausible and effective in removing the first Theoretical Obstacle, for unborn people are assumed to participate in an agreement in this hypothetical meeting as if there were actual 'conversation between generations'. Even Rawls himself admits that this way of construction has one advantage[57] with respect to the problems of his own theorisation around 'the motivational assumption', which will be mentioned below. In fact, at least one theorist (David Richard) followed this alternative line of thought, notwithstanding Rawls' eminent influence on him.[58] This hypothetical meeting can be called 'Trans-Generational' or 'Trans-Temporal Meeting'; similarly, this alternative original position is a 'Trans-Generational (Temporal) Original Position', and the consequent contract is a 'Trans-Generational (Temporal) Contract'.

Attractive as this idea may be, it is quite another matter whether it can constitute a consistent theory. In addition to the objection of Rawls himself ('too fantastic'), Barry pointed to a logical incoherence 'in combining the idea that people in the original position are choosing among policies which will produce different total numbers of people with the idea that they know at the outset that they are all the people who ever have existed or ever will exist'.[59] This criticism means that the first Theoretical Obstacle does not disappear completely, though the conception of Trans-Generational Original Position might appear to remove it at a stroke.

After refuting the idea above, Rawls emphasised that 'it is important that the original position be interpreted so that one can at any time adopt its perspective. It must make no difference when one takes this viewpoint, or who does so'.[60] This leads to the important assumption that people in the original position are contemporaries.[61] This can be called 'the Contemporary Condition (of the original position)'. That is, Rawls' original position can be called more accurately 'the Contemporary Original Position', and his contract is 'the Contemporary Contract', even though these are also regarded as universal along the temporal dimension.

To be precise, these are unable to be called 'intergenerational original position' or 'intergenerational contract'. This is an important point: if the range of the contract is restricted like this, there can be no 'Justice Between Generations' at all. Rawls himself wrote about the original position as follows:

> The one case where this conclusion *fails* is that of saving. Since the persons in the original position know that they are contemporaries (taking the present time of entry interpretation), they can favor their generation by refusing to make any sacrifices at all for their successors; they simply acknowledge the principle that no one has a duty to save for posterity. *Previous generations have saved or they have not; there is nothing the parties can now do to affect that.* So in this instance the veil of ignorance fails to secure the desired result. Therefore I resolve the question of justice between generations in a different way by *altering the motivation assumption.*[62] (italics mine)

Notice that 'previous generations have saved or they have not: there is nothing the parties can now do to affect that'.[63] This indicates nothing else but the third Theoretical Obstacle 'Asymmetry'. Because of this, the hypothesis of *Contemporary* Original Position fails to work for the care of future generations.

This compels Rawls to an important modification of his basic assumption: the motivation assumption. Rawls has postulated the 'rationality' of people in the original position: people try as best they can to advance their own interests; they prefer more primary social goods rather than less.[64] Moreover, Rawls made an additional assumption that a rational individual does not suffer from envy, and then developed it to the additional assumption of 'mutually disinterested rationality'. It runs as follows:

> The persons in the original position try to acknowledge principles which advance their system of ends as far as possible. They do this by attempting to win for themselves the highest index of primary social goods, since this enables them to promote their conception of the good most effectively whatever it turns out to be. *The parties do not seek to confer benefits or to impose injuries on one another; they are not moved by affection or rancour.* Nor do they try to gain relative to each other; they are not envious or vain. Put in terms of a game, we might say: they strive for as high an absolute score as possible.[65] (italics mine)

If Rawls had stuck to this assumption of 'mutually disinterested rationality' on intergenerational relations, the conclusion of no duty to future generations would have been inevitable. Rawls could not help abandoning this assumption in the case of intergenerational justice. Although he softened this impression by using the expression 'adjust the motivation condition',[66] this is not actually a slight modification. This is the only alteration which he mentioned in one of the most important sections of the book, 'The Veil of Ignorance' (§24). This proves the special and challenging character of 'The Problem of Justice Between Generations' (§44) against the basic logic of *A Theory of Justice* as a whole. It is not too much to say that it poses the question whether there is *one* theory of Justice or *two* theories of Justice: one on intra-generational justice, and the other on intergenerational justice.[67]

If so, we have to distinguish 'A Theory of Intra-generational Justice' and 'A Theory of Inter-generational Justice'. These two (theories of) Justice will be also called '(The First Theory of Synchronic (Contemporary) Justice', and '(the Second Theory of) Diachronic (Temporal) Justice'.

What, then, is the assumption of 'the Second Theory of Justice'? Rawls himself explained it like this:

'The parties are regarded as representing family lives, say, with ties of *sentiment* between successive generations. This modification seems *natural enough,* and has been used already in the argument for equal liberty (§33). Although the savings problem presents a *special situation,* the characterisation of *justice remains the same.* The criteria for justice between generations are those that would be chosen in the original position.'[68] (italics mine)

If Rawls had explicitly introduced a motivational assumption such as what he called 'elements of social solidarity' or 'perfect altruism',[69] the answer would have been clear: these assumptions would have contradicted the original one of rationality, and would have destroyed the consistency of the whole argument. In this case, there would have been obviously 'Two Theories of Justice'.

To be sure, Rawls avoided this obvious inconsistency. Instead of commitment to this disastrous failure for his system of logic, he introduced a restricted modification which incorporated familial ties of sentiment into the original rational motivational assumption. This means that 'it is assumed that a generation cares for its immediate descendants, as fathers say care for their sons, a just savings principle, or more accurately, certain limits on such principle, would be acknowledged'.[70] Rawls himself regarded this alteration as the adjustment within the original assumption of rationality and expressed this new assumption together with the original sub-assumption as 'mutual disinterestedness (limited altruism)'. [71] This can be schematised as follows:

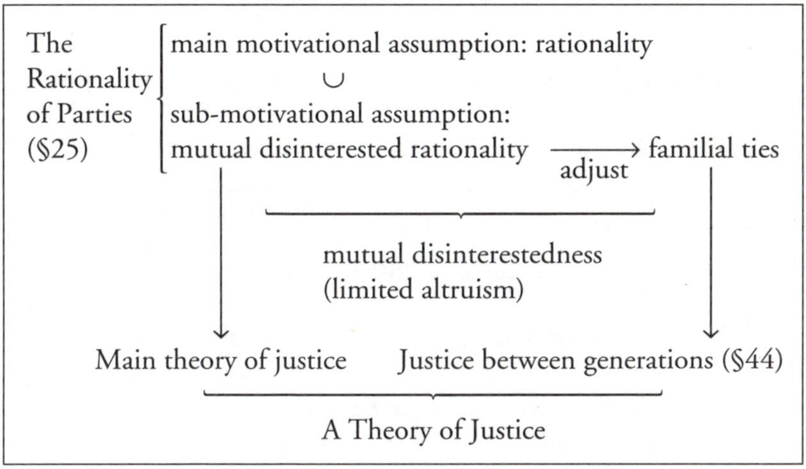

Figure 1. A Theory of Justice (Rawls' own explanation)

It is still unsure whether his justification for this formulation is sufficiently convincing, because it cannot be denied that ties of familial 'sentiment' are not only inconsistent with, but also logically opposite to the sub-assumption of mutual disinterestedness to some extent. It would be better to distinguish the new assumption of familial ties from the assumption of mutual disinterested rationality by calling the former that of 'Familial Interested Rationality'.

The estimation of the consistency of the Rawls theory depends upon whether this modified rationality can be considered to be included in the range of the original rationality or not. If the postulate that 'each tries as best he can to advance his interests'[72] is to be strictly interpreted, the modified rationality should be posited outside the original rationality. In this case, the previous schema changes like this:

original motivational assumption	↔	modified motivational assumption
|		|
rationality	↔	modified rationality
|		|
mutual disinterested rationality	↔	familial interested rationality
|		|
intra-generational justice	↔	inter-generational justice
|		|
the first theory of synchronic justice	↔	the second theory of diachronic justice

Figure 2. Two Theories of Justice (critical interpretation)

Laying aside the question which schema is correct as an explanation of the Rawls theory, let me stress the importance of this modified argument for it. In order to overcome the third Theoretical Obstacle, familial sentiment and interests were introduced as 'natural' human reality as (or, as if) this is (or, was) only a supplementary assumption or argument. These will be called a 'Supplementary Familial Assumption (Argument)'.

This Supplementary Familial Argument is usually proposed to secure a theory for the benefit of future generations beyond theoretical impasse, as was the case with the Rawls contractual theory. He defined intergenerational justice by the just savings principle. This is to say, people in the (contemporary) original position are to decide how much they will save at each stage of advance on the assumption that all other generations are to save at the same or the proposed rates, though the rates of each stage may be set beforehand to change depending upon the state of society. As Rawls also assumed that people in the original position have no pure time preference (§45), 'all generations are *virtually* represented in the original position, since the same principle would always be chosen'.[73] (italics mine) Thus, despite the hypothesis of *Contemporary* Original Position, Intergenerational or Trans-temporal Justice is supposed to be realised beyond the third Theoretical Obstacle, 'Asymmetry', in Rawls' imaginary universe.

In this universe, each generation passes on to the next generation a fair equivalent in real capital as defined by the just savings principle[74]: 'The equivalent is in return for what is received from previous generations that enables the later ones to enjoy a better life in a more just society'.[75]

It is worth emphasising that Rawls 'observe[s] that there is a peculiar feature of the reciprocity principle in the case of just savings'.[76] He wrote as follows:

> Normally this principle applies when there is an exchange of advantages and each party gives something as a fair return to the other. But in the course of history no generation gives to the preceding generations, the benefits of whose saving it has received. In following the saving principle, *each generation makes a contribution to later generations and receives from its predecessors*. The first generations may benefit hardly at all, whereas the last generations, those living when no further saving is required, gain the most and give the least.[77] (italics mine)

This is obviously the consequence of the third Theoretical Obstacle, 'Asymmetry'. Although the Supplementary Familial Assumption enabled Rawls to surmount the obstacle, Asymmetry survived by transforming its forms: from 'Asymmetry of power' to 'Asymmetry of reciprocity'. This 'peculiar' reciprocity could be called 'Asymmetrical Reciprocity' or 'Unilateral Reciprocity', although it can be doubted if this really deserves the name of 'reciprocity', which originally implied a mutual relationship.[78]

Rawls himself defended this reciprocity as follows:

> It is a natural fact that generations are spread out in time and actual exchanges between them take place *only in one direction.* We can do something for posterity but it can do nothing for us. *This situation is unalterable, and so the question of justice does not arise.* What is just or unjust is how institutions deal with natural limitations and the way they are set up to take advantage of historical possibilities.[79] (italics mine)

Whether we agree with his justification or not, it is a noteworthy fact that the just saving principle was stipulated by Rawls himself as involving this kind of reciprocity. This argument will be called 'the Argument of Unilateral (Asymmetrical) Reciprocity'. Securing this special reciprocity by introducing the just saving principle[80], Rawls declared that:

> *We can now see that persons in different generations have duties and obligations to one another just as contemporaries do.* The present generation cannot do as it pleases but is bound by the principles that would be chosen in the original position to define justice between persons are different moments of time. In addition, men have a natural duty to uphold and to further just institutions and for this the improvement of civilisation up to a certain level is required. The derivation of these duties and obligations may seem at first a somewhat far-fetched application of the contract doctrine. Nevertheless these requirements would be acknowledged in the original position, and so the conception of justice as fairness covers these matters without any changes in its basic idea.[81] (italics mine)

Rawls here believed that he had succeeded in solving 'The Problem of Justice between Generations', in other words, the 'The Problem of Intergenerational Justice'. His solution can be formulated as shown in fig. 3.

As has already been explained, his concept of original contract is constituted as a 'Contemporary Contract'. Therefore, this theory cannot be called 'intergenerational contractual theory', but should be termed 'a Theory of Contemporary Contract (on Intergenerational Justice)', or in brief, 'a Contemporarily Contractual Theory'.[82]

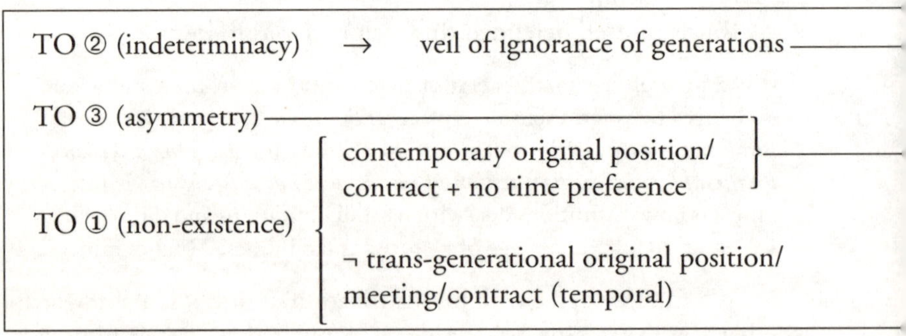

Figure 3. Rawl's Solution to the Problem of Intergenerational Justice

§7. The Essential Limit of Atomistic Contemporarily Contractual Theories

Without doubt, the Rawls theory is full of original insights on intergenerational justice as well as intra-generational justice, and is a prototype or even a paradigm of successive contractual arguments. Naturally, many critiques have already been made of it in proportion to its huge impact. In particular, at the third stage mentioned at §2, controversies stimulated by the Rawls theory (the second stage) played a central role. As there is no need to iterate them here,[83] let me focus on the major criticisms of Rawls by editors of the two seminal collections, namely, B. Barry (with R. I. Sikora, ed., *Obligations to Future Generations*, 1978) and E. Partridge (ed., *Responsibilities to Future Generations*, 1981).[84]

First, both of them criticised the limit of the 'just savings principle' for intergenerational justice. As a result of 'taking investment as the paradigm of relations between generations' (Barry),[85] intergenerational justice tends to be reduced to 'primarily, if not exclusively, an economic issue' as embodied in the terms 'saving' and 'capital' (Partridge).[86] In spite of Rawls' additional reference to 'knowledge and culture', the legitimacy of these criticisms cannot be denied.

Secondly, in consequence of the first defect, both of them also objected that Rawls missed the importance of negative obligation to avoid harm (forbearance), while this is considered to be stronger than any positive duty to make better off (active commissions),[87] on which he concentrated.

modified motivational assumption
familial interested rationality
supplementary familial argument

just saving principle
= intergenerational justice
||
unilateral reciprocity (asymmetrical)

As a corollary of this, thirdly, Partridge rightly indicated that 'Rawls has little to say about our ecological responsibility as stewards of this planet and its life community'.[88] Indeed, considering the importance of environmental problems in the world today, it is quite strange that Rawls seldom mentioned such problems in the context of intergenerational justice, with the exception of only one line as an example of the problem of justice.[89] Partridge tried to make up for the second and the third lacunas of the Rawls theory by proposing several concepts: principle of negative utility, critical Lockean proviso, just anticipation, just forbearance, and just stewardship.[90]

Fourthly, Barry underscored the fact that Rawls has nothing to say on obligations to remote descendants[91] because Rawls postulated familial concern about merely immediate descendants in his modified familial motivational assumption. Therefore, his theory is unable to settle the problem of the ecological 'sleeper-effect' that 'we set off now with no ill effects for some hundreds of years and then catastrophic effects'.[92] Moreover, Barry suggested, if the present generation takes care of the interests of remote future generations, there is no guarantee in the Rawls theory that intervening generations will also respect such interests.[93] Rawls could perhaps reply to the latter criticism that any generation including intervening generations should agree with the same conditions of intergenerational justice like the 'just savings principle', but it is definitely impossible to clear up the former doubt within his logic.

Finally, Barry objected to the modified motivational assumption itself. He argued that this modified assumption was unfounded because there is no reason for relaxing the original postulate of self-interest but for the fact that 'it enables Rawls to derive obligations to future generations'[94]; he raised a severe question, 'if it is acceptable to introduce desires for the welfare of immediate descendants into the original position simply in order to get them out again as obligations, what grounds can there be for refusing them to put into the original position a desire for the welfare of at least some contemporaries?'[95] This alteration of the assumption results in the weakening of his logical argument that the establishment of fair society can be deduced from the simple assumption of self-interest. This is exactly the same kind of criticism as was explained in the last section.

We can now distinguish two classes of problems: the *incidental* first three and the *essential* last two. Although the first three drawbacks are critical for the Rawls theory itself, it may not have been impossible for the subsequent theorists to surmount these: as these limits accompany Rawls' unique conception of a 'just savings principle', once theorists are liberated from this idea, they are able to put forward new contractual constructions without these defects. Contractual theories need not be circumscribed within the realm of economics (the first defect), but they can be responsive to the negative kind of obligation to avoid harm (the second defect) and the environmental problems (the third defect).

Therefore, these three shortcomings can be called 'Incidental Defects'. However, it is a completely different case with the latter two criticisms. These two concern the 'motivational assumption'. The last or fifth criticism affirmed the dubiousness of Rawls' modified motivational assumption, and even if this modified assumption were to be acceptable, the fourth criticism would show that the Supplementary Familial Argument involves an inherent limit. Since the original assumption of rationality is restricted to the modified motivational concern within the interests of immediate descendants, it is in principle impossible to theorise for the benefit of remote posterity beyond the first and second generation at the most.

Therefore, there is no glossing over these two defects so long as we wish to maintain the basic assumption of rationality; these can be called 'Essential Defects', and they are at the core of Rawls' failure. Nevertheless, contractual theorists after Rawls have tried in vain to improve the Rawlsian prototype so that its weak points would be surmounted, because they have failed to discriminate between these two kinds of Rawlsian defects.

For example, Gauthier's theory, which is one of the most well-known subsequent contractual theories, succeeded in escaping from the first three incidental defects: as there is no special 'just savings principle', it does not manifest these defects. However, his failure concerning the last two defects is even more conspicuous than the Rawls theory itself, for Gauthier made a stronger postulation than Rawls: maximisation of individual self-interests.[96] Such *entirely* self-interested individuals are supposed to enter the process of rational bargaining to reach an agreement. Assuming also his interpretation of the Lockean proviso, it follows that 'a rational contractor has no duty to avoid harming further generations nor to compensate them for his harmful actions, since he cannot now commercially interact with the persons'.[97]

This means that a cruel conclusion ensues from the first Theoretical Obstacle. Gauthier provided three additional arguments to avoid this untenable conclusion, but, one critic (K. Sauvé) proved that these arguments were insufficient for this purpose. In particular, what was termed the 'Inheritance Argument'[98] by Sauvé is virtually the same as the Supplementary Familial Argument:

> Here Gauthier characteristically suspends his *fundamental* assumption of mutual concern by asking us to suppose 'as is clearly the case, the most persons ...wish to share with spouse and provide for offspring'.[99] (italics original)

As Gauthier's postulation of maximisation of individual self-interests is stronger than that of Rawls, this Supplementary Argument more clearly contradicts his own postulation than Rawls' case.[100] In short, Gauthier fell into the same or even deeper pitfall of the Essential Defects, though he leaped over that of the Incidental Defects.

Sauvé concludes that to pass over the pitfall, some degree of affective concern for future generations[101] beyond immediate offspring must be assumed. This implies the necessity of reconsidering fundamentally the motivational assumption of rationality. The same comment could be applied to the Rawlsian theory. I shall term this problem 'the Theoretical Motivational Problem (of Rawlsian theory)'.

Once we begin to think of this problem, as Partridge wrote, we have to face a troublesome question: 'Have we actually the psychological capacity to do what our moral duty requires?'[102] In fact, this has already been argued as a 'Motivation Problem' in general since the third stage, though it has not necessarily been connected with the criticism of the Rawlsian theory itself. Let me call this the 'Practical Motivational Problem' to differentiate it from the 'Theoretical Motivational Problem'. Examining this problem, Norman Care doubted the existence of the required motivation in present human beings.[103]

This suspicious view on the Practical Motivational Problem has more affinity with the motivational assumption made by Rawls himself than with fundamental criticism of it[104]: both views reflect the orthodox way of thinking in the present Western society. Practical policy-makers may stop thinking in front of so-called reality, but the privilege to contemplate beyond it has traditionally been ascribed to philosophy.

To recapitulate: the basic Theoretical Obstacles for the classical conception of contractual theories are the first (Non-Existence) and third (Asymmetry). Rawls is no exception. Though he succeeded in the second Theoretical Obstacle (Indeterminacy) by the ingenious hypothetical assumption of the Veil of Ignorance of Generations, he had to face the other two obstacles inherent in contractual constructions.

He then tried to overcome the first obstacle by the Contemporary Original Position with the additional assumption of no time preference. As all generations including future generations are regarded as represented in the Contemporary Original Position, the necessity of reaching an agreement with real future people is considered to disappear: The problem of Non-existence is thus solved. While this problem is philosophically associated with the empiricism of Western science, the idealistic construction of the Rawls theory apparently managed to tide over the actual difficulty. Rawls, however, had to face the last Theoretical Obstacle: Asymmetry. In front of this problem, he abandoned the attempt to maintain the original motivational assumption of rationality, and grafted the modified motivational assumption of Familial Rationality into it.

To be sure, this theoretical operation seemingly enabled him to surmount the last obstacle in the formula of Asymmetrical (Unilateral) Reciprocity. Rawls justified this peculiar reciprocity by reference to natural causality, namely, the philosophical substance of the last obstacle. However, it cannot be denied that some inconsistency is contained in the grafting together of assumptions which brought this success. Indeed, it is questionable whether there is one unified theory of justice based on the motivational assumption of rationality, or two co-existent different theories of justice, one of which is based on the original assumption, the other on the modified version.

Rawls achieved a notable success in overcoming the three Theoretical Obstacles by his original and creative ideas, but these contrivances resulted in the fundamental contradiction of the Theoretical Motivational Problem. This remained as the last, but unsurpassable *aporia* for the Contemporarily Contractual Theory after its long journey towards the solution of the three obstacles.[105] In my view, however, the problem embodies not a last minute difficulty, but the first and the most fundamental feature of contractual theories: Atomism, discussed in §5. Rawls' original assumption of rationality is nothing else but a typical axiom of what can be named 'Individual Rationality', or more generally, 'Atomistic Rationality'.[106] Accordingly, his motivational assumption is an 'Atomistic Motivational Assumption'.

Let me quote his words once again. Each person is assumed to try 'as best he can to advance his interest'.[107] Individual or Atomistic Rationality means taking care merely of one's own individual interests. Rawls' world should be regarded as an 'Atomistic Universe' composed of 'Atomistic Persons', though it is a somewhat weaker version than that of Gauthier, in that the maximisation of individual interests is not necessarily postulated in Rawls' Atomistic Rationality. Moreover, Rawls' original sub-assumption of 'mutually disinterested rationality' signifies that 'The parties do not seek to confer benefits or to impose on one another: they are not moved by affection or rancour'.[108] In this universe, Atomistic Persons are postulated to have no affective concern or motivation towards other people, other atoms: it can be termed 'The Totally Atomistic Universe' comprised of 'Totally Atomistic Persons'. Similarly, the sub-assumption of 'mutually disinterested rationality' can be called that of 'Totally Atomistic Rationality': there is no rationality at all beyond the scope of an individual atom.

A totally Atomistic Person cannot or must not care about the interests or welfare of others, including future generations. Therefore, Rawls had to weaken his original assumption of totally Atomistic Rationality to avoid the unwelcome conclusion. As the familial concern is the most or the only remaining 'natural' human tie beyond individuals, atomistic thinkers such as Rawls have no other means than depending on kinship. This most basic, primitive and minimum humane relationship is the last saviour for them. Nevertheless, the Essential Defects indicated by criticisms of Rawls prove that he could not escape in the last analysis the impasse. In order to transcend this predicament, it may be required to transform completely his motivational assumption, from that of atomistic 'mutual disinterestedness' (limited altruism) into that of either 'elements of social solidarity and good will' or 'perfect altruism' according to his own terms,[109] but this is what he did not wish to admit: here is the 'Essential Limit of the Atomistic, Contemporarily Contractual Theory'. The essential limit of the Rawls theory should be realised to be a sub-problem of a far broader philosophical problem, which has enormous theoretical implications: that should be called 'The Problem of Atomism'.

4. Conclusion: The Encounter between East and West on Future Generations in the Global Overview

§8. Five criticisms of early Western theories

In this article, the impasse of Western theories on Future Generations has been ascribed to the fundamental attributes of modern science through examination of three Theoretical Obstacles: the source of these obstacles, namely, 'Non-Existence', 'Indeterminacy' and 'Asymmetry' lies in 'Empiricism', 'Determinism' and 'Causality', which feature in science. Thus, the first conclusion is that studies on Future Generations require philosophical reflection upon modern sciences in general: the limits of the science should be somehow transcended in order to overcome the Theoretical Obstacles.

Secondly, it goes without saying that modern science originally developed in the West: the central characteristics of Western modern science are described as the atomism or mechanism represented in Newtonian Classical Physics.

Thirdly, then, by the scrutiny of the Rawls theory as the representative argument at the early (first three) stages, it is concluded that the Essential Limit of Contemporarily Contractual Theories on Future Generations derives from Western Atomism. Rawls' theory assumed the Atomistic Person, which is the reason why he had to introduce the Supplementary Familial Argument based on the modified motivational assumption: an assumption that may be inconsistent with his original assumption of rationality.

The theoretical assumption of the Atomistic Person is closely related to the person's own self-image which should be termed the 'Atomistic Self'. Therefore, fourthly, it should be concluded that the problem of self is important and inevitable in furthering studies of Future Generations: the conception of the Atomistic Self should be reconsidered to provide a positive basis for studies on Future Generations.

As a result of these shortcomings, it is difficult for Western theorists to develop positive theories for the benefit of future generations. Thus, fifthly, though some managed to propose positive theories, others, including Golding, failed to do this and, in fact, developed negative arguments.

Hence, this chapter concludes that the present impasse of Western theories necessitates:

① a fundamental philosophical reflection on Western modern science, in particular,

② that on the Problem of Atomism,

③ some kind of non-atomistic theory,

④ a kind of non-atomistic conception of self or identity,

⑤ a new attempt to create positive theories overcoming the existing negative arguments.

As the arguments in this chapter have been restricted to the first three stages, some of these criticisms are irrelevant to the last two stages, which can be regarded as the present summit. As will be explained in chapter 8, Derek Parfit's Quasi-Utilitarian argument (at the fourth stage) even contains a radical philosophical attack on Western Orthodox theories, in particular, the conception of the Atomistic Self. Therefore, Parfit's argument is quite in tune with the first four criticisms: it contains ① serious philosophical reflection on ② Western theories such as the Self-interest Theory and Non-Reductionist View, and proposed ③, ④ a Reductionist View of Self or Identity. The only remaining, but serious problem is that ⑤ he elaborated a negative argument, but failed to propose a positive theory.

As for the contractual tradition, it is obviously necessary to investigate theories of intergenerational contract, which could be an alternative for the Contemporary Contract. The work of examining minutely the theories of Peter Laslett (and A. Baier) requires another paper, but it is sufficient here to say that these theories based on some kind of concept of trust[110] should not be regarded as *totally* atomistic.[111] This is the reason why these attempts at the fifth stage are, in the main, excluded from my criticism of Western Atomistic Theories. In other words, 'the Atomistic Theories' in the title of this chapter refers mainly to those in the first three stages: this chapter is 'a critique of the *early* Western theories'.

To be sure, as Laslett's theory can be considered to embody a Western tradition, this does not contain ① deep philosophical reflection upon Western modern science, in particular, ② atomism. As a result, he is ③ sympathetic with contractual construction, which is often atomistic, and ④ seldom mentions or puts little importance upon the issue of 'Self' in the context of intergenerational problems.[112] However, at the same time, his theory cannot be interpreted as totally ③ an Atomistic Theory presupposing ④ only the Atomistic Persons. Therefore, the non-atomistic element can be considered to enable him to succeed in proposing ⑤ a genuine positive theory beyond negative arguments. Thus, Peter Laslett's theory of 'Intergenerational Tricontract', can be considered to be a good starting point for a discussion between East and West on Future Generations, because Eastern tradition can be characterised by being more or less non-atomistic. Let me introduce briefly, in the final sections of this paper, the background of this 'intercultural conversation', that is, a recent development in studies on Future Generations in the Far East.

§9. A Philosophical Movement from within Japan[113]

It is generally difficult today to realise a genuinely intercultural conversation between West and East, in particular with Japan, because of the Westernisation of contemporary Japanese society itself, including the academic world. Moreover, as regards social sciences, such academic dialogue involves still more difficulty: as the post-war social scientists were profoundly affected by serious self-reflection on Japanese engagement in the Second World War, most of them today tend to disregard Eastern cultural tradition wholesale, because it was considered to have played some part in the nationalistic stream which advanced the pre-war propaganda of the 'Great East-Asian Region of Co-Prosperity'. Masao Maruyama, mentioned in §1, gave a lucid and critical analysis of pre-war 'ultra-nationalism' and Japanese culture behind it; and naive adoration of Eastern culture is reminiscent of the nightmare of the pre-war nationalism for most academics including myself.

Consequently, after the war, most Japanese social scientists turned their eyes to Western theories, and have tended to ignore their own cultural tradition and their classics. As a result, fruitful *intercultural* academic dialogue between East and West has become rare and difficult. Japanese researchers have earnestly adopted Western theories, and sometimes have applied or revised them, but they have little to say from their own *cultural* viewpoint. In actual discussion with Western academics, then, they tend to behave as if they were wise pupils, or learners who question academic authorities: the reason can be ascribed not only to notorious linguistic inability, but also to the historical situation of contemporary Japanese social sciences.

In understanding the character of the philosophical movement outlined below, it would be useful to bear this background in mind. The forerunner of the Future Generations Alliance Foundation, the still-existing Kyoto Forum, was inaugurated in 1989 under the chairmanship of a nuclear physicist, Sakae Shimizu. This Forum is a gathering for lectures and discussions, involving various people such as academics (in particular, natural scientists), thinkers, artists and journalists. It focuses especially on environmental issues and life-long education. The Forum is motivated and financially supported by the secretary-general Katsuhiko Yazaki, a former successful businessman in the mail-catalogue industry. He was inspired by the traditional Mahayana Buddhism through his experience of meditation in 1988 under a Zen master Kido Inoue.[114] Zen is a traditional school of Japanese Buddhism, historically introduced from China in the Kamakura period (especially, 12-13 C).

As is epitomised by the city of Kyoto, a historical and cultural metropolis of Japan for more than 1000 years, people surrounding the Kyoto Forum value highly traditional Eastern or Japanese thought and values in contrast to the modern Western 'rational' way of thinking. For example, some of them, including Shimizu, have been in sympathy with the Kyoto School, represented by Kitaro Nishida, the greatest philosopher in pre-War Japan, who proposed the original Eastern metaphysics inspired by his experiences of Zen. Despite or due to his knowledge of modern science, Shimizu explained that the purpose of the Kyoto Forum was to create a new civilisation of mankind by introducing profound

Eastern thought, which had been relatively unfamiliar to the Western civilisation. His words are all the more interesting because he has expert knowledge of modern physics. In this respect, several natural scientists around him could be regarded as intellectual successors of Hideki Yukawa, a Nobel-prize winner for his discovery of the neutron, who is considered to be a representative physicist in the Kyoto School[115]: in his later life, Yukawa was interested in the implications of traditional Eastern thought for modern physics. The period from 1989 to 1992 can be called the first stage of the Kyoto Forum which operated mainly in Japan. This cultural movement, which is still proceeding, had a general character at that stage: the themes of the gathering were not specific to Future Generations, but were concerned with many subjects such as religion, philosophy, medicine, home, education, psychology, ecology, economy, art, civilisation, and population.[116]

It seems to me that the original attempt of this group at this stage was the revival of the essential insights of the pre-war Kyoto School in the face of serious problems of civilisation such as environmental disasters, so that its intention could be characterised as the formation of, as it were, a 'Neo-Kyoto School': the name *Kyoto* Forum emphasises traditional culture in contrast to the contemporary metropolis, Tokyo. In my view, this enterprise contains noteworthy potential for contributing to the solution of world problems now by utilising half forgotten cultural resources; nevertheless, there was an attendant risk of becoming associated with the delicate problem of 'Original/Old Kyoto School'. The proposal for a new civilisation could remind us of the old call for 'surmounting the modern', and this movement could have become dubious if it had remained confined within Japan and begun to take on a nationalistic tone. Most of the eminent philosophers in the pre-war Kyoto School, for example, K. Nishida, Hajime Tanabe, and Tetsuro Watsuji, have been, more or less, criticised for their (usually, subjectively reluctant or unwilling, but) objective or resultant 'commitment' to the war: this trauma of the Old Kyoto School could be compared to the problem of Heidegger's commitment to Nazism, which seems to be more manifest than the Japanese counterpart.

Hence, the importance of the next stop: the movement seems to have passed the razor-edge, and entered a new stage through its co-operation in the 1992 Earth Summit (United Nations Conference on

Environment and Development in Rio de Janeiro).[117] Yazaki keenly felt in those days that we needed a new philosophy, enlarging his viewpoint through his experiences at the summit to that of 'citizen of the earth' and the perspective of 'future generations'. Thus, immediately after the summit, he established the Future Generations Alliance Foundation, which is 'dedicated to realising the happiness of the future generations who will live on this earth'[118]: the second stage can be characterised as such global or cosmopolitan orientation.

The manifesto of the Foundation at the time of its establishment (1992, published in 1993) explicitly stated as follows:

> 1. The Purpose of the Establishment: the philosophical foundation of the Foundation lies in the Mahayana-spirit of Buddhism. *However, we do not commit to any religious movements at all.* We attach importance to *forward-looking, open attitudes* in the research and activities of the Foundation.[119] (italics mine)

It is important to note that although the activities of the Foundation were inspired or grounded in the spirit of Mahayana Buddhism at this stage, so far as this manifesto declares, the mode of actual activities or discussions themselves have not been based on any religion, but have had an open or academic character. For this reason, the reference to Buddhism was omitted from the revised edition (1996) partly to avoid possible misunderstanding. This separation between the religious motive in the establishment of the Foundation and its actual mode of activities on a non-religious basis fostered the spirit of academic dialogue which underlay the Forum in Cambridge.

As a reflection of this separation, it seems to me that the Foundation proposes a philosophical principle of 'Universal Unity' rather than specific religious doctrines. The guiding principle has been explained in the pamphlet (1993) as follows:

> We are searching for a new way of self.
>
> In the past, as we pursued the convenience and rationality of a materialistic civilisation, we were directed towards fulfilling only our desires, realising self self-egotistically by separating it from people around us and the other beings. Distinct identities such as those attached to individuals, races, and states were necessary in doing this effectively; these are very powerful in almost all areas of the world. However, such

> a way of self has been the cause of conflicts and struggles in many parts of the world today. A fundamental transformation of our way of self is now required.
>
> We must re-realise that everything, including human-beings, on this beautiful Earth is connected with everything else in the dynamic, whole universal linkage, and we must practice this awareness in our everyday lives, for profound acts of all lives are interwoven with each other in concordance.
>
> We grasp this structure of inter-linkage and cohabitation in the great universe by a concept named Universal Unity, and employ it as a basic idea which we should try to actualise.[120]

This idea has laid the ground for a practical philosophy of 'Future Generations'. On the ground of the Universal Unity, we must realise that we owe our existence to the benefits accumulated since the infinite past, and that our actions will influence the infinite future: we can feel responsibility for the future on the basis of our recognition of our inheritance from the past. That is to say, 'The starting point of our practical philosophy is that we can realise the close inter-linkage between generations, based on the spirit of autonomy and mutual dependence, and that we can be aware of *"the pleasure of life which participates in the action of the great universe"*, by reconsidering our every act from the viewpoint of the expectation and well-being of future generations' (italics mine).[121]

Therefore, according to the Foundation's pamphlet, the philosophical conception of Universal Unity provides the ground of a practical philosophy for Future Generations. In my view, the former can be analysed as the key to overcoming the Three Theoretical Obstacles: the idea of existent 'inter-linkage between generations' requires us to care about interests of future generations, though they are, at present ① non-existent and ② indeterminate, and ③ they can do nothing for us. That is to say,

Universal Unity → ¬ (TO ①–③) → Philosophy for Future Generations

Although these concepts, in particular, Universal Unity, might not be interpreted as immutable doctrines, they can be regarded as the two philosophical axes of the Foundation, at least at the time of its establishment. We can call the period from 1992 onwards the second stage of this Eastern movement. The movement, originating in Kyoto, has extended its activities into the whole world and concentrated on the theme of Future Generations. Coincidentally, the year 1992 is the same point as the beginning of the Western fifth stage, when *Justice between Age Groups and Generations* was published.

Since then, the Foundation has promoted various intellectual and social activities in various parts of the world. In particular, philosophical exploration stands out. Though the Chairman, Yazaki is not a professional philosopher, he is a great learner, and sometimes proposed interesting concepts from his own experiences, for example, of his business: the idea of Universal Unity occurred to him, for he had already advocated, as a key concept for his company, *Felissimo (Felicity +ssimo,* the highest), 'Global Identity' and, moreover, 'Universal Identity', which transcends the conceptual limit of 'corporate identity'.[122] Furthermore, he formulated his ideas into 'Five Beyonds': Beyond Egoism, Economism, Now-ism, Nationalism, and Scientism. He also put these ideas around the concept of *Li'ang Zhi* (good wisdom, innate knowledge of the good) proposed by an idealist Chinese Confucian Wang Yang-Ming[123] in the 16th century: as a former entrepreneur, Yazaki naturally has great sympathy with Wang's active doctrine of 'polishing and training in actual affairs'.

Inspired by the lecture of a leading Buddhist businessman in Japan, Kazuo Inamori (Kyosera Corporation, Honorary Chairman of the Foundation), Yazaki repeatedly emphasises that we are all born as philosophers and that all of us can or should live as a philosopher.[124] To be sure, his philosophy is a that of a layman, not of a professor. However, it may be remembered that Socrates did not speak to professional philosophers in seminar rooms, but rather daily with citizens of Athens: the purpose of his activity is to make people love wisdom *(philo-sophia).*

In Christianity, Martin Luther had to free religious knowledge from being the preserve of the Catholic priesthood; creating 'the priesthood of all believers'. The universalisation of priesthood in Protestantism corresponds to a similar idea in Neo-Confucianism, especially the teaching of Wang Yang-Ming (1472-1529), who coincidentally lived in the same age as Luther (1483-1546): all people (on the street) can be 'sages' by the moral attainment of *Li'ang Zhi* (clear wisdom). Now, my proposal has been that philosophy should be extended from scholastic professional philosophers to everyone: this proposition can be called 'The Philosopherhood of All People (Everyone)'. This concept has indicated my ideal for philosophy, and it seems to me that Yazaki himself has advocated a similar idea. Of course, his work cannot be compared to that of Socrates, but one could call him a 'philosopher' in its etymological sense (*philosophus,* lover of wisdom), or more precisely, 'lover of good wisdom' (*Li'ang Zhi*), and the activities of his Foundation seem to be motivated by such an ideal: in short, Yazaki is a 'philosophical entrepreneur' for future generations.

Nevertheless, the activities of the Foundation have not been confined to such an everyday or popular philosophy. The Foundation established The Institute for the Integrated Study of Future Generations, and invited, as its President, the Korean academic Tae-Chang Kim, former Dean of the Graduate School of Public Administration at Chungbuk National University, who had inspired or committed himself to the movement since 1991. He has been devoting his whole activities to the development of studies for Future Generations with marvellous energy and vigour. He is an initiator of the *original* studies in the Far East, and it may not be too much to say that such Eastern academic studies on Future Generations have been developed almost entirely by him.

As he emphasises that 'Philosophy for Future Generations' is not only developing now but also never stops progressing dynamically, it is difficult to summarise his philosophy at this point. His written articles, however, show that, first, he is critical of modern civilisation in its characteristics of 'discontinuity, denial and destruction'[125] of spatial or temporal others. He associates these features with Newtonian and Cartesian world-views which 'tend to emphasize the aspect of separation, independence, and mechanistic relationship', and proposes alternatively 'the metaphysics of (universal) interconnectedness' which stress organic relationship, suggested by modern quantum physics and bio-sciences.[126]

On the ground of this metaphysics, secondly, he proposes to 'recover solidarity with others across space and time',[127] and not only to pass the legacy from the past generations to the future generations, but also to make an effort for greater happiness for future generations on the basis of gratitude to the past generations: this attitude conforms to the traditional ethics of Northeast Asian countries, namely, the Confucian aesthetic virtues, and according to 'the aesthetic view of solidarity, benefits may be cross-generational and unidirectional',[128] in contrast to the contractual view which presupposes a reciprocal reward.

These two components of Philosophy for Future Generations roughly correspond to the original two axes of the Foundation. Thus, the simple idea of the latter can be considered to have been first developed into an academic philosophy by Kim. Moreover, while he raised several proposals for Global Governance, a security system, a system of global values and organisational principle,[129] his main emphasis has been to construct 'an ecological philosophy', in particular, 'a New Theory of Value for the Global Age'[130]: This is a kind of 'Universal Ethical Relativism', which is intended to overcome both relativism and absolutism.

The basic ideas are first, that 'a truly viable system has to be explored through the process of ever-renewed value-building efforts – the continuous process of deconstruction and reconstruction', and secondly, that the concept of 'the minimum basic value', instead of 'supreme value', should be adopted in order to avoid conflicts or even wars arising from differences of views concerning supreme values such as freedom and equality. Whatever supreme values some people hold, this can be the cause of serious conflicts with others who believes in other supreme values; therefore, it is necessary to establish an ethical minimum and build a consensus based on it.[131]

As 'Universal Unity' is proposed mainly as a kind of religious or intuitional insight, it could be criticised as a new 'dogmatic metaphysics' (Kant) from the viewpoint of modern Western science; in contrast, this Universal Ethical Relativism may be regarded as a more sophisticated Eastern approach. Though the relation between Kim's own metaphysics (or the concept of Universal Unity) and Universal Ethical Relativism might be a little unclear, the latter seems to deserve attention as an ethical theory in its own right: comparison with recent sophisticated Western moral relativism such as that of Bernard Williams would be an interesting theme for ethical theorists. Kim insists that ecological awareness and ethical response towards it (eco-ethical conscience) necessitate such minimum basic values: 'Ecologically-Oriented Formulation of Minimum Values', namely, 'Ecological Peace (*oeco-pax*) as a Basic Value', 'Ecological Justice *(oeco-justitia)* as a Minimum Regulative Value' and

'Ecological Happiness *(oeco-felicitas)* as a Minimum Common Goal'. In addition, he described the 'Personal Formation for the Global Age' as a 'Gaian/Orphean person' in contrast to an 'Appollonian person' (Pre-modern Era) or a 'Promethean person' (Modern Era), and concludes that the Gaian/Orphean Person is a 'Global Family Person'.

Kim is an elegant speaker on Future Generations and has led discussions on this subject in many parts of the world.[132] His philosophical method is not that of monologue, produced in a closed study room, but that of a dialogue or 'trilogue', in such overseas seminars: he asserts that he regenerates the original dialogical way of philosophy practised by Socrates and Confucius.[133] In addition, Kim's role in the movement seems to be important also in having offset the danger over the pitfall of nationalistic turn of the movement simply because he came from Korea, one of the countries most damaged by the pre-war Japanese nationalistic regime: many Korean people are still hostile to Japan, and such a close co-operation between a Korean and Japanese is indeed rare and remarkable. Though it is too early to evaluate the academic achievements of this group, at least, the basic ideas, proposed by its pioneers such as Yazaki and Kim, seem to contain noteworthy potential for elaboration: *as long as* the cosmopolitan attitude is maintained, avoiding the trap of nationalism, the group could contribute to global studies for future generations from an Eastern perspective.[134]

Thus, it seems to me that the movement around the Foundation now (1997) intends to enter the third stage with the gradual emergence of an intellectual circle or network, comprising more or less sympathetic academics gathering around the Foundation and the Institute for the Integrated Study of Future Generations. The elements of the earlier stages have not necessarily disappeared, but this new stage could be considered to be built on or alongside the earlier attempt. In other words, the present movement is not only academic, but also cultural (special characteristic of the first stage) and philosophical (that of the second stage): it has a multi-layered structure of culture, everyday or popular philosophy, and multi-dimensional academic studies. Though this multi-layeredness might involve some tension within them, it could bring about dynamic development. Though this academic experiment has not yet been widely recognised in Japanese official (sometimes rather inward-looking) universities, a 'Far Eastern School for Future Generations' could emerge in the future in Japan just as the Frankfurt School has evolved around the Institute for Social Research in Frankfurt, Germany.

Just as the relation between theory and praxis is one of the central issues in the Frankfurt School, the Eastern movement is very eager to link the two. The Foundation has already encouraged several social and practical projects for the benefit of future generations: afforestation and greening of deserts in India, education in Thai farmland, a private school of *Li'ang Zhi* in China. This is important for the movement, because they have put their emphasis on 'practice' rather than abstract theory in the discussions since the first stage, and they have wished to contribute to the real world as the result of their academic activities: Kim emphasises the importance of the 'action model' rather than the Western 'thinker model', and such an emphasis seems to be reinforced by the Foundation's recent focus on Neo-Confucianism, in particular on the moral philosophy of Wang Yang-Ming, who proposed the doctrine of the unity of knowledge and action.[135]

§10. The (Far) Eastern Perspective and dialogues with its Western Counterparts

Of course, so long as this could be called a 'school', there might be some differences of opinions within its theories. Moreover, Kim emphasises that the Philosophy for Future Generations is not, or should not be a fixed doctrine like the dogmatic tenets of a religion. However, the overall characteristics of the school may be discerned as follows:

1. The value and relevance of philosophical or meta-physical arguments for studies on Future Generations are appreciated: philosophy for everyone (Yazaki) and the Philosophy for Future Generations (Kim).

2. While they are generally critical of modern Western science, rationality, and the civilisation based upon them, they are often inspired by some traditional Eastern religion or philosophy: Mahayana Buddhism (Shimizu, Inoue), Beyond Scientism and

Li'ang Zhi in Wang Yang-Ming's philosophy (Yazaki), and Northeast Asian Confucian aesthetic virtues (Kim).

3. In particular, whilst they are critical of Western atomism or individualism, they value highly the non-atomistic insights such as unity, interconnectedness, solidarity in Eastern philosophy or culture: Beyond Egoism, Universal Unity, and Dynamic Wave of Interconnectedness (Yazaki), Metaphysics of Interconnectedness (Kim), holistic ideas such as 'Emptiness' and 'Dependant Origination' in Buddhism. *Lì* (principle, form, pattern), the forming principle in 'the Great Ultimate' in Neo-Confucianism, particularly, in Chu Hsi's philosophy, together with the concept of 'field' in the philosophy of the Kyoto School, especially K. Nishida.

4. Amongst these non-atomistic elements, they tend to focus especially upon the non-atomistic human view, namely non-atomistic Self or Identity: autonomy and interdependence, Universal Identity (Yazaki), relation-formational existence, and the Gaian/ Orphean Person as a Global Family Person (Kim), and holistic virtue such as '*jen* (humanity) forming one body with all things' in Wang's teaching.

5. They propose, with conviction and passion, positive theories or practical philosophy for the benefit of Future Generations over time and place, on the grounds of the philosophical arguments: Beyond Now-ism and Beyond Nationalism (Yazaki), The Philosophy for Future Generations (Kim).

These five characteristics clearly correspond to the five characteristics of the Western early theories described in §8. Besides, some other features can be pointed out.

6. While Western positive theories usually focus on the concept of rights / obligations derived from utilitarianism or contractarianism, the Eastern positive theories or practical philosophies tend to emphasise voluntary, moralistic or ethical motivation or virtue such as gratitude for the past generations and responsibilities for the future generations: Buddhism (Inoue), Neo-Confucianism and Universal Ethical Relativism (Kim).[136]

7. As a result of this, though they appreciate the value of institutional arguments for Future Generations, they tend to give priority to the transformations and actions of individual persons stimulated by the efforts of NGOs, rather than institutional innovations at governmental or intergovernmental level, at least, at this stage: various academic or educational activities.

8. The name of the Institute for the Integrated Study of Future Generations seems to suggest that they aim to develop interdisciplinary approaches to Future Generations. Though the conference in Cambridge was organised according to three fields, namely, philosophy, sociology and politics, they also invite or collaborate with academics in other disciplines both of natural sciences such as nuclear physics and of social sciences such as economics. As a result of such multi-dimensional collaboration, several noteworthy concepts in social sciences have been proposed or illuminated: 'Sociology of Happiness', inspired by Aristotle, opportunity development, and Beyond Economism (Yazaki), 'Responsible Politics' in contrast to 'Responsive Politics', for future generations (Takeshi Sasaki)[137]; 'Fraternal Economy, Society, Politics', together constituting 'Fraternal Civilisation' (Yaroku Kobayashi and myself); and sustainable development.

These characteristics may be considered to constitute 'The (Far) Eastern Perspective'. It is clear that the (Far) Eastern Perspective forms a pronounced contrast with Western Atomistic Theories on future generations. In fact, in the fifth stage, several remarkable positive attempts with non-atomistic elements, besides Laslett's theory, have been made in the West, though not in Britain. The Foundation has already held several conferences with scholars or futurists concerned with such developments:[138] the principal figures of each seminar have mostly written important books or articles concerned with future generations since the late 1980s.[139] Some of these people might be considered to be the core of a kind of circle or network on future (generations): theoretically, the Washington, Toronto, Australia, and Malta Circle/Network on future (generations), though these may naturally overlap to some extent. In fact, they are sometimes associated with some research units or centres concerning future studies in these places: Foresight Research Unit (Institute of Education, University of Melbourne) and Futures Study Centre (Melbourne), Future Generations Programme (International Environmental Institute, University of Malta), Alternative Futures Option (Department of Political Science, University of Hawaii) and Hawaii Research Centre for Future Studies. Some of these groups are closer to the perspectives of the Far Eastern Group than most British theorists including Laslett.

In particular, the works of E. Agius in the especially distinct Malta Group has much in common with the Far Eastern Perspective. First, it is based upon Whitehead's process philosophy, or relational metaphysics. Secondly, though the Whitehead philosophy obviously does not originate in the East, he is critical of the mechanical world-picture and modern individualism, and his perspective is similar to some aspects of Eastern philosophy such as Nishida's philosophy. Thirdly, Agius proposes 'the Relational Theory of Intergenerational Ethics', applying, from Whitehead's philosophy, the organic, dynamic, interconnected, and relational perspectives upon reality: the understanding of the universe as an interconnected way of relations. Fourthly, Agius points to Whitehead's conception of 'the ontological nature of the relational self', that 'relatedness is the very "essence" of the self', because 'the self is in a process of becoming'. Thus, 'human existence has a communal character'. Fifthly, as the 'relations extend not only over space but also across time', the scope extends to the whole organic family or community of humankind ('generality of outlook'), which includes past, present and future generations ('intergenerational community'). Therefore, 'the present generation does have responsibility for mankind as a whole'. Sixthly, this responsibility is deduced from 'the future-orientation of the Whiteheadian ethical perspective' ('morality of outlook'), though Agius also proposes 'the relational concept of social justice'.[140]

Thus, in spite of the fact that both perspectives developed independently of one another, there are striking parallel and common views between the Malta Group, in particular E. Agius, and the Far Eastern Group on the first six characteristics. The fact that Whitehead was a co-author of the monumental *Principia Mathematica* may symbolise the possibility that these approaches can be an alternative to Anglo-

American mainstream theories, which are more or less closer to the view of the other co-author Bertrand Russell. There is, however, a substantive difference within the two groups around the seventh point: as social justice requires a 'moral duty to respect the claims of future generations',[141] who are in a disadvantaged position, Agius has advocated the appointment of a Guardian (an authorised person or organ, such as an ombudsman, to represent future generations at various international forums, particularly the United Nations) in line with the proposal of Government of Malta made in 1967 ('common heritage of mankind'),[142] while the Eastern Group has preferred encouragement and collaboration with the activities of various NGOs to entering directly into the maze of the political arena.[143]

In this respect, it is noteworthy that R. Slaughter in Australia has proposed 'the foresight principle' that 'one does not need to wait for final evidence (of a danger or threat) to act in a timely and effective fashion', and he endorses moreover 'institutions of foresight' such as the 'Council for Posterity' proposed in Britain. He is conscious of 'the worldview problem' widely overlooked by mainstream futurists: he is critical of Western modern culture with its short-term views and anticipates the contributions of non-Western culture with long-term perspectives, advocating an espousal of 'a new world view' with the steward ethic and notion of interconnectedness, inspired by quantum mechanics or 'new science'.[144] Similarly, A. Tough in Toronto has proposed more practically a 'Council for 2020', a group exercise which aims to foster empathy with future people, and the notion of making a pledge to future generations.[145]

Though these efforts in Malta, Australia and Toronto may not agree completely with the Far Eastern Perspective, there is no doubt that the perspectives of the former have many common aspects with those of latter. These are situated outside the mainstream of Anglo-American countries, but are still in the West. Thus, the Foundation has already held several discussions between East and West, but this Cambridge Forum on Future Generations can be considered to have a special symbolic meaning in this context. Needless to say, the reason is that the University of Cambridge is obviously one of the greatest academic centres, associated with a number of outstanding thinkers and scientists who could be said to represent modern Western civilisation. For example, a cursory look at a book interestingly entitled *Foundation for the Future: University of Cambridge,* published by Cambridge University Press in 1995, reveals its glorious past: philosophers such as Bacon, Sidgwick, Russell, Moore and Wittgenstein; economists such as Marshall, Keynes, Pigou; and natural scientists such as Harvey, Newton, Darwin, Maxwell, Watson and Crick, and Hawking.

In particular, Sir Isaac Newton himself, the central figure of the modern *atomistic* natural science, was a fellow of Trinity College, when he discovered the Law of gravitation (1665-6); Bertrand Russell, being also a fellow or a lecturer of Trinity College, proposed 'logical *atomism*' and contributed to the development of analytical philosophy today. In this sense, despite the existence of holistic thinkers such as the Cambridge Platonists, British Idealists (especially J. E. McTaggart), and Whitehead, Cambridge can be regarded as the alma mater of modern *atomistic* science, and therefore, it is one of the most appropriate or stimulating places for the dialogue between East and West. In spite of the fact that this forum is not an official conference of the University, since the Cambridge participants are mostly eminent scholars, representative of current Cambridge studies on philosophy, sociology, and politics, the tradition or spirit of Cambridge could be considered to be alive in the debate. Whilst the other positive schools at the fifth stage in the West are more or less critical of the Western tradition itself so that some of these may be positioned somewhat outside the orthodox modern Western science like the Far Eastern group, Cambridge can be considered to embody the orthodox Western tradition itself, and therefore, the highest positive attainments *within* the scope of the Western tradition. It might be difficult to reconcile or integrate completely the Eastern Perspective and the Western tradition, but the discussion between them may, at least, enable us to co-operate practically for the benefit of future generations despite the apparent theoretical gap: some differences seem to be what Bernard Williams calls a 'notional confrontation' rather than a 'real confrontation', and others could be, as it were, a 'productive confrontation'.[146] Hence, it is keenly hoped that this encounter between East and West will contribute to the next stage of studies for future generations, which constructs the global 'academic foundation for future generations'.

Notes

1. Masao Maruyama, 'Man and Politics' in his *Thought and Behaviour in Modern Japanese Politics,* ed. by Ivan Morris (Oxford University Press, 1963). Translation is mine, Japanese edition, 1964, Part 3, Ch.2, p.360. There is also a chapter entitled 'Man and Politics in the Modern Age', Part 3, Ch.8.

2. From the title of his well-known book. See note 1 above.

3. For example, Takashi Kato, *Politics and Man* (Tokyo, Iwanami,1993).

4. Similar views in this respect can be found in the contributions of John Dunn and Onora O'Neill in this volume.

5. Peter Laslett and James S. Fishkin, eds, *Justice Between Age Groups and Generations* (New Haven, Yale University Press, 1992), p.vii.

6. Ibid., p.l4.

7. Ibid., p.6.

8. I have given a full analysis in an unpublished treatise 'Synthetic Public Philosophy for Future Generations: Spatio-Temporal Neo-Republican Paradigm'. A summary of this is 'Synthetic Neo-Republicanism: New Public Philosophy for Future Generations', in *Hogaku Ronshu* (Chiba Journal of Law and Politics), vol.13, n.1 (1988), 249-290.

9. J. Narveson, 'Utilitarianism and New Generations', *Mind,* 76 (Jan. 1967); idem, 'Moral Problems of Population,' *The Monist,* 57 (1973), 69-78; Martin P. Golding, 'Ethical Issues in Biological Engineering,' *U.C.L.A. Law Review,* 15 (1968), 443-479; idem, 'Obligations to Future Generations,' *The Monist,* 56 (1972), 85-99.

10. John Rawls, *A Theory of Justice* (Oxford, Oxford University Press, 1971).

11. Laslett and Fishkin, op.cit., 'Introduction', p.l.

12. New Haven, Yale University Press.

13. R.I. Sikora and B. Barry, eds., *Obligations to Future Generations* (Philadelphia, Temple University Press, 1978); E. Partridge, ed., *Responsibilities to Future Generations: Environmental Ethics* (New York, Prometheus Books, 1981).

14. Brian Barry, 'Justice Between Generations' in P.M.S. Hacker and J.Raz, eds., *Law, Morality and Society: Essays in Honour of H.L.A. Hart* (Oxford, Clarendon Press, 1977); idem, 'Future Generations and the Circumstances of Justice' in Sikora and Barry, eds., op. cit.; idem, 'International Justice in Energy Policy' in D. MacLean and P.G. Brown eds, *Energy and the Future* (Rowman and Littlefield, 1983); J. Passmore, *Man's Responsibility for Future* (London, Duckworth, 1974), David Gauthier, *Morals by Agreement* (Oxford, Clarendon Press, 1986).

15. Parfit, *Reasons and Persons* (Oxford, Clarendon Press, 1982).

16. Samuel Scheffler in *The Times Literary Supplement* (from the back cover of the book, 1987 edition).

17. *The Sunday Times* (as above).

18. Section 44 ('The Problem of Justice between Generations') and section 45 ('Time Preference').

19. For example, Parfit, op. cit., p.416.

20. Laslett and Fishkin, op. cit., p.vii.

21. Cf. ibid., p.20.

22. Tyler Cowen and Derek Parfit, 'Against the Social Discount Rate', in ibid., Ch.7, pp.l44-161. This could be considered a elaborated version of Appendix F 'The Social Discount Rate' of Parfit's *Reasons and Persons* (pp.480-486).

23. Peter Laslett, 'The Conversation between the Generations' in G.N.A. Vesey, ed., *The Proper Study: Royal Institute of Philosophy Lectures, vol.4, 1969-70, 1972,* in P. Laslett and James Fishkin, eds, *Philosophy, Politics and Society, Fifth Series* (New Haven, Yale University Press, 1979), pp. 36-56.

24. After writing the manuscript of my papers, I discovered an important new book published in 1995: Avner de-Shalit, *Why Posterity Matters: Environmental Policies and Future Generations* (London, Routledge). Though I cannot mention this book sufficiently for this reason, I commented upon this in my unpublished paper and its summary (§3 Beyond 'Holistic' Communitarianism: Alternative Attempt, see note 8 above): this seems to share so many arguments with E. Agius and the Far Eastern theorists including myself (see §10) that these theories may be regarded as those of the sixth stage.

25. The actual contents of the conference were as follows:

12th November, 1996

1) Opening Remarks (P. Laslett/K. Yazaki)

2) The First Session: Philosophical Contributions to the Well-being of Future Generations (i) (Moderator J. Dunn)

Preliminary Remarks on the significance of the Conference (T. Kim)

Presentations (R. Harrison/Y. Chung)

3) The Second Session: Philosophical Contribution to the Well-being of Future Generations (ii) (Moderator D. Cope)

Presentations (O. O'Neill/M.Kobayashi/P. Laslett)

13th November

4) The Third Session: Sociological Contribution to the Well-being of Future Generations(Moderator R. Harrison)

Summary of the discussions of the first day (E. Page)

Presentations (A. Giddens/T. Imada/P. Baert)

5) Luncheon Speech (K. Inoue)

6) The Fourth Session: Political Contribution to the Well-being of Future Generations (Moderator T. Kim)

Presentations (J. Dunn / T. Sasaki)

7) Free Discussions

14th November

8) Final Discussions (Moderator T. Kim)

Summary of the discussions of the second day (E. Page)

9) Closing Remarks (K. Yazaki/P. Laslett)

I am very grateful for the valuable suggestions and help of the British people in arranging this project: those of the Cambridge scholars such as Peter Laslett, John Dunn, Anthony Giddens, Ross Harrison, Geoffrey Hawthorn, Raymond Geuss and Patrick Baert; those of Derek Parfit (Oxford University), David Cope (Parliamentary Office of Science and Technology, formerly, UK Centre for Economic and Environmental Development), Andrew Johnson (The White Horse Press), Edward Page (University of Southampton, formerly, Ph. D. student Warwick University) and Cathy Taylor (language editor).

26. It is important that not only Laslett but also Parfit contributed to the collection. Although Laslett's influence is obviously conspicuous in it, Parfit's impact can be also discerned especially in Chapter 4 'Future People, Disability, and Screening' (Jonathan Glover) and Chapter 5 'Consequentialism Implies a Zero Rate of Intergenerational Discount' (David Cowen).

27. Laslett, op. cit.

28. For example, Terrance Ball, 'The Incoherence of Intergenerational Justice,' *Inquiry,* vol. 28, n.3 (Sept. 1985), 321-338, cf. p.327.

29. This is the most common definition. Though it is possible to extend the range of future generations to younger generations who have already been born, this article, to simplify the argument, uses the usual definition.

30. For example, Golding, 'Obligations to Future Generations', op. cit. p.89; William Grey, 'Possible Persons and the Problems of Posterity'. *Environmental Values,* vol.5 n. 2. (1996), 161-180, p.l63.

31. Barry, op. cit. p.270.

32. For example, see J. Passmore, op. cit.

33. Narveson, op. cit; Parfit, op. cit.

34. John Passmore, op. cit. p.86, quoted from B. Barry 'Justice between Generations', op. cit.

35. Barry mentioned 'the asymmetry of power' and 'determinism', while Page listed explicitly (1) the contingency of future individuals (2) uncertainty or ignorance about the future (3) the lack of reciprocity between present and future persons. Barry, op.cit; Edward Page, 'Is Intergenerational Justice an Oxymoron?' 'Intergenerational Justice, Reciprocity and Posthumous Harms' (unpublished papers).

36. Golding, 'Obligations to Future Generations', op.cit.

37. Ball, op.cit., pp. 330-333. Ball regards Golding's argument as an intergenerational variation on a general theme developed by Michael Walzer. Michal Walzer, *Obligations* (Cambridge, Mass: Harvard University Press, 1970); idem, *Spheres of Justice* (New York, Basic Books, 1983).

38. Ball, op.cit., p.322.

39. Ibid.

40. 'from the fact that we are unable to treat them justly by their lights it does not follow that we are entitled to treat future generations in ways that are unfair or unjust by our lights'. Ibid., p.333.

41. Joel Feinberg, 'The Rights of Animals and Unborn Generations,' in *Philosophy and Environmental Crisis* ed. by William Blackstone (Athens, University of Georgia Press, 1974), 43-68, and Feinberg, *Rights, Justice and the Bounds of Liberty* (Princeton, N.J., Princeton University Press, 1980); idem, 'Harm and Self-Interest' in Hacker and Raz ed., *Law, Morality and Society,* op.cit., 284-308; J. O'Neill, 'Future Generations: Present Harms,' *Philosophy* (Jan. 1993); idem, *Ecology, Politics and Policy* (London, Routledge, 1995). Cf. Ernest Partridge, 'Posthumous Interests and Posthumous Respect', *Ethics,* Vol. 91, n.2 (Jan. 1981), 243-264.

42. Page, op. cit. For him, this is 'only one horn of the Symmetry View'. Another horn is to doubt the 'ground assumption that present persons can harm the future,' citing the Non-Identity problem raised by Parfit, op. cit., p.73.

43. Edward Page gives details of this issue, using the words of Parfit: Mental State Theories, Desire Fulfilment Theories, and Objective (List) Theories. The former two correspond to what I refer to here as 'empirical philosophy', whilst the third is the 'new theory'. Page. op.cit; Parfit, op.cit., p.493f; L. Temkin, 'Harmful goods, harmless bads,' in R.G. Frey and C. Morus, eds, *Value, Welfare and Morality* (Cambridge University Press, 1992).

44. Barry, op. cit, p. 284; Annette Baier, 'The rights of past and future persons,' in E. Partridge, ed., op. cit, p. 178.

45. Though Barry explicitly refers only to TO ③, his explanation about 1-3 is considered to assume TO ①.

46. This is the argument developed by J. Passmore as 2 is the argument of M. Golding. Though Barry himself is critical of Passmore's logic, Barry also denies universal utilitarianism for another reason: It is too great a demand that the present generation should 'always act in such a way as to maximise the sum of happiness over the further course of human (or maybe scientist) history'. Barry, op.cit., p. 275.

47. Barry's objections to Rawls' theory, one of the central points of his article, are too complicated to summarise here: some of these are related either to Rawls' postulate that people in the 'original position' are all contemporaries (against TO ①) or to indeterminant behaviour of the intervening generations (TO ②).

48. This process of extraction is parallel to what I examined about the development of theories on clientelism in my Japanese monograph, and such a way of criticism could be generalised into a 'Methodological Criticism of Atomistic Theories'.

49. R.M.Hare, 'Abortion and the Golden Rule', *Philosophy and Public Affairs,* vol.4 (1975), 201-222; William Grey, 'Possible Persons and Problems of Posterity', *Environmental Values,* vol.5, n.2 (1996), 161-180, especially, pp.169-171.

50. Rawls denies the relevancy of utilitarianism for a rather similar reason to that given by Barry: 'Thus the utilitarianism doctrine may direct us to demand heavy sacrifices of the *poor* generations for the sake of greater advantages for later ones that are far better off'. Rawls, op.cit., p.287.

51. Ibid., p.288.

52. Ibid., p.289.

53. Ibid.

54. Ibid., p.288.

55. Ibid., §.24, p.137.

56. Ibid., p.l39.

57. 'If we imagine that the original position contains representatives from all actual generations, the veil of ignorance would make it unneccesary to change the motivation assumption'. Ibid., p.291.

58. David A.J. Richard, *A Theory of Reasons for Action* (Oxford, Clarendon Press. 1971); cf. Barry, op.cit., pp.280-281. I detailed other similar attempts in the unpublished treatise (see note 8).

59. Barry, ibid., p.281.

60. Rawls, op.cit., p.l39.

61. Ibid., p.l40, also p.292. cf. p.l46, concerning 4 (Time and Entry), the interpretation of the original position is not c (all possible persons simultaneously), but a (anytime during the age of reason, for living persons).

62. Ibid., p.l40.

63. See also p.292. Almost the same sentence.

64. Ibid., §.25, pp.l42-143.

65. Ibid., p.l44.

66. Ibid., p.292, but he wrote more frankly at page 140: 'altering the motivation assumption'.

67. This line of criticism has already been made by several writers: Peter Danielson, 'Theories, Intuitions and the Problem of World-Wide Distribution Justice', *Philosophy of the Social Sciences,* vol. 3, n. 4 (Dec. 1973), 331-338; Gregory S. Kavka, 'Rawls on Average and Total Utility', *Philosophical Studies,*vol. 27, n. 4 (April 1975), 237-253; Brian Barry, 'Rawls on Average and Total Utility: A Comment,' *Philosophical Studies,* vol. 31, n. 5 (May 1977), 317-325; idem, 'Justice Between Generations', op. cit.; idem. *Theories of Justice* (London, Harvester, 1989), p.24; D. Clayton Hubin, 'Justice and Future Generations,' *Philosophy and Public Affairs,* vol. 6, n.1 (Fall, 1976), 70-83; Jane English, 'Justice Between Generations', *Philosophical Studies,* vol. 31, n. 2 (Feb. 1997), 91-104; R. and V. Routley, 'Nuclear Energy and Obligations to the Future', *Inquiry,* vol. 21, n. 2 (Summer, 1978), especially pp.l68-171; Stephen Bickham 'Future Generations and Contemporary Ethical Theory', *Journal of Value Inquiry,* vol. 15 (1981), 169-177, especially p. 174; Robin Attfield, *The Ethics of Environmental Concern,* 2nd edn. (Athens and London, The University of Georgia Press, 1983/1991), especially, pp.105-107; Emmanuel Agius, 'Towards a Relational Theory of Intergenerational Ethics', *Bijdragen,* vol. 50, n. 3 (1989), 293-313, especially, pp.298-299.

68. Rawls, op.cit., p.292.

69. Ibid., p.146, b and c of 8 (Motivation of the parties). Cf. note 61 above.

70. Ibid., p.288.

71. Ibid., p.146, a in 8, cf. note 69 above.

72. Ibid., p.142.

73. Ibid., p.288.

74. Ibid.

75. Ibid.

76. Ibid., p.290.

77. Ibid.

78. This reciprocity could be interpreted as generalised exchange (Levi-Strauss), which is the central concept of my Japanese monograph 'Political Clientelism and Political Syncretism: The Structure of these Concepts'. This point will be hopefully elaborated in the future.

79. Ibid., p.291.

80. Rawls finally combined the just saving principle with his two principles of justice. Ibid., p.292.

81. Ibid.

82. A term 'contemporary contractual theory' is avoided, for it can be mistaken for a modern contractual theory.

83. As for the details, cf. my unpublished treatise, see note 8 above.

84. Ernest Partridge 'Posterity and the "Strains of Commitment"' in *Creating A New History For Future Generations,* ed. by Tae-Chang Kim and James A. Dator (Institute for the Integrated Study of Future Generations, 1994), pp. 263-278, cf. pp.268-271. Its origin is his Doctoral Dissertation 'Rawls and the Duty to Posterity' (University of Utah, 1976);Barry, op.cit.

85. Ibid.,p.278.

86. Partridge, 'Posterity and the "Strains of Commitment"', op. cit., p.268.

87. Barry, op. cit., p.276; Partridge, op. cit., pp.268-269.

88. Ibid., p.269.

89. '... for example, the question of the appropriate rate of capital saving and of the conservation of natural resources and the environment of nature', Rawls, op. cit., p.l37, in §24 'The Veil of Ignorance'. However, there is no reference in §.44 'The Problem of Justice Between Generations'.

90. Partridge, op.cit., pp.269-291.

91. Barry, op.cit., p.279.

92. Ibid,p.277.

93. Ibid., p. 276.

94. Ibid., p.279.

95. lbid., p.279-280.

96. Gauthier, op. cit; Kevin Sauvé, 'Gauthier, Property Right, and Future Generations,' *Canadian Journal of Philosophy,* vol.25, n.2 (June, 1995), 163-176. The following argument mainly relied on Sauvé's brilliant critique.

97. Ibid., p165.

98. Ibid., pp. 166-167. The other arguments were named 'Productive Investments Arguments' and 'Continuing Contract Arguments'.

99. Ibid., p.166. cf. Gauthier, op. cit., p.166.

100. cf. Sauvé., op. cit., p.175.

101. Ibid., p.176.

102. Partridge, op. cit., p.271.

103. Partridge mentioned Rawlsian theory in a section named 'Future Policy for a Society of Saints,' distinguishing it from 'The Motivation Problem' in our real world. However, it is doubtful whether the motivational assumption of Rawls can be regarded as that of saints. Ibid., p.270.

104. Norman Care, 'Future Generations, Public Policy, and the Motivation Problem,' *Environmental Ethics,* Vol. 4, n.3 (Fall, 1982), 195-214; idem, 'Future Generations and the Motivation Problem,' in Kim and Dator, eds., op. cit., pp.293-336; Robert L. Heilbroner, 'What has Posterity ever done for me?' and Thomas H. Thompson, 'Are we Obliged to Future Others?' both in Partridge, ed., op. cit.

105. In response to the criticism of this point, Rawls changed his formulation on the just saving principle, in his *Political Liberalism* ; however, his new attempt involves a logical flaw and, therefore, he is unable to escape from this impasse. J. Rawls, *Political Liberalism* (New York, Columbia University Press, 1993), p.274, note 12. Cf. my unpublished treatise, see note 8 above.

106. The following atomistic concepts are based on my presentation 'A Criticism of Rationalistic Political Theories: A Prospect towards a New-Rationalistic Theory,' The Japanese Political Science Association, on 2nd October 1994, at the University of Kansai. The central object of the criticism is public choice theories, and the Rawls' theory at this stage could be classified in the category.

107. Rawls, *A Theory of Justice,* op.cit., p.142.

108. Ibid., p.144.

109. Ibid., p.146. cf. note 69 in this paper.

110. Laslett, 'Is there a Generational Contract?', op. cit., pp.30-46; Annette C. Baier, *Moral Prejudices* (Cambridge, Mass., Harvard University Press, 1995).

111. Peter Laslett stated at the conference to the effect that he was neither an individualist nor an atomist. I deeply appreciated the explicit statement upon my presentation, and agreed to this on the ground of his previous articles.

112. This was confirmed in my private conversation with him in organising this conference.

113. The explanation in this section is written merely with the role of the organiser of this specific conference, sponsored by the Future Generations Alliance Foundation. Therefore, my articles are written as an academic independent of the Foundation, and the statements which follows in the text are not officially provided by the Foundation itself. As my knowledge of the Foundation is basically limited to that concerning this conference, the following account mainly depends on the publications of the Foundation, in particular, on the 1993 pamphlet of the Foundation; Tae-Chang Kim and Allen

Tough, 'Thinking About the Well-Being of Future Generations: A One Year Learning Effect,' and Katsuhiko Yazaki, 'Going Beyond Boundaries for Our Future Generations', both in *Thinking About Future Generations* (Kyoto, Institute for the Integrated Study of Future Generations, 1994),pp.17-54, and pp.273-285; Katsuhiko Yazaki, *Path to Liang Zhi: Seeking an Eternal Philosophy* (Japan, Future Generations Alliance Foundation, 1994). I am grateful to Professor Kim, Mr Naoki Shiomi, Miss Akiko Tobitani and other staff of the Foundation, who provided information on the Foundation in response to my questions, and also for the various documents provided by the Foundation. Publications of the Foundation or the Institute are usually available by direct order to them: the adresses are (1) 5th Floor, 88, Kankoboko-cho, Muromachi-Higashi-Iru, Shimogyo-ku, Kyoto 600 Japan, or (2) 10 West, 56th Street 5F, New York, NY, 10019 U.S.A..

114. See also, his 'Ever-Changing Life and Ever Lasting Existence: The Eternal Path of Mankind Toward Tranquility of Mind' in *Thinking About Future Generations,* op. cit., pp.151-159.

115. Sakae Shimizu, 'Foreword' and 'Why should we think about Future Generations?' in *Thinking About Future Generations,* op. cit., pp.7-16, 233-246. He is a Professor Emeritus of Kyoto University. With respect to other natural scientists, for example, T.and H. Hirai, N. Hokkyo, W. Unno; as for a philosopher, Eiko Hanaoka.

116. The Kyoto Forum had held 16 conferences by 1991 (51 by 1996), and edited, in Japanese, 'The Kyoto Forum Lecture Series' entitled *In Pursuit of New Values* (1991), *Cohabitation and Life Cycle on Earth* (1992). 'Cohabitation and Cycle' is a key concept proposed by Takeshi Umehara, a representative philosopher both of contemporary Kyoto School and of Contemporary Japan. The recent themes of the Kyoto Forum seem to have been co-ordinated with Future Generations: Kyoto Forum, ed., *Seeking Solidarity with Our Future Generations* (1994).

117. The Kyoto Forum published the Japanese translation of the pre-conference official newsletter *Earth Summit News* and *Our Country, the Planet* (the official book for the summit by Sir Shridath Ramphal), and became joint publisher with T. W. Kheel of the *Earth Summit Times.* Shridath Ramphal, *Our Country, the Planet* (Washington. D.C., Island Press, 1992), translated by Yoko Eguchi, *Earth Ethics* (Japan, Kodansha Publishing, 1992); Kyoto Forum, ed., *Voices from Kyoto Forum in Earth Summit Times* (1992) and idem, *Earth Summit Leadership Dialogue: UNCED Special Event* (1993). Both are bilingual editions (Japanese /English). cf. Theodore W. Kheel, 'Future Generations and the Next 50 years', in *Thinking About Future Generations,* op.cit., pp.161-168.

118. Yazaki, *Path to Li'ang Zhi,* op.cit., p.44.

119. Pamphlet *Future Generations,* 1993, p.1. This is a direct translation by myself. English translation of this clause in the pamphlet is so free that it could lead to the misunderstanding that the Foundation undertakes some kind of religious or evangelistic activities. In reality, this is what the clause explicitly denies.

120. Pamphlet, op. cit., p.2. Translation is mine. Also, see the manifesto of the Foundation, 4.

121. Ibid., p.5.

122. Katsuhiko Yazaki, *Felissimo: The Sociology of Happiness* (Japan, 1990), in Japanese.

123. For example, he developed the principles of his mail-catalogue business, 'gathering the value of a wide area' and 'taking advantage of future value now', into 'Beyond Nationalism' and 'Beyond Now-ism'; also, the idea of 'ultra store' was developed into 'ultra conference' and Five Beyonds. Yazaki, 'Going Beyond Boundaries for Our Future Generations,' op. cit., Yazaki, *Path to Li'ang Zhi,* op. cit., especially, pp. 32-40, p.69.

124. Ibid., p.116, 122. Inamori became a monk in 1997.

125. Tae-Chang Kim, *Thinking About Future Generations,* op.cit., pp.l69-196, in particular, pp. 178-181.

126. Ibid., p.183. See his reference to Donah Zohar in his own article in this volume.

127. Ibid., p.l86.

128. Ibid., p.l92.

129. Ibid., pp.l92-196. Kyoto Forum translated *Our Global Neighbourhood: the Report of the Commission on Global Governance* (Oxford University Press, 1995). Japanese version was entitled *Global Leadership:In Search for a New World Order* (NHK publications, 1995).

130. Kim, 'Toward a New Theory of Value for the Global Age,' in *Creating A New History For Future Generations,* ed. by T.C. Kim and J.A. Dator (Future Generations Studies Series 2, Institute for the Integrated Study of Future Generations, 1994), pp.319-342.

131. Ibid.

132. See Kim's article in chapter 12 of this volume.

133. As records of these dialogues, the Institute for the Integrated Study of Future Generations has already published two volumes containing papers presented in such conferences: 'Future Generations Studies Series', namely, *Thinking About Future Generations* (Series 1, 1994), op. cit.; Kim and Dator, eds, *Creating a New History for Future Generations* (Series 2, 1994), op. cit. The Foundation published also *Why Future Generations Now?*(1994) and *From Hiroshima to Future Generations* (1994): both books are bilingual editions, and most important articles are included in 'Future Generation Series 1-2'.

134. The cosmopolitan orientation which embraces a kind of communitarianism based upon a criticism of Western individualism reminds me of an important Japanese political philosophy of Shigeru Nanbara, the teacher of Masao Maruyama: such cosmopolitanism enables me to co-operate with the group.

135. The Foundation sponsored an international conference on the significance of Wang Yang-Ming's philosophy for the 21st century, at the Third Global Future Generations Kyoto Forum in 1997.

136. Regarding the discussion around this theme, Christopher Jones, 'Cosmic Gaia and Future Generations' and the contribution in Section 3 'Philosophical and ethical issues concerning acting on behalf of future generations', in Kim and Dator, eds, *Creating a New History for Future Generations,* op. cit., pp.43-60, 263-342.

137. Takeshi Sasaki, 'The responsibilities of politics for future generations', in ibid., pp. 87-101, also in this volume, ch. 9.

138. In 1994, Washington Seminar (organised by H. F. Didsbury, addressed by Edith B. Weiss, Amitai Etzioni, Harvey Cox and others), Toronto Seminar (organised by Allen Tough, attended by Norman Care, Duane Elgin and others), Sydney Seminar (organised by Richard Slaughter, attended by Charles Birch, Ian Lowe and others), and Malta Seminar (co-sponsored by the Foundation for International Studies, University of Malta, and attended by Emmanuel Agius, Salvino Busuttil, Christopher D. Stone and others). Cf. Kim and Tough, 'Thinking About the Well-Being of Future Generations', op.cit.

139. Edith Brown Weiss, *In Fairness to Future Generations: International Law, Common Patrimony And Intergenerational Equity* (Japan, The United Nations University; Transnational Publishers, Inc., 1989); Allen Tough, *Crucial Questions About the Future* (Lanham University Press of America, 1991); Richard Slaughter, *The Foresight Principle: Cultural Recovery in the 21st Century* (London, Adamantive Press, 1994); Emmanuel Agius, *The Rights of Future Generations: In Search of an Intergenerational Ethical Theory* (Leuven, Belgium, Catholic University, 1986); E. Agius and Busuttil, eds, *Our Responsibilities Towards Future Generations* and *What Future for Future Generations?* (Malta, Union Press, 1990 and 1994); James Dator, *The Future of Development* (Paris, Unesco, 1991).

140. Emmanuel Agius, 'Towards a Relational Theory of Intergenerational Ethics,' *Bijdragen,* vol. 50, n.3, 1989, 293-313, especially, pp. 301-310, cited from p.303, 302, 304, 307, 305; idem, 'Germ-line Cells – Our Responsibilities For Future Generations', *Concilium,* 203 (1989), D. Mieth and J. Pohier, eds, *Ethics in the Natural Sciences* (T.&T. Clark Ltd, Edinburgh, 1989).

141. Agius, 'Towards a Relational Theory of Intergenerational Ethics', op.cit., p.310.

142. Agius, 'What Future for Future Generations?: The 'Quality of Life' of the Future', in *Thinking About Future Generations,* op. cit., especially, p.67.

143. This issue was especially discussed in the Malta Seminar. Kim and Tough, op.cit., pp.41-48, especially, p.45. cf. Christopher Stone, 'Should we establish a guardian to speak for future generations?', in Kim and Dator eds, op. cit., pp.l27-140; Bruce E. Tonn 'The Court of Generations: A proposed amendment to the US Constitution', *Futures,* Vol.23, n.5 (June, 1991), 482-498.

144. Richard A. Slaughter, 'Why We Should Care About Future Generations Now?' in *Thinking About Future Generations,* op. cit., pp.247-271, cited from, p.256, pp.264-65; idem, 'How Institutions of Foresight Protect Future Generations', in Kim and Dator eds., op.cit., pp.181-201; idem, 'Changing Images of Futures in tbe 20th Century', *Futures,* vol. 23, n.5 (June, 1991), 499-515; idem, 'Looking for the real "megatrends"', *Futures,* vol.25, n.8 (October, 1993), 827-849; idem, *The Foresight Principle,* op. cit. He (and H. Disbury) addressed at the Kyoto Forum in 1993, and their lectures are included in *Seeking Solidarity with Our Future Generations,* op. cit.

145. Tough, *Crucial Questions About the Future,* op. cit., especially, Ch.10; idem, 'What future generations need from us', *Futures,* vol.25, n.l0 (December, 1993), 1041-1050.

146. Bernard Williams, 'The truth in relativism', in his *Moral Luck* (Cambridge, Cambridge University Press, 1981), Ch.11, especially p.l38.

3

Distant Strangers and Future Generations

Onora O'Neill

Distance in Space and in Time

I want to consider what we can learn about obligations to future generations by looking at certain analogies with our obligations to distant contemporaries. Should we look at our obligations to others who are distant in space and who are distant in time in the same way, or do spatial and temporal distance have profoundly different implications for moral relations? My suggestion will be that the two sorts of distance can be looked at in similar ways, and that they have parallel implications for our moral thinking, and in particular for our thinking about justice.

I shall present these points without any attempt to consider how we might best think about justice or about other forms of moral concern. I shall assume simply that these are matters on which we can reach some reasonable and usable conclusions. I shall investigate only the question of the *range* or *scope* of those conclusions. If we owe justice to others, then, I shall argue, we owe it to all beings on whom we believe our action impinges or will impinge, even if they are distant in space or in time.

Traditional Western thought is not, I think, very helpful here, because it has been concerned less with distance in space or time than with the question whether others are to count as *strangers* or as *neighbours.* In Christian thought the parable of the Good Samaritan has played an important role. In this parable the Samaritan helps the wounded stranger whom he encounters on the lonely road between Jerusalem and Jericho.

One striking thing about the story is that it is not about distance. The stranger and the Samaritan were side by side, face to face. The moral of the story is supposed to be that strangers too are neighbours and to be treated well – but the context in which they can be treated well is when they are close at hand.

Much other traditional Western thinking about obligations to strangers was not concerned with distance. It construed obligations to strangers as a matter of *hospitality* to those strangers while they were near by, and of *rescue* or *succour* of strangers in danger who were near enough to be rescued.

The reason why traditional thought concentrated on *strangeness* rather than on *distance* is not hard to see. Until recently action-at-a-distance was difficult or impossible. It took great and exceptional effort to affect the lives of far distant others. Only the most powerful individuals and organisations could affect distant others intentionally, for example by conquest and conversion. Other effects on distant others, such as those produced by the spread of diseases and technologies were usually unintended.

However, with the advent of long distance, then of global travel, trade, economies, power politics and telecommunications, action-at-a-distance that affects the lives of distant others has become a ubiquitous feature of all our lives.

The same is true of action-across-time. Human action has always affected the future in limited ways, above all by having or not having children and descendants, but also by cultivating or by damaging the natural and the man made worlds – the fields, forests and cities. The difference today is that we have capacities to affect the further future in more radically destructive or transformative ways by action that affects the environment.

The Scope of Moral Concern

To which others, whether familiars or strangers, nearby or far off, contemporaries or future generations, should we direct our moral concern? To which of them do we have obligations? To which of them do we have the obligations of justice? I do not think that it is at all obvious how this question is to be answered, nor that it is obvious that we begin with the case of nearby contemporaries. There are great divisions of opinion in many traditions of thought about the *scope* of moral concern, quite apart from the differences about the *content* of moral requirements, about which I shall say nothing in this paper.

Do we owe moral concern to all other humans – as many moral cosmopolitans think? Or only to those humans to whom we have some sort of special relationship (our fellow countrymen, members of our own community, our own clan or family) – as anti-cosmopolitans of many sorts think? Moreover, do we owe moral concern to certain non-human beings, such as certain animals, and if so to which? We are all familiar with the range of issues that bioethics has brought to our attention as possible (but, according to some, controversial) objects of moral concern: in the human case the foetus and the senile, the retarded and the comatose; in the non-human case ranging from the higher primates to bacteria, as well as certain abstract aspects of the environment such as biodiversity and gene pools, the ozone layer and the CO_2 level, habitats and species. Although there are many writers who hope to instruct us on the proper basis of moral concern, and to enable us to discriminate the beings to which we owe it from those to which we do not, I am not confident that convincing arguments can be produced.

In contemporary Western philosophy these questions are often posed by asking who or what has *moral standing*, and by asking what feature or characteristic confers that standing. A traditional religious and metaphysical view was that moral standing has been a matter of possessing an immortal soul. More recent views have maintained that it is a matter of having the capacity to reason, or the capacity to suffer, or perhaps the prospect of developing one or both of these capacities. Whichever of these views we look at it seems that we will find difficult border-line cases. Those who think that moral standing is a matter of rationality or of the prospect of rationality will find that there are some human beings who by this standard would not have moral standing. Those who think that moral standing is a matter of sentience or of the prospect of sentience will find that they will need to explain why they value human life more than the lives of bacteria, and why they assign any value to abstract entities such as species or biodiversity, as opposed to valuing the sheer number of sentient lives. Those who claim that they value all life will have difficulty in identifying any way of living that lives up to their claim.

In short, it seems that many of the claims that are made about the basis and the extent of moral standing require an account of the metaphysics of the person or of the self, of the reasons why certain characteristics are essential for a being to merit moral concern, and lack of those characteristics an appropriate reason for denying moral concern.

Yet it is hard to know how to reach agreement on any metaphysics of the person or self.

A Practical Approach to Moral Standing

There may be ways forward which do not require us to reach agreement on the metaphysics of the self or the person; I shall sketch one such way.

Another more practical way of looking at the matter might be to consider the assumptions to which we are already and unavoidably committed in acting. When we act we already view certain other beings as agents and as subjects. Our views may sometimes be mistaken, and they may often be held without any clear, let alone well-grounded, account of the basis of moral standing. We lead our lives with little concentration on the metaphysics of the person. Yet it is quite clear that we view many other as agents and as subjects of experience. Although we do not always articulate or establish the assumption that others are agents or subjects of experience, these assumptions are embedded in our action.

In some cases we make assumptions about *particular* other beings, whom we see as agents or as subjects. For example, in giving a present to a friend, or in preparing a meal for one's family, or in marking a particular student's essay we take a definite view that those particular, individual persons are capable of pleasure, or that they need to eat well, or that they are able to learn. These and many other interconnected assumptions that we standardly make commit us to viewing those particular others as agents and as subjects of experience, or in some cases simply as subjects who can experience although they cannot act.

It may seem to be a difficulty that we do not, indeed cannot make assumptions about *particular* distant or future individuals. However, this is not a problem that arises only in the case of action that affects distant and future others; and on reflection I think it is not a problem at all. The vast majority of the assumptions we make in daily life and activity are about *specifiable* and not about *particular* others. For example, when a hotel manager prepares meals he does not always assume that identifiable, particular people will come to the hotel to order, eat and pay for those meals. For he usually does not know who will come. Rather he assumes that some others, who will he assumes have a certain standard range of capacities to act and to experience, but whom he cannot pick out as individuals, will come, eat and pay. Or when a shopkeeper displays certain goods at a certain price she may make no assumptions about who is going to buy which item. She assumes simply that various customers, with broadly predictable characteristics, whom she undoubtedly assumes will be agents and subjects of experience, will like and will buy at the price offered. Or when a university advertises for laboratory technicians, nobody knows which individuals will reply to the advertisement, or prove to have the best qualifications, but the advertisement is placed on the assumption that there are competent and perhaps excellent persons who could and probably will apply.

The fact that our action is often designed to take account of *specific types of agent and subject*, rather than of *particular, individual agents or subjects*, is indispensable for a convincing account of our action and interaction with nearby others; it is even more basic for our action, or interaction with distant others, and for our action on future others.

When a company is exporting a product to a distant market, the managers need not and often cannot assume anything about individual customers: they assume that there will be some customers with abilities to negotiate and to enter ordinary commercial relations. Or if a householder protects her house against burglars she will usually make no assumptions about any particular burglar, but she will assume that somebody or other, she knows not who, might seek to enter her house if she did not take certain sorts of precautions. The company and the householder are inevitably committed to viewing others whom they can specify only in fairly vague terms as beings who might, hence could, act in certain ways and so who have certain capacities to experience and to act.

Whenever we act we make complicated assumptions about the capacities of specifiable others, whom we usually cannot identify individually, and specifically about their capacities to act and to be on the receiving end of action. Since our action is based on these assumptions, we cannot simply drop them when considering the ethical demands that are relevant to our action.

A practical approach to moral standing is simply the view that what we assume in acting we cannot selectively reject or neglect in making moral judgements about that action,

However, a practical approach will not provide us with all the conclusions that we might have reached if we had succeeded in establishing a metaphysics of the person. In particular it will point to a less comprehensively cosmopolitan account of the scope of justice and of other forms of moral concern. Nevertheless, I do not think that the fact that a practical approach has these limits is likely to have significant implications for action.

A Practical Approach to the Standing of Distant Others

For example, consider the peoples of East Asia and those of Western Europe 2000 years ago. There was no contact. In acting nobody made any assumptions at all about others inhabiting those distant, unknown parts of the world. No doubt if our ancestors had had an appropriate metaphysics of the person they might have concluded that the inhabitants of all remote regions, if there were any, had moral standing. However this hypothetical conclusion would have been without practical import for the way in which they acted.

The fact that a practical approach leads us to more limited conclusions – it implies nothing when we genuinely make no assumptions about others whom we take to be agents and subjects – *may* make no practical difference. Since our remote ancestors could not in any case act on one another across the distances that separated them, we need not ask or answer the question whether they behaved appropriately or inappropriately, justly or unjustly, to one another.

Of course, sometimes we act on false assumptions. Those who colonise an inhabited island may falsely assume that it is without inhabitants. However, once they discover their mistake, their assumptions will change. At that point they will be assuming either that there are others who accept their presence or that there are others who will resist it. The ways in which they act will be testimony enough of the revised assumptions on which they now act. If they no longer think that their action affects no others, they may assume that their action harms and perhaps defeats and dispossesses, or at the limit exterminates, others whom they view as agents and subjects of experience. Alternatively, they may revise their plans to take account of the reality that their invasion is not without danger, that they may meet resistance: once again their assumption that the original inhabitants are agents and subjects of experience will be evident from their action. A third possibility is that they will accept that they must not treat the original inhabitants of whom they now know unjustly, and will revise their plans and action accordingly. Once new assumptions of these or other sorts are made, the invaders will in effect have assumed that the inhabitants of whom they were formerly ignorant are ordinary agents and subjects of experience. They will then have to accord the moral consideration which they think appropriate to other ordinary agents to those on the island, or to offer some special (non-arbitrary) reason why the islanders do not merit moral consideration (at this point self-deception is common). The point I wish to make is simply that as we adjust our views of what we are doing and whom we affect, we must accept the implications of those revised views for an account of the scope of our obligations to others.

A Practical Approach to the Standing of Future Others

An analogous approach to the standing of future persons is also possible. Even if we cannot settle the disputes that have been conducted about the metaphysics of the person, or the basis of moral standing, it is plain that in acting we make assumptions about future persons.

In the first place, we make assumptions about particular persons whom we can identify. We may make assumptions about our children or grandchildren who already exist. But far more often we will make assumptions about persons whom we cannot pick out as individuals, but whom we can specify.

For example, I may consider the needs of students who will be at my College in 25 or 50 or 100 years time. They have not yet been born. We can have no way of knowing which particular individuals will become those students. Yet it makes perfectly good sense for me to think about the needs of those future students whom I cannot identify as individuals. If I believe that the College should adopt policies which enable it to educate all its students, then I must conclude that the College has reason to follow policies which will enable it to educate those future generations of students, that it must preserve its buildings and its financial status, despite the fact that nobody can now say who the future beneficiaries of these policies will be.

We make assumptions about future persons either when we think that there will be a chain of connected individuals – the descendants of a certain family, or the future students of a certain university – or when we act institutionally in ways that would make no sense unless we thought that there would be future agents and subjects of experience.

When we build businesses or establish foundations, when we cherish and maintain schools or universities, when we write books or poems or music, when we work to establish and to hand on traditions of civic and personal life, we act in ways that assume that there will be future persons to join in and to benefit, to be customers and students, to read and to listen, to grow up in the traditions that we shall have kept alive. Equally when we engage in very long term enterprises like soil conservation or planting trees, like scientific research or constructing buildings that are to last for centuries, we assume a future of agents and subjects of experience who will use and benefit from the still fertile land, from the slowly maturing forests and from robust buildings and from accumulated knowledge. If we are making these assumptions in some areas of our lives we can hardly assume that the future can be discounted on the basis of our lack of any proven metaphysics of the person.

It is, I think, true that we do not base action on assumptions about others in the very far future: but the time horizon of the assumptions to which we are committed is one of many generations, indeed centuries, and therefore one which (I believe) is sufficient to require us to take stringent account of the environmental impact of any action we propose and to reject any proposal that would be a source of injury to whichever future others our proposals assume.

Once again a practical approach may not reach all the conclusions that a metaphysics of the person would provide. But I believe that it will provide a framework which, in conjunction with ethical reasoning, will require us to accept substantial conclusions about our obligations to future generations as well as to distant strangers.

4

Politics and the Well-being of Future Generations

John Dunn

Because they are wholly unreciprocal, the political relations between ourselves and future generations are in one respect radically unlike our political relations with our contemporaries. They also differ drastically from our political relations with our human predecessors. It is plausible in the first instance to see our relations with past persons as a mirror image of those with future persons, as, in temporal terms, they presumably must be. But the key political respect in which the two differ is in the reversal of the direction of power. The dead have a kind of external power over us through the world which they have left us; and at least some older human beings (living or dead) have a kind of internal power over us, embodied in what we are (in the persons who we have become). It is a nice point where this power ends, if indeed it ever does end. But a power, however external initially, which has come to be embodied in what we just are is external no longer. The future, by contrast, has no power over us at all. Any capacity to move us which it possesses must derive from causal characteristics already internal to us and ex hypothesi formed either by our own choices, or, perhaps more plausibly, from the impact upon us of the past. Its power, where it has any, its capacity to prompt us to act to its denizens' advantage, or, in more strained hypothetical mode, as they would (or will) wish us to have done, it can obtain only by courtesy of our sentiments, judgments and choices.

It is coherent, both metaphysically and practically, to think of power as running forwards from the past, through the present, into the future. But it is certainly not coherent, at least within the modern western world view, to see it as running backwards from the future even into the present, let alone back on into the past. In terms of political causality, we can be confident that this simple relation is of very considerable importance. But it is less obvious what moral significance it has. Hence, amongst other matters, the difficulty for a prominent school of Anglo-American political philosophy today[1] of determining how we should see it as bearing upon relations of justice. It is metaphysically inane to think of a purely temporal relation as either just or unjust. But a relation which is defined in purely temporal terms can still readily generate opportunities for action and motives for acting which are profoundly unjust. It cannot be in itself unjust that the human future is at our mercy. (On any coherent theistic view, as the Book of Job unforgettably conveys, this would be quite the wrong sort of human quarrel with God.) But the all too apparent probability of our treating it both fecklessly and with purposeful selfishness means that what is structurally neither just nor unjust is virtually certain in practice to issue in very grave injustice. Because we are all in some sense free agents, any of us could always choose to avoid such injustice when we come to act[2]. But it is hard to see strong grounds for expecting that most, on balance, will.

What we individually expect about the human future over any period no doubt largely reflects our personal temperaments and more or less idiosyncratic experiences.[3] But whatever their causal antecedents, the expectations themselves have at least a measure of epistemic structure. That structure consists largely in beliefs about social, economic and political causality; and, on any sane interpretation of their character and significance, the attempt to identify such causalities must form a large part of the point of the social sciences. Political scientists, partly from habit and epistemic convenience, and partly perhaps for other and more compelling reasons, study principally political relations between contemporaries and focus to a considerable degree upon their relative power. For a very long time the great majority of human societies have consisted of human beings with very unequal power. But only in extreme, if politically instructive, cases[4] have large numbers of human beings been at the mercy of others in the same sense and to the same degree as the human future is at our mercy.[5]

The human world, during the period within which we really know anything at all intimate and reliable about it, has always been pretty unjust; and at an individual level and in detail relations between generations have often been perceived as, and felt to be, acutely unjust. But, as human powers to modify the natural world have increased ever more dramatically, the most important locus of potential injustice in relations between present and future human beings has stretched ever further, shifting inexorably from the domestic and lineal to the international and global. All very young humans have always been at the mercy of at least some much older humans, not infrequently to their grave jeopardy. But the picture of entire human populations in the future as effectively in jeopardy to their (still relatively youthful) present day ancestors is comparatively unfamiliar. If political scientists should study political causality, and if it is professionally open to them, or even incumbent upon them (as I believe it is), to study such causality with particular care and attention as it bears painfully upon human prospects for receiving justice from one another, it is clear that political scientists today should at least be trying to discover how to capture more reliably just what this dependence of the future on our limited generosity and comprehension implies for the level of injustice which our successors can anticipate (and should therefore fear) from us (and we, accordingly, as moral and political agents, can anticipate and should fear from and in ourselves and each other). As free agents, we may in some sense choose to prescind from anticipating our own prospective actions when we assess the good or bad news. But only the genuinely demented could opt, when they try to assess this, to prescind from anticipating how other human beings are likely to behave.

It is neater (and perhaps in some ways clearer) to think of political relations as paradigmatically relations between contemporaries, who could in principle disagree directly with one another in real time about what is or is not just, and who can all, however modestly, exert some degree of power over some other living humans. Seen thus, political relations, however substantively unequal, have some element of reciprocity – of acting and being acted upon by turns within a shared span of time. In the end, however, this is never a sufficient analysis. In my view, quite clearly ever since the invention of nuclear armamaments, but probably, if far less clearly, over a very much longer period, the most important political relation in the human world has been one between a set of current agents and the actual or potential consequences of their actions for many future actual or possible human beings. For much of the period in which the thermonuclear arms race was still going on, as potentially in any future in which it happens to revive, those consequences could at the limit have included or still include there being no actual set of future human beings. There could hardly be a greater exertion of power between human beings than that; and it is hard to see how there could be a more profound injustice either. So for both political scientists and moral and political philosophers this age-old but now permanently worsening imbalance of power between present and future humans has a claim to far greater salience than it has yet been accorded.

The power in question, to be sure, is a matter of exposure and vulnerability, not one of effective control by the past over the future. Whatever future human beings there prove to be will, as far as we can reasonably surmise, be free agents just as we are. Nothing in human experience, as child or parent or directly encountering or encountered adult, is as familiar as the incapacity of the older in most instances to cause the younger to act as they would wish. But exposure and vulnerability lie at the very centre of the human condition, so the enhancement of our collective capacity to harm (and perhaps even to benefit) our descendants is of awesome political importance. Asymmetries of power between human beings are always perilous, and, in the absence of strong countervailing pressures of sentiment (as optimistically presumed to obtain within, for example, the nuclear family), they are very likely to issue in grave abuse. All power corrupts, and absolute power corrupts absolutely.

Our collective power over the human future is certainly not absolute, since it is a power to wound (or, at the limit, to eliminate), not a power to enforce compliance. It is a power to shape the circumstances within which future human beings will have to act (and, altogether more whimsically and individually, to determine what future human beings there will in fact be). It is not a power to determine how any future human beings will in fact act. But even if it plainly is not (and as far as we can now tell, never could become) absolute, what is clear is that our collective power over the future has increased, is increasing, and could scarcely in principle be diminished by anything short of wholesale destruction. The political implication of this is that this is a power which it is of ever greater moral urgency for us to edify, precisely because it is one which we could scarcely in principle forego.

Edifying power is a hazardous and elusive project under the best of circumstances – under political conditions in which there exists a measure of reciprocity. It is bound to prove (as it very obviously has proven) even more difficult under conditions in which it does not even make sense to conceive of reciprocity.

One way of dramatising the political extremity of the task is to note the strong analogies, in terms of power, between our relations with future human beings and our relations with our contemporaries amongst other animal (or even sentient) species. In both instances, the vulnerability is all too conspicuous, there is little or no reciprocity in interaction, and the prospects for edification at any given time depend solely on the susceptibilities of the current generation of humans.

The task of edification can be seen from at least two angles. It can be viewed as essentially one of enhancing our generosity and diminishing our selfishness (of improving our characters). But it can also be viewed as one of enhancing our comprehension of the consequences which are likely to follow from our habitual ways of acting. It is a fair bet that substantial shifts in either respect will modify the other considerably. But there are good reasons for supposing that political action – terminating as it must in a shift in (or a failure to shift) the incidence of coercive power – is a less promising approach to modifying our moral sensitivities than it is to enhancing our causal understanding of what we really are doing and leaving undone, as we pursue our daily purposes. Governments are drastically better placed than single individuals to amass and refine pertinent information, and communicate the results of their inquiries effectively to the population at large. They are, on the evidence, far from well placed to improve our characters.[6]

I have deliberately refrained thus far from focusing even momentarily on the idea of the self. This is a controversial omission, but one which I am anxious to defend with some vigour. Conceptions of the self, or of what exactly it is to be a person, have varied very widely across time and space.[7] They play a prominent role in the organisation of human cultures, and can plausibly be seen as carrying powerful implications for how human beings have good reason to act. The most distinguished recent western analysis of any aspect of how we have good reason to act in the light of other human lives, Derek Parfit's *Reasons and Persons,*[8] presents its positive arguments on the issue as following from its analysis of what it is to be one particular person. (Part 4 of Parfit's book presents an elaborate treatment of the implications for one key aspect of the problem of justice to future generations.) Similarly, one of the more influential criticisms of the leading contemporary theory of justice in social, political and economic relations amongst human beings has also taken its stand on the supposedly erroneous conception of personhood which it sees that theory as presupposing.[9] If conceptions of personhood can be pivotal for the understanding of practical rationality and social justice, why should they not offer a strategic key to the wholesale edification of our political, economic, social,and ecological agency ?

The reason why, in my view, they cannot hope to is the causal character of that agency. Even if it is true, as I have argued, that the power of the human present over the human future is increasingly malign, that malignity is only unequivocal from the viewpoint of the future itself. In the present, we can be reasonably confident, even the most cumulatively feckless conduct makes, in detail, at least subjective rational sense for the agents in question.[10] There is no entirely convincing extant method of distinguishing subjective practical rationality from objective practical rationality[11]: too large a target, too many potentially pertinent considerations, probably also too much weakly disciplined emotion.

In part at least in consequence, there is also no dependable way of specifying either the causal character of human political, economic, or social agency at a given time or the content of human interests at that time. But we can at least be confident that what any of us has good reason to do politically must depend extensively on what others have recently done and are now doing: on the myriads of other human purposes with which our own purposes must interact if they are to find expression in action at all. Even if we see our present political situation as constrained solely by the economic and political history of the world thus far and the logic of collective action, that is more than enough to require that very much of our political conduct must be aimed (if it is not to be completely self-indulgent, and if it is to to avoid being either utterly inconsequential or essentially aleatory in its consequences) at responding to these constraints. No way of envisaging the self could be of much help here.

In the face of a drastic asymmetry of power in an overwhelmingly and pervasively important human relation, it is hopeless to try to rectify matters by anything other than an overtly political response. What defines our interests is largely the causal pressure upon them of the ways in which other human beings pursue their supposed interests. It would be spiritually suicidal to permit that pressure to define our own interests in their entirety. (Probably also self-contradictory.) But it is certain to prove practically incoherent for the great majority of us to seek to define our interests without a wary and well-informed regard for the practical implications of that pressure.

There are three serious contenders for potentially effective responses to recognising the increasing malignity of the power of the human present over the human future: our understanding of justice, our understanding of the nature of a political community, and our understanding of the practical causality of our impact upon that future. I do not myself believe that interpretations of selfhood or personhood offer the key to any of them. But there have been strong recent defences of the view that they certainly do provide the key to the first[12]; and there have been appreciably more powerful defences far longer ago, notably by Aristotle and Burke, of the claim that they provide a key to the second.[13] What I wish to argue is that no one could readily defend the view that such interpretations give any effective purchase on the third, and that it is plain that it is the third which essentially drives an economic, social, political and ecological process whose net consequences are ever more patently malign. (It is worth reminding ourselves that it is only insofar as they are malign that there is any urgent need for us to bother our heads about the consequences. What, after all, has the future ever done for us?)

The optimistic political hypothesis is that many of the most malign of these consequences are malign by inadvertence: outcomes of far worse actions than we realise ourselves to be performing, and outcomes which we might well prove unable to bring ourselves to will if we recognised that they were what is really at stake in the actions which we are in the habit of performing. This may be over-optimistic. (Introspection on this point, if at all energetic, is not invariably reassuring.) But at least it is optimism where optimism might prove well-founded, and where, for things to go better, it is certain to be required.[14] In the other two respects, by contrast, there are, in my view, no grounds whatever for anticipating that optimism will prove well-founded, and no obvious reason for supposing that it will be required.

The reasons for supposing that an understanding of justice should drastically inhibit the harms which we knowingly inflict on the human future are simple and intuitively obvious. They rest on the values of impartiality and equality. Just ways of acting are ways in which we treat all other human beings equally as valued, discriminating between them only on genuinely pertinent grounds. Impartiality is a conceptual precondition for justice.[15] In any distributive setting – conviction or punishment for offences, need-satisfaction – to treat other human beings differently because of the ways in which we happen to feel about them is always potentially unjust. Over much of human life partiality is permissible; and over some of it (reasonably intimate relations, for example), it may even come to be required (a duty, or a causal precondition for a virtue). Love is as partial as you can get; and it is far easier to act well towards another person from love than it is from a sense of justice. But in some aspects of human life, justice is a very plain duty; and wherever it is a duty, impartiality is a precondition for discharging it with any reliability.

In our relations with future human beings we fail in justice if we fail to treat them with as much concern as we should treat those of our contemporaries towards whom we have no partiality whatever. The dimension of time is no better an excuse for partiality in the wrong case than the dimension of space. The readily foreseeable infliction of serious harm on others is certainly a wrong case. There are two possible qualifications to this simple moral intuition, one metaphysical and the other political. The metaphysical qualification is bemusing, but not in the end, in my view, morally very important. In the future, unlike the past and present, there is no fact of the matter as to the identity of its inhabitants.[16] If we definitely owe a duty to future human beings, there are no determinate beneficiaries of that duty. I doubt whether this is of much moral consequence.[17] The fact that we do not and cannot know the identity of our victims, if we can know that there will be many victims of our actions, does nothing whatever to excuse those actions. But it does, of course, bear on the potential political force of impartiality.

Politics is largely defined in practice by the interaction of partialities. The asymmetry of power between present agents and future victims is the polar case of the asymmetries of power which pervade (and perhaps constitute) politics. The modest degree of reciprocity which obtains even between the very weak and the very mighty, or the very poor and the very rich (amongst persons, groups, countries and continents), disappears completely in the relations between future human beings and ourselves. If we ask how far claims of justice in distribution have prevailed politically in modern world history, the answer must be, to a severely limited extent. If we ask why that extent has been so limited, there are two possible types of explanation, one formal and the other substantive. The formal answer is a trifle flippant – that in a domain largely constituted by the interaction of partialities, the causal force of the claims of impartiality is likely, ceteris paribus, to prove weak. The substantive answer,[18] at present perhaps more important and certainly very far from flippant, is that in the economic, social and political format of capitalist production the trade-off between efficiency and justice has proved pretty merciless towards justice. This may be simply an instance of moral bad luck, or it may be just a consequence of failure in practical intelligence (which could, or will, in due course be reversed).[19] But in either case even the less axiomatically pessimistic substantive explanation of the political inefficacy of claims of justice gives no reason as yet for supposing that considerations of justice are likely to have much practical effect in edifying how we conduct ourselves towards the human future.

More imaginatively stimulating, but, I fear, practically still less promising, would be to approach the question of how we have good reason to act towards the human future by interpreting what it is (or should be) to belong to a political community. An Aristotelian (or perhaps Habermasian) construction of political membership at least defines a space in which for moral imagination to exert itself on the significance of our relations with other human beings through time.[20] A Burkean construction of political membership does so still more emphatically.[21] But the evidence of recent history is that the human world constructed by capitalist production (with its dynamic radicalisation of the logic of partiality) is profoundly inimical to any of these visions of political community.[22] I believe that there are deep (if somewhat treacherous) truths in the visions of both Aristotle and Burke. But I see nothing whatever in the practical organisation of the world today which gives either vision any serious prospect of practical political efficacy.

I will end, therefore, by saying something very brief about one narrow but potentially instructive political relation which has become far more salient throughout the industrialised world in the last few years: the funding of post-retirement life chances for the population. In themselves the arrangements for pensions and social security for the elderly are just a special case of the encroachment of efficiency on justice in the economics and politics of the wealthier countries over the last three decades. In Italy at present there are more pensions being drawn than there are officially declared members of the active labour force.[23] In the United States in 1950 there were sixteen active American workers for every pensioner. In 1996, there are three; and in 2030 there are now expected to be two. What began as an apparently practically coherent promise, made in perfectly good faith, has turned, as a result of unanticipated demographic shifts and intervening political history, into a patently unsustainable structure, in which, sooner or later, and by now much sooner, the promissor is going to be compelled to default.

The demographic, political, and economic history of these arrangements offers an apt parable for the problem of identifying our duties towards future generations. It shows the slide from mild ingenuousness into radical cynicism, and the extreme political difficulty of reversing that slide on any basis other than unmistakable force majeure. It also shows the practical importance of improving our collective foresight, insofar as this is possible, and the overwhelming political merit of grasping what we are doing early, when the costs of amending this are reasonably modest, rather than late, when they have already become too grim to contemplate except under extreme duress.

The conceptual relations between cynicism, ignorance, stupidity and imprudence in these processes are very hard to plot. But I doubt very much whether any way of interpreting the self will help us to plot them with greater accuracy. In my view the best approach to learning to see them clearly is to concentrate our minds with greater energy on just what it is that we are bringing about by our actions. Even if we learnt to understand this as well as human beings could understand it, we would still be left with an ample residue of partiality which is beyond edification. But the component of partiality on which we have any practical reason to concentrate (in politics most nakedly of all) is the component which is within reach of edification. My bet is that how large that component is in turn depends quite considerably on how well we understand what we really are doing. Insofar as it does not, I suspect that it depends exclusively upon the past, and is therefore safe from our attentions and conclusively beyond our reach.

Notes

1. John Rawls, A *Theory of Justice*, (Cambridge, Mass.,Harvard University Press, 1971); R.I.Sikora & Brian Barry(eds), *Obligations to Future Generations,* (Philadelphia, Temple University Press 1978). For excellent commentary on Rawls see Brian Barry, *Theories of Justice,* (Hemel Hempstead, Harvester-Wheatsheaf, 1989) pp. 183-212.

2. Cf. John Dunn, 'The Contemporary Political Significance of John Locke's Conception of Civil Society', *Iyyun* (*Jerusalem Philosophical Quarterly*), July 1996, pp. 327-48.

3. There is, however, unfortunately no ground whatever to expect that these experiences will prompt us to anticipate wisely what the future will be like, or that the consequences of our several anticipations will come out felicitously at a political level. See, for example, all too distressingly, Russell Hardin, *One for All: The Logic of Group Conflict* (Princeton, Princeton University Press, 1995).

4. Compare, for example, the analysis of slavery in the ancient world – M.I.Finley, *Ancient Slavery and Modern Ideology*, (London, Chatto & Windus, 1980); M.I.Finley (ed), *Slavery in Classical Antiquity:Views and Controversies* (Cambridge, W.Heffer & Sons, 1960), or perhaps, more adventurously, Hegel's *Phenomenology.*

5. We, within our own current powers, can do to it more or less whatever we choose. It has no current powers and so can do nothing whatever to us. As Lenin said: 'Who whom?'. It is not difficult in such an encounter, to see who is likely to get hurt.

6. John Dunn, The *History of Political Theory* (Cambridge, Cambridge University Press, 1995) cap. 13.

7. Michael Carrithers, Steven Collins, & Steven Lukes, (eds) *The Category of the Person* (Cambridge, Cambridge University Press, 1985); cf Steven Collins, *Selfless Persons: Imagery and Thought in Therāvāda Buddhism* (Cambridge, Cambridge University Press, 1982); and Charles Taylor, *Sources of the Self* (Cambridge, Mass., Harvard University Press, 1989).

8. Derek Parfit, *Reasons and Persons* (Oxford, Clarendon Press, 1984).

9. Michael Sandel, *Liberalism and the Limits of Justice* (Cambridge, Cambridge University Press, 1982).

10. It would, of course, be clinically paranoid to see the power of the human present over the human future as exhaustively malign at any point short of the complete elimination of that future. But it is important, as already noted, to remember that there was a period

in the past when we came at times very close indeed to that outcome – Paul Bracken, *The Command and Control of Nuclear Forces* (New Haven, Yale University Press, 1982).

11. Robert Nozick, *The Nature of Rationality* (Princeton, Princeton University Press, 1993).

12. Parfit, op.cit.

13. Aristotle, *Politics,* tr. H.Rackham (Cambridge, Mass., Harvard University Press, 1932); Edmund Burke, ed L.G.Mitchell, *The Writings and Speeches of Edmund Burke, Vol VIII (The French Revolution 1790-1794),* (Oxford, Clarendon Press, 1989).

14. cf. John Dunn, *Western Political Theory in the Face of the Future* , 2nd ed., (Cambridge, Cambridge University Press, 1993), Conclusion.

15. Brian Barry, op.cit.

16. Parfit, op.cit.

17. But cf. Parfit, op. cit.

18. Dunn, op.cit. (1995), cap. 7.

19. For the urgency of the need to assess the proportions between these possibilities see Amartya Sen's helpful contribution to Paul Barker (ed.), *Living as Equals* (Oxford, Oxford University Press, 1996).

20. Aristotle, op.cit. (1932) 1251b, ll 1-2, p. 2; 1253a ll 1-18, pp. 8-10, ll 30-39, p. 12; 1263b, ll 30-41, p. 90; 1276b, ll 1-2, p. 184, especially 1253a, ll 1-18.

21. The classic text is the *Reflections on the Revolution in France*(1790). But the theme resonates throughout the remainder of Burke's works up till his death. See especially Burke, op.cit. (1989), p. 147:

'...the state ought not to be considered as nothing better than a partnership agreement in a trade of pepper and coffee, callico or tobacco, or some other such low concern, to be taken up for a little temporary interest, and to be dissolved by the fancy of the parties. It is to be looked on with other reverence; because it is not a partnership in things subservient only to the gross animal existence of a temporary and perishable nature. It is a partnership in all science; a partnership in all art; a partnership in every virtue, and in all perfection. As the ends of such a partnership cannot be obtained in many generations, it becomes a partnership not only between those who are living, but between those who are living, those who are dead, and those who are to be born. Each contract of each particular state is but a clause in the great primaeval contract of eternal society, linking the lower with the higher natures, connecting the visible and invisible world, according to a fixed contract sanctioned by the inviolable oath which holds all physical and all moral natures, each in their appointed place'. etc

(Contrast John Rawls, *Political Liberalism* (New York, Columbia University Press, 1993), Lecture 1, especially pp. 40-43: 'Neither a Community nor an Association').

22. cf. John Dunn, *Interpreting Political Responsibility* (Cambridge, Polity Press, 1990), caps. 11 and 12.

23. Barry Riley, *Financial Times* 26/10/96.'Weekend Money', p. 1, 'All Work and No Pension".

5

My Interest in Future Generations

Ross Harrison

In this paper I shall consider whether pure self-interest could ever give someone a reason for concern for future generations. The best reasons for concern for future generations are, no doubt, not based on self-interest but upon something else, such as respect for inter-generational justice. However, in the West self-interest has been taken to provide powerful reasons for action; indeed, it has often been held to be what constitutes rationality. So, even if it may not provide the best reasons, it is important to see whether any reasons at all for concern for future generations could be provided by this familiar and powerful kind of reason. Part of the importance of doing this is that it is initially implausible to think that there could be such reasons; to think, that is, that whatever maximises someone's individual, personal, or selfish interest could ever give that person a reason for considering future generations. Yet it would be rather wonderful if it were true.

At first sight it might just seem to be obvious that someone could not have a self-interested reason for concern for future generations. Self-interested reasons mean that the actual and possible future states of myself give me reasons for action which they do not give to others and, conversely, that the states of others give me no such reasons. However, future generations are other people. Hence the states of future generations are states of other people. So the answer to the central question which I am considering would seem at first sight to be quite straightforward. It would seem to be that there could be no such reasons. To repeat: future generations are other people; what happens to other people, by definition can give me no self-interested reasons for action; therefore I can have no reasons based on self-interest for concern for future generations.

Of course, sometimes I have self-interested reasons for concern for others. Because I want them to be kind to me, I may be kind to them. But here my kindness to them is because they are capable of affecting my interests. Because they can damage me, I have to exercise care in how I treat them. However, or so at least it seems, nothing like this is true for future generations. Future generations live after my death. After my death I have no interests. They cannot help or harm me; hence, or so it seems, I can have no self-interested reasons for action for concern for them.

Whichever version of the argument is used, therefore, the answer would seem to be quite simple. It would seem to be that I cannot have self-interested reasons for concern for future generations. Nevertheless in this paper I shall try to show that it is not, after all, quite so simple. In fact, and by contrast, I shall try to show that there can indeed be self-interested reasons for concerning oneself with future generations.

The over-simple arguments with which I started depend upon a familiar conception of the self and a familiar conception of a self-interested reason. One way to subvert them would be to criticise either of these familiar conceptions. The initial argument would then be subverted either by producing a more subtle (and less familiar) idea of the self; or else by a more subtle (and less familiar) idea of a self-interested reason. I do not in fact want to adopt this approach in this paper. By contrast I aim to take the ideas of self and self-interested reason in their standard, simple or familiar form and show that, even so, we can have self-interested reasons for concern for future generations. However, before going directly on to this argument I should outline these more subtle forms of subversion, which depend upon producing a different idea of the self or of self-interested reason. This is because these may be ways of subverting the original argument which appeal to other people.

For example, one such subverting strategy would be to deny the application just made of the distinction between self and other to future generations. In the simple argument with which I started, I assumed that future generations were other people; that future people were not myself. On a different metaphysical view of the self, however, this might be denied. It might be claimed, that is, that I survive my bodily death and become reincarnated in the body of another, future, person. Were this to happen then one or more members of future generations will also actually be me, the me who is now here in the present. But if the future generations are me, then I have a perfectly normal, self-interested reason for concern for them.

This alternative strategy assumes an important and determinate distinction between self and others, but claims that the application of this distinction is mistaken (so that what are conventionally called future people are in fact really me, the me who exists in the present). Alternatively, in a different way of subverting the initial assumptions, the determinacy and depth of the distinction itself might be contested. What is taken to be the self, or person, might be taken to be built up out of a series of prior psychological relations between states of mind. On this view of the self, rather than the trajectory of the self through time explaining my present concern for my future, instead things I am concerned about in the future thereby become part of myself. That is, instead of what is the self explaining self-concern, a particular kind of concern makes the self. Therefore, on this view, if I have a particular kind of concern for what are conventionally called future generations, this would thereby make those future generations myself. Hence, on this metaphysical picture, I could again have a straightforward, self-interested, self-regarding, concern for future generations.

These are two ways in which a different metaphysics could deliver normal self-interested reasons for concern for future generations. I only mention them here and do not wish to discuss them further as they are both unusual, or highly contested, metaphysical pictures. Instead, as I said, I wish in the central argument of this paper to keep to the normal, or common sense, assumptions that there is such a thing as selves persisting through time; that what these selves are explains their concern for the future rather than vice versa; and that members of future generations are not myself.

However before I move to the main argument and examine directly whether on these normal assumptions there could be self-interested reasons for concern for future generations, I should mention another way in which the original problem might be subverted. This would be not by changing the standard picture of what the self is but, rather, by changing the standard picture of what a self-interested reason is. For example, it is sometimes thought that there is a close analogy between supposed self-interested behaviour directed at other times and supposed altruistic behaviour directed at other people. These, it is claimed, should be considered in the same way. That is, either they both should provide good reasons or else neither should. The latter option, it is supposed, is absurd, because it is rational to show prudential concern for our own futures. Hence we get that those people who believe in prudence (i.e. a concern for the future of themselves) are thereby rationally driven to altruism (or a concern for the future of others). In this way the distinction between self-interested and other-interested reasons gets subverted. Instead, it is claimed that there are just reasons for action: future good states of affairs provide me (just like anyone else) with reasons for action, no matter whose states they are. If this account of reasons works, then I have perfectly good reasons for concern for future generations, and any classification into self-and other-interested reasons is pointless and marks no distinction in the power of the reasons.

Again, I only wish to mention this attempt to subvert the original question and do not myself wish to discuss it further in this paper. For I want to see whether the original question can be answered directly and without supposing a different idea either of the metaphysics of the self or of the nature of self-interested reason. I wish to maintain the normal, or common sense, assumption that there is an important difference between self and others and that there is an important form of reason based upon pure self-interest which is different from concern for others. Of course the attempts at subverting the original question which I have just listed may work, or may attract a reader; and if they do, these subversions would succeed in removing the sting of the original problem. They would remove its sting, however, either by a bold metaphysical move or else by a boldly creative account of prudential reasons. This boldness makes them controversial and I wish here to see if anything can be done with less bold, or eccentric, assumptions.

For the rest of the paper, therefore, I shall assume that the metaphysical distinction between self and others is real and deep and that there is a special, identifiable, self-interested kind of rationality. I shall assume, therefore, that there are states which we can call future states of a particular person, and that these states provide that person with self-interested (or prudential) reasons for action. I shall assume that, by contrast, future generations are other people, and that states of these other people do not in the same way provide such self-interested (or prudential) reasons for action. Reasons of the prudential kind which give a particular person a reason for action which they do not give to someone else can be called 'person-relative'. If the great weight is going to fall on me and not on the people who come after me, then there is a person-relative reason for me to do something which these other people do not have. The central question of this paper now therefore becomes the question of whether there are any person-relative reasons for concern for future generations.

In arguing directly for my main claim that there are such reasons, the first important thing to notice is that death is not necessarily a limit to matters of purely self-interested concern. It seems at first sight that it must be, as I suggested at the start of the paper. For, it is natural to say: after death I no longer exist; non-existent people have no interests; hence after death I can have no interests. But this perfectly natural claim is refuted by the fact that people often show great concern for what will happen to such things as their projects, possessions, body, or memory after they are dead. This concern is for aspects of themselves (their projects; their body...); and so it is self-interested concern. A concern for posthumous reputation, for example, seems a concern by someone for how they are thought of by others. That is, it is a concern for an aspect of themselves, their reputation. Yet since it is posthumous reputation, it is a (self-regarding) concern for something which only happens after they are dead. Therefore death is not a limit to matters of purely self-interested concern.

One way to test this is by trying the question of whether a deterrent theory of punishment could provide successful punishments to deter suicide. A deterrent theory of punishment appeals to the purely self-interested motivations of people to stop them doing those things which are thought to be socially or politically undesirable; for example, it stipulates punishments which make it in people's interests not to commit murder, rape, or whatever. So, supposing that a state wished to outlaw suicide, the question is whether they could provide a punishment which deterred people from committing suicide by threatening their interests. At first sight, again, the answer might seem to be that they could not. For, as before, successful suicides are dead; they have no interests; hence punishment cannot work against their interests; hence they can have no self interested reasons produced by threatened punishment for not committing suicide. However, history shows that procedures were in fact used against the bodies of suicides in many communities, such as their bodies being paraded naked through the town, or being staked out at cross roads. These procedures were intended to deter suicide, and it does seem perfectly conceivable that someone might be deterred from suicide by the thought of their body being made an exhibition after their death. Yet this deterrent thought is a self-interested thought. That is, people have an interest in what happens to their bodies after they are dead.

It is not just the body for which this is true. The concern for the body in this example connects with a concern many people have for their posthumous reputation. They do not want an exhibition made of their body; they are worried about how people will regard them once they have departed. This is a purely self-regarding (or self-interested) concern: their concern for their posthumous reputation is a concern for themselves. Yet, obviously, it is independent of any concern for painful future state of themselves. Once dead, they feel no pain. So this shows that my self-interested concern about the future is not restricted to concern about future mental states of myself. It is not, that is, restricted to worry about my future pleasures and pains. Yet, once this link is broken it is open for me to have concern about future times after I no longer exist. It is true that I am not going to feel anything at those times; that I will have no pleasures or pains. Nevertheless I can still be concerned. Self-interested concern is therefore not restricted to concern about possible future states of one's own mind. It is not restricted to possible pleasures and pains.

Another example which shows that self-interested concern does not necessarily depend upon concern about possible sensations is that I, like most people, do not want it to be the case that other people say bad things about me behind my back and without my knowledge. It might be thought, of course, that my concern that this does not happen is merely a concern that I should not find out; that is, it is a concern about the pain I would suffer on discovering the nasty things which people thought about me. This is obviously a proper matter for concern. Yet I think that most people would also be concerned about whether other people thought badly of them, whether or not they were ever going to find this out. That is, it is a concern independent of possible perception. The concern for reputation is not just the concern to avoid the painful sensation of finding that you are disliked. Yet, again, if this is so, I can have a (self-interested) concern for my reputation after my death; for, again, this concern is not just a concern to avoid a particular kind of suffering. I do not want people to think bad things about me after I am dead; and this is quite independent of whether I might suffer from finding out about it.

However, once we see that concern for reputation can extend after someone's death, we see that my self-interested concern may extend far into the future long after I have ceased to exist. Consider, for example, the benefaction of educational, charitable, or religious institutions. Benefactors give these large sums of money enabling them to exist and flourish long after the death of the benefactor. Sometimes, of course, the reason for the benefaction is purely altruistic; but self-interested reasons can be presumed in other cases. Endowing an Oxford or Cambridge college in the Middle Ages meant endowing also a college chapel in which masses could be said for the soul of the benefactor. Here the benefactor believed that they (or their soul) continued to exist after their death, so they had a straightforward interest in the benefaction, based on the kind of (now unusual) metaphysical view which I mentioned and set aside above. However, quite independently of whether there were chantry chapels praying for their soul, endowing a college preserved the benefactor's memory. The colleges bear their names, or otherwise remember their benefactors. Hence the benefactors get remembered. Their names live after their death. If someone has an interest in their name living after their death, this is therefore one way in which they can achieve it: they can purchase posthumous memory or fame. It seems clear that this should properly be classified as a self-interested concern; it is a concern for their name, their fame, their memory; that is, themselves. Yet, equally clearly, it extends after their death. So we can after all have purely self interested concern in things which happen long after our deaths.

The next thing to notice is that although the motive for a particular benefaction might have been self-interested, it may still be a genuine benefaction in the sense that it is of genuine benefit to people other than the giver. The result of the benefaction is to benefit people living long after the death of the benefactor; the self-interested gift is of benefit to future generations. Furthermore this is not just an unintended spill over effect of the original act. The benefactor gave the gift explicitly and expressly to benefit future generations. Nevertheless the reasons for the giving might have been purely self-regarding. The benefactor wants explicitly to benefit future generations; but wants to do so because they are concerned that those future generations think well of them. The benefactor wants to leave behind after death a memory; a reputation.

There can, therefore, be actions which both benefit and are intended to benefit others and yet whose prime motivation is self-interested. The important thing is to distinguish between the motive and the content of the action. The motive of the action can be something to do with the self; so that its perpetrator has a particular reason for performing it which others do not. Just as my possible future pain gives me a (self-regarding) reason for action which is not a reason for others, so my possible future reputation can give me a (self-interested) reason for action which is not a reason for others. Yet the content of the action may be distinct from its motive. The content of the action could be to do something which benefits others.

If I have a particular project, then I have a particular reason for action which others do not. It is my own particular project, it is not the project of others. Hence I have a reason to try and bring it into effect (because it is my project) which they do not have. This, again, is respect to the motive, or reason for performing it. Yet the content of the project (what it actually is) could be anything. It could, for example, be to benefit future generations in particular ways. My project is to leave a college after me, benefiting all future members of that college; yet it is my particular project, which gives me a reason for action, which it does not give to others.

This is to put the matter purely generally. Yet I would like to end by mentioning certain natural relationships which give me a reason (as opposed to people generally) to do something, yet where that thing is of advantage to people who only live after my death. All that is needed for this to be the case is that I am a member of (and identify myself with) something which exists both before and after my own existence and in which many generations participate: for example, families, cities, firms, universities. These are all things in which I can have pride: that is, they are mine (my family, my city); and they give me reasons for action. Non-members, that is, could not be proud; could not identify; and would not have such self-regarding reasons for action. Yet, obviously, members of my family or city may live long after I am dead. I can do things therefore to benefit them where the motive is the self-regarding one of benefiting something which is (already and naturally) mine: my family or my city. So here we get specific and perfectly natural examples of where someone can act (knowingly and explicitly) for the benefit of future generations, and yet where the (perfectly understandable) motives may be self-interested or self-regarding ones. I conclude, therefore, that, contrary to first appearances, it makes perfectly good sense to think that there can be self-interested reasons for concern for future generations.

6

Self, Time and Separability

John O'Neill

How should we value projects and activities over time? Standard cost benefit analysis offers a clear answer to that question. In cost benefit appraisal of a project over time, the value of the project (PV) over a time period t = 0 and t = n is calculated by the following formula:

$$(1) \quad PV = \sum_{t=0}^{t=n} \{B_t - C_t\}(1 + r)^{-t}$$

where B_t is the benefit at time t
C_t is the cost at time t
r is the discount rate.

If PV > 0 then the project is acceptable. Given a choice of projects, the project with the highest total PV is taken to be the best. The use of this formula for project appraisal involves three assumptions:

1. **Discounting the future**. The future should be discounted: future costs and benefits of any proposed option are valued at less than those of the present using some specified discount rate, r, the more distant into the future, the lower the value.

2. **Additive separability**. The values of events at different moments of time are additively separable. Informally, to say they are separable is to say that the value of what happens at some point in time, t_i, is independent of the value of what happens at another point, t_j, and to say that they are additively separable is to say that the total value of a project over a period of time is the sum of these independent values.[1]

3. **The irrelevance of the past.** The formula assumes some form of consequentialism. What has happened in the past is irrelevant to the value of the project. We always start now, t = 0, and consider only the future.

Most of the discussion of the environmental implications of cost benefit analysis has focused upon the first assumption, and for obvious reasons: it appears to fail tests of equity between us and future generations. Given a discount rate r, a preference measured at \$n now is valued in t years time at $\$n/(1 + r)^t$. This has clear implications for our treatment of future generations for it magnifies the value we place on current benefits and diminishes the value we place on future costs: we are justified in shifting costs into the future for our current benefit. However, while I discuss discounting in this paper, it will not form the central object of concern. My main purpose is rather to question the second and third assumptions and to draw out their implications for our relation to future generations. The paper is in two parts. In the first I consider the use of assumptions in the appraisal of personal projects for a single person. I shall argue that the use of any such account assumes a particular mistaken view of personal identity over time: the picture of the self and its relation to the future that it presupposes is indefensible. In the second section I will draw out the implications of these arguments for the relations of present generations to those of both past and future: if we are to have some sense of community over generations, then the assumptions of additive separability and the irrelevance of the past should be rejected.

The self and its future

One of the central arguments for discounting the future starts from assumptions about individuals' preferences. The argument runs that individuals have pure time preferences – they are impatient: they prefer benefits now to benefits tomorrow and costs tomorrow to costs now simply in virtue of the time they occur; the more distant the future, the less costs and benefits are counted. The argument continues that, since it is the task of social policy to aggregate the preferences of affected parties, time preferences must be incorporated into public policy. Any aggregation of preferences in cost benefit analysis must reflect these pure time preferences. Now this argument is open to a number of objections. Even if is accepted that social policy should be simply a matter of aggregating given preferences, and I believe it should not,[2] there is clearly something objectionable about the shift in the argument from intrapersonal preferences to interpersonal preferences. Individuals who have pure time preferences for the present over the future consumption of goods have preferences about their own future preference satisfaction. The aggregation of those preferences does not licence any social discount rate in which the preferences of a distinct future population are counted for less than those of existing populations. There is also, however, a prior issue about the rationality of pure time preferences themselves.

There is a standard debate about the rationality of pure time preferences which runs something as follows. The defender of pure time preferences claims we have to respect these preferences. If well-being consists in preference satisfaction, then we must include these preferences in arriving at the policy that maximises well being. Each individual will have a welfare function that corresponds roughly to the formula give earlier. In considering acts at any point t = 0, and looking forward over a probable remaining lifetime to t = n, the personal welfare value (WV) will be calculated by the following formula:

$$(2) \qquad WV = \sum_{t=0}^{t=n} \{B_t - C_t\}(1 + r)^{-t}$$

The opponent of pure time preferences holds that a concern with maximising well-being demands that we ignore pure-time preferences since to include them would be to fail to maximise the satisfaction of preferences over persons' lifetimes. In the words of Pigou, time preferences only show that 'our telescopic faculty is defective'.[3] One should take a temporally neutral perspective on the satisfaction of preferences across an individual's life time. Pure time preferences are irrational. The welfare value will be represented rather by a simple sum:

$$(3) \qquad WV = \sum_{t=0}^{t=n} \{B_t - C_t\}$$

Both of these perspectives share the assumptions that the value of events at different moments of time are additively separable and that the past is irrelevant. Are these assumptions defensible? Consider first the assumption of additive separability, the claim that the value of what happens at some point in time, t_i, is independent of the value at what happens at another point, t_j, and the total value over a period of time is the sum of these independent values. Is this assumption defensible? Consider the following examples that I have used elsewhere.[4]

A. A newly married couple, couple A, go on a two week honeymoon. The holiday begins disastrously: they each discover much in the other which they had not noticed before, and they dislike what they find. The first four days are spent in an almighty row. However, while they argue continuously over the next eight days, they begin to resolve their differences and come to a deeper appreciation of each other. Over the last two days of the holiday they are much happier and both feel that they have realised a relationship that is better than that which they had before their argument. The holiday ends happily. Sadly, on their return journey, the plane that carries them explodes and they die.

B. A newly married couple, couple B, go on honeymoon. The first twelve days proceed wonderfully. On the thirteenth day their relationship deteriorates badly as each begins to notice and dislike in the other a character trait which they had not noticed before, at the same time realising that the other had a quite mistaken view of themselves. On the last day of the holiday they have a terrible row, and sit on opposite ends of the plane on the return journey. They both die in an explosion on the plane.

Which lives go better? Or, to stay with the language of consumer choice, given a visitation on the day before the holiday begins by an angel who presents you with a choice between the two lives, which would you choose? (The visitation and the choice itself will be instantly forgotten, so can be ignored.) Given the assumption of additive separability, then whether or not one discounts the future, the answer looks as if it should be B. Thus given a temporally neutral perspective, we have a sum given by (3) above. We are to tot up the days of dissatisfaction – in the case of A, the first 12 days, in the case of B the last two days – and the days of satisfaction – in the case of A the last two days and in the case of B the first twelve days – and the total value is the sum of these. Given rough equality in dissatisfactions from arguments and satisfactions from enjoyable times together, holiday B comes out as the better choice. If one adds a discount rate and employs the formula given in (2) the value of B over A is simply magnified: since the dissatisfactions in B happen later, they count for less at the point of choice on the visitation by my angel. So given additive separability and a few assumption about the costs over benefits scores for each day of the holiday, B looks like the best consumer value.

However, many individuals (although not all as I have discovered in offering the choice to some of my more hedonistically inclined students), given a visitation from my angel would choose holiday A; they characterise the story of holiday A as a happier one than that of holiday B. They do so because the temporal order of events is neither irrelevant nor is it the case that it is always better to have goods sooner rather than later. What counts in favour of holiday A is the narrative order of events, and crucial to that order is the way in which that story ends.

However, to assume the additive separability of value through time is to assume that the order of events does not matter. The total value of a project over a period of time is simply taken to be the sum of the value of each moment taken in separation. The sequence of events is irrelevant to its total value. The value of each event in a moment of time can be ascertained separately, in isolation from what occurs before and after. Now clearly there are theories of value which entail such separability. Thus, as I noted above, some of my more hedonistically inclined students are inclined to choose holiday B, and from within a hedonistic perspective this makes sense. If one assumes, with Pigou, a subjective state account of welfare, that 'the elements of welfare are states of consciousness',[5] be these states of pleasure or satisfaction, then one can treat the value of events in time as separable for whether or not the event was pleasurable or painful can be ascertained independently of what happened before or after. Thus while it might be the case that the anticipation or recollection of an event causes pain or pleasure, its characterisation as painful or pleasurable at the time at which it occurred cannot be altered. From with a hedonistic perspective, the order of events as such cannot matter. However, this simply gives us I believe one more reason for rejecting a hedonistic account of value. For the narrative order of events does matter, and that it does entails that the assumption of additive separability has to be rejected.

There are characterisations that we make of events in a person's life that can only be made in the context of a larger narrative order. Thus the way we characterise the days in my honeymoon stories depends on their place in a larger narrative frame. In holiday A, the argument at the start of the holiday is not simply a 'cost' – a moment of pain or desire dissatisfaction. Rather, taken in context, it might be taken to be a 'turning point' in the relationship, one which clarifies the relationship and lays the foundation for the ensuing happiness. Within the context of the individuals' entire lives, it has another significance. For that reason one can also talk of the earlier event having been 'redeemed' by the later reconciliation to which it gave rise. Likewise, the moments of happiness in holiday B are not 'benefits' – feelings of satisfaction. Rather, within the context of the whole story, they are moments of illusion, when each person has a false view of the other, an illusion shattered by the final argument. Had their lives continued, the argument also may have become something else, but the ill fortune of untimely deaths robs the participants of such a future. Whether moments of pain and pleasure are goods or evils depends on their context of a life as a whole. They do not come ready-tagged as such.

To make these claims is to deny the separability of the value of moments of time. An evaluation of what happens at one moment in time cannot be made independently of what happens at others. An argument can only be characterised positively as a 'turning point' in a person's life given that the events that follow are of a certain kind. A reconciliation counts as a 'redemption' of events only given its particular relation to those past events from which it grew. For that reason, when we are living through events, painful or pleasurable, it is often difficult to ascertain what their final value will be. It depends upon their place in the larger story of our lives and whether this turns out well or ill depends upon the way that story unfolds and ends: the genre to which the story belongs depends upon the way it concludes. Given that this is the case temporal separability, and more specifically additive separability, fails. One cannot treat the total value of a person's life over a period of time by totting up the values of individual moments taken in isolation.

Because temporal separability fails in this particular way so also does the irrelevance of the past. Given the place of narrative orders in evaluation, it makes sense to make decisions that refer not just to the future, but also to the past. The argument here is not that standardly invoked against consequentialism – that there are acts in the past such as promising that lay upon us current obligations. Rather, it is that we can act now in ways that make intelligible or redeem our past. A farmer might quite rationally shun the enticements of a good life with his children in a city and live out his days alone and in hardship on a hill farm, in virtue of the fact that the farm represent his life work: to leave and to let it go to ruin would be to render his life pointless. A student with a terminal illness may continue to an examination at the end of the course because it is the culmination of her past studies, even if it looks on a strictly consequentialist reasoning to make no sense at all.

The principle of additive separability of moments of time presuppose a particular picture of the self and its continuity over time. Given additive separability the relation between my self and my future takes on a strangely impersonal aspect. A strong sense of identity over time that is given by narrative unity or continuity is lacking. Life is treated as a series of discrete episodes, and our relation to the future begins to look like a relation to other persons. The only argument is how much I should care for the future selves that follow me. For the defender of time preferences at any moment t_0 O'Neill cares for O'Neill_0 who exists now more than O'Neill_1 who exists at t_1 who is a physically related relative of O'Neill_0 who in turn is cared for more than the more distant relative O'Neill_2 and so on as time stretches out into the future. The critic of pure time preferences assumes the same picture but is an economic maximiser who demands equal consideration for future preferences on the basis of an oddly impersonal perspective. A life is still a series of discrete acts of consumption, but the maximiser asks for any future O'Neill, O'Neill_n to be given the same consideration as the current O'Neill, O'Neill_0. The life still lacks internal coherence. The only relation between the various O'Neills is one of physical continuity. The relation of a person to the future becomes one of self to others.

This picture of temporal neutrality has indeed been exploited by utilitarians. Sidgwick raises the following objection to the Egoist understood in the uncommonsensical sense as one who refuses the Utilitarian principle of universal benevolence:

> If the Utilitarian has to answer the question, 'Why should I sacrifice my own happiness for the greater happiness of another?', it must surely be admissible to ask the Egoist, 'Why should I sacrifice a present pleasure for one in the future? Why should I concern myself about my own future feelings any more than about the feelings of other persons?'[6]

The thought, developed in detail by Nagel and Parfit, is that a self-interest theory of rationality, according to which each person aims at the world which makes his or her life go as well as possible, is vitiated by the fact that it is agent-relative i.e it gives reasons that are reasons only for the agent, but not time-relative i.e. it aims to maximise well-being across time. The claim is that the rejection of impersonality and the acceptance of temporal neutrality cannot be happily combined. My relation to my future selves is not in principle different from my relation to others.[7] Any future 'self' is an other like any other.[8]

This account of the self to its future needs to be rejected. The picture of identity over time it assumes is in error. What is absent is precisely a view of human lives as ones that have a narrative structure – as stories of physical and mental growth and development, of decline, of the success and failure of projects and relationships. It fails to allow any place for narrative order in our identity and correspondingly in the evaluation of a moment or period in our lives. The future of one's own life does matter for an appraisal of current life in a way that the current or future lives of strangers need not. What the future is like matters to how well we can say our present life is going. Our present life is part of a larger narrative and the shape of that whole life matters. In particular, the way matters turn out matters. Our lives are not or should not be a series of disconnected events between disconnected selves such that at any moment we can say now whether our lives are going well or badly. Our own future matters to us because it determines what appraisal we can give to the present. Hence the truth in Solon's dictum that we can call no man happy until dead.[9] The problem with Solon's dictum is only the point of death is too soon to make an evaluation: a person's death is not the end of the narratives of which they are part.

Between past and future generations: community, environment and public decisions

The assumptions of the additive separability in the value of different moments of time and the irrelevance of the past may fail in the valuation of how well an individual's life can be said to go. It does not follow immediately that they fail also for public social decisions about projects over time. Hence it does not follow immediately that there is any problem with cost benefit analysis as a decision procedure for assessing the value of projects over time. Do the arguments in the last section about intrapersonal relations of past, present and future have any implications for interpersonal relations between individuals in different, albeit overlapping, generations?

One initial reason for thinking it may have such significance is the way in which considerations about the past are peculiarly relevant to deliberations about the environment. A feature of deliberation about environmental value is that history matters and constrains our decisions as to what kind of future is appropriate. This is true of the conservation of natural objects. We value natural objects, forests, lakes, mountains and ecosystems, specifically for the particular history they embody. The very ascription of 'naturalness' to them depends upon the specific history we can tell of them. The block on 'faking' nature[10] lies not just in the origin of natural objects but also in the history that takes us from their origin. However, the significance of history is still more evident in the problems that are typical of nature conservation in the European context. Many have arisen as a consequence of too abrupt changes in the use of the land – the loss of meadowland and pastures with the use of nitrogen and intensive farming techniques, radical shifts in patterns of grazing, the disappearance of hedgerow and copses to make way for efficient use of new machinery, the drainage of old wetland rescued from the sea. Most of these nature conservation problems are concerned with flora and fauna that flourish in particular sites that are the result of a specific history of human pastoral and agricultural activity, not with sites that existed prior to human intervention. Nor is this a typically 'old world' phenomena. Many of the conservation issues in the new world have the same form: indeed their presentation as problems of 'wilderness preservation' are misleading if one means by a wilderness a landscape or habitat that is undisturbed by human activity. Rather, many new world 'wildernesses' in Africa, Australia and America are the old world pastoral landscapes shaped by indigenous people whose activities are rendered invisible and their memory lost. That this is so has been a source of many of the practical problems in 'managing wilderness' for the 'wilderness' as discovered by Europeans was a landscape that depended upon pastoral activities such as burning.[11]

This relevance of the past is evident also in the conservation of the embodiments of the work of past generations that are a part of the landscapes of the old world: stone walls, terraces, thingmounts, old irrigation systems and so on. And at the local level past matters in the value we put upon place.[12] The value of specific locations is often a consequence of the way that the life of a community is embodied within it. Historical ties of community have a material dimension in both human and natural landscapes within which a community dwells. The city is an environment that has suffered its own dislocations: hence the complaint 'I no longer know the place'. Place is also valued on a more individual level – the local familiar walk, stream, pond or landscape that invokes a very specific past of one's childhood, parents, friends, or whatever. Hence the strong reactions roused by external changes that transform those places. In all these case, the past is relevant to our current evaluations. It is because a particular place embodies a particular past that they cannot be substituted for by new artificial replacements. The history matters. Place, like nature, cannot be faked. We aim to preserve a ancient meadowland, a thingmount, an ancient stonewall and not modern reproductions. As such the past does constrain our current decisions.

The constraint that the past places upon us is best understood as one founded in the significance of the narrative orders objects and places can have for us. We enter worlds that are rich with past histories, the narratives of lives and communities from which our own lives take significance. The problem is, or should be construed as, the problem of *how best to continue the narrative*; and the question we should ask is: *what would make the most appropriate trajectory* from what has gone before? The value in these situations which we should be seeking to uphold lies in the way that the constituent items and the places which they occupy are intertwined with and embody the life-history of the community of which they form a part. This is the perspective which lies behind the following attempt to characterise (not define) the objectives of conservation: 'conservation is .... about preserving the future *as a realisation of the potential of the past.....* [it] is about negotiating the transition from past to future in such a way as to secure the transfer of maximum significance'.[13] It is because it is about the negotiation of a narrative order between past and future, that it is not simply about 'preserving the past'. Indeed once the significance of the role of a narrative order is understood, we can understand more clearly just what is wrong with that approach. One major problem with the heritage industry is the way it often attempts to freeze historical development. A place then ceases to have a continuing story to tell. The object becomes a mere spectacle, a museum piece, taken outside of any common history.

Public decisions, no less than private choices, do not start from year zero. They are, or should be, expressive of a particular understanding of relation of past and future and the communities to which we belong. They are contested for that reason. For the same objects and places often embody quite *different* narratives which sometimes point to different and conflicting trajectories between which we must adjudicate. There are different histories to which we have to be true – and there are histories that, when they are unearthed, change our perceptions of the nature of a place and what it embodies. For example the empty hills of highland Scotland embody not just a wild beauty but also the absence of those who were driven from their homes in the clearances. Their memory must also be respected. The argument over the fate of the 100 foot high statue to the Duke of Sutherland on Beinn Bhraggie Hill near Golspie is about which history we choose to acknowledge. Between 1814 and 1819, the 'Black Duke', as he was known, played a leading role in evicting the indigenous people from their homes.[14] We should perhaps support its removal not just on aesthetic grounds but also for what it represents to the local people, some of whom are descended from those who were driven out. For the same reasons, the now dilapidated cottages which their ancestors left behind should perhaps remain. More controversially, such histories form a proper part of the debate as to how far the highlands of Scotland should remain unpopulated.

Finally, it needs to be noted that in discussing the transition from past to future we are not mere conduits through which history flows. The future matters not just to the past but to us – for the characterisation of how well our own lives go depends upon what happens after we have gone. There are a variety of projects in which we engage and relationships in which we are involved which are such that how well our lives can be said to go can depend on what happens to the projects and relationships that occur beyond our lifetime. Hence my remark at the end of the last section, that Solon is wrong: at death it too soon to say how well a person's life has gone. Consider what it is to engage in the sciences and the arts. The status of a piece of scientific work depends on its relation to both a particular past and a particular future. In relation to the past, a piece of scientific work only makes sense within a particular history of problems and theories to which it makes a contribution. Its success or failure depends on its capacity to solve existing problems where others fail. However, it also depends on a projected relation to the future in terms of its capacity to solve not just existing problems, but also problems unenvisaged by its author, and in its fruitfulness in creating new problems to be solved and new avenues of research beyond anything a scientist may have considered. Correspondingly, that there exist future scientists educated in a discipline and able to continue work within it matters for current scientific activity.

Likewise the greatness of many works of art lies in their continuing to illuminate human problems and predicaments in contexts quite foreign to that in which they were originally constructed. Many of the aesthetic qualities of a work of art may only become apparent in virtue of its relation to future works. Hence the truth in Eliot's comment: 'the past should be altered by the present as much as the present is directed by the past'.[15] For this reason, it is of significance for us now that there be future generations able to appreciate the arts and contribute to them. Similar points apply to more everyday activities, raising and educating children, tilling soils, creating towns and cities in which the future can be happily lived. In all such activities, the future matters to us now. This is apt to sound paradoxical, especially when stated in terms of our being 'harmed after our deaths':[16] the phrase conjures up implication of backward causation and is resisted for this reason. However, this worry misses the point, for no such implication is involved. The point is rather that how we characterise the value of an event depends upon a larger narrative frame in which it occurs and that frame itself depends upon a particular future. It is because in our lives both public and private, the value of different events does not answer to the assumptions of additive separability.

It is just this point that highlights the problem with utilitarian decision making procedures like cost benefit analysis. As I noted at the outset of this paper, cost benefit analysis assumes additive separability of moments of time and the irrelevance of the past. As such it disrupts proper deliberative reflection of our relation of past to future. It involves the introduction of particular assumptions about the public appraisal of projects that are central to institutions in commercial society. In the world of costs and benefits in a competitive commercial society the past is irrelevant, for the survival always depends upon future profitability. The past and long term future count only to the extent they may be represented in immediate consumer preferences. Moreover, specifically commercial values, the prices individuals are willing to place on objects and events at specific moments of time, are additively separable over time.

Cost benefit analysis takes these commercial norms into the world of public choices. However, whatever the appropriateness they have for the economic sphere, and I leave this aside in this paper,[17] they are inappropriate for public choice. They disrupt the social narratives that make possible community over time. Hence, decision procedures like cost benefit analysis are apt to foster forms of development and planning that are ahistorical and placeless. The justification of the road that runs through copse, woodland and ancient meadowland to save a few minutes on travel time, expresses an attitude to time as a series of separable moments that come as cost or benefit, not as the narrative order of a life. Such results are not accidental. Given the assumptions of additive separability and the irrelevance of the past, one can expect decision that fail to appreciate the significance of places that bind communities over time. In public choices about the environment we express the kinds of relations to past and future we want as a society: the very assumptions of cost benefit analysis rule out proper expression of those values.[18]

Notes

1. For a detailed and more technical discussion of the concept of separability and the different dimensions over which separability can be considered see J. Broome *Weighing Goods* (Oxford, Blackwell, 1991).

2. See J. O'Neill *Ecology, Policy and Politics: Human Well-Being and the Natural World* (London, Routledge, 1993), ch.5.

3. A. Pigou *The Economics of Welfare* 4th edn. (London, Macmillan, 1952), p.25.

4. See J. O'Neill *Ecology, Policy and Politics: Human Well-Being and the Natural World* p.53.

5. A. Pigou *The Economics of Welfare* 4th edn. (London: Macmillan, 1952), p.107.

6. H. Sidgwick *The Methods of Ethics* (London, MacMillan, 1907), p.418

7. T. Nagel *The Possibility of Altruism* (Oxford, Oxford University Press, 1970) and D. Parfit *Reasons and Persons* (Oxford, Clarendon Press, 1984), part two.

8. A similar thought underlies recent work of economists on the possible parallels between temporal and spatial discounting, where the latter involves weighting costs and benefits differently in proportion to their geographical or cultural distance from oneself. See C. Perring and B. Hannon, 'A Sense of Time and Place: An Introduction to Spatial Discounting', paper given to Ecology, Society, Economy: The Inaugural Conference of the European Branch of the International Society for Ecological Economics, 1996.

9. See Aristotle *Nicomachean Ethics* (Indianapolis, Hackett, 1985), Book I, chs.10-13.

10. Robert Elliot, 'Faking Nature', *Inquiry* vol. 25, 1982, pp. 81-93.

11. Thus consider the history of the management of one of the great symbols of American wilderness, Yosemite National Park. In the influential report of the Leopold Committee, Wildlife Management in the National Parks, we find the following statement of objectives for parks:

> As a primary goal we would recommend that the biotic associations within each park be maintained, or where necessary recreated, as nearly as possible in the condition that prevailed when the area was first visited by the white man. A national park should represent a vignette of primitive America'. (Cited in A. Runte, *National Parks: The American Experience* 2nd edn. (Lincoln, University of Nebraska Press, 1987) pp.198-9.)

The 'primitive' condition experienced by the first white visitors to the area is reported thus:

> When the forty niners poured over the Sierra Nevada into California, those who kept diaries spoke almost to a man of the wide-space columns of mature trees that grew on the lower western slope in gigantic magnificence. The ground was a grass parkland, in springtime carpeted with wildflowers. Deer and bears were abundant. (Ibid. p.205.)

This 'original' and 'primitive' state was not a wilderness, but a cultural landscape with its own history. The 'grass parkland' was in part the result of the pastoral practices of the Native Americans, who had used fire to promote pastures for game and black oak for acorn. After the Ahwahneeche Indians were driven from their lands by Major Savage's military expedition of 1851, 'Indian style' burning techniques were discontinued and fire suppression controls introduced. The consequence was the decline in meadowlands under increasing areas of bush. When the Totuya, the grand daughter of chief Tanaya and sole survivor of the Ahwahneeche Indians evicted from the valley, returned in 1929 she remarked on the landscape she found, 'Too dirty; too much bushy'. (Cited in K. Olwig, 'Reinventing Common Nature: Yosemite and Mt. Rushmore – A Meandering Tale of a Double Nature', in W. Cronon *Uncommon Ground: Toward Reinventing Nature* (New York, W.W. Norton, 1995)) It was not just the landscape that had changed. In the Giant Sequoia groves the growth of litter on the forest floor, dead branches and competitive vegetation inhibited the growth of new Sequoia and threatened more destructive fires. Following the Leopold report, both cutting and burning were used to 'restore' Yosemite back to its 'primitive' state. However to talk of restoring a park to a 'primitive', 'natural' or 'wilderness' condition simply disguises the nature of the problems. Reference to wilderness suppresses one part of the story that can be told of the landscape: the non-European native occupants of the land are themselves treated as part of the 'natural scheme', of the 'wilderness', without history and not as dwellers in a landscape which embodies their own cultural history. Moreover, the language also disguises the way in which the history of the landscape is being artificially frozen at a particular point in time: 'The goal of managing the national parks and monuments should be to preserve, or where necessary recreate, the ecologic scene as viewed by the first European visitors'. (Cited in A. Runte op. cit. p.200.) To refer to mythical 'natural' or 'wilderness' states avoids the obvious question 'why choose that moment to freeze the landscape?'.

12. On this see the work of 'Common Ground': S. Clifford and A. King *Holding Your Ground London,* Temple Smith, 1985); S. Clifford and A. King eds. *Local Distinctiveness: Place, Particularity and Identity* (London, Common Ground, 1993).

13. A. Holland and K. Rawles, 'The Ethics of Conservation', report presented to The Countryside Council for Wales, p 37, Thingmount Series, No.1. (Lancaster University: Department of Philosophy, 1994). For a discussion see A. Holland and J. O'Neill 'The Ecological Integrity of Nature over Time: Some Problems' *Global Bioethics,* forthcoming.

13. See David Craig, *On the Crofters' Trail* (London, Jonathan Cape, 1990).

14. T.S. Eliot 'Tradition and Individual Talent', in *Selected Essays* (London, Faber and Faber, 1951) p. 15.

15. I use this formulation in 'Future Generations: Present Harms', *Philosophy,* 1993, no.68, pp. 35-51.

16. I discuss the issue in detail in J. O'Neill, 'Time, Narrative and Environmental Politics', in R. Gottlieb, ed. *Ecological Community* (London, Routledge, 1997).

17. This point arises in protests respondents make in contingent valuation surveys on being asked to put a price on environmental goods which express our relations to past and future. Typical is the following:

> ...it's a totally disgusting idea, putting a price on nature. You can't put a price on the environment. You can't put a price on what you're going to leave for you children's children...It's a heritage. It's not an open cattle market. (J. Burgess, J. Clark and C. Harrison, *Valuing Nature: What Lies Behind Responses to Contingent Valuation Surveys?*, London, UCL, 1995, p.44)

I discuss the point in detail in J. O'Neill, 'King Darius and the Environmental Economist', in O'Neill and Hayward, eds, *Justice, Property and the Environment: Social and Legal Perspectives* (Aldershot, Avebury, 1997).

7

Global Warming and the Non-Identity Problem

Edward Page

I

Substantial evidence exists that continuing release of greenhouse gasses into the atmosphere will have grave consequences for the long-term health of the earth's environment and its human inhabitants. In its most recent authoritative report, the Intergovernmental Panel on Climate Change (IPCC) concluded not only that 'the balance of evidence suggests discernible human influence on climate change',[1] but also that the long-term impact of global warming, in virtue of the disturbances it will cause for the functioning of physical systems, will have a considerable impact on the health of future human populations.[2] Concern about the *ethical* implications of climate change has been manifest in both the language of the IPCC's latest assessment and the text of the Framework Convention on Climate Change (FCCC).[3] Both emphasise the fact that climate change policies – in virtue of influencing the distribution of benefits and, particularly, burdens across generations – raise important ethical questions. The IPCC observes that climate change issues raises 'particular questions of equity between generations',[4] while article 3.1 of the FCCC states that 'the parties should protect the climate system for the benefit of present and future generations of humankind'.[5]

A common view to hold in the light of these issues is that to the extent that a government, institution, or individual acts so as to compound the global warming problem, they act *unjustly.* And they act unjustly at least partly because in so doing they *harm*, or affect adversely, the interests, welfare or well-being of those that are not yet born.[6] However, it does appear that the extension of various familiar, and well established, norms of justice which serve us well in thinking about justice *within* generations to issues of distribution *between* generations is problematic.[7] In this paper, I want to explore just one of these problems, which has been called the *Non-Identity Problem*.[8] The Non-Identity Problem suggests that the claim that persons in the distant future will be harmed by the present generation's profligate burning of greenhouse gasses – on some familiar moral views – is much more difficult to defend at the *theoretical* level than it is to believe at the *intuitive* level. In the following, I present an analysis of the Non-Identity Problem, and go on to consider the strengths and weaknesses of some responses to it, using the expanding scientific and ethical literature on global warming as the context for the discussion.

II

I begin with an example.[9] Consider the *Two Climate Change Policies*. A society faces a choice between two mutually exclusive, and exhaustive, climate change policies. The first, the Depletion Policy, involves a continuing commitment to non-renewable, fossil-fuel, energy sources and associated greenhouse gas emissions; the second, the Conservation Policy, involves a move towards heavier reliance on renewable energy sources, and tight restrictions on greenhouse emissions. Adopting the Conservation Policy, it is known, will limit the damage caused by global warming significantly. However, because the Conservation Policy will rely primarily on 'no regrets'[10] measures, it would demand only moderate sacrifices of present and immediate generations. The Depletion Policy would demand little or no sacrifice of present persons, and, in virtue of failing to check the increase of anthropogenic (that is, human originating) greenhouse emissions, would have serious long-term consequences – such as the high social and health costs of adapting to higher levels of global warming.[11]

We suppose that, one or two centuries after the choice has been made, all of the people who would later live if Depletion is chosen will enjoy a much lower quality of life than those who would live if the Conservation choice is adopted. We also suppose, however, that the long-term problems associated with choosing Depletion are not so severe that the persons who will come into existence if this option is chosen will lead lives which are not worth living – i.e. they will not on balance regret that they had ever been born.

Suppose, lastly, that at the final meeting of elected representatives responsible for making the choice, one of those present puts forward the following argument. 'Because of the profound influence it will have on the smallest details of all people's lives whatever decision we take will indirectly, if predictably, affect who mates with whom and when, and thus which individuals will be born in the future. This is because all persons owe their personal identity to the coming together of a singular egg and a singular sperm. In fact, after a few generations, and depending on which policy we choose, completely different sets of people will come into existence and these sets of people will owe their existence to this prior choice – that is, they would not have been born if this choice had not been made. Now, as we know that the adoption of neither policy will result in any of our distant successors leading lives which are not worth living, I submit that we will be harming no one in the future by choosing to adopt the Depletion Policy. We will, on the other hand, benefit many in the present generation by doing so – for even the limited sacrifices Conservation will demand of us will be on balance harmful to us. I urge, therefore, that we choose the Depletion Policy.'

Is there an objection to this line of argument, and, if so, what is it? Parfit calls the need to answer these questions, the *Non-Identity Problem*.[12]

Take as a starting point for our inquiry into the implications of the Non-Identity Problem, the influential theory of moral motivation and reasoning proposed by T.M. Scanlon. According to Scanlon's 'contractualist' view, the source of moral motivation is 'the desire to be able to justify one's actions to others on grounds they could not reasonably reject'; and an act is wrong *only* if its performance 'would be disallowed by any system of rules for the general regulation of behaviour which no one could reasonably reject as a basis for informed, unforced general agreement'.[13] Scanlon holds, firstly, that for a person to reasonably reject, that is raise a decisive objection to, an act, he must be harmed by this act; and, secondly, that the complaint based on this harm must be *unanswerable.* As Parfit puts it, on the Scanlonian view, 'an act cannot be wrong unless it will affect someone in a way that cannot be justified – unless there will be some complainant whose complaint cannot be answered'.[14]

Applying Scanlon's view to the above example, then, would require that the policy we should adopt is the one in respect of which the strongest complaint is weakest. Let's call this the 'Unanswerable Complaint Principle'. The problem with applying this principle to the Conservation-Depletion Policy choice is that there appear to be no *particular* people in the example whom our acts will affect, and will have a complaint against us, if we choose Depletion, as it appears that no particular future person's interests will be jeopardised by this choice.

Let us, for clarification, call all those who will exist in the future if we choose Depletion, the *Depletion People*, and all those who later exist if we choose Conservation, the *Conservation People.* Who would be made worse off if we chose Depletion – and relative to what alternative? Not the Depletion People, it seems, for their only alternative to being born into the polluted future world would be non-existence, and not to have been born cannot be considered better than leading a life which is worth living.[15] Next suppose, as Parfit occasionally invites us to, we imagine away the identity problem – that is, we assume that the same people will exist in the future whatever we do.[16] In such circumstances, we could provide a contractualist objection to the Depletion Policy which would not also apply to the Conservation Policy. This would be that many future persons will be worse off when they come into existence than they might otherwise have been, that is, in the one possible future (of Depletion) they will inherit a world in which vector-borne diseases, rising sea-levels, and extreme weather events customarily injure and kill many more of them than in the alternative possible future (of Conservation). When we re-introduce ourselves to the reality of the precariousness of human origins, however, this objection – and the complaints which sustain it – seems to disappear. So the problem is that it is unclear how contractualism can cope with the problem raised by future people who owe their existence to actions which worsen the conditions in which they live.

Scanlon is aware of this problem, for at one point he asks: 'Do [the Depletion] people have reasons to reject principles allowing these actions to be performed?'[17] The answer we give to Scanlon's question has implications beyond our views about *intergenerational* justice. If we answer 'no', and still entertain the strong conviction that the choice of Depletion would be wrong regardless of the inapplicability of the 'reasonable rejection' test, this would seem to undermine Scanlon's whole construction. This would be because, as Parfit observes, it is a major failing that the 'fundamental principle of Scanlon's theory draws a distinction where, on our view, no distinction should be drawn'.[18] That is, while we think it morally irrelevant that the test of reasonable rejection is not applicable in such cases, Scanlon's view suggests that it is morally relevant, and in fact it shows that we would be doing no wrong by choosing Depletion and thereby worsening the conditions in which many of our successors will live.

I have focused on the disconcerting questions raised by the Non-Identity Problem for Scanlon's view. Such questions should disconcert many contemporary moral and political philosophers, not least because Scanlon's account of moral reasoning is widely influential.[19] However, similar questions will be raised for numerous other *complaint-based* moral views when they are extended so as to cover future generations.[20] This is because our policymakers appear neither to be *harming* nor *wronging* any particular future people whichever policy they adopt. If it is wrong to adopt the Depletion Policy, then, this is not because it harms particular future persons, but because it is a sort of harmless wrong, a wrong without a victim, or, if you wish, a somewhat rare example of 'harmless non-wronging wrong-doing'.[21] As such, the Non-Identity Problem presents a stiff challenge for those who subscribe to a common view about wrong-doing which holds that acts are wrong only if they harm the interests of some particular person more than any alternative. This can be called the *Person-Affecting View.*[22] The Person-Affecting View appears to be one of a mutually exclusive, and exhaustive, pair of views of morality. The other is the non person-affecting, *or Impersonal*

View. This holds that acts can be considered wrong even if they do not harm any particular persons.[23]

The intractability of the Non-Identity Problem might best be explained by the way it tempts the proponent of the person-affecting view into subscribing to three mutually inconsistent claims. These are (1) adopting the Depletion Policy is wrong because it harms future persons (the *Intergenerational Harms Claim*); (2) an act harms somebody only if it makes a particular person worse off than they would have been had the act not been performed (the *No Worse off Claim*); and (3) the adoption of the Depletion Policy is a remote, but necessary, condition of the Depletion People coming into existence and leading lives which are worth living (the *Identity Dependence Claim*).

If we are inclined towards the Person-Affecting view, then, we appear to be caught in the horns of a powerful *trilemma*. The trilemma suggests that we must revise the Intergenerational Harms Claim – thus abandoning our intuitive commitment to a harm-based approach to intergenerational justice – or revise the No Worse Off Claim – thus abandoning the person-affecting view in favour of the alternative view that acts, such as choosing the Depletion Policy, can be wrong even if they harm no one.[24]

Sure enough, both of the above options have been canvassed in the recent literature on the Non-Identity Problem. Canvassing the former revision, Heyd endorses a view he calls *volitionism*, which holds that moral obligations can be owed only to persons whose identities are beyond the reach of the Non-Identity Problem. But because persons whose identities do not depend on present decisions will almost invariably belong to our own generation, Heyd believes that we have no moral obligations to *most* future individuals.[25] We do, on Heyd's view, possess significant obligations to our contemporaries, and we also have various prudential reasons to act so as not to lower future quality of life in virtue of certain 'empirical constraints' – such as the desire to save for our nearest descendants, and the desire to transcend our time-frame by involving ourselves with projects which will survive our death.[26] But we would, on Heyd's view, have no direct duties to the Depletion People not to choose the Depletion option. Heyd's response to the trilemma, then, is to drop the Intergenerational Harms Claim and retain the No Worse Off and Identity Dependence claims.

Parfit, on the contrary, canvasses the alternative revision. He thinks that our initial intuition that adopting the Depletion Policy would be wrong is correct, and in this sense he thinks the Non-Identity Problem ought to make no difference to our evaluation of the wrongness of this choice.[27] However, Parfit thinks that we need impersonal principles, which recall are not restricted to tracking concerns about the harming or wronging of particular persons, to explain this evaluation at the theoretical level. He offers the following *impersonal* principle which he calls the 'Same Number Quality Claim', or Q, as a stab in this direction. Q states that, 'if in either of two outcomes the same number of people would ever live, it would be bad if those who live are worse off, or have a lower quality of life, than those who would have lived.'[28]

Q, though, cannot explain what would be wrong with choices which lead to different numbers of persons existing than their alternatives. It would not, for example, explain why choosing Depletion would be wrong if different numbers of people would exist in the future under Depletion than under Conservation. Given such *Different Number Choices*,[29] the proponent of impersonal principles appears forced to abandon – or at the very least supplement – the comparative principle, Q. Suppose, as seems natural, that we appeal to a straight-forward, utility maximisation strategy, when faced by Different Number Choices. The problem then would be that such an approach could as well imply that the choice of Conservation would be the morally wrong one to make. Putting aside problems associated with making interpersonal comparisons of well-being, suppose that so many more people would live in the future Depletion world than in the future Conservation world that the Depletion People, although much poorer on average, had a greater combined utility. In such a scenario, the total utility-maximiser would appear, counter-intuitively, to view the adoption of the Depletion Policy to be morally preferable to the adoption of the Conservation Policy.[30] Although I have not the space to demonstrate this, there are also various problems awaiting those who attempt to fall back an average utility-maximising strategy.[31]

To conclude this section, in one way or another both Heyd's and Parfit's approaches seem unsatisfactory. Heyd's view invites the charge that it is repugnant, or at the very least entails counter-intuitive revisions at the practical level. Parfit's view, on the other hand, is at best an incomplete approximation to a theory of intergenerational justice, and would appear to suggest extensive revisions to principles of justice *within* generations. These worries suggest that, even if Heyd's or Parfit's views prove satisfactory ultimately, we have reason to canvass further views.

III

Recall the question which Scanlon raises but does not answer, namely, do the Depletion People have reasonable grounds to reject principles allowing the Depletion Policy to be chosen? In the remainder of the paper I will sketch two alternative approaches to answering this question. The first trades on an ambiguity in Scanlon's question over whether, in order for a (future) individual to have a complaint against an action, he would have to be at the very least rendered worse off *all things considered* by the action. Here it is argued that the person-affecting view can be interpreted as holding that a person can be harmed only if they have been made worse off *in at least one respect*, then there might be grounds for the Depletion People to complain about the actions of the Depletion option. The second focuses on a different ambiguity arising from Scanlon's question. It exists since Scanlon's talk of 'future people' might be stretched to include human collectivities, in addition to individual human beings, within the class of (potential) complainants.

The first of these two additional approaches to the Non-Identity Problem is in essence an intermediate position between the extremes which Parfit and Heyd represent – that is between pure *impersonalism* and pure *person-affectingness*. The Specific Rights Approach, as I will call it, denies the claim that choosing Depletion will not harm any particular future person. It does so by focusing on a different *dimension* of the future person who will be harmed by adopting depletion. Rather than focusing on a person's welfare as grounding various rights claims, it focuses on the way in which certain specific interests are the basis of rights claims – interests which are not simply reducible to a single more general *all things considered* interest. Examples of these specific interests might include the interest in having promises made to one kept, in avoiding physical injury, or in not being deceived, or in breathing clean air.[32]

One attraction of the idea of specific, as opposed to all-things-considered (or welfare), interests is the following. Take as our starting point the influential *interest-theory of rights.*[33] Here, a person has a right only if an aspect of his well-being is a sufficient reason for holding some other person to be under a duty to him[34] – as Raz puts it, 'rights are always to what is in the interest of the right-holder'.[35] The merit of making space in such a theory for specific rights and interests is that the possession of certain rights appear to be in one's interests in some respects but not in others. As Raz writes, 'One may have a right to some valuable property which may make one a target for criminals or for temptation. It may be in one's overall interest not to have it, but as having the property is on one's interest *in some respect* one can have a right to it.'[36]

One might illustrate these comments with an example. Suppose Smith, who is a member of a religious sect which regards blood transfusions as both unholy and immoral, requires a transfusion in order to save his life. Although he is lying unconscious after a road accident, the medical authorities are aware of his views, and decide to proceed with the transfusion regardless. Although Smith is livid when he regains consciousness, claming that the operation ought to have been delayed in order for his permission to be sought, let us suppose that sometime after the transfusion he *predictably* comes to feel grateful for his continued existence, and accepts that the transfusion was *all things considered* in his interests. Raz's comments show that it is plausible to say that Smith had at least *one* of his rights violated by the medical authorities – namely, the right to be consulted – even if the actions which led to this right being violated rendered Smith no worse off in the process all things considered.

Now turn to the case of Jones. Jones is a dweller of 21st century Britain, and who was born with a mild handicap as a result of his mother's long-term exposure to heat exhaustion (a necessary condition of which, we suppose, was anthropogenically induced global warming). As we have seen, it seems implausible to suggest that Jones's interests have been set back *all things considered* by his being born handicapped. Had the anthropogenic warming not occurred, he would never have been born, and his handicap, we suppose, is not of a severity which calls into question the fact of whether he will, on balance, lead a life which is worth living. However, as in the case of Smith, Raz's view suggests that this need not be an insurmountable obstacle to our claiming that at least *one* of his rights had been violated by the various human acts or decisions which brought about the warming, specifically, the right not to be conceived with a serious, but not devastating, handicap as a result of the environmentally profligate actions of descendants. And this is the case despite Jones predictably, if indirectly, owing his existence to these actions.

Cases such as these suggest that we should abandon the view that actions cannot be wrong if their net effects are to render no particular person worse off than they would otherwise have been *all things considered.*[37] This need not, however, entail abandoning the person-affecting view altogether, because this view is opaque. It might, for example, refer to the view that 'an act cannot be wrong *in any respect* if it is not worse for people than any alternative *in any respect'* or that 'an act cannot be wrong *in any respect* if it is not worse for people than any alternative *all things considered*'.[38] The Specific Rights Approach holds that a right-based objection to Non-Identity Problem cases can survive our subscription to the former but not the latter interpretation; and that the latter implausibly assumes that all moral requirements pick out, or only serve to protect, their owners' all things considered interests.

The upshot of the above line of argument is that some future persons' interests, and the rights they ground, confer obligations upon their predecessors not only to refrain from harming these interests once they have come into existence, but in addition to refrain from adopting courses of action which result in bringing persons into the world whose specific interests will thereby be unavoidably harmed. Suppose that included amongst these specific interests is the interest in having access to (i.e. in order to breathe) clean air. If it could be shown that the adoption of the Depletion Policy (as seems plausible[39]) will result, many decades later, in much of the earth's atmosphere being contaminated, and this compromises the ability of various obligation-bearing institutions to protect the rights grounded in these interests, then there would appear to be some (though not necessarily a decisive) objection to the Depletion Policy. The adoption of the Depletion Policy would be objectionable here because it resulted in many persons coming into existence with specific rights which could not have been fulfilled or protected. If, on the other hand, the Conservation Policy had been chosen, let's suppose, widespread air pollution would have been averted and no (or at least far fewer) people would have been brought into existence bearing rights which could not have been fulfilled. It would not matter on this view that the Depletion and Conservation People will be different individuals; and it would make no moral difference that the Depletion and Conservation peoples' identities were tied to the Depletion and Conservation Policies' prior adoption. The Specific Rights Approach, then, responds to the trilemma by revising the No Worse Off Claim in order to retain the Intergenerational Harms and Identity Dependence claims.

One problem with this approach is that it does not seem able to provide a *consistent* objection to the Depletion Policy. Suppose that it could be predicted that the Depletion Policy, although lowering the quality of life for future generations relative to the alternative, would not result in any future persons being subject to great poverty, and we suppose to specific interests violations. Then there would seem to be no specific interest-based objection to this choice. But in that case, there would be many hypothetical cases which could be constructed such that our intuitions still point to the choice of Depletion being wrong, but where it would not be considered wrong on the Specific Rights Approach. Indeed, variations on the case of Jones might constitute one such set of cases, for it might be doubted that people have rights *not* to be born handicapped, as opposed to rights *not* to born into a world where one cannot breath clean air.[40]

A different problem arises when we adopt the perspective of the potential recipient of these specific rights. Consider again the case of Jones. Parfit suggests that the main defect in a rights-based objection to Depletion in the Jones case would be that we might expect Jones, or indeed any other person in a similar position, to be grateful – rather than resentful – that he had been born. So long as the Depletion People lead lives worth living, and do not therefore regret their existence, Parfit surmises, we can assume that they would *waive* any claims they might possess which require us not to choose the Depletion Policy on their behalf.[41] And if we can predict that future persons would waive their rights not to be born rather than be born with rights that could not possibly be fulfilled, then there would be no – or possibly reduced – force to a specific-rights based objection to the earlier acts. Perhaps a response to this objection might be found in the thought that these specific rights are inalienable in some sense – that is they *cannot* be waived by their owners – but more needs to be said here about this suggestion.

Finally, suppose we grant the basic premise of the approach – that some rights protect interests which are not in their holders' all things considered interest to have respected. Many of the goods which we are concerned to preserve for posterity are public goods. Public goods, such as (the access to) clean air, are goods whose benefits are distributed throughout a society such that they are 'not subject to voluntary control by anyone other than each potential beneficiary controlling his share of the benefits'.[42] However, on the interest-theory of rights, it is problematic to argue that individuals possess rights to public goods such as clean air. This is because the interest-theory does not generate rights to all interests which individuals possess, rather only those which are sufficiently important to hold others under a duty to protect those interests. But it seems unlikely that the interest of single individual in a public good is important – and *weighty* – enough to make it the case that all other members of society are under a duty to do something about this interest. Indeed, Raz himself is skeptical about the idea of an individual possessing a right to a public good, and suggests that separate individuals' interests in such goods are best thought of as grounding *collective* rights.[43] So it seems that the idea of the specific rights (or interests) of *individuals* will need to be supplemented by some appeal to the specific rights (or interests) of *collectivities* if we are to make sense of the idea of rights to environmental public goods such as clean air. In short, the Specific Rights Approach seems unlikely to provide a full solution to the Non-Identity Problem.

IV

The drawbacks associated with the approaches considered above might not necessarily show that a solution to the Non-Identity Problem is out of reach. At first glance, at least, it might suggest rather that approaches to the Non-Identity Problem which take an *individualistic* form are implausible. But this is not quite right. What the Non-Identity Problem renders implausible, I think, are objections to Depletion which focus on the rights and interests of *particular persons* as central to the moral wrongness of choosing Depletion over Conservation. As a new piece of terminology, call all similar accounts of morality – which rest on the rights and interests (or more generally moral status) of particular value bearing entities – *token-affecting accounts.* The Non-Identity Problem appears to undermine any account which takes the relevant, value bearing, token to be a particular person. But rather than implying that we ought to abandon a token-affecting approach altogether, this result might rather suggest that we ought to appeal to the interests or rights of a different token if we are to formulate an objection to the Depletion Policy's adoption (or at least it does not at this stage rule out this possibility). The main candidate for this substitution is, I think, the token of 'particular human collectivity', however there are other possibilities. Each substitution would of course have to be evaluated on its own merits – most obviously in terms of the way it makes sense of our convictions about cases such as Conservation-Depletion example.

Consider figure 1, which attempts to explore diagrammatically the intricacies of the *token-affecting* view – consider particularly the position I call the Wide Token-Affecting View. The proponent of this last view canvasses a view different from those proposed by Heyd and Parfit. The revised view is compatible with the claim that the Non-Identity Problem blocks a *person-affecting* account of the wrongness of choosing Depletion, but instead claims that Depletion is objectionable in virtue of harming the interests of future collectivities.[44]

So whereas the Specific Rights Approach revises the *dimension* by which we claim future persons are harmed – made worse off – by our prodigious choice of Depletion, the Group Affecting Approach (as we might call it) revises the identity of the *victim* of this choice. This approach suggests that we can reconcile all three of the claims identified earlier by revising the Intergenerational Harms and No Worse Off claims by focusing on the way in which future collectivities are harmed – made worse off by – Depletion rather than particular persons. Moreover, because this strategy is agnostic on the issue of whether the No Worse Off Claim should be cashed out in terms of 'all things considered' or 'specific' interests (of groups or individuals) it is worth emphasising that it is compatible, indeed complementary, to the Specific Rights Approach.

Consider the way in which climate change is expected to alter the cultural and social fabric of certain nations. There is possibly no better example of this than the way in which global warming will cause significant mean sea-level rises in the coming decades and centuries. In its latest assessment, the IPCC concluded that there will be an increase in global mean surface sea-levels of around half a meter on 1990 levels by the year 2100.[45] Moreover, it predicts that this will have serious consequences for many nations in the future, but in particular for nations which are entirely, or have regions which are, low lying. Indeed, these sea-level increases are expected to inundate much of the world's lowlands, damage coastal cropland, and displace millions of persons from low-lying and coastal communities.[46] Just some of the lowlying nations that the IPCC thinks are in danger are the north-east coastal nations of Latin America, Bangladesh, Egypt and Holland.

But consider, even more worryingly, the small island states of the South Pacific. The IPCC singles out these nations for special attention because of the especially grave, and largely adverse, effects that sea-level rises will have on these states – culminating in the worst case scenario in complete disappearance. Here, the combined effect of warming and sea-level rises is expected to reduce soil fertility, push agriculture inland, and thereby exacerbate soil erosion. It will be massively expensive to undertake even moderate mitigation responses for all these effects, and even if the resources could be found (from international humanitarian assistance, for example) the costs to the community in terms of maintaining access to traditional ways of life, and adapting to new ways of living, would be profound. These are all projections which the IPCC make with some confidence.[47]

With these observations in mind, consider the case of *The Displaced Islanders.* Suppose world-wide policies of Conservation are not implemented, and that the IPCC's best estimate of global sea level rise of a half a meter by the year 2100 is proved accurate. Towards the end of the 21st century, the elder statesmen of the Pacific island state of *Globalwarmia* have assembled to assess the damage which global warming has caused their small community. In line with the IPCC's projections, their island has been all but submerged by the Pacific Ocean, and their agricultural industry had been destroyed by a combination of soil erosion and infertility. Because of the lack of employment prospects and general social upheaval, moreover, the indigenous population has been cut to a small percentage of its twentieth century level. Finally, because

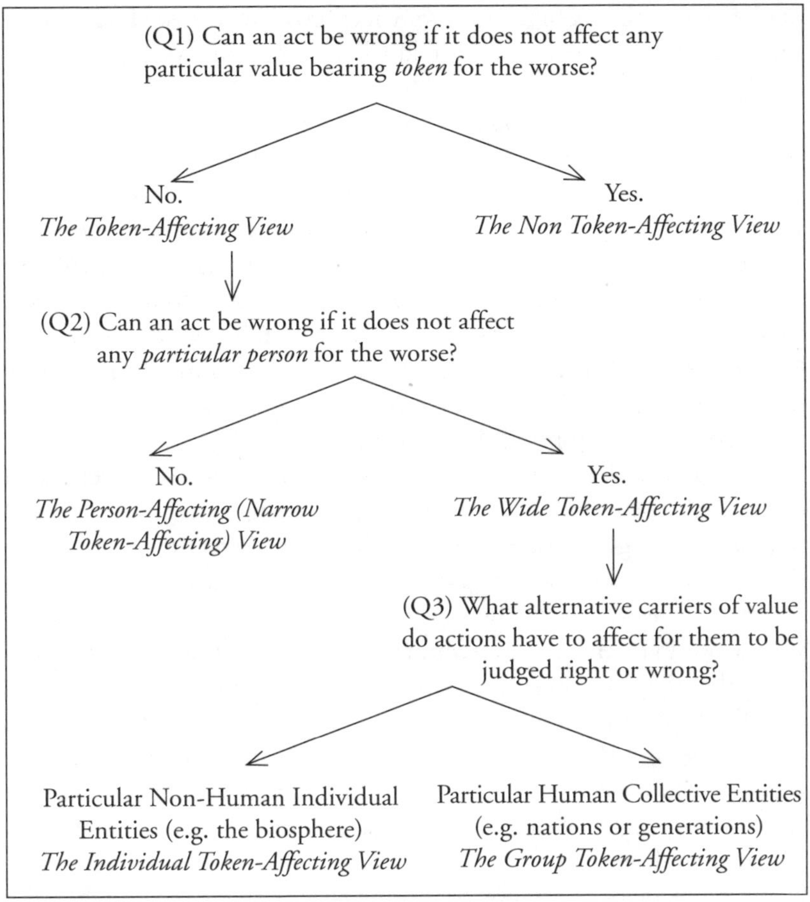

Figure 1. The Token-Affecting View

of the combined impact of population displacement and other impacts, many cultural practices – practices which had been handed down through the generations – have been abandoned. The community, the elders agreed, was on the verge of collapse.

Let us put aside the economic, social and health impacts of climate change on existing islanders, and in particular the important issues of *international* justice which this case raises. Has the island community *itself* been harmed by – has it a complaint against – previous generations' failure to implement climate change policies to prevent the worst effects of global warming? On the Group Affecting View, it has. Here, despite the fact that no particular individual will exist in the future where Depletion is adopted who would have existed had it not been, various collectivities and associations will, and are thus candidates for complaint-bearing status. Indeed, even if the community of Globalwarmia ceased to exist following a catastrophic increase in sea levels, this would not mean that we could simply assume that it had never existed. Rather, it would be because the nation had been destroyed primarily as a result, we are supposing, of the impact of climate change on its viability. The idea, then, is that the interests of the collectivities which constitute Globalwarmia – including, but not merely, the political community itself – generate certain requirements which we can say were violated as a consequence of adopting the Depletion Policy.[48]

Suppose that the community was, prior to the sea-level rise, a traditional community dedicated to preserving a rich cultural and linguistic heritage. Assume, however, that the preservation of the native language is not a necessary condition of the survival of the Globalwarmian community as such.[49] As the warming, and consequent sea level rises, would result in the impoverishment of the Islanders' linguistic and cultural heritage (most of the population bar the Elders, let's suppose, have fled to the mainland and now need to speak a different language in order to get by) the interests of the Islanders *as a collectivity* might be thought to have been harmed by this – the group, collectively, at the very least had its right of access to an integral and undamaged cultural language undermined.

Note that we are not proposing – as is suggested esewhere by Kymlicka – that the adoption of Depletion type policies would be wrong in virtue of undermining the needs of *specific individuals* to have access to a flourishing cultural structure, in order that they are in a position to pursue their own conceptions of the good. Kymlicka argues that persons belonging to disadvantaged minority cultures can, from the liberal point of view, be afforded additional rights and resources to compensate for their damaged needs. He claims that commonality – namely a shared language, history, and membership in a cultural community – does not constrain individuality: 'membership in a cultural structure is what enables individual freedom, what enables meaningful choices about how to lead one's life.'[50]

Rather, the claim here is that the communities which future people belong to are deserving of concern and respect *in their own right.* And if present actions have the result either that these communities die out altogether, or are damaged in the sense that various communal practices are undermined, they are morally objectionable at least in this one important respect.[51] Thus, despite the fact that no future individual islander will be harmed by the Depletion Policy's adoption – they all lead lives which are at least worth living and owe their existence to it – the Islanders *as a collectivity* are harmed. Here we appear to have the basis of an objection to Depletionist policies which survives the Non-Identity Problem, and is framed within token-affecting terms. It is important here to note that the Group Affecting Approach is still atomistic – or non-holistic – in the sense Masaya Kobayashi uses the term, as it is particular (or individual) groups which possess interests in (and thus rights to) maintaining an undamaged heritage of cultural goods, such as viable linguistic structures. The value of cultural preservation, here, is not owed 'to the world' abstracted from the way it connects to the flourishing, and continued survival, of human communities. Indeed, groups – together with their individual members – can equally be thought of as atoms of the whole which Kobayashi seeks to exploit as a basis for a solution of the Non-Identity Problem.[52]

Furthermore, because it is framed in token-affecting terms, the Group-Affecting View is reconcilable with Scanlon's contractualist view. Recall that contractualism is the view that the fundamental moral motive is 'the desire to be able to justify one's actions to others on grounds that they could not reasonably reject'[53] and an act is wrong only if its performance 'would be disallowed by any system of rules for the general regulation of behaviour which no one could reasonably reject as a basis for informed, unforced general agreement'.[54] As noted earlier, if interpreted as a person-affecting doctrine, contractualism seems an unpromising approach to the Non-Identity Problem. This is because the Depletion People, taken person by person, do not seem to have a legitimate complaint against the Depletion Policy's adoption.

Scanlon's construction does not appear to be formally tied to the idea that the complaints it considers must be restricted to those arising from harms, or wrongs, done to particular *persons.*[55] Indeed, I suspect that if the contractualist approach is in the final analysis to offer a coherent orientation to intergenerational issues, it will take on a mixed, or pluralist, form. That is, it will appeal to both person-affecting and impersonal-principles. However, putting aside impersonal principles at this point, it seems that contractualism could be bolstered somewhat if it made room for unanswerable complaints of certain human (and possibly non-human) groups. The view which I have been exploring, then, suggests that we should revise Scanlon's account of moral reasoning to read that 'an act is wrong only if it affects some particular *individual or group* in a way that cannot be justified'. We might call this the *Wide Unanswerable Complaint* principle.[56]

I have space only to mention one significant problem with the Group Affecting Approach. Suppose that a course of action which we think will harm a certain future group's interests would also be a necessary condition either of that group's coming into existence or its continued survival. In such cases it might be that the approach will be plagued by a new *group-affecting* version of the Non-Identity Problem. Take, as an historical example of what I mean, the enforced transportation of West African peoples to North America in previous centuries.[57] Suppose that a present-day African American individual suggests that he had been harmed – and deserves compensation – in virtue of being born into a community which had been created by the enslavement of his ancestors. The Non-Identity Problem suggests that he was not harmed by the slavers' activities as he owed his existence, in part, to their actions (as all of us do, I suspect). Suppose next that the complaint had been made on behalf of the present-day African American *community*. The enslavement again appears to have been a necessary condition of the existence of the present-day African American community. If this grave injustice – or series of injustices – had never occurred there would be no African American community in quite the same sense as there is today. There would no doubt be some Africans who had emigrated to the United States, for example, but it is unlikely that there would be the rich diversity of African American linguistic and cultural heritage that there is today. This new version of the Non-Identity Problem suggests that a representative of this present-day community could not argue that his *community* had been harmed by the original enslavement.[58] If parallel cases can be constructed in the Depletion-Conservation example, then, various group based objections to choosing Depletion might similarly fall away.

These and other worries suggest that the Wide Unanswerable Complaint Principle would certainly stand in need of supplementation – perhaps with both specific-rights and impersonal principles. Questions would then be raised as to how these different principles would stand in relation to one another. For example, would token-affecting principles have (lexical) priority over impersonal principles in our pluralist theory? – or would the principles be weighted differently? Such important issues are beyond the scope of this chapter.[59] My aims have been more modest. I hope to have sketched *two* relatively neglected lines of thought which might be appealed to in order to solve the Non-Identity Problem in an important range of cases.

Notes

1. J.T. Houghton et al. (eds), 'Summary for Policymakers', *Climate Change 1995: The Science of Climate Change*, (Cambridge, Cambridge University Press, 1995), p.5.

2. See A.J. McMichael et al., 'Human Population Health', in R.T Watson et al. (eds) *Climate Change 1995: Impacts, Adaptations, and Mitigation of Climate Change: Scientific-Technical Analyses*, (Cambridge, Cambridge University Press, 1995), p.564ff.

3. This was adopted at the United Nations Conference on Environment and Development, Rio de Janeiro, 1992 – otherwise known as the Rio Earth Summit.

4. K.J. Arrow et al., 'Intertemporal Equity, Discounting and Economic Efficiency', in J.P. Bruce et al. (eds), *Climate Change 1995: Economic and Social Dimensions of Climate Change*, (Cambridge, Cambridge University Press, 1996), p.130.

5. Quoted in T. Banuri et al., 'Equity and Social Considerations', ibid., p.90.

6. Onora O'Neill, for example, writes that 'by burning fossil fuels prodigally we accelerate the green-house effect and may *dramatically harm successors*, who can do nothing to us' (O'Neill, *Towards Justice and Virtue*, (Cambridge, Cambridge University Press, 1996), p.115 – emphasis added).

7. These problems are mirrored in many ways by the formidable problems facing those who wish to extend domestic norms of justice in order to approach issues of international justice.

8. See D. Parfit, *Reasons and Persons*, (Oxford, Clarendon Press, 1984), p.351f.

9. Which is a variant of a case discussed by Parfit, ibid., pp.361-64.

10. The IPCC defines these as measures whose benefits 'equal or exceed their cost to society, excluding the benefits of climate change mitigation', J.P. Bruce et al. (eds), 'Summary for Policymakers', op. cit., p.15.

11. As a rough and ready parallel to this hypothetical policy choice, one might think of the decision of whether or not to ratify - and adopt policies consistent with - the requirements of the Kyoto Protocol to the Framework Convention on Climate Change.

12. Parfit, *Reasons and Persons*, p.359.

13. T.M. Scanlon, 'Contractualism and Utilitarianism', in A. Sen and B. Williams (eds), *Utilitarianism and Beyond*, (Cambridge, Cambridge University Press, 1982), p.116; 110.

14. Parfit, 'A Reply to Sterba', *Philosophy and Public Affairs*, 16, 1987, p.193.

15. In fact, if we think that causing someone to exist who will lead a life worth living thereby benefits them, we might think the Depletion people ought to be grateful to the policy-chooser's for being born at all. For the purposes of the paper, however, I put this possibility to one side.

16. See Parfit, *Reasons and Persons*, p.365-6.

17. Scanlon, 'Contractualism and Utilitarianism', p.115.

18. Parfit, *Reasons and Persons*, p.523.

19. As evidenced by its adoption by Brian Barry in recent work. See Barry, *Theories of Justice*, (Berkeley, University of California Press, 1989), p.284f; and *Justice as Impartiality*, (Oxford, Clarendon, 1995), especially pp.67-72.

20. Take the view proposed by Onora O'Neill in this volume. O'Neill claims that the scope of our duties extend not only to those whom can be identified with ease - such as our proximate coevals and fellow countrymen - but in addition to all those whom we in some way premise our agency upon. We habitually make assumptions about distant strangers when we decide how to act, she argues, and accordingly we are required not to harm *them* even if we are not in a position to determine exactly who *they* are. There is an important problem with her analogy between our dealings with *distant contemporaries* and *distant noncontemporaries* though. Suppose that the society's adoption of Depletion would lead, predictably, to a radical lowering of the quality of life for *both* presently existing and future persons. Suppose next that some of the existing persons whose lives go worse because of the policy are noncompatriots. The fact that some of the people we would affect are distant strangers – on some agent-relative view – might entail that we violate no serious moral requirements by affecting these people adversely. However, even on an extreme agent-relative view the claim would *not* be that we have harmed no particular people by choosing the policy, but rather that because of some view of the relative moral unimportance of the well-being of noncompatriots, these persons' interests do not ground any strong requirements against us. When we turn to future persons, however, even the idea that we *harm* future persons is undermined. Put differently, suppose we grant, to O'Neill, that we have some imperfect – that is non-rights grounding – obligations to future persons not to adopt Depletion. *Which* particular persons will benefit from such an obligation being respected as opposed to disrespected? O'Neill's view appears to imply that we have obligations to (future) persons who could not possibly benefit from these obligations being respected, or harmed by their *not* being respected.

21. See J. Feinberg, *Harmless Wrongdoing*, (Oxford, Oxford University Press, 1988), p.xxviii.

22. Clearly the full implications of endorsing a person-affecting view of moral reasoning will depend in part on whether or not one holds that causing a person to exist who leads a life worth living thereby benefits that person. As stated in note 14, I am assuming here that causing to exist *cannot* benefit. However, for a discussion of this issue, and especially of the implications of abandoning this assumption, see Parfit, *Reasons and Persons*, pp.393-401; and pp.487-90. Interestingly, Masaya Kobayashi (this volume, chapter 8) appears to embrace the claim that causing to exist *can* benefit. Kobayashi remarks that a Depletion type policy 'is simply bad for the [Conservation] Virtual Persons because they are deprived both of the (possible) benefit caused by being born, and of the possible life worth living' (p. 181).

23. On the distinction, see D. Heyd, *Genethics: Moral Issues in the Creation of People*, (Berkeley, University of California Press, 1992), p.80f.

24. Although it is essentially a *trilemma* - the third option being to revise the Identity Dependence Claim – I want to put this possibility to one side. While I have not the space here to discuss the issue of personal identity in detail here, it does seem that dispensing with the Identity Dependence Claim in order to retain the other two claims is at the very least counter to the ethos of the most familiar theories of personal identity.

25. Heyd refers to this view as *generocentrism*. According to generocentrism, requirements of intergenerational justice are grounded 'exclusively by reference to the interests, welfare, ideals, rights, and duties of [actual persons]' – see D. Heyd, op. cit., p.xi, 80f; Schwartz, writing some years earlier, defends substantially the same view. See T. Schwartz, 'Obligations to Posterity', in R.I Sikora and B. Barry (eds) *Obligations to Future Generations*, (Philadelphia, Temple University Press, 1978), p.3ff.

26. See Heyd, op. cit., p.193f.

27. Parfit calls this the *No Difference View*. See *Reasons and Persons*, p.367.

28. Ibid., p.361.

29. Parfit contrasts these with *Same Person Cases* and *Same Number Cases*. The former choices lead to the same persons living as their alternatives, the latter choices lead to the same number, but not same individuals, living as their alternatives. See ibid., p.356.

30. Similar worries are raised by Sidgwick and Parfit. See H. Sidgwick, *Methods of Ethics*, (London, MacMillan, 1901), p.415-6. Parfit takes this line of reasoning to its logical, and he thinks *repugnant*, conclusion when he observes that on the impersonal-maximising view, 'for any possible population of at least ten billion people, all with a very high quality of life, there must be some much larger imaginable population whose existence, if other things are equal, would be better, even though its members have lives that are barely worth living' (*Reasons and Persons*, p.388).

31. Suppose all who live in some society are uniformly very happy. Impersonal average-utilitarianism would appear to require that additional people be added to the society's population if they are on balance happier than presently existing persons, and condemn

additional persons being added to the population if the are on balance slightly less happy than existing persons.

32. See J. Woodward, 'The Non-Identity Problem', *Ethics*, 96, 1986, p.810f; and 'Reply to Parfit', *Ethics*, 97, 1987, p.802.

33. I do not consider the alternative, *choice-theory*, as it is straightforwardly incompatible with right-based norms of intergenerational justice for reasons quite apart from the Non-Identity Problem. For discussion, see H.Steiner, 'The Rights of Future Generations', in D. MacLean (ed.) *Energy and the Future*, (Totowa, New Jersey, Rowman and Littlefield, 1983), esp. p.154f.

34. See, for example, J. Raz *The Morality of Freedom*, (Oxford, Clarendon Press, 1986), p.166f

35. Raz, *Ethics in the Public Domain*, (Oxford, Clarendon Press, 1994), p.46.

36. Ibid., p.46.

37. See Woodward, 'Reply to Parfit', *Ethics*, 1987, p.802.

38. As suggested by L. Temkin, 'Harmful goods, harmless bads', in R.G. Frey and C. Morris (eds) *Value, Welfare, and Morality*, (Cambridge, C.U.P,. 1993), pp.295-98.

39. Climate Change Policies can have both direct and indirect effects on air pollution levels. Firstly, and directly, reducing the combustion of fossil fuels will reduce one of the main sources of various air pollutants, most significantly CO_2. Secondly, and more indirectly, global warming is expected to amplify levels of pollution in certain circumstances, particularly in urban areas. For example, if, as appears likely, warming causes an increase in the frequency of occasions where very hot, and humid, weather is combined with low wind speeds, there will be many more occasions where air pollutants will not be rapidly dispersed. This is expected, among other things, to exacerbate the urban asthma problem. Action to reduce anthropogenic radiative forcing – such as tight(er) restrictions on anthropogenic greenhouse gas emissions – therefore, would be expected to reduce the severity of these effects relative to the alternative (see McMichael et al., op. cit., p.577-79).

40. See Woodward, 'The Non-Identity Problem', note 12; and 'Reply to Parfit', p.809.

41. See Parfit, *Reasons and Persons*, p.365.

42. Raz, op. cit., p.198.

43. Ibid., pp.186-90.

44. Interestingly, Heyd at one point remarks that person-affectingness 'is not necessarily committed to individualism; the "carrier" of value, the entity for whom something can be good, can be a group of people, a collective' (Heyd, op. cit., pp.84-85).

45. See R.A. Warrick et al., 'Changes in Sea Level', in J.T. Houghton et al. (eds.), op. cit., p.365ff. Therein the authors report that global mean sea level has 'already risen 10-25 cm over the last 100 years' and, on the most researched anthropogenic 'emissions scenario', is expected to rise by between 38 and 86 cm – with a 'best estimate' of 49 cm – by the year 2100. See ibid., pp.381-85.

46. See L. Bijlsma et al., 'Coastal Zones and Small Islands', in R.T. Watson et al. (eds.) op. cit., pp.295-297. The authors project, with 'high confidence', that sea-level rise 'would have negative effects on a number of sectors, including tourism, freshwater supply and quality, fisheries and aquaculture, agriculture, human settlements, financial services, and human health.' They also project that 'adaptation to sea-level-rise and climate change will involve important trade-offs, which could include environmental, social, cultural values' (ibid., p.292).

47. See ibid., pp.296-98.

48. Compare with the view Charles Taylor takes of the good of communities in *Multiculturalism: Examining the Politics of Recognition*, (Princeton, Princeton University Press, 1994), pp.40-1. Therein Taylor criticises the view – attributed to Will Kymlicka – that the worth of communities is derived from the value they have in securing the 'cultural needs' of individuals, such as their seeking to give meaning to their lives. This individualistic view, Taylor thinks, firstly neglects the importance of these communities *qua* communities rather than just associations of value-bearing individuals; and, secondly, that it cannot account for the fact that what many Quebecois, for example, want is that their community survive into the future for reasons quite apart from the positive impact that this will have on the well-being of its members. According to my account, Taylor is advocating a *wide* token-affecting view to Kymlicka's *narrow* token-affecting view.

49. This seems a reasonable assumption, for there may well be other distinctive and well-rooted cultural traditions enjoyed by the Islanders which can be continued, and preserved for future generations, without their being pursued in a particular language.

50. See Kymlicka, *Liberalism, Community, and Culture*, (Oxford, Clarendon, 1989), p.208. Kymlicka, like Heyd, adopts a solely person-affecting view of intergenerational morality, according to which 'non-existent people don't have claims – we don't have a moral duty to them to bring them into the world' (ibid., p.27). Note that Yoon-Jae Chung (this volume, chapter 11) appears to subscribe to Kymlicka's view when he claims that various institutions ought to 'utilise their transnational networks for the good purposes of providing children and new generations with opportunities to experience a variety of cultures' (p. 279). It is unclear, though, how this claim links with Chung's other main claim that 'individuals are trans-individuals who are intrinsically related to God, cosmos, and all animate and inanimate objects in the universe' (p. 280).

51. Taylor argues that 'Kymlicka's [person-affecting view] is valid (perhaps) for existing people who find themselves trapped within a culture under pressure, and can flourish within it or not at all. But it doesn't justify measures designed to ensure survival through indefinite future generations. For the populations concerned, however, that is what is at stake' (Taylor, op. cit., p.41).

52. Notice also that my claim is not that we ought to be concerned for posterity because posterity at least partly constitutes our identities. This would reduce the requirements of intergenerational justice to a matter of extended self-interest. The claim I am defending is rather that certain groups should be seen as interest-bearing entities in their own right, and as a result are deserving of our concern and respect when it comes to deciding between

competing *culturally sensitive* public policies. Put another way, the intergenerational requirements which I am seeking to explore are *agent-neutral* as opposed to *agent-relative.*

53. Scanlon, 'Contractualism and Utilitarianism', p.116.

54. Ibid., p.110.

55. According to Scanlon's view of the scope of contractualism, 'morality applies to a being if the notion of justification to a being of that kind makes sense...the being must have a good, that is, that there be a clear sense in which things can be said to go better or worse for that being...the being [must] constitute a point of view; that is there be such a thing as what it is like to be that being' ('Contractualism and Utilitarianism', pp.113-14). The analysis of the interests of groups in the text is intended to convey the thought that there can be such a thing as a group point of view or perspective of things, and that things can indeed go better or worse for these groups.

56. Suppose we do formulate such a group-affecting objection in terms of rights-language. Then note that it is not subject to the problem that no *particular individual's* interest in securing access to a public good such as clean air will be important enough to hold everyone else to be under a duty to provide that good. Here it is the interest of the group *qua* group which grounds the right of the group to certain public goods, such as access to a flourishing cultural resource base or linguistic heritage, and is *ex hypothese* sufficiently strong to hold other groups (and individuals) to be under a duty not to violate this right.

57. Which is discussed by J. Fishkin 'Justice Between Generations', *Nomos XXXIII: Compensatory Justice*, J.Chapman (ed), (New York, New York University Press, 1991), pp.91ff.

58. I put to one side here the injustices which the original enslavement perpetrated on the African slaves and the communities to which they belonged to at the time of this enslavement.

59. For a seminal discussion of these matters, see J. Rawls 'The Priority Problem', *A Theory of Justice*, Oxford, O.U.P., 1973, pp.40-6.

8

Holistic Self and Future Generations: A Revolutionary Solution to the Non-Identity Problem

Masaya Kobayashi

1. Great Riddles from within the Utilitarian Tradition

§1. The Radical Attack Against Atomistic 'Reasons and Persons'

In Chapter 2, it was made clear that there are essential limits derived from atomistic construction in Western theories on future generations at the first three stages of development, and in particular, in contemporarily contractual theories including that of Rawls. The problem of atomism was later illuminated from the other important tradition, utilitarianism, at the fourth stage by Derek Parfit. The title of *Reasons and Persons* signifies the subjects of his masterpiece: 'reason' to do with morality and rationality, and 'person' in terms of our identity or unity over time, as distinct from others. In concordance, the first three Parts are named, 'Self-Defeating Theories', 'Rationality and Time', 'Personal Identity', and the last part concerns the present subject, 'Future Generations'.

In this chapter, the discussion is concentrated upon Parfit's arguments, including that of the well-known 'Non-Identity Problem': the purpose is to propose a revolutionary solution to this problem from an Eastern holistic perspective.

Although most articles referring to Parfit's work on 'Future Generations' discuss merely the fourth part, it is necessary to describe the outline of the other three parts briefly in order to explicate the whole implication of his argument, because the first three parts compose the background to the final part. In particular, it should be emphasised that the most important purpose of the first two parts can be regarded as refuting what Parfit calls 'the Self-interest Theory', a theory about rationality. He stated that the central claim of this theory was that 'For each person, there is one supremely rational ultimate aim: that his life go, for him, as well as possible'.[1] This 'rational supreme aim' equates with 'the outcomes that would be best for himself', namely 'self-interest' itself, although there are three kinds of 'theories about self-interest': 'Hedonistic Theory' including the utilitarianism of Bentham and Sidgwick, 'Desire-Fulfilment Theory' and 'Objective List Theory'.[2]

Though it is impossible to give a full account of Parfit's long argument here, it is worth noting that 'Time' has already played a central role in his refutation of 'Self-interest Theory', especially in Chapter 8 in Part 2, 'Different Attitudes to Time'.[3] First, he argued against the theory from the point of view of morality in Part 1, and then from 'the Present-aim Theory' in Part 2, 'Rationality and Time'. In brief, he denied the orthodox view that it is rational for persons to act according to their self-interest, whichever theory may be adopted about self-interest. Accordingly, his conclusion was that 'we must reject S [the Self-interest Theory] and accept P [the Present-aim Theory]', changing our view about rationality (instead of that about self-interest).[4] Whether we consent to the Present-aim Theory or not, his rejection of the Self-interest Theory is itself remarkable, because 'The Self-interest Theory has been believed by most people for more than two millenia'.[5] Raising an analogy between the Self-interest Theory and Newton's Law, he insisted that we should search for a different theory now, though the former had been accepted because it was partly correct, just as Newton's law had been in physics.[6]

Despite the fact that he referred to this analogy as perhaps being 'too grandiose',[7] it may be more appropriate and substantive than he himself realised: as the Self-interest Theory has dominated modern Western social sciences, it can indeed be regarded as a paradigm in the same way as Newtonian physics was in the past. Moreover, it is the Self-interest Theory that should be regarded as the core of atomism in contemporary social sciences, just as classical physics was the intellectual source of atomism in modern sciences and in society as a whole. The former may be seen as an equivalent in social sciences for the latter in natural sciences in that the world-view influenced by classical physics can be considered to have had an indirect influence on the transformation from medieval society to the modern world.

Thus, Parfit's criticism of the Self-interest Theory represents a tacit rejection of the core of atomistic social and political theories. Indeed, the first three parts of the book can be interpreted as a consistent radical challenge to orthodox Atomistic Theories. In Self-interest Theory, the atomistic entity is, of course, a 'person' who rationally seeks 'self-interest'; as Parfit himself uses the expression 'a theory of individual rationality' about the argument of individually/collectively 'self-defeating' theory,[8] the Self-interest Theory is nothing other than 'Atomistic Theory of Rationality'. Let me call this concept the 'Atomistic Concept of Self' or, in short, 'Atomistic Self'. These interests, then, are 'the Atomistic Self-interests' of Atomistic Persons, which have already appeared in the axiom of the Rawls theory; actually, the Rawls theory, based as it is on the motivational assumption of rationality, may be classified as a Self-interest Theory, though Parfit did not mention Rawls explicitly in this context. Therefore, Parfit's argument can be considered to undermine the philosophical validity of Rawls' basic assumption.[9]

Moreover, Parfit explored far further than Rawls the 'Selfhood' of a person. In Part Three, 'Personal Identity', questioning the nature and criterion of personal identity over time, he proposed a 'Reductionist' view that identity 'consists in the holding of certain more particular facts': physical and psychological continuity. Therefore, 'A person's existence just consists in the existence of a brain and body, and the occurrence of a series of interrelated physical and mental events.'[10] This view is opposed to the 'Non-reductionist' view that we are 'separately existing entities' (such as a purely mental entity like a Cartesian Ego, or an unknown physical entity) distinct from our brain, bodies and experiences, unless the personal identity is a further fact beyond physical and/or psychological continuity ('Further Fact View'). In this Non-Reductionist view, the existence of these entities must be all-or-nothing.

A Reductionist, on the other hand, might not necessarily presuppose the identity or even the existence of a 'person' in describing the reality and thus it could be described in an 'impersonal' way.[11] For the Reductionist, therefore, what matters is not 'personal identity' but 'Relation R' (psychological connectedness and/or continuity, with the right kind of cause), while, for most Non-Reductionists, personal identity is what matters.[12]

Parfit's Reductionist argument is an extremely striking one, for he is attempting to deny the importance and certainty of personal identity which is usually believed to dwell in a separately existing entity, that is, a 'person' itself. What else can be more challenging to our belief? This must be one of the most radical attacks on the atomistic view of persons in the history of Western thought, because a 'separate existing entity' is nothing but the atomistic entity usually called a 'person': to be exact, an Atomistic Person. As most Non-Reductionists believe that personal identity is immanent in this atomic entity and that the two are indivisible, this identity may be called 'the Atomistic Personal Identity', or in short, 'the Atomistic Identity'. Thus, the Non-Reductionist View could be summarised as 'the Atomistic View (on personal identity)', apart from the minor case of the Further Fact View.

Parfit disavowed this 'common sense' view. Illustrating his argument by fantastic thought experiments such as those of teletransportation and the mad neuro surgeon, he insisted that a personal identity is different or divisible from the atomistic entity usually perceived as a person like me, he or she. If this is the case, what is a personal identity in his Reductionist View? Parfit's answer is that it consists in merely physical and/or psychological connectedness or continuity, namely Relation R. This is identified to be what makes a person the identical person over time: roughly speaking, 'I am not a person of an atomistic entity whom I tend to believe I am, but the continuity or the Relation'. Accordingly, 'the descriptive equivalent of the concept of a person was on my proposal the concept, not of a single self, but of a series of successive selves.'[13] Although Parfit does not use the word 'essence', this continuity or the Relation R might be expressed as 'the (continuous or relational) Essence of a (so-called) Personal Identity', which remains after the philosophical 'reduction'.

Therefore, the solid visible atomistic entity in the Non-Reductionist View dissolves into the mere essence of the continuity or the relation in Parfit's Reductionist View. Though the latter view might also be called 'a Continuity or Relation View', it is clear that this is definitely a 'Non-Atomistic View'. Although it is impossible to discuss the validity of his

Reductionist View here, it might be worth pointing to the interesting similarity between his Reductionist View and the Buddhist View of 'Not-Self' (*anattā)*, especially in the content of this dialogue between East and West. Parfit himself wrote as follows:

> As Appendix J shows, *Buddha would have agreed.* The Reductionist View is not merely part of one cultural tradition. It may be, as I have claimed, the true view about all people at all times.[14]

Strictly speaking, 'Buddha's View' quoted in Appendix J might not be necessarily the view of the historical Gautama Buddha himself, but may be the view of some of the most important philosophical schools of Buddhism: although the doctrine of Not-Self is embraced by most schools, there have been various interpretations of this fundamental doctrine.[15] Nevertheless, the value of Parfit's insight is not diminished by this possibility: rather, this may confirm the universality of the 'Non-Religious Ethics' advocated by Parfit in the final section of the 'Concluding Chapter',[16] because those schools were more distinguished in philosophical and scholastic (namely, non-religious in Parfit's terms) argumentation than Buddha himself [17].

The intellectual context within which Parfit stands, however, is totally different from Buddhism: viz., utilitarianism. To be sure, Parfit refuted the classical Self-interest Theory once again on the ground of the Reductionist View: as psychological connectedness holds over time to reduced degrees, it cannot be irrational to be less concerned about our future, against the argument of classical Self-interest Theory.[18] However, this refutation of the classical Self-interest Theories induding those of Bentham and Sidgwick seems to be co-existent in Parfit with some sympathy with the broader utilitarian tradition itself. Moreover, it can be inferred that the tacit motive of his Non-Atomistic View may be the defence of the utilitarian stream against criticism by Atomistic Theories such as the contractual arguments. In this context, Parfit's criticism of Atomistic Theories can be regarded as an effective countercharge against such theories, including that of Rawls.

For example, Rawls wrote against utilitarianism:

> Utilitarianism does not take seriously the distinction between persons.[19]

Similarly, he wrote two pages later as follows:

> To do this is *not to take seriously the plurality and distinctness of individuals,* nor to recognise as the basis of justice that to which men would consent. Here we may note a curious anomaly. It *is customary to think of utilitarianism as individualistic,* and certainly there are good reasons for this. The utilitarians were strong defenders of liberty and freedom of thought, and they held that the good of society is constituted by the advantages enjoyed by individuals. *Yet utilitarianism is not individualistic,* at least when arrived at by the more natural course of reflection, in that, by conflating all systems of desires, it applies to society the principle of choice for one man.[20] (italics mine)

As seen here, Rawls criticised utilitarianism in that it is 'not individualistic', because it fails 'to take seriously the plurality and distinctiveness of individuals', though 'it is customary to think of utilitarianism as individualistic'. As an atomistic theorist, Rawls attacked the non-individualistic, in other words, non-atomistic aspect of utilitarianism. Against this charge, Parfit, quoting these words of Rawls,[21] vindicated the non-atomistic aspect of utilitarianism on the grounds that the Reductionist View undermines the importance of the separateness, or non-identity of different people,[22] because the fact of personal identity is considered to be 'less deep' in this view. For example, he defended the utilitarian rejection or disregard of the principle of equality against Rawls, in that 'it is more plausible to give less weight to distributive principles', for the 'less deep' identity.[23] In this context, he carefully wrote as follows:

> I claim that, on the Reductionist View, it is *more plausible* to give these principles less weight, or even no weight... The argument that I have given cannot show that we must accept the Utilitarian View. It can only yield *conclusions about relative plausibility*. When we cease to believe that persons are separately existing entities, the Utilitarian view becomes *more plausible.* Is the gain in plausibility great or small? My argument leaves the question open.[24] (italics mine)

Thus, Parfit cautiously avoided a definitive assertion of utilitarianism, explicitly stating that it cannot be logically deduced from his Reductionist View, despite the relative affinity between them. Although his sympathy or familiarity with utilitarianism was obvious, his intellectual sincerity and rigorousness prevented him from a simple affirmation of his own prejudgement. This is all the more important because he had proposed, in a previous article, a partial, but stronger defence of utilitarianism – that the Reductionist View might support a 'pro-utilitarian view' on principles concerning distributive justice, desert and commitment.[25] Bold as it may be, the impressive argument in the first three parts of this monumental book can be judged to have achieved great success in refuting atomistic theories such as the Rawlsian argument. This is indeed one of the most radical philosophical attacks on orthodox atomistic concepts such as, for example, as self-interest and persons: Radical Attack against Atomistic 'Reasons and Persons'. However, it has also to be appreciated that Parfit failed to testify to (or at least did not succeed in demonstrating) the validity of utilitarianism itself, for recognition of this fact will be important in the interpretation of the fourth part, 'Future Generations'.

§2 The Theoretical Obstacle Termed 'The Non-Identity Problem'

The first chapter of Part 4, 'The Non-Identity Problem', begins like this:

> There is another question about personal identity. *Each of us might never have existed.* What would have made this true? The answer produces a problem that most of us overlook.[26] (italics mine)

This problem, namely, Parfit's 'Non-Identity Problem', remains one of the central points of controversy surrounding future generations. There is, however, no avoiding the other important implications contained in these brief sentences. To begin with, he calls this conundrum 'another question about personal identity'. This implies that the Non-Identity problem can be regarded as an extension of the question about personal identity (over time) discussed in the previous parts. Next, it is a question concerning the idea that 'Each of us might never have existed'. Here are the first two Theoretical Obstacles, 'Non-Existence' and 'Indeterminacy' (see Chapter 2, §3). Put together, these two imply that the Non-Identity Problem is crystallised where the problem about 'Personal Identity' is transposed in a temporal dimension to the time of 'Non-Existence'.

It has already been mentioned in Chapter 2 that temporal utilitarianism such as that of Sidgwick faced particularly the second Theoretical Obstacle of Indeterminacy (and imposed too many demands on the present generation). As Parfit has denied the Self-interest Theory of classical utilitarianism, he does not follow the typical utilitarian logic. Instead, while corroborating the relative plausibility of utilitarianism, he embraces it within a broader theory named 'consequentialism': 'There is one ultimate moral aim: that outcomes be as good as possible.'[27] Within this general framework, he proposed the 'Principle of Beneficence' as a substitute for the Principle of Utility: though substantive content, the net sum of benefit minus burdens, has not been much changed, this generalised new principle, unlike the Principle of Utility, is assumed to be compatible with or complementary to the deontological concept of people's rights.[28] The Principle of Beneficence is supposed to enable one to compare the consequences of two alternative social or political policies, where an appeal to people's rights is not sufficient for this purpose. Thus, this new principle should be considered as playing the role of a transformed utilitarian principle in Parfit's world. Although Parfit himself differentiated this from normal utilitarianism for the reason mentioned above, his version of consequentialism might be termed 'Quasi (Revised)-Utilitarian Principle', if not 'Quasi (Revised)-Utilitarianism' itself.[29] So far as he developed his arguments assuming this principle, they can collectively be called 'Quasi (Revised)-Utilitarian Arguments'. Although he seems to adopt pluralism of moral principles in some places,[30] there is no doubt that the major principle amongst them is the Quasi-Utilitarian Argument. Therefore, though he seems to avoid calling himself utilitarian, the most appropriate term for his theoretical stance may be 'Pluralistic Quasi-Utilitarianism' within consequentialism in general.

However, Parfit's argument does not result in demonstrating the validity of this Quasi-Utilitarian Principle, but rather leads to an impasse even for this new principle. Here appears the 'Non-Identity Problem': Parfit's version of the 'Non-Existence Problem', the first Theoretical Obstacle. The basic logic of this problem is as follows:

No-one would have existed in their present form if he/she had not been conceived within a month of the time of the actual conception. 'We can easily affect the identity of future people, or *who* the people are who will later live.'[31] Future people who owe their future existence to us benefit from us so long as their subsequent lives are worth living, if causing them to exist itself can benefit them: if causing them to exist is not considered to benefit them, at least, future people are not worse off because of us so long as their lives are worth living. If a choice between two social policies affects the potential existence of future people, all the people at some future time will ultimately owe their existence to our choice of these policies. Therefore, even if we take the policy of 'Depletion', which will cause a great lowering of the quality of life, our choice of Depletion will be worse for no one in terms of existence itself. If we assume that a choice cannot have bad effects when the choice will be worse for no one, this leads to the intuitionally unacceptable conclusion that we cannot object to this policy.[32] In the case of the 'Risky Policy', which is likely to cause a catastrophe killing thousands of people, the unreasonableness of such a conclusion is more obvious.[33]

This Non-Identity Problem is a quasi-utilitarian problem about 'Non-Existence': roughly speaking, since existence itself is benefit (some kind of positive utility) or, at least, not harm (lack of negative utility) for non-existent future people, the present generation may do whatever they like without considering any interests of future generations in the world. If we imagine away the Non-Identity Problem, the revised utilitarian principle, the Principle of Beneficence, provides us with reasonable judgements. For example, the Depletion Policy will cause less beneficence than the 'Conservative Policy' on resources. If non-identity is supposed to make no moral difference ('No Difference View'), this conclusion should be maintained even when we take the fact of non-identity into account, while the Principle of Beneficence actually leads to the diametrically opposed conclusion, as explained above.

Therefore, Parfit wrote, we have to revise the Principle of Beneficence. Although one revised Principle of Beneficence ('the Same Number Quality Claim') can provide us with reasonable judgements in the restricted cases of comparison between the outcomes on the same number of people, this is not applicable to other cases concerning different numbers of people. Accordingly, he concluded that we have to search for a new theory about beneficence in order to find a general solution to the Non-Identity Problem, and he called this desired theory 'Theory X'.[34]

Parfit used the '(too grandiose) analogy' once again here. That is, 'In ordinary cases we can accept Newton's Laws. But not in all cases. And we now accept a different theory.'[35]

Whilst he likened the Self-interest Theory to Newton's Law in Part 2, this time, 'Newton's Law' indicates the Quasi-Utilitarian Principle of Beneficence: using 'our general moral reason to benefit other people, and to protect them from harm'.[36] Thus, the Non-Identity Problem is regarded as an exceptional, but important, difficult case to solve, which may cause a theoretical revolution in general moral reason. William Gray made an insightful comment on this important point: 'For Parfit, the Non-Identity Problem provides a moral counterpart to the Michaelson-Morley experiment, revealing the limitation of traditional moral principles, in particular the principle of utility.'[37] The role of the Michaelson-Morley experiment for Special Relativity was here alloted to the Non-Identity Problem for a new moral theory which is to replace the Quasi-Utilitarian Principle.

To sum up, in Chapter 15, 'The Non-Identity Problem', Parfit impressively demonstrated the seriousness of the first Theoretical Obstacle 'Non-Existence' for the utilitarian tradition (as well as for the contractual tradition).[38] He tried, in vain, to solve the problem by various revised versions of the Principle of Beneficence *within* the utilitarian tradition, although he did foresee the necessity of a great new theory comparable to the Revolution of Relativity in physics. This tragic intellectual quest is the theme of the next section.

§3. The Puzzling Predicament of the Quasi-Utilitarian 'Adventures in Wonderland'

Parfit presented several wonderful puzzles in his attempts to solve the Non-Identity Problem. Let me briefly summarise his complicated arguments full of paradoxes and colourful imaginary worlds: 'Parfit's Wonderland'.

One of the most important assumptions of the Non-Identity Problem is that 'what is bad must be bad for someone'.[39] This leads to the confusion that a Depletion or Risky policy cannot be objected to, for the people will not be worse off from the point of view of coming into existence. Parfit described this assumption as 'Person-Affecting', because this appealed to 'what is good or bad for those people whom our acts affect'.[40] He insisted that so long as we maintain this assumption, we will be unable to solve the Non-Identity Problem.

Now, in order to solve it, Parfit proposed the adoption of different kinds of Principles of Beneficence: 'The Impersonal Average principle' and 'The Impersonal Total Principle'. These are formulated as follows:

> If other things are equal, the best outcome is the one in which
>
> ① people's lives go,on average, best (The impersonal Average Principle).
>
> ①′ there is the greatest average net sum of happiness, per life lived (the Hedonistic Version of ①)
>
> ② there would be the greatest quantity of whatever makes life worth living (The Impersonal Total Principle)
>
> ②′ there would be the greatest quantity of happiness—the greatest net sum of happiness minus misery (the Hedonistic Version of ②).[41]

These are called 'Impersonal' because these are not 'person-affecting'.[42] It goes without saying that these have much common with utilitarian principles: the Hedonistic Versions (①′ and ②′) have the classical utilitarian forms, while the other two (① and ②) are the revised forms of the Quasi-Utilitarian Principles offered by Parfit himself.

Certainly, as these are not person-affecting forms, we can avoid the ridiculous conclusion of the Non-Identity Problem. However, Parfit attested that each principle would lead to unacceptable conclusions for our moral sense in some cases.

To begin with, the Impersonal Total Principle (②, ②′) implies 'The Repugnant Conclusion': 'For any possible population of at least ten billion people, all with a very high quality of life, there must be some much larger imaginable population whose existence, if other things are equal, would be better, even though its members have lives that are barely worth living.'[43] This unacceptable conclusion can be typically illustrated by 'A < B < C … < Z' in Figure 1.

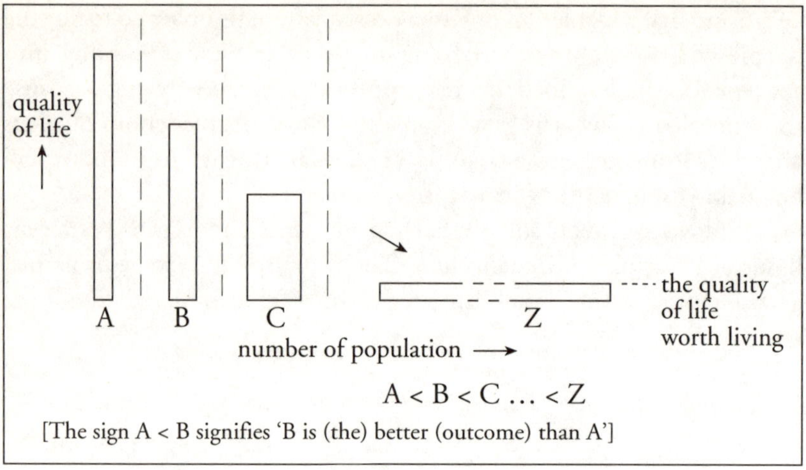

Figure 1. The Repugnant Conclusion (Parfit's Reasons and Persons, *p.388; supplemented by myself).*

Therefore, we have to reject the Impersonal Total Principle to avoid the Repugnant conclusion.[44] The Total Principle is particularly related to the 'quantity' of life, while only 'quality' of life has value in the Average Principle. It is natural to think that Theory X, the best theory about beneficence, may claim that both quality and quantity have value. (As for the quality, the simplest form is, 'The Two-Level Quality Value').[45] We may call this 'the Mixed Principle', though Parfit did not use this term.

Parfit showed, however, if we assume, in order to avoid the Repugnant Conclusion, that there must be an upper limit to the positive value of quantity within a certain time-scale ('The Limited Quantity View'), supposing there would be no such limit to the negative value of quantity, then, we would have to face another unacceptable conclusion, namely, 'the Absurd Conclusion'.

Roughly speaking, this can be illustrated by two cases. In the first, in some future century, while some people would live on Earth, a number of extra people would enjoy a high quality of life on other Earth-like planets, though there are very rare unfortunate people amongst the latter; in the second case, the extra people in the first case would not live in the same future century on the other Earth-like planets, but they, including the same rate of unfortunate people, would spread out over many future centuries only on the Earth itself.

In the first case, the positive value of quantity would reach the upper limit in the assumption, and this value may be outweighed by the badness of suffering of the unfortunate people, because there is no limit for the negative value. In contrast to this, in the second case, the positive value of quantity, which would not reach the upper limit, may outweigh, in each century, its negative value, because the latter is equal to value of the negative value in the first case divided by the number of future centuries. Therefore, the first outcome would be very bad, while the second outcome would be very good, although all the lives that are ever lived in the two cases would be identical both in number and quality.[46]

As this 'Absurd' Conclusion is the consequence of the asymmetry of the limit concerning positive and negative quantity, we have to abandon this assumption. Alternatively, however, if we assume plural scales of value such as those in 'The Appeal to the Valueless Level', and 'The Lexical View', we cannot avoid variants of the Repugnant or Absurd Conclusion.[47]

Therefore,the only remaining possibility is the Average Principle focusing merely on the quality of life. However, as this principle gives no weight to the quantity of happiness (in other words, to whatever makes life worth living), its implications are too extreme to believe in in some cases. For example, according to this principle, the best possible history might be for only the most blissful person or for only Adam and Eve to have ever lived, because if a greater number of people have lived, the average quality of life would be lowered even though the quality of life of the other people would be merely slightly less than that of the original one or two persons.[48]

Finally, Parfit presented a further paradox termed 'The Mere Addition Paradox': while an outcome A+ with merely additional people (who have a life worth living, who affect no one else, and whose existence does not involve social injustice) should be considered to be not worse than the original outcome A, Divided B, which is substantially equal to the B in Figure 1, shall be considered to be better than A+ both on any principle of equality and on any plausible Principle of Beneficence (for example, The Total Principle, The Average Principle). Though Parfit did not use mathematical signs, this can be expressed as:

$$\left.\begin{array}{l} A+ \gtreqqless A \\ \\ B > A+ \end{array}\right\} \rightarrow \quad A \lesseqqgtr B \text{ (not } A < B)^{49}$$

where $\gtreqqless$ signifies 'not worse than', while $\geqq$ signifies 'at least as good as'

Similarly,

$$A \lesseqqgtr B \lesseqqgtr C \ldots \lesseqqgtr Z$$
$$\therefore A \lesseqqgtr Z \qquad \text{(not } A < Z)$$

Though this is not exactly the Repugnant Conclusion itself (not A < Z), Parfit showed that versions of The Mere Addition Paradox led to 'The New Repugnant Conclusion' (A < Z).[50] If we appeal to the Valueless Level or the Lexical View to avoid the Repugnant Conclusion, this will lead to the result of B < A, which is inconsistent with the result above $A \lesseqqgtr B$. This is the 'Mere Addition Paradox' (Figure 2).

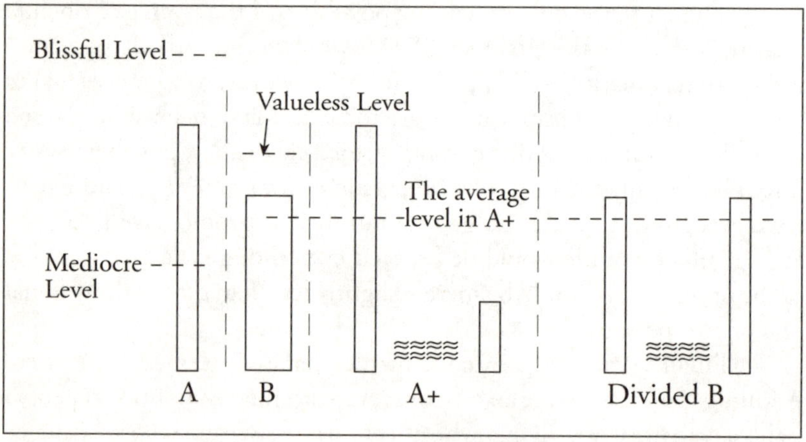

Figure 2. The Mere Addition Paradox (Parfit, Reasons and Persons, *p.419; supplemented by myself).*

Hence, though Parfit 'made progress of a negative kind'[51] in proving that all 'possible theories' (§137) involve their own untenable conclusions or paradoxes (and are, therefore, not the sought after Theory X), he failed to discover Theory X itself. In the first paragraph of his 'Concluding Chapter', Parfit wrote as follows:

> When he was asked about his book, Sidgwick said that its first word was *Ethics,* and its last *failure.* This could have been the last word of my Part Four. As I argued, we need a new theory about Beneficence. This must solve the Non-Identity Problem, avoid Repugnant and Absurd Conclusions, and solve the Mere Addition Paradox. **I failed to find a theory** that can meet these four requirements. Though I failed to find such a theory, I believe that, if they tried, others could succeed. [52] (Italics original, bold mine)

This is Parfit's conclusion. Like 'Alice's Wonderland', Parfit's fantastic world is filled with colourful paradoxes and unreasonable conclusions. In case we might succumb to these anti-intuitional or anti-ethical conclusions – the present generation may do whatever they like without thinking of the benefit of future generations –, it is important to point out that Parfit himself refused to submit to such temptation, appealing to our healthy intuition (the 'Low Road', in contrast to the 'High Road' of Meta-Ethics).[53] It is also important that he rejected 'Moral Sceptism' (§153) and maintained his hope for 'the Unified Theory that would remove our disagreement',[54] despite his own failure to find it.

As has been explained in the last section, by the Non-Identity Problem, Parfit emphasised the importance of the first Theoretical Obstacle, 'Non-Existence'. As he acknowledged the Person-Affecting view to be the source of the problem, he tried to overcome it by the Impersonal Quasi-Utilitarian Principle. However, first, the Total Principle led to the Repugnant Conclusion. Secondly, the Average Principle was too extreme to accept. Finally, the mixed principle consisting of these two involved the Absurd Conclusion or some variants of the Repugnant or Absurd Conclusion.

While the most serious problem for classical utilitarianism is considered to be the second Theoretical Obstacle 'Indeterminacy', Parfit's Quasi-Utilitarian Principle of Beneficence seems to manage to avoid this, because he was content with 'only rough or partial comparability'.[55] As a substitute for accurate calculation, he compared several possible (but sometimes extreme) cases as thought experiments, and indicated logical predicaments involved in them. So, the second Theoretical Obstacle can be said to be transformed into a 'logical puzzle' in Parfit's arguments. Finally, as for the third Theoretical Obstacle 'Asymmetry', Parfit said little apart from his remark about 'The Direction of Causation' (§65), because in the end, he was unable to reach the point of theorising realistically for future generations, blocked as he was by the other obstacles, especially the first.

Hence, Parfit's arguments on Future Generations can be summarised as in Figure 3. This Wonderland full of puzzles of moral calculation is reminiscent of the well-known *Alice's Adventures in Wonderland,* whose author Lewis Carroll was a mathematician at Oxford. Carroll wrote his fantasy for the real Alice Liddell, a daughter of the Dean of Christ Church College, and his 'Alice' finally awoke from her land of dream. How can we awake from Parfit's land of dream where Parfit's Riddle entangles us, and escape from the maze of his 'moral mathematics',[56] created in Oxford?

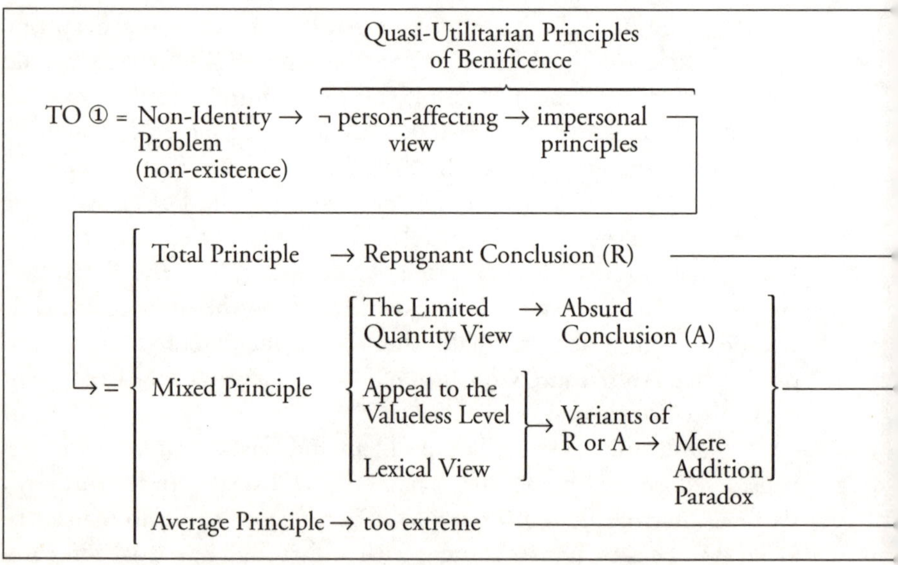

Figure 3. Parfit's Wonderland

2. A Holistic Revolution around the Riddles

§4 The Logical Hiatus around 'Impersonality' in Parfit

The most indolent response to the Non-Identity Problem is to conclude that the present generation has no obligation for future generations, for the reason that existence itself is of benefit or, at least, of no harm for them. This is a negative kind of response, similar to that of Golding to the Theoretical Obstacles (Ch.2, §4). In this view, the first Theoretical Obstacle, the 'Non-Existence Problem', finally prevents us from theorising for the sake of future generations. Though this is not a rare attitude towards The Non-Identity Problem,[57] it should be noted that it is not, at least, a result originally intended by Parfit himself.

If we try to overcome Parfit's perplexities, the first possible option open to us is to dissolve the problem or subsequent puzzles by pointing to logical or technical defects in Parfit's arguments. For example, some have challenged the assumption that causing someone to exist benefits

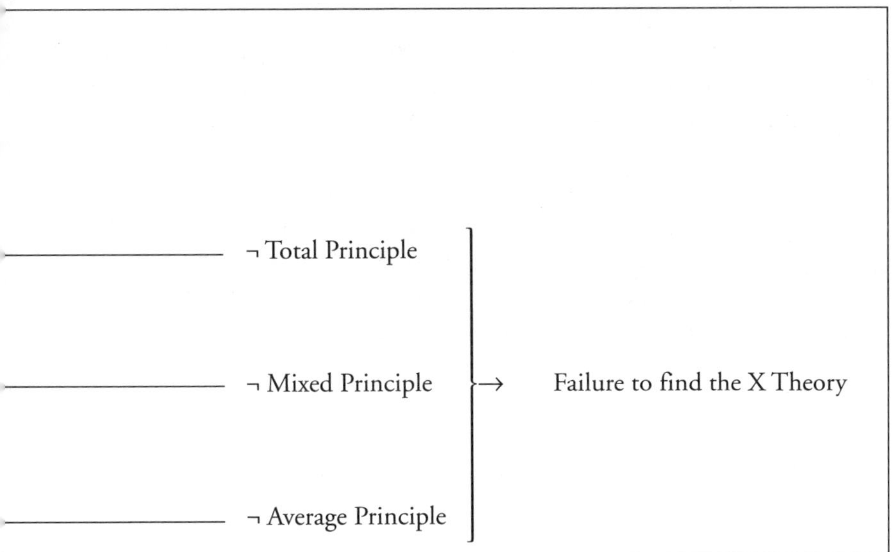

the person;[58] some have doubted the practical relevance of Parfit's examples and the validity for this issue of the 'Consequentialist' Principle of Beneficence itself ('misguided strategy'), insisting that considerations of rights and fairness ('rights-based approach') can cope with most of Parfit's problems;[59] others have attacked the Mere Addition Paradox by suggesting that A and A+ are not strictly comparable[60]; yet others have diagnosed Parfit's problems as being caused by mistaking one chronological perspective (such as the present) for another chronological perspective such as the future, and proposed that we explicate obligations to the future in terms of an 'impersonal' principle subject to 'retroactive person-affecting' constraints.[61].

Although the details of these arguments cannot be discussed here, it should be mentioned that most of the writers themselves admit beforehand that their arguments are unable to solve Parfit's puzzles completely [62]: their responses should be regarded as, at most, 'partial solutions' to his great riddles. These writers have grasped the importance of the problems raised by Parfit, but tried to solve them without making fundamental changes to previous orthodox theories. The partial character of their solutions can be considered to be the result of this kind of reaction. If, however, the conundrums indicate the necessity of a new theory as Parfit himself thought, they may be temporising in such a way that their attempt hinders a deeper quest for a complete solution with a full-scale transformation of previous theories. As it were, these arguments may play a role comparable with the Lorentz solution (to the Michelson-Morley Experiment), which blocked scientists from progressing towards the Einstein theory of Special Relativity.

Thus, let me take Parfit's own upshot more seriously. Though he professed his failure to discover Theory X in the 'Concluding Chapter', he extracted 'one common feature' amongst the various conclusions in his book: viz., 'Impersonality' (§150).

According to his own summary,[63] in Part One, as the revised version of 'Common Sense Morality' is a partial move towards rational altruism, it follows that we must be more 'impersonal'. In Part Two, as we should reject the Self-interest Theory (about Rationality), which gives most importance to 'the separateness of persons' based on 'different lives' as fundamental units, our theory must be more 'impersonal' in disregarding the boundaries between lives – though the Critical Present-aim Theory is more personal than the Self-interest Theory in a different way. In Part Three, Parfit shows that on the Reductionist View which denies that we are separately existing entities (distinct from our brains and bodies, and our experiences), we could describe a person's life in an 'impersonal' way, which does not claim that a person *fundamentally* exists. This view is more 'impersonal', because it gives less importance both to the unity of each life and to the boundaries between lives, or the separateness of persons; In Part Four, since we should not appeal to a Person-Affecting principle in solving the Non-Identity Problem, Parfit's conclusion is 'in the clearest and strongest sense impersonal'.[64] Thus, all his arguments could be regarded as being in favour of Impersonality, both in 'Reasons' (Parts 1and 2) and in 'Persons' (Parts 3 and 4).[65]

Indeed, it is not too much to say that insistence on 'Impersonality' is not only the clearest but also the only definite conclusion in his 'Concluding Chapter' (§150–§154), amongst his failure to solve the Non-Identity Problem, vague sympathy for utilitarianism and plain prospect of a Unified Theory and Non-Religious Ethics in the rest of the chapter. This conclusion may disappoint some readers, but it should be noted that a precious clue for further arguments is tacitly hidden here. This is the wider possible implications of 'Impersonality'; the substance of these implications, however, remains to be explored.

On Parfit's own account, Impersonality is closely related to his sympathy for utilitarianism. As was explained in §1 above, Parfit rejected the Atomistic Theory both of Rationality (the Self-interest Theory) and of Persons (the Non-Reductionist View) in the first three Parts, and he argued for the relative plausibility of impersonal utilitarian views in Part Three. Moreover, in Part Four, he presented the Theoretical Obstacle of the Non-Identity Problem for the Quasi-Utilitarian Principle of Beneficence, and searched for the alternative (impersonal) principle Theory X without success.

However, it must be stressed that there is a jump in logic between the first three Parts and Part Four. As has been pointed out above, Parfit neither offered any proof of utilitarianism nor insisted upon its truth in Part Three. Nevertheless, he developed his argument in Part Four assuming the relevance of the Quasi-Utilitarian Principle of Beneficence.

So, in Part Four, he *suddenly* appears as a Pluralistic Quasi-Utilitarian without any testimony for utilitarianism in the previous three Parts. Certainly, impersonality is a common aspect of the conclusions of the previous three Parts and the Pluralistic Quasi-Utilitarianism of Part Four. But, while this may be partial evidence for the relative plausibility of the latter, it cannot be a proof. The missing link is the proof. Here surely is the logical hiatus in the structure of arguments about Impersonality in the masterpiece *Reasons and Persons*, though one cannot go so far as to call it a logical inconsistency.

Therefore, there is a logical rupture between the end of Part Three and the beginning of Part Four: although Parfit acknowledged that he had not succeeded in demonstrating utilitarianism in Part Three, he assumed the relevance of the Quasi-Utilitarian Principle of Beneficence as if it had already been proved. This is a structural dislocation, so that Part Four could be regarded as an independent, separate argument from the first three Parts – as if the book were called 'Reasons and Persons (the first three Parts), or Future Generations (Part Four)', rather than 'Reasons (Parts 1, 2) and Persons (Parts 3, 4)' (See, Figure 4, next section). Indeed, reflecting the logical leap over the fission, there is almost no reference to the Self-interest theory or Reductionist View of personal identity in Part Four, in contrast to the previous three Parts – as though there were no use in considering 'Reasons' and 'Persons' now that he had arrived at his Quasi-Utilitarian destination. In fact, it may be wondered whether Parfit needed to contemplate 'Reasons' or 'Persons' in order to think of 'Future Generations', though he himself wrote that the Non-Identity Problem is 'another question about personal identity', as mentioned before. Actually, his presentation in Part Four bears no reminder of the Self-interest theory or Reductionist View, as if the Non-Identity Problem were a totally different kind of question about personal identity: those arguments elaborated in the previous Parts vanish into the air of Future Generations.

Since Part Four cannot be considered to be the logically necessary development of the previous three Parts, it follows that the failure to find a new theory in Part Four cannot necessarily be imputed to the other three Parts. In reality, the Quasi-Utilitarian Principle assumed in Part Four is merely one possibility included in the wider sphere of Impersonality induced from the first three Parts. In other words, it could be posited that the failure to find Theory X in Part Four is the consequence of Parfit's slightly arbitrary assumption of the Quasi-Utilitarian Principle of Beneficence, which is not an inevitable upshot of the previous arguments.

Parfit's predisposition for utilitarianism may have misled him into a 'Wonderland' without definite solutions: the acknowledgement of this fact may be a key to the way of escape from his wonderful Oxford labyrinth.

§5. From More-Atomistic to Less-Atomistic Impersonality

Facing Parfit's perplexities, some have found them an ideal pretext for abandoning consideration of Future Generations; others have tried technically to solve the puzzles. However, once we take account of the logical hiatus, the most natural way is probably to examine the unfounded assumption of Part Four itself. As in Figure 4, the whole structure of Parfit's book could be schematised as 'Reasons, Persons and Future Generations' rather than 'Reasons and Persons'. 'Impersonality' involves plural possibilities: Parfit picked up merely one of them. This, the Principle of Beneficence, has proved to lead to untenable conclusions. Thus, the logical way out of the difficulty is to abandon the search for the elusive Theory X and relinquish the source of these perplexities itself.

Now, what could form an alternative hypothesis sharing the characteristic of Impersonality? It is important here to meditate on the development of Parfit's arguments from our philosophical point of view. 'Impersonality' is a common characteristic of Parfit's arguments against both the Self-interest theory and the Non-Reductionist view, whilst, at the same time, these arguments could be characterised as 'Non (or even Anti-)Atomistic Arguments' from our viewpoint, as has already been explained. Both interpretations are compatible, because Impersonality is indeed Non-Atomistic in the human world. So far, so good: there is no contradiction or discrepancy up to the hiatus at the end of Part Three, except in the actual terms used.

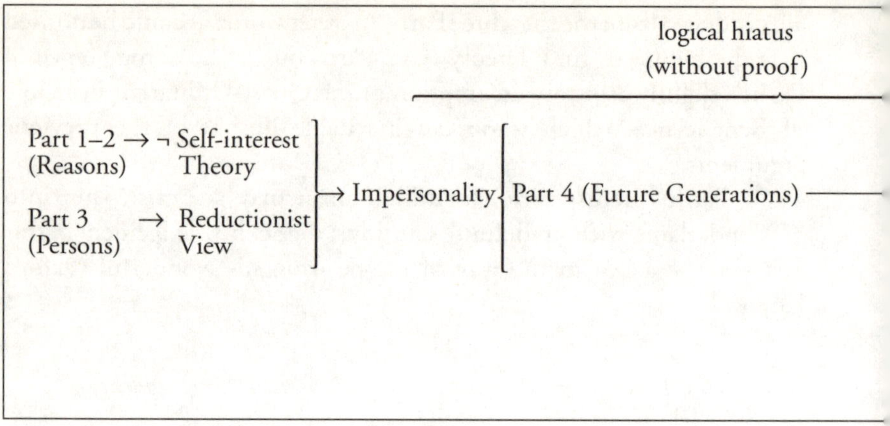

Figure 4. Reasons, Persons and Future Generations

However, the two interpretations diverge at the beginning of Part Four, or to be more precise, at the beginning of Parfit's defence of utilitarianism in Part Three. The reason is that utilitarianism is impersonal in Parfit's sense, whilst it is not totally non-atomistic in another sense: as Rawls has pointed out, 'It is customary to think of utilitarianism as individualistic' (§1 above). Though it is finally regarded as impersonal in aggregating the amount of happiness or desires (minus burdens), it retains the individual or atomistic feature that the aggregation is grounded on those amounts for each atomistic individual. So, utilitarianism is halfway impersonal or halfway non-atomistic, but neither completely impersonal nor non-atomistic: it could be called a 'Halfway Atomistic/ Non-Atomistic Theory'.

It has been argued in Chapter 2 that Rawls' atomism prevented him from developing a consistent fully-fledged theory of intergenerational justice. Therefore, Parfit hit the mark[66] when he criticised Atomistic Arguments including that of Rawls, favouring impersonal or non-atomistic utilitarianism. In particular, his focusing on Self or Personal Identity is a distinguished achievement, reaching beyond other Western theories concerning the theme of Future Generations.

If the Quasi-Utilitarian Principle of Beneficence is still too personal or atomistic to solve the Non-Identity Problem and its corollar-

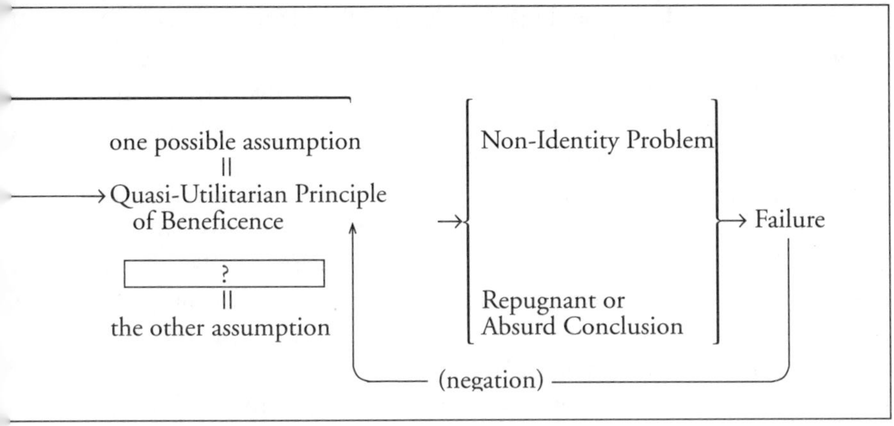

ies, the various puzzles,[67] it would be better for us to search for *less* personal or, more precisely, *less* atomistic theories than utilitarian principles.

Paradoxically, the Reductionist View can itself give rise to a *kind of* atomism, as is referred to in Part Three 'Personal Identity'. As the Reductionist View supposes that personal identity merely consists in physical and psychological continuity, some Reductionists such as J. Perry and M. Wachsbery make 'the Extreme Claim' (§102) that we have no reason to be concerned about our own futures, for the futures are nothing more than those of a complete stranger.[68] Similarly, in 'a More Extreme Argument' (§342), as the relevant units for distributive principles are in the Reductionist View not complete lives but the states that people are in at particular times, some such as Wachsbery claim that we should give no weight to principles such as compensation over time (for past suffering, for example). Parfit distances himself from these extreme views, endorsing, against the Extreme View, 'the Moderate Claims' that Relation R gives us reason for special further concern, for example, our special concern for our children or for anyone we love[69]; and arguing, against the More Extreme Argument, more cautiously, that the principles become less plausible.[70] However, the Moderate Claim is not a definite judgement linked with the Reductionist View, because Parfit says it is logically defensible both to claim and to deny these extreme arguments.[71]

As these arguments demonstrate, the Reductionist View implies that a personal identity may be reduced to the (physical and/or psychological) continuity at the present or at particular times within the life of the person as a whole. To be sure, in negating the atomistic entity usually supposed to be able to survive for several tens of years as one person, this view is not atomistic. However, the concept of successive selves within one person can be regarded as *more* atomistic along a temporal dimension than the usual atomistic view. In this sense, there is sufficient reason for the Reductionist View, in particular that of the Extreme Claim, to have been described pejoratively by Samuel Scheffler as 'Atomistic (Utilitarian)', though the usage of atomism is to be distinguished from ours.[72]

These relations can be shown as in Figure 5:

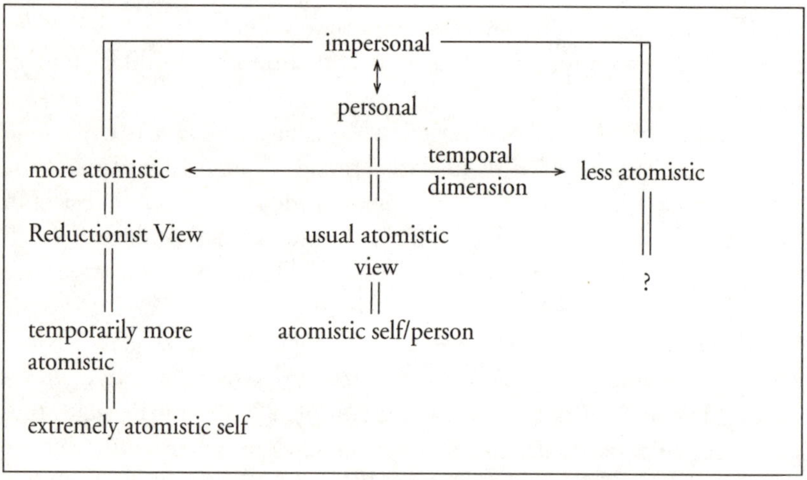

Figure 5. Atomism/Impersonality

The conventional concept of a person has already been named the Atomistic Self or Person. This is of course a 'personal' concept. Though the Reductionist View is 'impersonal', it is more atomistic in the temporal dimension, namely, 'Temporally More Atomistic'. This momentary or discontinuous self can be called 'the Extremely Atomistic (concept of) Self' (not person).

However, Impersonality comprises both *more* and *less* atomistic directions. That is to say, Non-Atomism, which is equal to Impersonality, contains both 'More or Extreme Atomism' and, of course, 'Less Atomism'. The 'More Atomistic Reductionist View' can be considered to be in tune with utilitarian principles, because it still retains an atomistic element while being impersonal. Now that the 'more' atomistic direction in conjunction with the Quasi-Utilitarian Principle has proved to lead to the impasse, it would be better to turn to the other direction: 'the Less Atomistic Way of Impersonality'.[73]

§6. Revolutionary Axioms of Duality

As Parfit used the expression 'less deep' about personal identity, I used the phrase the 'Less Atomistic way of Impersonality'. The terms of '*less* deep', '*less* atomistic', '*im*personality' are of course negative expressions which deny the positive contents of 'deep', 'atomistic', 'personality'. There are, however, convincing antonyms of the former two, while it is difficult to find one for the last. For example, 'shallow' is the antonym of 'deep'. Why not make use of such convenient terms in such cases as do not carry pejorative connotations? The antonym of 'Atomistic' is 'Holistic' and that of 'Atomism' is 'Holism': these are the terms which I shall use hereafter in place of 'less atomistic'.

As has been expounded, Parfit rejected Atomistic Theories such as the Self-interest Theory and the Non-Reductionist View, but postulated the Quasi-Utilitarian Principle of Beneficence without solid philosophical underpinning. Utilitarian principles, in general, share some atomistic aspects, though they are impersonal compared with typical Atomistic Theories such as contractual arguments: utilitarianism is a Halfway Atomistic Theory as well as a 'Halfway Holistic Theory'. When we investigate Parfit's arguments in Part Four, two distinct phases can be discerned.

The first phase, the Non-Identity Problem, is the Quasi-Utilitarian version of the first Theoretical Obstacle 'Non-Existence', which is philosophically associated with the empiricism of Western modern science (see Chapter 2, §5). While the Non-Identity Problem is grounded on the assumption that causing existence by itself guarantees benefit or, at least, no harm for a person, this assumption entails the empiricism underlying the Non-Identity Problem: it is justified on condition that we take only empirical, observable persons into account whilst ignoring non-empirical, non-observable 'possible-persons'. On this empirical condition, the Non-Identity Problem negates the Person-Affecting principle. Moreover, this principle reveals plainly the atomistic character: affected persons are considered to be atomistic individuals for whom our acts would be good or bad. In other words, the negated Person-Affecting principles assume separate or 'Atomistic Identity'. Thus, the Non-Identity Problem can be considered to be the consequence of both empirical and atomistic assumptions.

The next phase is the unsuccessful quest for a new theory. Since Parfit forsook the atomistic, person-affecting principle, his arguments moved to Impersonal principles such as the Total or the Average Principle. However, it has been established that these Quasi-Utilitarian Principles comprehend their own atomistic elements, which are correlated with the Extremely Atomistic Concept of Self in the Reductionist View. In sum, the Impersonality of the utilitarian principles might be called 'Atomistic Impersonality'.

Thus, both phases contain some kinds of atomistic assumptions, whether in a person-affecting form or as utilitarian principles. If we have to adopt a new impersonal assumption to avoid contradictions or paradoxes grounded on those atomistic assumptions, then the most rational and fundamental solution must be to introduce holistic kinds of impersonal assumptions.

A dictionary defines 'Holism (Wholism)' philosophically as 'the theory that certain wholes are to be regarded as greater than the sum of their parts'.[74] This is usually considered to be the antonym of Atomism, which is 'the theory that all matter consists of tiny individual particles'.[75] If these 'tiny individual particles' are physical entities, the atomistic theory is that of natural science, especially as expressed in Newtonian classical physics. If those particles are persons or human mental states, the atomistic theory is that of social sciences: Self-interest Theories and the Non-Reductionist View. Under the huge influences of both Atomistic

Theories, 'Holistic Theories' have dwindled away into almost nothing in the modern world, except for rare cases such as the philosophy of the Romantics, Hegelianism or American transcendentalism. Even in the West, however, holistic theories existed in ancient medicine or philosophy including that of the Eleatics or (Neo-)Platonists.[76]

There appears to be nothing more appropriate than this Holistic tradition, if we look for an alternative to Atomistic Theories such as the Self-interest Theory or the Non-Reductionist View. Although Parfit likened these theories to Newton's Laws and searched for a Unified Theory, he failed to discover Theory X, perhaps because he confined his quests within the narrow limit of utilitarian halfway atomistic tradition. If the Non-Identity Problem is comparable to the Michaelson-Morley experiment, the new Theory X should transcend the boundary of Atomistic Theories. It is not surprising then if this theory is holistic in nature: Theory X is nothing other than a new paradigm comparable in impact to the theory of Relativity.

As has been explained in Chapter 2, Atomistic Contractual Theories need Supplementary Familial Arguments to overcome their limits. In fact, as the concept of a family contains some holistic element, this can be interpreted to the effect that Atomistic Theories require a kind of holistic component to theorise for future generations.

Now, it should be apparent that it is strategically better to posit the holistic element explicitly than to steal it into the Atomistic Argument. Thus, I shall introduce Holistic Arguments clearly, and develop them in parallel with Atomistic Arguments. Let me briefly outline what can be called 'the Holistic Argument' in contrast to the Atomistic Argument. The procedure of these two arguments can be regarded as symmetrical: the form is the same, though the content is opposite. These parallel arguments may be called 'the Dual Argument'[77] in contrast to 'the Single Argument' of Atomistic Theories (Figure 8). Although these two directions are apparently exclusive, it will be necessary to integrate dialectically or synthesise the two arguments in explaining our reality. Therefore, our theory/argument should ultimately be called a 'Dialectical or Synthetic Theory/Argument',[78] although the expression 'Holistic Theory/Argument' is acceptable because of the convenience of contrasting it with existing Atomistic Theories. For a start, the standard definition in the dictionary can be restated as two general principles:

- The Atomistic View (AV): A certain unit is only the sum of individual atoms.
- The Holistic View (HV): A certain whole is greater than only the sum of its parts.

(AV and HV are the abbreviations of each principle, and will be used below.)

As these views, however, are manifest in various forms in reality, it would be better to break up the logic into several axioms and postulates. From the perspective of the Dual Argument, the first point to be considered is that, strictly speaking, holism is not the exact *antonym* of atomism in this definition: the formulation of HV does not accurately parallel that of AV, because HV is the comparative and premises AV. 'The sum of its parts' in HV is merely another expression of 'the sum of individual atoms' in AV, and the formulation of HV is, as it were, logically dependent upon that of AV. Therefore, in order to make the contrast in the Dual Argument clearer, the essential core within each view should be extracted as the following polar axioms.

- The Atomistic Axiom (AA): Each atomistic entity is separate from the other within a certain unit.
  – The (Atomistic) Axiom of Separateness
- The Holistic Axiom (HA): All of a certain whole is one unitary entity.
  – The (Holistic) Axiom of Oneness

As the central element of each Axiom is 'separate' (plural or different) and 'one' (same or unitary), these can be called 'The (Atomistic) Axiom of Separateness' and 'The (Holistic) Axiom of Oneness': separateness is the exact antonym of oneness (=non-separateness), and HA can be considered to be diametrically opposed to AA. Since Gödel's incompleteness theorems show that, for any member of a certain class of formal systems such as that of mathematics and of logic, 'there is a sentence formulable in its language that it cannot prove, but that it would be desirable for it to prove',[79] it is regarded as necessary for any logical system to pose at least one axiom that cannot be proven. Accordingly, most Atomistic Theories such as utilitarianism, contractrarianism and pluralism can be considered to premise implicitly the Atomistic Axiom; public choice theories, in which the Rawls theory in *A Theory of Justice* could be counted, explicitly introduce AA or atomistic postulates. As against this, since such atomistic construction leaves some parts of 'reality' in this world unexplained, another axiom HA should be introduced. Although, for some, HA may seem to contradict common sense, its truth has been long affirmed in holistic traditions including some of Eastern metaphysics. While AA is often taken for granted, HA has sometimes been regarded as profound (existential) reality. Therefore, just as AA should be theoretically considered to be an axiom, HA can be posited as another axiom: just as Atomistic Arguments are theoretically based, as it were, on 'Hypothetical Atomism', Holistic Arguments are grounded upon 'Hypothetical Holism'.[80]

When separate entities are observed within a unit, we tend to regard the unit as the aggregation of the entities. Accordingly, the Atomistic Axiom is the ground of the Atomistic View. When a certain whole is observed as one entity, we tend to regard the whole as greater than the sum of its parts. Accordingly, the Holistic Axiom is the ground of the Holistic View. As has been mentioned, HV involves the dichotomy of whole/part, and contains some atomistic division between the two: HV is grounded not only upon HA but also upon AA, and its nature is not purely holistic but also synthetic. Therefore, strictly speaking, HV should be called 'Synthetic View' (SV); however, for simplicity, this subtle difference between 'holistic' and 'synthetic' will sometimes be ignored in this paper.

Moreover, several versions of each axiom can be discriminated in principle, for example: ①the 'Totally' version; ② 'Ultimately'/②′ 'Superficially' version; ③ 'Rigidly'/③′ 'Roughly' version; ④ 'Mainly'/④′ 'Auxiliarily' version; ⑤ (Qualitatively/Quantitatively) 'Half' version.

• The [① Totally / ② Ultimately/②′ Superficially / ③ Rigidly/③′ Roughly / ④ Mainly/④′ Auxiliarily / ⑤ (Qualitatively/Quantitatively) Half] Atomistic Axiom:

Each entity is [① totally / ② ultimately/②′ superficially / ③ rigidly/③′ roughly / ④ mainly/④′ auxiliarily / ⑤ (qualitatively/quantitatively) half] separate from another (or the other) within a certain unit …
AA ① – ⑤

• The [① Totally / ② Ultimately/②′ Superficially / ③ Rigidly/③′ Roughly / ④ Mainly/④′ Auxiliarily / ⑤ (Qualitatively/Quantitatively) Half] Holistic Axiom:

All of the certain whole is [① totally / ② ultimately/②′ superficially / ③ rigidly/③′ roughly / ④ mainly/④′ auxiliarily / ⑤ (qualitatively/quantitatively) half] one unitary entity …
HA ①–⑤

The 'Totally' version (①) is supposed to explain all reality totally without any exception, without any modification. The 'Ultimately/Superficially' version (②/②′) is strong/weak in principle, but weak/strong in application to reality; it means '– ultimately/superficially separate/one, but apparently/ultimately non-separate/separate –'. The 'Rigidly/Roughly' version (③/③′) is qualitatively strong/weak or strict/loose; in Atomistic Axioms, the degree of separateness is strong/weak or strict/loose, while the degree of unity is so in the Holistic Axiom. The 'Mainly/Auxiliarily' version (④/④′) is quantitatively strong/weak. In this version, each axiom is supposed to explain only 'main/auxiliary' cases; in other words, this version admits that other cases may be explained by other auxiliary/main axioms or principles. In addition, the '(Qualitatively/Quantitatively) Half' version (⑤) indicates the middle cases in the previous two versions, either between a 'Rigidly' and a 'Roughly' version or between a 'Mainly' and an 'Auxiliarily' version.

Of these versions, the 'Totally' version is most useful to theorise simply or purely, but it can be criticised as being too rough, or irrelevant. For example, in the Rawls theory, while the basic postulate of rationality corresponds to an Atomistic Axiom, the assumption of mutually disinterested rationality corresponds to a 'Totally Atomistic Axiom'. This is logically desirable, but in practice proves to be impossible to maintain.

Rawls' modified assumption of familial rationality agrees with the 'Ultimately Atomistic Axiom' (if his modified assumption can be interpreted as consistent with the basic assumption of rationality; see Ch. 2, §6). In this case, his theory is 'ultimately' atomistic, but actually modified slightly in a holistic direction through the introduction of 'natural' familial ties. Such modification plays the role of a secondary axiom. As this hidden axiom is considered to be superficial in contrast to the ultimate axiom, it can be called a 'Superficial Axiom' as opposed to an 'Ultimate Axiom'. As an Ultimate Axiom is the 'Ultimately' version (②), the Superficial Axiom can be termed an axiom of the 'Superficially' Version (②′).

As has already been argued in the context of the Rawls theory, the problem is how to explain the other 'superficial' element which is opposed to the 'ultimately' atomistic (or holistic) character. If we are unable to elucidate a relation between the two versions, the axiom should probably be classified as a 'Roughly' or 'Mainly' version. If his theory should be regarded as 'two theories of justice' rather than 'a theory of justice', Rawl's postulate of rationality might be a 'Roughly Atomistic Axiom' or 'Mainly Atomistic Axiom'. In these cases, his basic postulate of rationality is only 'roughly atomistic' or 'mainly atomistic', because his Supplementary Familial Argument has a weak holistic direction, restricted within familial relations. As is exemplified in this case, 'Mainly' versions of each axiom need be supplemented by the other (or another) minor axiom. The opposite axiom is an 'Auxiliary Axiom' as opposed to the 'Main Axiom'. As a Main Axiom is a 'Mainly' version (④), the Auxiliary Axiom can be termed an axiom of an 'Auxiliarily' version (④′).

In contrast to the 'Totally' version (①), the two pairs of versions (② Ultimately/②′ Superficially, ④Mainly/④′ Auxiliarily) alike consist of both Atomistic and Holistic Axioms, whichever has more weight (② Ultimately, ④Mainly). In this sense, while the 'Totally' version comprises only one axiom, these two cases, the pairs of versions, are really comprised of 'Dual Axioms': The former can be called 'A Single Axiom of Atomism (or Holism)' or 'An Axiom of Singularity', whilst the latter are termed 'Dual Axioms of Atomism and Holism' or 'Axioms of Duality'.

The difference between the 'Rigid/Rough' version (③/③′) and the 'Mainly/Auxiliarily' version (④/④′) is that the former (③/③′) is principally associated with a qualitative degree of separateness/oneness, while the latter (④/④′) is connected with the quantitative (Main/Auxiliary) importance of each axiom. With regard to each case, it can be conceived that the qualitative or quantitative weights are equal to one another: this would be 'a (Qualitatively/Quantitatively) Half Axiom' and a '(Qualitatively/Quantitatively) Half' version (⑤). Our critique of Rawls indicates that, in order to bring the interests of future generations into the picture, Rawls had to introduce tacitly the Dual Axioms of either the 'Ultimately' or 'Mainly' version by modifying his original assumption of rationality. In other words, in order to theorise for the benefit of future generations, even a convinced atomist is forced to introduce some kind of Holistic Argument. Parfit's conclusion of Impersonality and his failure to find the Theory X takes us further in this direction, so that it would better for us to adopt the Holistic Axiom at least as one of the two fundamental axioms. If we were to propose that the 'Single Axiom of Holism' is the only relevant axiom, denying totally the Atomistic Axiom, some might contend that this would be too unrealistic and ignore manifest atomistic actuality. However, our proposal is only that we should take account of the Holistic Axiom as one of the Dual Axioms, since the 'Single Axiom of Atomism' has proved to lead to the impasse. It is hoped that this argument will be regarded as reasonable even by Western people, most of whom have been unfamiliar with the holistic way of thinking.

§7. The Variety of Holistic Postulates and Conditions

Our proposal might sound like the 'Egg of Columbus': as contractual theorists like Rawls had to appeal to the Supplementary Familial Argument, intergenerational issues require us to introduce some kind of Holistic Argument. As the Theoretical Obstacle led Atomistic Theories into the predicament, it would be better to adopt the Dual Axioms of Atomism and Holism in place of the Single Axiom of Atomism.

If there is still a resistance to this simple logic, the objection may be that the concept of Holism is too broad and vague to be applied to actual intergenerational problems. In response to such concerns, let me classify Holistic Arguments by four viewpoints: two postulates and two conditions.

§7.1 The Holistic Postulate of (Philosophical) Reasoning (HPR)

The first viewpoint is associated with the philosophical attribute of reasoning. Firstly, according to a standard explanation of holism, in the context of description for example, in biology or psychology, 'holism with respect to some system maintains that the whole has some properties that its parts lack'; it is further held, in the thesis of *descriptive emergentism,* that 'these properties of the whole cannot be defined by properties of the parts': this view which denies the deducibility of the whole from the parts is known as 'metaphysical or methodological holism' as against 'descriptive or methodological individualism'. Secondly, in epistemology and philosophy of language, 'doxastic or epistemic holism' focuses on the close and indivisible interconnection in a person's belief, and 'semantic or meaning holism' denotes the tight and inseparable interrelation concerning the meanings of all terms or sentences in a language.[81]

These two kinds of holism can be formulated as follows:

① The Holistic Postulate of Ontology (HPR ① =HPO): All of a certain whole, as being itself, is (ontologically) one unitary entity in reality.

② The Holistic Postulate of Epistemology (HPR ② =HPE):All of a certain whole should be observed or appreciated as one unitary entity.

②′ The Holistic Postulate of Semantics (HPR ②′ = HPS): All of certain terms or sentences in a language should be understood as one unitary whole.

In this article, these three will be termed 'Ontological Holism', 'Epistemological Holism' and 'Semantic Holism': Semantic Holism could be regarded as a corollary of Epistemological Holism. As Ontological Holism insists that a certain whole is ontologically one unitary whole in reality, that is, beyond appearances, the Holistic View with descriptive emergence naturally follows. Epistemological Holism implies that once we try to observe or appreciate a certain whole as one entity, the relevance of the Holistic View is revealed: the whole is greater than the sum of its parts. The philosophy of the Eleatics including Parmenides belongs to the former, while most modern holistic theories such as some kinds of functionalism and structuralism are examples of the latter. In particular, structuralism, which is sometimes described as 'a theory without subject', can be considered to have a characteristic of impersonality as extracted by Parfit.

In addition, Ontological Holism is often proposed on the basis of Epistemological Holism, because only studies or appreciation of Holistic Epistemology can illuminate what can be called the 'Ontologically Holistic Reality'. This form can be especially named 'Onto-Epistemological Holism'. Hegelian philosophy should be included in this category.

- The Holistic Postulate of Onto-Epistemology (HPR ③ = HPO-E): As all of a certain whole, as being itself, is (ontologically) one unitary entity in reality, all of the whole should be observed or appreciated as one unitary entity.

§7.2. The Holistic Condition of Objects (HCO)

The second viewpoint regards the range or the object of the 'certain whole' in each Holistic Argument. Though the 'certain whole' can signify anything we want to consider, the most basic standard of classification is whether the whole is related to (only) humans. The representative type is,

- The Holistic Condition of Object, namely, ① Everything, ② Human, ③Non-Human, (HCO ①–③): 'A certain whole' signifies ① everything, ② human entity, ③non-human entity.

When we apply these conditions to the Holistic Axiom, we can obtain ① 'Pan-Holism' (Holistic Condition, HCO ①), ② 'Human Holism' (Holistic Condition, HCO②), ③ 'Non Human Holism' (Non-Human Holistic Condition, HCO③).

The logical pole of Pan-Holism insists that the whole universe is one unitary being. The Ontological version of this Holism, namely, 'Ontological Pan-Holism' includes pantheism, which has existed in many parts of the world: this has especially flourished in the East, for example, in Hinduism or Taoism, though it appeared also in the West in various forms.

Pan-Holism comprehends both Human Holism (②) and Non-Human Holism (③), but the latter two versions of Holism do not necessarily presuppose the existence of the former, Pan-Holism. A certain whole consisting of a human entity in Human Holism includes that of various levels, for example, a person, a family, a society, a country, the world (see Figure 6), while that of a non-human entity in Non-Human Holism could be not only various materiality or non-human organism(s), but also abstract entities like space and time. Amongst these, as Human Holism (②) is naturally the most important to consider for future generations, this will be focused upon in the following.

§7.3. The Holistic Postulate of Subjective Consciousness or Awareness (HPS)

The third viewpoint is related to the way of thinking of ordinary subjects themselves.

① The Holistic Postulate of Conscious Whole (HPS ①): A certain whole is conscious or aware of its wholeness.

② The Holistic/Synthetic Postulate of Conscious Part(HPS ②): A part is conscious or aware of the wholeness of its whole.

③ The Holistic/Synthetic Postulate of Conscious Duad(HPS ③): A certain entity is conscious or aware both of its own wholeness (against its parts below) and of its own partialness (against its whole above).

These postulates constitute what can be termed 'Subjective Holism' in contrast to 'Objective Holism'. The wholes and parts of Subjective Holism can be called the '(Holistic) Conscious Whole' and the '(Holistic) Conscious Part'. So far as the Holistic Postulate of Conscious Duad is valid in appropriate conditions, the dual relation of part and whole can extend to many layers. As has been referred to, the dichotomy part/whole premises some atomistic element, HPS ② and HPS ③ can also be called Synthetic postulates: then, Holistic/Synthetic Postulates (for simplicity, the word 'synthetic' will be omitted in the following postulates).

As an entity which is both a part and a whole has recently been called a 'Holon' by A. Koestler,[82] the entity which is conscious both of its own wholeness and of its own partialness can be called the 'Subjective Holon': the postulate is also the 'Holonistic Postulate of the Conscious Holon' or the 'Consciously Holonistic Postulate'.

Though these postulates can be applied to everything, the clearest case for us may be those about human society: Human Holism.

To begin with, as a person can be regarded as a whole of the parts of his/her body, in contrast to Parfit's Reductionist View, the Postulate of Holistic Conscious Whole is relevant to conventional personal identity. The person is a Holistic Conscious Whole on one level, which can be called 'a Person Level'. This whole, however, can be regarded as a part of wider or greater communities such as those of 'family', 'society', 'state', 'world', and 'universe'.

The Conscious Whole at the person level is also the Conscious Part of these various higher levels. The person, then, is a Conscious Holon; there are multi-layered communities, which are hierarchically structured, in Human Holism. These can be called 'Holistic Communities' as opposed to 'Atomistic Communities'.[83]

The advantage of those postulates is that we can explain psychological and mental aspects in this framework. First, people do sometimes feel or think that they are the parts of greater wholes, whether this subjective feeling is objectively true or not. Besides, they may act for the

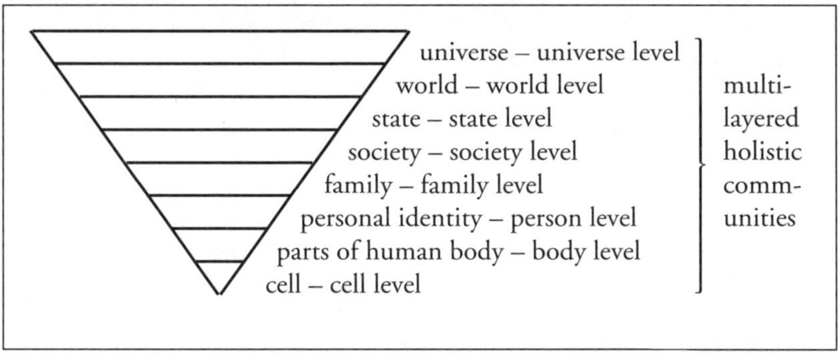

Figure 6. Multi-layered Human Holism

benefit of the whole according to this feeling or thought, even if this action makes a victim of themselves. The person with such feeling is explained as the 'Conscious Part of Subjective Holism at the Person Level'. As such a case is important for our purpose, this kind of subjective holism may be specially termed '(Human) Psychological Holism', and/or '(Human) Mental Holism', which are sub-types both of Human Holism and of Subjective Holism.

In fact, these types of holism have been advocated not only by religious thinkers but also by many philosophers, psychologists, physicians, social and political theorists who have highly valued spiritual solidarity and social co-operation. For example, in the collectivistic tradition of social and political theories, Rousseau emphasised the importance of moralistic solidarity, and the young Marx insisted upon 'species-being' and criticised 'alienation'; recent communitarians such as A. MacIntyre, M. Sandel and C. Taylor criticised atomistic liberalism, and emphasised the importance of Holistic Communities; idealistic psychologists such as Erich Fromm and A.H. Maslow regarded wholeness as one of the characteristics of the higher psychological state, and C.G. Jung discovered the universal 'Self' in the human collective subconsciousness; recent transpersonal psychologists such as Ken Wilber have further explored the 'transpersonal' layer of human psychology; similarly, the current of holistic medicine urges physicians to realise the 'holistic' constitution of human bodies as opposed to the atomistic and mechanical understanding of orthodox modern Western medicine. In general, collectivistic connotations of words such as fraternity, solidarity, and unity imply the existence of some kind of Psychological or Mental Holism, though this may be weak Holism like the 'Roughly' or 'Mainly' version.

§7.4. The Holistic Condition of (Phenomenal) Dimensions (HCD)

As already discussed, Parfit criticised the atomistic, Non-Reductionist View, and advocated the Reductionist View, which is *more* atomistic along the temporal dimension. Since the Holistic Arguments are being explored as, alternatively, the *less* atomistic direction of Impersonality, we have to consider one more viewpoint. The final viewpoint listed here is

- The Holistic Condition of Phenomenal Dimensions, namely, ① Space, ② Time, ③ Space-Time (HCD ①–③):
  'A certain whole' is ① synchronic spatial entity, ② diachronic temporal entity, ③ spatio-temporal entity.

These conditions can be called ① 'Spatial Axis', ② 'Temporal Axis', ③ 'Spatio-Temporal Axis'. The axes can be collectively called 'Phenomenal Dimensions', after Kant's expression of 'the phenomenal world' associated with 'pure forms of intuition': ① the first three (phenomenal) dimensions, ② the fourth (phenomenal) dimension, ③ the four (phenomenal) dimensions.

When we apply these conditions to the Holistic Axioms, we can obtain the following postulates.

- The Holistic Postulate of Phenomenal Dimensions, namely, ① Spatiality, ② Temporality, ③Spatio-Temporality (HPD ①–③):
  All of a certain whole ① in space, ② over time, ③in time-space, is one unitary entity.

These postulates express what can be called ① 'Spatial Holism', ② 'Temporal Holism', ③ 'Spatio-Temporal Holism'. Many-layered synchronic wholes as depicted in Figure 6 are classified as Spatial Holism: for example, entities such as family. While we tend to think of 'Holism' in terms of Spatial Holism, Temporal Holism is also important. Of course, Spatio-Temporal Holism is the synthesis of the two, and, an actual entity certainly exists always in the coordinates of Space-Time. When we deal with human problems such as intergenerational issues, these types of holism are called, together with Human Holism, 'Spatial (Temporal, Spatio-Temporal) Human Holism'.

With regard to Parfit's explanation on the Extreme Arguments, the conventional conception of a person in the spatially atomistic Non-Reductionist View is, along the temporal dimension, classified as '*restricted* Temporal Human Holism' within the person's life, while the Extreme Arguments of the Reductionist View can be called symmetrically 'Temporal Human Atomism'. When we consider intergenerational problems, it would be useful to conceive of Temporal (or Spatio-Temporal) Human Holism beyond the length of a person's life.

Now that the, somewhat troublesome, taxonomy is complete,[84] we can return to Parfit's 'Wonderland' with various holistic instruments in our hands.

3. The Holistic Solution for 'Future Generations'

§8. The Theorems of Holistic Identity, Person and Self

The key to solving the Non-Identity Problem is to focus on the following two pivots of logic: first, the assumption that causing to exist is itself a benefit or at least no harm for future people, and secondly, the assumption that what is bad must be bad for someone. Let me call the first the 'Assumption of Causing Existence', the second the 'Person-Affecting Assumption'.

To illustrate the issue, it is convenient to quote Parfit's simple example called 'The 14-Year-Old Girl': the 14-year-old girl who chooses to bear a child now is so young that this will be detrimental to the quality of the child's life, though that life will predictably be worth living. If she had waited for several years, she would have had a different child, to whom she would have given a better life.[85]

We can call the child who is born now 'the Actual Child (A)', the potential different child 'the Counter-factual Child (C)'. Similarly, we can generalise the dyad as 'the Actual Future Person (A)' and 'the

Counter-factual Future Person (C)'. Parfit's logic is that as causing the existence is itself benefit or at least no harm for A, the choice of this girl is not bad, for this is bad for no one including A, even though A's life would be worse than that of C.

This argument obviously excludes the theoretical relevancy of comparison between A and C. The reason is that C, the Counter-factual Future Person, different from A, is not actually existent. This is a manifestation of empiricism as has already been maintained, but it can also be considered to be the consequence of atomistic logic, in which separation is pre-supposed between A and C: here is a tacit atomistic assumption in Parfit's reasoning.

However, this logic is very different from our usual way of thinking in everyday life. As Parfit himself remarked, most of us would oppose the choice of the girl, for we intuitionally compare the prospect of A's life and C's life. Our intuition recommends us to compare these two. The reason is that most of us do not feel that C, the Counter-factual Child, is a totally unrelated existence from A,[86] the Actual Child: we tend to imagine that the same coming child will be born either as A or as C. In short, the existence of a kind of identity is conceived between these two.

Therefore, our everyday reasoning can be considered to involve some kind of non-atomistic identity. Now, can we identify this with a holistic logic ? In answering this question, it is necessary first to develop the theorems following from the axioms and postulates explained. First,

- The Holistic Theorem of All Parts: All parts of a certain whole are one unitary entity (of the whole). ··· Holistic Theorem of Part, 1 (HTP 1)

This theorem directly derives from the Holistic Axiom (HA). As all of a certain whole is one unitary entity, all parts are the entity. In other words,

- The Holistic Theorem of Each Part: Each part of a certain whole consists in the one unitary entity. ··· Holistic Theorem of Part, 2 (HTP 2)

The problem is the connotation of the expression, 'consists in', in this theorem. If each part is regarded as an entity independent of the whole, this is the Atomistic View. The feature of the Holistic View is that each part is not independent of or different from the whole: it is an essential, indivisible constituent. As the whole is a single entity, the indivisable constituent of the whole 'is' the whole itself. This leads to the following simple theorem.

- The Holistic Theorem of Each Part: Each part 'is' the one unitary certain whole. ··· Holistic Theorem of Part, 3 (HTP 3)

Therefore,

- The Theorem of Holistic Identity: Each part is 'identical' with the one unitary whole. ··· Holistic Theorem of Identity, 1 (HTI 1)

This is the important sequel of Holism, though it may seem strange from the Atomistic standpoint. Though this section focuses on 'Holistic Theorems' between Dual Arguments to save space, we can also develop 'Atomistic Theorems' in parallel with the former. For example,

- The Atomistic Theorem of Each Atom: Each atom is separate from the others in the unit. ··· Atomistic Theorem of Atom, 3 (ATP 3)[87]

- The Theorem of Atomistic Identity: Each atom is identical only with itself. ··· Atomistic Theorem of Identity (ATI 1)[88]

In other words, the Atomistic Identity is 'Separate Identity', while the Holistic Identity is 'Non-Separate Identity'. As the Atomistic Axiom presupposes the separateness of all entities, the part cannot be the whole; as the Holistic Axiom presupposes the non-separateness or oneness within the certain whole, the part 'is' at the same time the whole. This seems to contravene the logical law of identity (and those of contradiction and excluded middle), but this classical law itself should be regarded as part of 'Atomistic Logic', which has long dominated since Aristotle. The theorems above actually require another kind of logic, 'Holistic Logic' or 'Synthetic Logic'. The use of inverted commas in these Holistic Theorems indicates that 'is' and 'identical' are used in compliance with this new logic, not with the usual Atomistic Logic. These signify the existence of 'identity' on a deeper level as opposed to the usual concept of identity: the former may be called 'Deeper Identity' in contrast to the latter, so to speak, 'Usual Identity'.

In the history of Western philosophy, in my view, such a concept of Deeper Identity was first proposed by Parmenides, and, in the modern age, it was put forward by Spinoza, Schelling and Hegel. In particular, Schelling's ontological concept 'Absolute Identity', which is the starting point of 'indifference' in his 'System of Identity', can be regarded as a specific kind of ontological Deeper Identity in Holistic Logic. Further, Hegel criticised Schelling's idea, and defined 'the Absolute' as the identity between identity (indifference) and non-identity (difference): this concept may be considered to be Deeper Identity in Synthetic logic rather than in Holistic Logic. In Eastern philosophy, in particular, Buddhist philosophy, there has been an important idea that 'one', is (is equal to) 'many'; 'many' is 'one'. This can be considered to provide us with a model of Holistic/Synthetic Logic, and the Japanese philosopher Kitaro Nishida, whom I mentioned in Chapter §9, has already developed such logic, and proposed the concept of 'Absolutely Contradictory Self-Identity', which unites, for example, 'one' and 'many'.

The next theorem is a corollary of the theorems above. As each part is 'identical' with the unitary whole, through the common entity,

- The Theorem of Holistic Identity Between Each: Each part of a certain whole is 'identical' with every other part. ··· HTI 2 (HTI/ATI signifies 'Holistic/Atomistic Theorem of Identity' in the following.)

Besides, on the grounds of the argument in the last section, we can develop several versions of these theorems. For example,

- The Various Theorems of Holistic Identity: Each part is ① totally, ② ultimately/superficially, ③ rigidly/roughly, ④ mainly/auxiliarily, ⑤ half, 'identical' with the one unitary whole. ··· HTI 3(①–⑤)

- The Various Theorems of Holistic Identity Between Each: Each part is ① totally,...⑤half, 'identical' with the other parts within a certain whole. ··· HTI 4 (①–⑤)

Thus, even if some versions, such as the 'Totally' one, sound too extreme to accept, we can adopt another weaker version. For simplicity, the discussion will hereafter be restricted to Human Holism, in particular, that of the Person Level. 'Each Part' in these theorems, then, will signify 'a person'. The next step is to consider the condition of the Phenomenal Dimensions, ① space, ② time, and ③space-time.

- The Theorems of ① Spatial, ② Temporal, ③ Spatio-Temporal Human Holistic Identity: Each person is 'identical' with the ① spatial, ② temporal, ③ spatio-temporal, one unitary whole. ··· HTI 5 (①–③)
- The Theorems of ① Spatial, ② Temporal, ③ Spatio-Temporal Human Holistic Identity Between Each: Each person is ① spatially, ② temporally, ③ spatio-temporally, 'identical' with every other within a certain whole. ··· HTI 6 (①–③)

The most typical case of Spatial Holism is that a certain diachronic whole consists of two closely related persons such as a loving couple: let me call this case 'the Loving Couple'.

Applying the Theorems of Holistic Identity, HTI 2 and HTI 6 ①, it follows that each lover is 'identical' both with the couple and with one another (within the two).

This might sound a little strange, but we can modify this by applying the Holistic Postulate of Conscious Part, HPS ② : each lover is conscious of his/her identity both with the couple and with the other.

This is reasonable. It seems to me that this describes the reality of intense lovers better than the following atomistic explanation: each lover is conscious of his/her identity only with him/herself, and of no identity with the other (ATI 2, ATI 6 ① , and 'the Atomistic Postulate of Conscious Atom', APS ②). The latter is nothing but the description of an unhappy or lonely couple.

This example is easily transferred to other cases such as the 'Happy Family' and the 'Fraternal Society'. Stated generally,

- The Theorem of Human Holistic Identity of Conscious Parts: Each person is conscious of his/her 'identity' both with a certain whole community and with the other persons in it. ··· HTI 7

Such a person should be termed 'the Holistic Conscious Person' or, simply, 'the Holistic Person': it will be appropriate to call the other persons in the community the 'Community (Fellow) Members' or, in short, 'the Fellows'. As such persons feel or associate with their 'personal identity' with the whole community or the people in it, they *voluntarily* try to contribute to the community or co-operate with the Fellows with fellow-feeling, namely, brotherhood/sisterhood, or, so to speak, 'siblinghood'.[89]

Note that the person is still an autonomous, active agent or individual. This is the important difference from heteronomous, passive subjects under coercive power, for example, those under a totalitarian regime. Holism, as a philosophical concept, must be rigidly distinguished from the political concept of totalitarianism.

The Holistic Person is the opposite of the Atomistic Person assumed in Atomistic Theories such as the Self-interest Theory and the Non-Reductionist view. The Theorem above can be restated as that of 'Holistic Personal Identity':

- The Theorem of Holistic Personal Identity: The Holistic Persons 'identify' themselves with a certain whole community and with their Fellows (the other persons in it). ··· HTI 8

The parallel theorem of 'Atomistic Personal Identity' is,

- The Theorem of Atomistic Personal Identity: The Atomistic Persons identify themselves with only themselves, not with the others. ··· ATI 8

As the Holistic Persons 'identify' themselves with the whole community and the other Fellows, they can voluntarily devote themselves to the wider or higher well-being of the Community; as Atomistic Persons, on the other hand, identify themselves with nothing but themselves, they will not want to do anything voluntarily for the benefit of their 'community' if these actions conflict with their own self-interests.

This difference can also be explained by the question of self-identity. The Holistic identity implies that Holistic Persons regard (the interests of) others including the particular Community and their Fellows as (those of) *themselves* .

In the simple example of 'the loving couple', the lover regards (the interests of) the other as (those of) himself/herself: 'You 'are' I. I 'am' you. You and I 'are' one'.

Some lovers subjectively feel and insist that this is ontologically true. If this is the case, this is the subjective kind of Holistic Identity which entails the belief in Ontological Holism, in other words, 'the Subjective Ontologically Holistic Identity'; similarly,such a self is a 'Subjective Ontologically Holistic Self'.

Others believe in a more moderate view. 'Your interests are my own. My interests are yours. Your interests and mine are the same.'

This is the subjective kind of Holistic Identity of Epistemological Holism, in short, 'the Subjective Epistemologically Holistic Identity', because the word 'interests' actually implies that the couple epistemologically regard themselves as one, even though they hesitate to affirm the ontological belief above. Accordingly, such a self is a 'Subjective Epistemologically Holistic Self'.

This example shows that, in considering self-interest, the concept of self in the Holistic Person is to be distinguished from that of the Atomistic Self. The fact that Holistic Persons regard others as themselves implies that their conception of self incorporates a certain whole (Holistic) Community and their Fellows. This broader, extended self will be termed 'the Holistic Self':

- The Theorem of Holistic Self: Holistic Persons incorporate a certain whole (Holistic) Community and their Fellows within their conception of the extended self. ··· Holistic Theorem of Self,1 (HTS 1)

The classical example of such a conception is *Àtman* (the Great Self, Real Self) in Hinduism. This concept can be interpreted as the 'Ontologically Holistic Self' when the Holistic Community is 'identified' with the whole universe. Just as *Àtman* is considered to be realised when the usual selfhood is negated or transcended, the Holistic Self may manifest itself: this is, as it were, 'Selfless Self(hood)'.

Some may wonder if these arguments are too extreme: as we observe that strength of sympathy for others varies with actual situations, we have to consider this variety even if we accept the Holistic Axiom. This doubt may be relevant to the 'Totally' version of Holism, but it is irrelevant to the other versions. As the other versions presuppose degrees of wholeness, we can conceive of qualitative or quantitative degrees of identification: qualitatively/quantitatively 'more identical' or 'less identical', in other words, 'Strong(er) Identity' and 'Weak(er) Identity'. For example, each Loving Couple is 'more identical' with the other than are the Fellows of a 'Fraternal Society'.[90]

Others may be sceptical of the Holistic Self, if it is seen as meaning that there can be no element of the usual Atomistic Self in the Holistic Person. The extreme 'Totally' version of Holism may insist upon this interpretation, but most versions of Holism argue differently. As they adopt the Dual Argument comprising both Atomism and Holism, they posit the co-existence of the Atomistic Identity and the Holistic Identity: the Atomistic Self and the Holistic Self within the same person. These can be named 'the Dual Identity' and 'the Dual Self'; or, put more generally, 'Synthetic Identity/Self'. A convenient picture of these is,

Dual (Synthetic) Structure	surface structure – Atomistic Identity/Self deep structure – Holistic Identity/Self	Dual (Synthetic) Identity/Self

Figure 7. Dual (Synthetic) Identity/Self

Although the concept of dual or multi-layered structure is more fully understood in the context of neo-structuralism I propose in previous Japanese papers, this simple illustration is sufficient for the present purpose. Our conventional view of Identity or Self, which is called the Non-Reductionist View by Parfit, is formulated as the Atomistic Identity/Self. While Parfit proposed the *more* atomistic Reductionist View, we reach the *less* atomistic view, namely the Holistic Identity/Self. Holistic or Synthetic Persons[91] can take as much care of their own atomistic interests or rights through their Atomistic Identity/Self as Atomistic Persons. In contrast, Atomistic Persons are unable to concern themselves with holistic interests because they have no Holistic Identity/Self. Therefore, there could be no objection to supposing that Holistic or Synthetic Persons would posess morally more desirable or higher attributes than the Atomistic Persons. Such persons can be imagined to feel love or charity towards the whole Community and their Fellows through their empathy with them.

These Holistic Persons should not be excluded from social and political theory as being exceptional or even merely abnormal cases. If the Atomistic persons with only Atomistic Identity/Self are regarded as 'Normal Persons' with 'Normal Identity/Self' at the present stage of our civilisation, the Holistic or Synthetic Persons should be considered to be 'Superior Persons', for they have not only the 'Normal Identity/Self' but also 'Super Identity/Self': such a 'Double Selfhood' might be our ideal for the coming century.

§9. 'Identical' Solution to the Non-Identity Problem

Although the examples in the last section are drawn from Spatial form of Human Holism, the same general argument can be transposed into Temporal form: in other words, we can apply the above theorems not only to spatial cases but also to temporal (HPD②) or spatio-temporal (HPD③) cases.

- The Theorems of the ① Spatially, ② Temporally, ③Spatio-Temporally Holistic Personal Identity: The Holistic Persons 'identify' themselves with a certain whole (Holistic) Community ① in space, ② over time, ③in space and time, and with their Fellows (in it). ··· HTI 9
- The Theorems of the ① Spatially, ② Temporally, ③Spatio-Temporally, Holistic Self: Holistic Persons incorporate a certain whole (Holistic) Community ① in space, ② over time, ③in space and time, and their Fellows within their conception of extended self. ··· HTI 10

The Community in space(①) over time(②), or in space and time (③) can be called 'the Spatial Community', 'the Temporal Community', and 'the Spatio-Temporal Community' respectively. Similarly, these Fellows are 'Spatial Fellows', 'Temporal Fellows' and 'Spatio-Temporal Fellows'.

With regard to Temporal Holism, these theorems mean that the Holistic Persons are supposed to be able to 'identify' themselves with a 'Holistic Community' (a certain whole people) in the past or in the future. Thus, the Holistic Self extends not only over space, but also over time. The Temporal Community, then, can be differentiated from the synchronic 'Contemporary Community' and the diachronic 'Trans-temporal Community'.[92]

Though we face here the second Theoretical Obstacle, Indeterminacy, it can be assumed that indeterminate or 'possible persons' can be included in the Trans-temporal Community in accordance with the possibility of their future existence: the Trans-temporal Fellows in the future can also be called 'Future Fellows', while those in the past are 'Past Fellows'. Just as the Spatial Holistic Persons consider their Spatial Fellows to 'be' themselves, the Temporal Holistic Persons regard their Trans-temporal Fellows, namely, the Past and Future Fellows as themselves.

Now, recall the example of the 14-Year-Old Girl in the last section. The everyday reasoning about this case can be interpreted not only as non-atomistic but also as holistic along the temporal dimension: at that point in time, before the birth of A, the Actual Child (A) and the Counterfactual Child (C) belonged to the same imaginative Trans-temporal Community consisting of potential children to whom this girl could give birth. Note that potential A and C stood in the same ontological position before the conception or birth, while at a certain later point, A became actual and C became counterfactual, namely, non-existent. For the sake of future analysis, let us differentiate and label the hypothetical persons accordingly, namely, as Ab (before that certain point in time) and Aa (after), and Cb and Ca: Potentially/Really Actual Future Person (Ab/Aa) and Potentially/Really Counterfactual Future Person (Cb/Ca). Both Ab and Cb were Trans-temporal Potential Fellows of the same imaginative Trans-temporal Community. In fact, if we adopt a weak version of Holism such as the 'Roughly' and 'Mainly' versions, we can suppose that those two Potential Fellows are 'more identical' with each other than they are 'identical' with the Holistic Person herself: the weak versions recognise, as it were, the quantitative or qualitative 'Holistic Degree'.

This argument is nothing but Temporal Human Holism. Most people intuitively adopt a kind of holistic thinking on intergenerational issues. What we have to do is only to admit this obvious reality in our theory as a holistic element, relinquishing our attachment to the Single Atomistic Axiom.

The same words can be applied to the Supplementary Familial Arguments in Atomistic Contractual Theories. Though family has been mentioned as an example of Spatial Human Holism, this is actually a spatio-temporal entity, related both with space and with time. Those atomistic theorists can be considered to have reluctantly acknowledged that one inevitably has to suppose some kind of holistic component in theorising for future generations, for the 'natural' familial ties are regarded as holistic feeling within a certain whole called the 'family'. The adjective 'natural' implies that even they admit that the assumption of a certain holistic identity is 'natural' against the original atomistic assumption. Though they restricted the temporal scope of the family concerned to the immediate descendants, this only means that the Future Fellows of the same Temporal Community are confined to the subsequent few generations. It would be better to profess that some kind of Holistic Argument is necessary than to conceal it behind the façade of a 'modified' atomistic assumption.

Thus, it should be recognised that both everyday reasoning about the 14-Year-Old Girl and the Supplementary Familial Argument contain some kinds of holistic logic, though they may be weak versions. Once this fact is acknowledged, the Non-Identity Problem dissolves. According to the Holistic Theorems, Holistic Persons, in general, should care about their Future Fellows because these Fellows belong to the same Trans-temporal Community. Not only the potentially Actual Future Person (Ab), but also the Potentially Counterfactual Future Person (Cb) is a Potential Future Fellow when parents decide the time of a birth. Besides, Ab and Cb are especially 'identical' with each other: in weak versions of Holism, while they are 'less identical' with the Holistic Person, they are 'more identical' with each other. Therefore, it syllogistically follows that the interests of the Potentially Counterfactual Future Person (Cb) should be considered as much as those of the Potentially Actual Future Person (Ab). If we can and must choose between two policies which affect the two potential Fellows, it would be better for us to compare the results for each of them. Nothing prevents us from taking the interests of the Potentially Counterfactual Future Person (Cb) into account.

In the case of the 14-Year-Old Girl, the conclusion would be that she should not bear A, but rather bear C, because the advantages for Ca (Really Counterfactual Future Person) are probably greater than for Aa (Really Actual Future Person). In the case of the choice of the policies between Depletion (or Risky Policy) and Conservation, the Holistic Argument concludes that we should choose the Conservation Policy for the benefit of future generations.

There is nothing special in these conclusions. The Holistic Argument merely supports the common sense judgements of ordinary citizens, though they may not behave as they conclude. Since this was a logical puzzle, the important thing is not the above conclusion, but the way of solving the problem. This requires us to forsake the Single Atomistic Argument, in particular, the assumption of Atomistic Identity/Self. Instead, the Holistic Argument including the concepts of Holistic Identity/Self has been introduced. Though this result may sound simple, a long argument has been needed to prove the necessity. The clue to solving the problem is to transform fundamentally the concepts of Identity/Self into Holistic versions. Thus, this solution can be named the 'Holistic Solution'.

How, then, can we solve Parfit's puzzle? The Holistic Solution suggests that the Potentially Actual Future Person (Ab) and the Potentially Counterfactual Future Person (Cb) are strongly 'identifiable' with one another from the holistic point of view. In other words, they can be called 'the Potentially Actual Future Fellow' and 'the Potentially Counterfactual Future Fellow' of the same imaginary Temporal Community. Therefore, at a certain moment in time, for the decision-maker, the Potentially Counterfactual Future Person (Cb) has as much 'existence/identity' as the Potentially Actual Future Person (Ab), with whom Cb is strongly 'identifiable'. The Potentially Counterfactual Future Person (Cb) has, so to speak, 'Virtual or Invisible Existence/Identity'; he/she is a 'Virtual or Invisible Person'.[93]

Thus, it is justifiable to compare the interests of the two kinds of Potentially Future Persons, Ab and Cb. We need not deny Parfit's Assumption of Causing Existence in order to avoid his conclusion. To be sure, this is a benefit, or at least no harm, but not only for the Actual Future Persons (A), but also for the Counterfactual Future Persons (C), if the latter were born in place of the former. There is no difference between the two from our standpoint: either A or C would have the benefit (or no harm). Therefore, this point does not effect our judgement on the comparative desirability between the two options. How, then, should we think about the other important assumption, the Person-Affecting Assumption?

As Parfit assumes the total Non-Existence, in other words, the Non-Identity of Counterfactual Persons (with Actual Persons), he concludes that a certain policy cannot be bad because this is bad for no-one. However, now that Virtual or Invisible Existence/Identity is ascribed to the Counterfactual Persons, the policy is simply bad for the Virtual Persons because they are deprived both of the (possible) benefit caused by being born, and of the possible life worth living. There is no doubt about the disadvantage to the Counterfactual Persons. Therefore, we cannot immediately conclude that the policy is not bad, because it is surely bad at least for the Counterfactual Persons, even if the policy seems to be good for the Actual Persons. Therefore, in the holistic universe, the second assumption of Parfit also does not lead to the conclusion: we have to appeal to another principle to judge the desirability.

Futhermore, we can question whether the policy is not really bad even for the Actual Persons. To be sure, they have the benefit (or no harm) of being born. However, the (possible) benefit would be the same for the Counterfactual Persons if they were really born. Once we assume the 'identity' between the Actual Persons and the Counterfactual Persons, we can consider what both categories of persons lose by the choice of the Actual as opposed to the Counterfactual Persons: the lost possible benefit for the Counterfactual Persons minus the acquired benefit for the Actual Persons. In the cases of the 14-Year-Old Girl and the Depletion or Risky Policy, it is clear that there is a great deal of such loss. Though Parfit himself mentioned the same comparison as the Quasi-Utilitarian Principle of Beneficence, we can conclude differently from our holistic standpoint: this may not only be loss for the Counterfactual Persons, but also for the Actual Persons, for these two kinds of people may be 'identical' with one another, at least before the birth. Thus, the policies may be regarded as bad also for the Actual Persons.

Hence, once we adopt the Holistic Axioms, Parfit's two assumptions, namely, the Assumption of causing Existence and the Person-Affecting Assumption are unable to lead to the untenable conclusion that certain policies such as those of Depletion or Risk are not bad. Therefore, the Non-Identity Problem disappears. Parfit's riddle has thus been solved. This is a manifest Holistic Solution of the problem.

We appealed to the two arguments of Holistic Identity. First, in justifying the everyday reasoning, we appealed to the Trans-temporal Holistic Identity of present people who have 'identity' with Future Fellows, even if the degree of 'identity' is weak. Secondly, especially in solving Parfit's riddle, we appealed to the Trans-temporal Holistic Identity between the Actual Future Person and the Counterfactual Future Person: this is a stronger 'identity' between the two (Potential) Future Fellows of the same (imaginative) Trans-temporal Community. Hence, the clue to unriddling the Non-Identity Problem proved to lie hidden in the concept of 'identity': 'identical' relations of these two kinds. Thus, we can call the solution 'the 'Identical' Solution of the Non-Identity Problem'.

§10. The Dualistic Solution of the Other Riddles

In one sense, as the Non-Identity Problem has already been solved, there is no need to be annoyed by the other riddles such as the Repuguant Conclusion and the Absurd Conclusion. Since Theory X has been discovered, we need not be bewildered in Parfit's labyrinth any more.

However, in another sense, our solution takes a similar direction to Parfit's attempt. As Parfit supposed that the Non-Identity Problem could not be solved by the person-affecting principle, he looked for impersonal principles. Our solution is holistic, viz., impersonal: it shows that once we adopt the Holistic Axioms, the Person-Affecting Assumption loses its magical power to force us into untenable conclusions. How, then, can the other riddles of Parfit's 'Wonderland' be solved from our standpoint?

To begin with, the Holistic View endorses Parfit's abandonment of the Person-Affecting Assumption. From the Holistic Point of view, the assumption is, exactly speaking, 'the Atomistic Person-Affecting

Assumption', because it presuppposes that the basis of moral judgements rests on independent individuals.[94]

It supposes that what is bad/good must be bad/good for someone. This 'someone' is the 'Atomistic Person', and, therefore, the principle is the 'Atomistic Person-Affecting Principle'. However, under the Holistic Axioms, the person is 'identical' with all of the Fellows: the 'someone' is 'all'. Therefore, in the Holistic Argument, this assumption transforms into,

- The Holistic Person-Affecting Assumption: What is bad/good must be bad/good for all of a certain Holistic Community.

When we apply the assumption to the case of the 14-Year-Old Girl, we have to consider the interests of all, that is, both of the Actual Child and the Counterfactual Child: not separately, but collectively. Thus,we can avoid the unacceptable conclusion stemming from the Atomistic Person-Affecting Principle.

Nevertheless, this result does not mean that the 'Person'-Affecting Assumption is valid. The assumption is actually the 'Holistic Person'-Affecting Principle. The Holistic Person is 'impersonal' rather than 'personal', because of his/her holistic character. Therefore, Parfit's conclusion for Impersonality is confirmed by our solution. However, Parfit entered a dead-end street called the Repugnant or Absurd Conclusion, searching for the appropriate impersonal principle. How can we escape from this labyrinth ?

Let us recall that Parfit's Quasi-Utilitarian Principle of Beneficence is still considered to be atomistic to some extent: half-atomistic. The Total and Average Principle are finally grounded on the quality and/or quantity of happiness (minus misery) or whatever makes life worth living for each person. The person conceived of in the principle is the Atomistic Person. The amount which is attributed to each person in the quasi-utilitarian calculation or reasoning can be called 'the Atomistic Individual Amount'; the value for each is the 'Atomistic Individual Value'.[95] The total is calculated as the sum of the Atomistic Individual Amounts, while the average is the total amount divided out per person. Thus, the total amount can be called the 'Atomistic Total Amount', whilst the average amount is the 'Atomistic Average Amount'. Accordingly, the Total Principle is 'the Atomistic Total Principle', whilst the Average Principle is the 'Atomistic Average Principle': these principles are impersonal because the sum or the average is regarded as significant, but they are still atomistic because the means of calculation is atomistic in its basis or starting point.

It should be remembered here that the Atomistic View (AV) regards a unit as the sum of individual atoms, while the Holistic View (HV) regards the whole as greater than merely the sum of its parts. This is the most important difference concerning, so to speak, the *raison d'être* of atomism and holism. Thus, it necessarily follows that, if the Holistic View is valid for a certain case (call this 'a Holistic Situation' in the following), the value of the whole recognised in the Holistic View is greater than that of the simple sum of its parts, that is, the Atomistic Total Amount counted according to the Atomistic View. If we define the value of the whole in the Holistic View as 'the Holistic Total Amount' (of Value),[96] then this is formulated as follows:

- The Synthetic Theorem of Dual Total Amount: In a Holistic Situation, the Holistic Total Amount *(hta)* is greater than the Atomistic Total Amount *(ata)*. ··· Synthetic Theorem of Amount, 1 (STA1)

That is to say, $hta > ata$

To state conversely, this is the definition of a Holistic Situation. Moreover, if we define 'the Holistic Average Amount' as the Holistic Total Amount divided per person, then the theorem looks as follows:

- The Synthetic Theorem of Dual Average Amount: In a Holistic Situation, the Holistic Average Amount (*haa*) is greater than the Atomistic Average Amount (*aaa*). ··· STA2

$$haa = \frac{hta}{n} \quad , \qquad aaa = \frac{ata}{n}$$

$$haa > aaa \qquad \text{(n is the number of the persons)}$$

One significant upshot of these theorems is that if there is a Holistic Situation, we can count dually the Atomistic Amount and the Holistic

Amount. This can be named the 'Dual Count (of the Dual Amount)' against the usual 'Single Count (of the Single Amount)'. Parfit's puzzle is caused by the Single Count of Atomistic Amount. Thus, in the Synthetic Argument, we have to take the Dual Amount into account, while the Single Amount is the only factor considered in the Atomistic Argument. In other words, what can be named 'Holistic or Synthetic Analysis' requires dual analysis, while 'Atomistic Analysis' is a single, simple analysis.

Now, how can we consider the Repugnant Conclusion? In the case of 'over-population', the Atomistic Analysis led to the odd conclusion that the Atomistic Total Amount of Z (with an enormous population, whose members have lives that are barely worth living) is greater than that of A (for example, ten billion people with a high quality of life). The reason is that the value of the large quantity of Z outweighs the value of the high quality of A, because the former has no limit. This is the 'repugnant' result of the Single Count or 'the Atomistic Calculation'.

The ultimate source of this Repugnant Conclusion is that there is positive Atomistic Individual Amount for each Atomistic Person. Thus, the greater the population is, the greater the Atomistic Total Amount is. Accordingly, the amount of Z finally outweighs the fixed amount of A. It should be realised that the repugnance of the conclusion is the consequence of the Atomistic Analysis based on the Atomistic Individual Amount.

In contrast, the Holistic Analysis indicates that there may be another kind of value for a certain Holistic Community. For example, a family is considered to involve some holistic value which cannot be reduced to the Atomistic Individual Amount of its members. This value can be called 'Holistic Familial Value'. Similarly, civilisation is considered to have such 'Holistic Civilisational Value': generally, there is, as it were, 'Holistic Communal Value', and the amount of it can be called 'Holistic Communal Amount'.

In calculation, this amount can be formulated as:

- Holistic Communal Amount *(hca):* The Holistic Total Amount minus the Atomistic Total Amount.

$hca = hta - ata$

In other words,

- The Holistic Total Amount: The sum of the Atomistic Total Amount and the Holistic Communal Amount.

  $hta = ata + hca$

Here, we apparently face a similar problem to the Repugnant Conclusion. If the Atomistic Total Amount of Z grows without limit, it finally surmounts the high Holistic Communal Amount of A: consequently, the Holistic Total Amount of Z is greater than that of A (see Figure 1 on p.142). At first glance, this constitutes a holistic version of the Repugnant Conclusion. In this interpretation, the Atomistic Total Amount roughly corresponds to the value of quantity in the Atomistic Analysis, and the Holistic Communal Amount to that of quality.

However, this interpretation is not accurate, because the way of interpretation is still bound by atomism. Atomistic Analysis tends to suppose that there can be no restriction or limit to the size of possible population: people can be born as if they were born from nothing. For Holistic Analysis, on the other hand, there is a fixed given size of population, because Holism is always about a certain whole Community consisting of certain (actual and possible) Fellows. Thus, the problem of population is to ascertain the best way for the given Fellows to be born: the options are not restricted to the sphere of how many are born in a certain age, but are also spread along a temporal dimension.

Therefore, the Repugnant case in the Atomistic Argument transforms into the following question in the Holistic Analysis: which is the better way for the fixed number of Future Fellows, A or Z ? In Option A, it takes many years for all of the fixed Future Fellows to have been born, because the people of only limited number at the same age can construct a Holistic Community of high value. In contrast, in Option Z, this takes merely a few years, though the value of the Holistic Community is low.

The answer is probably that A is better than Z. If all Future Fellows finally will be born, even the Atomistic Total Amount of A may be higher than that of Z, to say nothing of the Holistic Communal Amount. The Repugnant Conclusion is thus dissipated here.

As a consequence, the Absurd Conclusion also disappears: since the Repugnant Conclusion has evaporated, we need not assume that there is a limit on the positive value of the Atomistic Total Amount like that of the quantity in Parfit's argument.

Moreover, we can avoid the too extreme conclusion of the Atomistic Average Principle. The extreme conclusion is that the state of the blissful one or two persons (Adam and Eve) is better than that of more people with a slightly lower standard of living. We can reasonably assume that while the Holistic Communal Value increases as the population of the Contemporal Community grows (up to a certain scale), it is extremely low in the cases of a few persons. Thus, despite the slightly higher Atomistic Individual Amount of very small community consisting of a few persons, the Holistic Average Amount of it is lower than that of a community with appropriate scale: the Holistic Count of the Average Amount does not lead to the extreme conclusion of the Atomistic Average Principle.

Furthermore, the Mere Addition Paradox also vanishes in the holistic perspective. Once again, the basis of the judgement that A+ is not worse than A (A+ $\gneqq$ A) consists in the positive Atomistic Individual Amount of extra people (see Figure 2 on p.144). When we consider this situation in the same way as we did in that of the Repugnant Conclusion, the paradox melts away: the extra people of the Holistic Community may wish to be born in the future with a higher standard of life. Thus, A+ is not necessarily 'not worse than A'. In other words, A+ may be worse than A. While (Divided) B is better than A+, there is no contradiction between these judgements and the view that B may be worse than A: B can be both better than A+ and worse than A, because A+ may be worse than A.

Hence, the Holistic Argument not only solves the Non-Identity Problem, but also dispels all the other unacceptable conclusions and paradoxes. This is nothing but what Parfit expected the Theory X to accomplish. The dawn of Holism may have awoken us from Parfit's Wonderland.

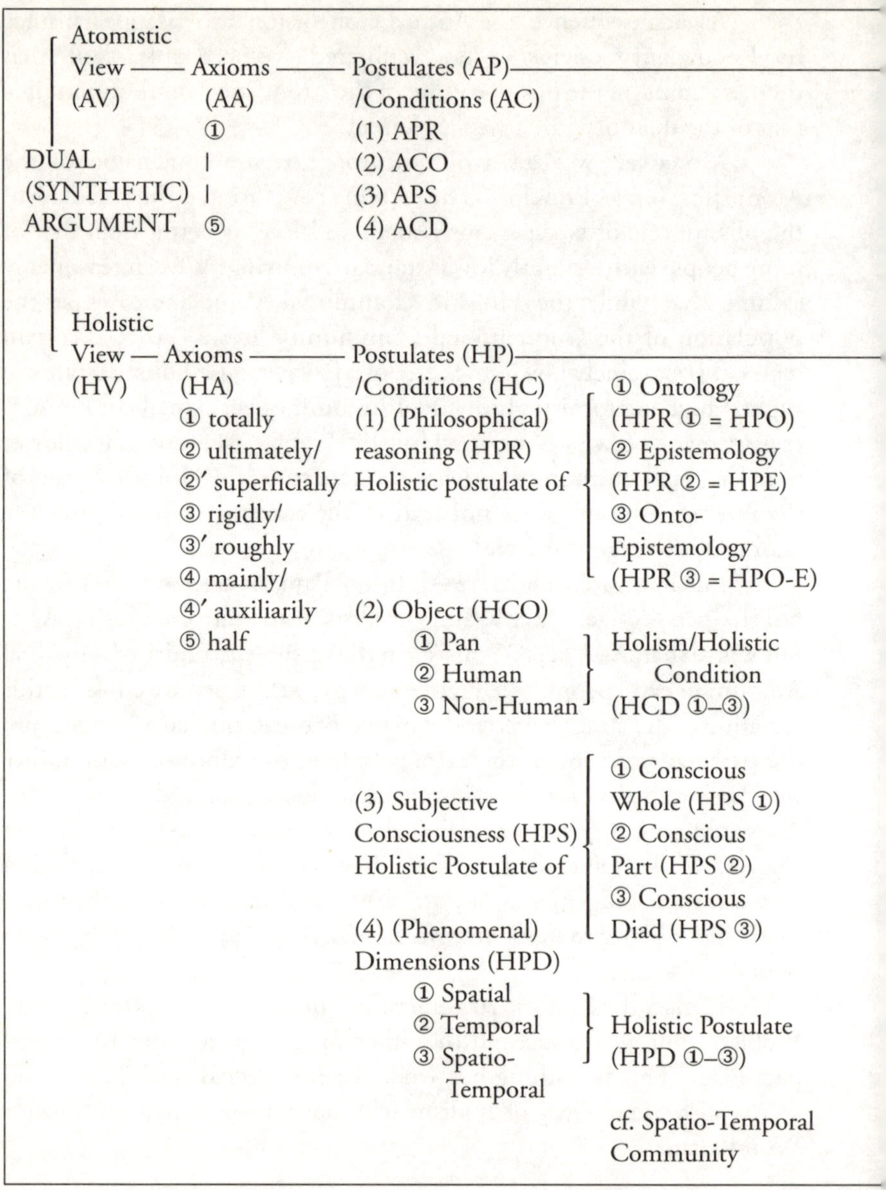

Figure 8. Dual (Synthetic) Argument

—Theorems—————————Analysis

(1) ATP
(2) ATI
(3) ATI
(4) ATS

Analysis:
(1) *ata*
(2) *aaa*

SYNTHETIC THEORY OF AMOUNT (STA 1,2)
cf. Holistic Communal Amount (*hca*)

—Theorems—————————Analysis

(1) The Holistic Theorem of All Parts/Each Part (HTP 1–3)
(2) The Theorem of Holistic Identity (HTI 1–4) (between Each)
(3) The Theorem of Human Holistic Identity (HTI 5–10) cf. Holistic Person, Fellow
(4) The Theorem of Holistic Self (HTS 1)

Analysis:
(1) Total Amount (*hta*)
(2) Average Amount (*haa*)

4. Conclusion: From Dialogue to Dialectical Synthesis

§11. Towards Global Moral Philosophy

The conclusion of this paper is that *some kind of* Holistic Theory, in particular, the concept of Holistic Identity/Self is required to further studies for future generations beyond the present impasse of Western Atomistic Theories. The limit of Atomistic Theories has been illuminated, in Chapter 2, by the critical examination of Rawls' Contemporarily Contractual Theory. Though Parfit radically rejected Atomistic Theories such as the Self-interest Theory, he could not resolve the Non-Identity Problem because of his unfounded bias towards the utilitarian tradition. It has been demonstrated that some kind of Holistic Argument can unravel the Non-Identity Problem and the other riddles.

However, this Holistic Solution neither signifies that a particular form of Holistic Theory has here been justified, nor that one Holistic Theory for future generations has been proposed. In this paper, I have refrained from developing my own theory of such a kind: I shall put this forward in my next paper.[97] Besides, it seems to be necessary to examine not only Parfit's negative argument but also the 'Intergenerational Contractual Theories' such as Peter Laslett's 'Intergenerational Tricontract' at the fifth stage, because these can be regarded as the most advanced of Western *positive* theories on future generations at present.

If a brief comment about them may be allowed: the concept of Intergenerational Contract, in particular, the Intergenerational Tricontract is very significant as an alternative contractual construction to the Rawlsian Contemporary Contract. However, the present argument seems to lack sufficient philosophical reasoning to prove its validity. The most important point is that, though, unlike Rawls, it managed to avoid explicit inconsistency because of this lack, it also introduced some kind of holistic component after all: by the analogical extension of the Familial Argument or under the key concept of trust. Although these approaches are valuable, I should argue that it is necessary to reconstruct such an Intergenerational Contractual Theory on the ground of the Dual Axioms, explicitly introducing a kind of Holistic Argument.

On the basis of the examination of Western theories, a new theory can be proposed. The ideal contractual construction such as the Veil of

Ignorance of Generations will be the legacy of the Rawls theory, especially against the second Theoretical Obstacle 'Indeterminacy'; Parfit's presumption of the necessity for Impersonality will be developed towards the Holistic Theory, especially for overcoming the first Theoretical Obstacle 'Non-Existence'; Laslett's Intergenerational Tricontract will be elaborated into a 'Temporal Exchange', especially for surmounting the third Theoretical Obstacle, 'Asymmetry'.

As the theoretical reformulation of concepts such as 'reciprocity' or 'exchange' plays a central role in my attempt at the theoretical reconstruction, the new theory might be called, for example, the 'Holistic Temporal Intergenerational Exchange Theory'—a variant of the Holistic Intergenerational Contractual Theory in a wide sense. This is a brief preview of my succeeding arguments, but it is the task of my future papers to explicate this.

Finally, let me mention a little about the sub-title of this book, 'an intercultural conversation'. On the one hand, as has been argued in Chapter 2, the various problems to do with future generations indicate the limits of modern Western science in general. If we take the three Theoretical Obstacles seriously, they seem to require us to meditate fundamentally on the nature of modern Western sciences themselves. In fact, the need for this kind of reflection is not restricted to intergenerational issues. Since Charles Taylor criticised 'atomism',[98] this recognition has gradually begun to spread even in the Western academic world. In this context, the most significant discussion within the West is that between liberalism and communitarianism. While liberalism is generally associated with the tradition of individualism or atomism, communitarianism has some affinity with the Holistic Arguments. This will also be an interesting theme for Holistic Analysis in the future, and the framework in this paper will provide the basis of theoretical development from so-called communitarianism to 'Synthetic Neo-Republicanism' founded upon the idea of 'Universal Dialectical Holism/Communitarianism'.[99].

On the other hand, there still remains much for us 'Easterners' to learn from the efforts of Western theorists in general. To be sure, as has been mentioned, the holistic tradition has flourished more in the East than in the West: in Hinduism, Buddhism, Taoism, and (Neo-) Confucianism.[100] However, there are not only these profound religious or metaphysical thoughts but also everyday ways of thinking such as 'familyism' and 'groupism'. Let me differentiate these two by naming them 'Profound (Metaphysical) Holism' and 'Shallow (Everyday) Holism' respectively. Masao Maruyama, mentioned in Chapter 2, emphasised the importance of Western individualism against these types of Shallow Holism in Japanese culture, reflecting that the source of the Japanese military regime, which in the Second World War contained some totalitarian component, can be traced to Everyday Holism in traditional Japanese culture. This view should be regarded as still relevant to and significant in contemporary Japanese society and politics.

However, it seems to me that the same holistic component in culture paradoxically enables us to accommodate future generations in our worldview more easily than Westerners, who are more accustomed to atomistic culture or theories. In fact, various publications of the Foundation vividly prove that Profound or Metaphysical Holism has been stimulating studies and action for the benefit of future generations. Although not all of them are academic in form, it is obviously desirable for us researchers to work in closer co-operation with practical thinkers or actors, concomitant with discussion within the confines of the academic community.

In conclusion, the issue of future generations seems to be a wonderful meeting point between East and West. Easterners often started from traditional holism and have advanced a little in the individualistic direction in the social and political sphere; Westerners departed from modern individualism and came up against the difficulties accompanying atomism. The two lines intersect in the issue of future generations. While we, in the East, can still learn much from the attempts of Western theories on this issue; on the other hand, Holistic Arguments stimulated by Eastern tradition could be presented as our contribution to the debate.

In recent Western philosophy, one of the most remarkable phenomena seems to have been the animated interaction between Continental philosophy and Anglo-American analytical philosophy. From the global point of view, this stimulating academic exchange is, however, still within the West. It can easily be imagined that the next significant phase will be the academic encounter between East and West.

This paper has argued that the encounter on future generations is characterised as one between Western Atomism and Eastern Holism. Parfit advocated Non-Religious Ethics, which are not confined within the West but universal, as his reference to Buddhism exemplifies. The present paper shares this global prospect. My last word in this paper is not 'failure' as the final words of Sidgwick and Parfit express, but 'hope': that this academic dialogue may lead not only to the next stage of studies for future generations (as I wrote in the final section of Chapter 2), but also to dialectical synthesis towards a universal 'Global Moral Philosophy'.[101] May readers from both East and West share this hope.

Notes

1. Parfit, *Reasons and Persons* (Oxford, Clarendon Press, 1984), p. 4.

2. Ibid., pp. 3-4, and Appendices C, pp. 464-468.

3. For example, §59 'Is It Irrational to Give no Weight to One's Past Desires ?'; §61 'Mere Past Desires'; §62 'Is It Irrational to Care Less About One's Further Future?'; §64 'Past or Future Suffering'; §65 'The Direction of Causation'; §66 'Temporal Neutrality'; §67 'Why We Should not be Biased towards the Future'; §68 'Time's Passage'. He mentioned Rawls' assumption of temporal neutrality in §63, p. 163.

4. Ibid., p. 467.

5. Ibid., p. 194.

6. Ibid., pp. 194-195. Besides, Parfit uses the words 'the Unified Theory' which reminds us of the same term in contemporary physics. Parfit's Unified Theory means a new Theory which combines revised versions both of 'Consequentialism' and of 'Common-Sense Morality'. Ibid., §42, pp. 112-113.

7. Ibid., p. 195.

8. Ibid., p. 111.

9. As for the response of Rawls, see J. Rawls, 'The Independence of Moral Theory' *Proceedings and Addresses of the American Philosophical Association,* vol.47 (1975), 5-22; S.Scheffler, 'Ethics, Personal Identity, and the Ideal of the Person', *Canadian Journal of Philosophy,* vol.12 (1982), 229-46; Bart Schultz 'Persons and Utilitarianism', *Ethics,* vol. 96, n.4 (July, 1986), 721-745, pp. 742-744.

10. Parfit, op.cit., pp. 210, 211.

11. Ibid., pp. 210-212.

12. Ibid., p. 215.

13. Derek Parfit, 'Lewis, Perry, and What Matters', in A. Rorty, ed., *The Identities of Persons* (Berkeley, University of California Press, 1976), pp. 91-107, p.106, n.25.

Quoted from Bart Schultz, op.cit., p. 724. cf. Parfit, *Reasons and Persons,* op.cit., § 101, 'Successive Selves'.

14. Parfit, ibid., §92, p. 273. Cf. Appendices J, pp. 502-503.

15. As the historical Buddha himself is basically considered to have avoided answering ontological questions in order to make his disciples concentrate on the way to salvation, the development or elaboration of such arguments was mainly left to various later Buddhist schools influenced by the scholastic Arbidhamma. Though it is impossible to give full details of Buddhist history here, Peter Harvey's *The Selfless Mind: Personality, Consciousness and Nirvana in Early Buddhism* (Richmond, Surrey, Curzon Press, 1975) and Sue Hamilton's recent book *Identity and Experience: The Constitution of the Human Being According to Early Buddhism* (London, Luzac Oriental, 1996) can be recommended as reliable studies of early Buddhism. In particular, Hamilton illuminates the point mentioned above as against S. Collin's *Selfless Persons* (Cambridge, Cambridge University Press, 1982), which can be regarded as one of Parfit's sources of information about Buddhism. Parfit, op.cit., p. 532; Collins, op.cit., especially, p. 177.

16. Parfit, op.cit., §154 'How both Human History, and the History of Ethics, May be just Beginning'

17. However, Parfit counted Buddha amongst the few atheistic predecessors of ethics, probably according to the Western popular interpretation of Buddhism. Ibid., p. 453,

18. Ibid., Ch.14, §102-105, also §118, pp. 346-347.

19. John Rawls, *A Theory of Justice* (Oxford, Oxford University Press, 1971), p. 27.

20. Ibid., p. 29.

21. Parfit, op.cit., p.341, pp. 520-521, note 109.

22. Ibid., p. 346.

23. Ibid.

24. Ibid., p. 342. Cf. §112-116, especially, §112, pp. 330-332. 'The Impersonality of Utilitarianism is therefore less implausible than most of us believe', ibid., p. 346, also, p. 446.

25. For example, Parfit, 'Later Selves and Moral Principles', in A. Montefiore, ed., *Philosophy and Personal Relations* (London, Routledge and Kegan Paul, 1973), pp. 137-168. On this point, see Schultz's 'lucid paper', op.cit., pp. 726-732; Parfit, 'Comments' in *Ethics,* vol. 96, n.4 (July, 1986), 832-872, p. 839.

26. Parfit, *Reasons and Persons,* op.cit., Ch.16, p. 351. Cf. Appendix to this chapter.

27. Ibid., §10, p. 24. See note 6 above.

28. Ibid., p. 366.

29. As the word 'Quasi-Utilitarian' is too grand or vague, 'Revised-Utilitarian' might be more suitable. However, as the latter expression can cause a confusion with Parfit's attempt to revise the Principle of Beneficence, the former (or, for example, 'Transformed [Neo-] Utilitarian') will be used in this article.

30. Ibid., §124, p. 366; also for example, p. 426.

31. Ibid., p. 377. Italics in original.

32. Exactly speaking, it is assumed here that we cannot discount the more remote effects of our acts and policies, at some rate of n per cent per year (Denial of the 'Social Discount Rate'). Ibid., p. 357.

33. Ibid., §129, pp. 377-378.

34. Ibid., p. 378.

35. Ibid., p. 371.

36. Ibid., p. 371.

37. William Gray, 'Possible Persons and the Problems of Posterity' *Environmental Values,* vol. 5, n. 2 (1996), p. 164.

38. Parfit criticised 'The Ideal Contractual Method' of Rawls for reasons associated with 'Non-Existence' or 'Non-Identity' as follows: 'This reasoning assumes that, whatever principle is followed, we shall certainly exist. This assumption violates the requirement of impartiality'. Parfit, op.cit., p. 382 In reality, this criticism should be directed towards the 'Atemporal Contract' rather than the 'Contemporarily Contract' of the Rawls theory. c.f. my unpublished treatise 'Synthetic Public Philosophy for Future Generations: Spatio-Temporal Neo-Republican Paradigm', especially Part 1 'Atomistic Liberalism: Crisis of the Present Paradigm' §2-5: a summary of this is 'Synthetic Neo-Republicanism: New Public Philosophy for Future Generations', in *Hogaku Ronshu* (Chiba Journal of Law and Politics), vol.13, n.1 (1998), 247-270.

39. Parfit, op.cit., p. 363.

40. Ibid., p. 378. This will be considered as a stronger form of 'The Personal Restriction'. Ibid., p. 394.

41. Ibid., pp. 386-387.

42. Ibid., p. 386.

43. Ibid., p. 388.

44. Although Parfit re-stated both the Impersonal Average Principle and Impersonal Total Principle as the 'Wide Average Principle' and 'Wide Total Principle' in person-affecting terms, these details can be omitted because this did not substantially affect the conclusion. Ibid., §134-§136.

45. Ibid., p. 404.

46. Ibid., §137-138, especially, pp. 410-411.

47. Ibid., §139-141, pp. 412-417.

48. Ibid., p. 416, §143, pp. 420-422.

49. Parfit differentiated 'not worse than' from 'at least as good as'. He thought that as the former means only 'rough comparability', it does not imply a transitive relation, whilst there is a transitive relation with regard to the latter ($A < B, B < C \therefore A < C$). Ibid., §146, pp. 430-432.

50. Ibid., §148 'The Second Version of the Paradox', p. 436.

51. Ibid, p. 416.

52. Ibid., p. 443.

53. Ibid., §151, p. 447.

54. Ibid, p. 453.

55. Ibid, p. 357.

56. Cf. ibid, Ch.3.

57. For example, see the debate in *Obligations to Future Generations,* ed. by R. I. Sikora and Brian Barry (Cambridge, The White Horse Press, 1978/1996), Part 1, especially, Thomas Schwartz, 'Obligations to Posterity', pp. 3-13

58. Cf. Parfit, op.cit., Appendix G, 'Whether Causing Someone to Exist can Benefit this Person'.

59. James Woodward, 'The Non-Identity Problem'. *Ethics,* vol.96, n.4 (July 1986), 804-831, p. 808; Parfit, 'Comment', ibid., pp. 854-862.

60. For example, Ronald Dworkin and A. K. Sen. See Parfit, *Reasons and Persons,* op.cit., p. 528, note 49.

61. Gray, op.cit.

62. Woodward, op.cit., p. 804, p. 818; Grey, op.cit., p. 174.

63. Ibid., §150, pp. 443-447.

64. Ibid., p. 447.

65. This is the extension of his own account only about 'reason'. Ibid., p.443.

66. See note 21 above. Cf. Parfit, ibid., §144, pp. 422-425.

67. Larry Temkin pointed out that 'the slogan' associated with Parfit's argument concerning a person-affecting form may be called 'the individualistic approach in ethics'. Temkin, 'Harmful goods, harmless bads', in R. G. Frey and Christopher W. Morris, eds, *Value, Welfare and Morality* (Cambridge: Cambridge University Press, 1993), Ch. 14, pp. 290-324, especially, pp. 315-316, quoted from p. 315.

68. Parfit, op.cit., §102, pp. 307, 308.

69. Ibid., p. 311.

70. Ibid., p. 344.

71. Ibid., p. 312.

72. S.Scheffler, op.cit., for example, p. 236.

73. In reality, as we see in Buddhism, these two directions are not completely incompatible if we take account of the possible difference of each dimension. See Appendix to this article.

74. The Concise Oxford Dictionary, Ninth Edition (Oxford, Clarendon Press, 1995), p.647. The medical meaning derives from this: 'The treating of the whole person including mental and social factors rather than just the symptons of a disease'.

75. Ibid., p. 79.

76. Though there is no space to explicate here, a holistic turn has already begun in modern, quantum physics.

77. Some may think that there can be more than three basic axioms, but the following arguments will be based on the assumption that these two directions are necessary and sufficient, as a starting point.

78. My 'Synthetic Public Philosophy for Future Generations', op. cit., especially, §8 'Dialectical Holism: Eastern Hegelesque Philosophy'; and my 'Synthetic Neo-Republicanism', §6, op.cit.

79. Michael Detlefsen, 'Gödel's incompleteness theorems', in *The Cambridge Dictionary of Philosophy,* ed. by Robert Audi (Cambridge, Cambridge University Press, 1995).

80. What is implied here is not philosophical relativism but possibility of a kind of realism: just as the content of AA can be a truth, that of HA may be also true.

81. Laird Addis, in Audi, ed., ibid., pp. 335-336.

82. Arther Koestler, *Tbe Ghost in tbe Machine* (London, Hutchinson, 1967).

83. Some of these arguments are applicable to Non-Human or Pan Holism.

84. This taxonomy is proposed for indicating an outline of the Holistic Argument in order to solve the Non-Identity Problem, and it should be considered to be merely tentative as a general taxonomy.

85. Parfit, *Reasons and Persons,* op.cit., §122, p. 358.

86. As regards Parfit's view, see, ibid., pp. 351-355, 'If any particular person had not been conceived within a month of the time when he was in fact conceived he would in fact never have existed', ibid., p. 352.

87. Not only Atomistic Theory of Atom, 3 (ATA3), but also ATA1 and 2 can be formulated similarly.

88. Exactly speaking, this identity is associated with 'numerical identity' which is different from 'qualitative identity', and the issue of 'identity of indiscernibles' is to discussed further.

89. I try to avoid sexist expressions taking account of recent feminist critiques, but it is difficult to accomplish this completely because of the present linguistic limit of English. There is no such sexist connotation to Japanese equivalents of 'Fellow' or 'Fraternity'. These words are so important to the expression of my ideas that I first write the words as neutrally as possible, for example, 'Community Membership' or 'brotherhood/ sisterhood', and then use usual or traditional words for convenience.

90. See note 89 above.

91. There can be a questionable case in which a person has too little Atomistic Identity/ Self because of the dominance of Holistic Identity / Self. This is the reason why I add 'Synthetic' to 'Holistic' here. As this possibility, however, is negligible in most parts of this article, I shall omit 'Synthetic' to simplify the expression unless this is necessary.

92. Avner de-Shalit has proposed a very similar concept ,'the transgenerational community', in his *Why Posterity Matters: Environmental policies and future generations* (London, Routledge, 1995), Ch. 1. Cf. my article in Ch. 2, note 24. For a detailed critique of this, see 'Synthetic Philosophy for Future Generations', op.cit., §6.

93. Such conceptions have affinity with some forms of Eastern thought such as Hinduism and Buddhism, because, in these world-views, there is the idea of reincarnation and, therefore, the concept of the existence of a soul before birth. Even in Christianity, there may be a similar idea such as in the 'community of souls', which can be associated with an 'imaginative virtual (invisible) community'.

94. Temkin, op.cit., see note 67 above.

95. Strictly speaking, it is necessary to discuss how the 'value' should be theorised: as subjective or objective value. Although, as against (classical) utilitarianism, I am inclined to assume the existence of a kind of objective value, the explication of this important issue is beyond the scope of this paper. Suffice it to say that the idea of objective value is compatible with Parfit's consequential framework, because this is classified under 'the Objective List Theory' amongst the three types he proposed. Since this type is deemed to be especially significant from my point of view, such a theory will be called 'Neo-Consequentialism' in my next paper. See note 2 above; my 'Synthetic Public Philosophy for Future Generations', §15(2), Holistic Consequential Ethics. Cf. John O'Neill, *Ecology, Policy and Politics: Human Well-Being and the Natural World* (London, Routledge, 1993).

96. See note 95 above.

97. My 'Synthetic Public Philosophy for Future Generations' and 'Synthetic Neo-Republicanism', op.cit.

98. Charles Taylor, *Human Agency and Language* and *Philosophy and Human Sciences* (Philosophical Papers 1 and 2, Cambridge, Cambridge University Press, 1985), especially, vol. 2, Ch.7 'Atomism'.

99. In this context, it is noteworthy that Avner de-Shalit has developed a 'Communitarian theory of intergenerational justice' inspired by communitarianism. See note 92 above, and my 'Synthetic Public Philosophy for Future Generations', §6, 'Intergenerational Communitarianism', and my 'Syntetic Neo-Republicanism', §3, op.cit.

100. Donald J. Munro, ed., *Individualism and Holism: Studies in Confucian and Taoist Values* (Ann Arbor, Center for Chinese Studies, The University of Michigan, 1985). Yoon-Jae Chung's article (Chapter 11 in this volume) vividly illustrates such an Eastern tradition in modern Korean philosophies: his key concept 'trans-individuality' can be considered to be closely associated with holism.

101. Cf. My 'Synthetic Public Philosophy for Future Generations', op.cit., especially §17, 'Synthetic World Philosophy', and my 'Synthetic Neo-Republicanism', op.cit., §7.

Appendix: Self/Identity in Hinduism and Buddhism

Professor Parfit kindly commented upon a draft of my paper as follows[1]:

> ...But one general comment did occur to me. You discuss two ways of departing from the ordinary assumption that the significant moral units are individual people. We can move in what you call the atomistic direction, or what you call the holistic direction. The holistic view treats different individuals as being, at a deeper level, united, and the atomistic view, in contrast, downplays the unity even of each individual. In their extreme forms, the holistic view reduces the number of individuals, or subjects, from many to only one, as in some forms of Hinduism; and the atomistic view reduces the number to none, as in the No Self View of some forms of Buddhism.
>
> My point is that, though the atomistic and holistic views depart from common sense in opposite directions, they are in fact closer to each other than either is to the common sense view. Both attach much less significance to the boundaries between individuals. And, in some contexts, it matters little whether we take the number of Selves to be one or none. (One analogy might be with the curving horns of some bull. These leave the bull's head in different directions, but because they curve they end up closer together.) For example, my response to the Non-Identity Problem – though it may seem very different from yours – is not, I believe, very different. Thus, if we deny moral significance to the fact that my 14-Year-Old Girl could have one of many different children, we can either express that view with an impersonal principle, such as my Q, or allow ourselves to treat these different children as if they were a single person – which is a very crude statement of some of your suggestions.
>
> ...I've often regretted the Non-Identity Problem because it makes it in some ways harder to argue that we have great obligations to future generations. That we do have such obligations I feel very passionately. It is unfortunate that the issue here isn't only that they are in the *future*, and that we are asymmetrically related to them. Though it is philosophically less interesting, I take the most important practical problem to be our tendency to give less weight to the further future. (In the early days of concern about global warming, there was much alarm about the

prospect of the melting of the Antarctic ice shelf, which would raise the oceans by as much as 20 metres, with disastrous effects. But then the scientists concluded that such melting would not start for about two centuries, and would take another three centuries. That led the problem to be ignored!)...

I completely subscribe to the second point; in terms of the first point, I also basically agree with Parfit's view, but it would be useful for Western readers to note this issue in terms of Eastern philosophies. To begin with, Parfit is quite right in comparing the holistic view/the (temporally) atomistic view to some forms of Hinduism/Buddhism. Next, as mentioned in my note (73), I deem that, as we see in Buddhism, the holistic direction and the atomistic direction (in the temporal dimension) are not incompatible, which is very similar to Parfit's view that 'though the atomistic and holistic view depart from common sense in opposite directions, they are in fact closer to each other than either is to the common view' .

Nevertheless, a subtle problem for this agreement lies in the understanding of the Eastern philosophies: while the compatibility or closeness between 'holistic' Hinduism and temporally 'atomistic' Buddhism is presumed here, Buddhism itself historically disagreed with Hindu philosophy in India especially with regard to the conception of the person. In reality, the relation between these two is more complicated or entangled than it appears at first glance: in order to elucidate this question, it would be better to give an overview of each position in turn.

1. Hinduism

The philosophical core of orthodox Hinduism as stated in the Upaniṣhads is that, behind the diversity of all appearances including gods and humans in the world, there is one impersonal and absolute spiritual entity called *brahman,* the ultimate essence or reality of the universe: moreover, the individual self (*ātman*) is considered to contain the universe within its depth, and, therefore, *ātman,* the essence of human individual self, is the same as the universal or cosmic spirit, *brahman.*[2] In my taxonomy in §7, the doctrine of *brahman* is considered to embody typically Ontological Holism (HPR ①) or Onto-Epistemological Holism (HPR ③), Pan-Holism (HCO ①), and Spatio-Temporal Holism

(HPD ③). In short, *brahman is* 'the Holistic Universe'. Moreover, the realised Self, *ātman,* is regarded as the Holistic Conscious Part (HPS ②) of the Holistic Community at the Universal Level in the perspective of Subjective Holism: *ātman* is, as it were, nothing but 'the Universal Holistic Self', and this is 'identical' with the Holistic Universe itself.

Later development in Hindu philosophy is closely associated with my argument concerning Axioms of Duality in §6. 'Hindu theologists have been interested in the relation of "the one" and "the many"':[3] the unique one/diversified many correspond to the Holistic Axiom/Atomistic Axiom in the Dual Axioms. In particular, in *Vedānta,* the most influential school of theology in India, there are three important traditions: Advaita (Non-Dualist) Vedānta, Viśiṣṭādvaita (Qualified Non-Dualist), and Dvaita (Dualist) Vedānta. In Advaita Vedānta, formulated by Śaṅkara (8-9c), the multiple many is regarded as the result of spiritual ignorance *(avidyā)* or illusion *(māyā),* and 'the reality of the one over that of the many'[4] is maintained: this 'non-dualist' view is deemed to be the typical 'Totally' version of the Single Holistic Axiom. In reality, Śaṅkara made concessions to the popular idea of devotion *(bhakti)* to a personal Lord *(Iśvara),* and insisted that 'in reading a sacred text there are two levels of truth in operation, one concerned with the higher truth of the unity of *brahman,* the other lower level representing *brahman* as a personal Lord'[5]: these two could be ascribed respectively to the 'Ultimately' version of the Holistic Axiom and the 'Superficially' version of the Atomistic Axiom in the transcendent sphere. As against this distinction by Śaṅkara, in Viśiṣṭādvaita Vedānta, advocated by Rāmānuja (1017-1137), 'both the one and the many are real; the many being the one's manifold mode of expression'[6]: this 'qualified non-dualist view' is equal to the 'Ultimately' version of the Single Holistic Axiom, which can be translated into a form of the Dual Axioms, in particular, the 'Quantitatively Half' version both of the Holistic and of the Atomistic Axiom – 'totally' Holistic in the transcendent sphere, and 'ultimately' Holistic but 'superficially' Atomistic in the phenomenal sphere (self, material world). Finally, in complete contrast to Advaita Vedānta, in Dvaita Vedānta, represented by Madha, the 'dualistic' interpretation of sacred scripture is proposed and the 'eternal distinction between the individual self and Lord'[7] is maintained: since the uniqueness of each thing and the difference between them are generally emphasised, this 'dualist' view should be regarded as the Dual Axioms consisting of the 'Mainly' version of Atomism especially in the phenomenal sphere, and 'Auxiliarily' version of Holism confined to the transcendent sphere.

2. Buddhist doctrine of not-self and personal identity

Thus, the orthodox Hindu philosophies represented by Vedānta are quite in tune with the framework of Dual Axioms because of their stress on the Holistic Universe, *brahman,* which is identified with the Holistic Self, *ātman.* It is an early form of such Hinduism, in particular, the exposition of *ātman,* that Buddhism challenged by the central doctrine of not-self *(anattā* in Pali, *anātman* in Sanscrit). It has been widely believed that the Buddhist doctrine of not-self *(anātman)* is philosophically opposed to the Hindu conception of self *(ātman),* and this understanding is historically right with regard to various Buddhist schools setting aside Buddha's teaching itself. Steven Collins regards the Buddhist doctrine of not-self as a 'soteriological strategy', and argues that its 'crucial importance is to provide an intransigent symbolic opposition to the belief system of the Brahmin priesthood, and therefore to the social position of Brahmins themselves'.[8]

Certainly, the doctrine of not-self involves the denial not only of the Hindu idea of self, *ātman,* but also of our usual notion of self; however, as Parfit suggested, while Hindu *ātman* extends the usual self to the Universal Holistic Self, Buddhist *anattā* seemingly reduces it to atomistic momentary self, and, ultimately to nothing.

The doctrine of *anattā* has usually been associated with that of five constituents of human beings: 'human beings *have* no self but only five consituent parts'. In this theory, individuality 'should be understood in terms of a combination of phenomena which appear to form the physical and mental continuum of an individual life': the five constituents or aggregates of states *(Khandhas)* constituting the human being are material form or body *(rūpa),* feelings *(vedanā),* cognition or apperception and conception *(saññā),* constructive or volitional activities *(saṇkhārā),* and discriminative consciousness or discernment *(viññāṇa).*[9] As Peter Harvey calls these 'personality-factors',[10] this analysis of personality can be regarded as the Buddhist theory of personal identity: people normally comprehend their personal identity by the five groups or factors.

As Sue Hamilton has recently suggested in the 'acknowledgements' of her solid study,[11] there are remarkable common elements between Buddhist arguments and contemporary Western philosophical discussions. Eric T. Olson has argued that there are two principal theories on personal identity in contemporary Western philosophy: the psychological approach and the biological approach. The psychological approach, the major view, maintains that some psychological relation or continuity is 'both necessary and sufficient for one to survive' and 'our persistence depends on some psychological relation' which has to do with 'mental contents and capacities'.[12] In contrast, the biological approach, the minor view, insists that 'What it takes for us to persist through time' is 'biological continuity': 'one survives just in case one's purely animal functions ... continue'.[13] While Olson himself puts forward a biological approach, Parfit's Reductionist View is counted as a psychological approach.[14]

Whichever approach is considered to be right, both may be compared to some personality-factors in the Buddhist analysis: roughly speaking, the biological approach corresponds to the first constituent, material form or body *(rūpa)*, and the psychological approach to the other four, namely, feelings *(vendanā)*, cognition (*saññā*), constructing activities *(saṇkhārā)*, and discernment *(viññāṇa)*. In this sense, it could be argued that most contemporary Western theories of personal identity contain components which have some affinity with the Buddhist doctrine of personality-factors, or even not-self: Parfit's insight on the similarity with Buddhism could thus be confirmed and even extended to some other Western theories. In particular, the 'Reductionist View' seems to imply that the usual conception of a person can be 'reduced' to some personality-factors called the 'Relation R', that is, physical and/or psychological connectedness or continuity: it follows that there is no self other than these factors. Thus, it is not to say too much that, from the Eastern Perspective, Parfit's argument can be deemed to be essentially a (at least, partial) revival of Buddhist ideas.

Moreover, similar problems have been discussed in terms both of the Reductionist View and of Buddhism. Parfit himself examined 'the Extreme Claim' that 'if the Reductionist View is true, we have *no* reason to be concerned about our own futures'[15]: as I discussed in §5 above, this is the problem arising from the temporally atomistic character of the

Reductionist View. In a similar vein, an inherent problem of Buddhism has been pointed out as follows: the doctrine of not-self logically undermines the subjective basis of moral responsibility and the continuity of character because of its ontological denial of the actual self itself, and, therefore, this doctrine involves a theoretical tension with the important Buddhist beliefs in *karma* and rebirth. Parfit avoided the Extreme Claim or a More Extreme Argument by adopting 'a Moderate Claim'; likewise, Buddhism eschewed the denial of moral responsibility and rebirth by arguing that a person who was reborn is neither the same as nor different from the person in the past life.[16] Just as Parfit used the word 'the Moderate Claim', this standard Buddhist view was described in Buddhist terminology as 'a middle way': it avoided both extremes, materialistic annihilationism, which insists that a person is annihilated in death, and Hindu eternalism, which maintains that a person continues as an eternal Self even after death.[17]

3. Original Buddhism

Thus, as Parfit himself acknowledges, his Temporally Atomistic Reductionist View has much in common with the popular interpretation of Buddhism, and these are opposed to holistic Hinduism. However, as I mentioned briefly in §1, especially in note 15, it should be noted that there are, both historically and contemporarily, various schools and interpretations of Buddhism: though the interpretation mentioned here as similar to Parfit's argument has been historically orthodox especially in Theravāda or Southern Buddhism (in Southeast Asian countries such as Sri Lanka, Burma, and Thailand) and is still endorsed by contemporary writers such as Steven Collins, this cannot be regarded as infallible.

First of all, the Buddha's own teaching and standard Theravāda Buddhism should be distinguished: the former will be called 'Original Buddhism' hereafter. In particular, as Hamilton has recently emphasised, as far as the earliest literature, *Sutta Piṭaka* of the Pali canon, is concerned, there is no suggestion that 'the Buddha had any concern with ontological matters; on the contrary, he dismisses all ontological questions as irrelevant and/or misleading'.[18] The Historical Buddha himself taught the working and the constitution of human beings 'in terms of processes and events', but he seems to have had no concern with ontological matters.[19] If Hamilton's observation is correct, the ontological view formulated in the standard Buddhist doctrine of not-self may be ascribed to the scholastic commentaries, *Abhidhamma Piṭaka,* and *Visuddhimagga* of Buddhaghosa rather than to Buddha's teaching itself: most Buddhist ontology both in Theravāda and Mahāyāna Buddhism seems to have been much influenced (or even misled) by these later literatures.

If this line of interpretation is correct, the apparent contradiction between orthodox Hinduism and Original Buddhism disappears: while the Hindu doctrine of *ātman* is clearly ontological, the Buddhist doctrine of *anattā* is not ontological. When the latter is interpreted to be the purely practical advice for the negation or extinction of an egoistic self for spiritual development towards *Nirvana,* the Buddhist doctrine of not-self is hardly contradictory to ethical precepts against egoism or selfishness in the Hindu tradition – or even in most religious traditions including Christianity.

Peter Harvey's recent book *The Selfless Mind: Personality, Consciousness and Nirvana in Early Buddhism* (1995)[20]is noteworthy in this respect. According to him, in 'early Suttas' which are considered best to preserve Original Buddhism, the doctrine of *anattā* can be interpreted as not implying the simple denial of any kind of self, metaphysical or empirical.[21] The basic purpose of the doctrine is, rather than to give ontological knowledge of not- self, to emancipate people practically from the deep-seated illusion of self, which he calls 'empirical self' consisting of the five personality-factors. These factors are 'a cluster of mental and physical processes centred on discernment, also seen as a succession of mind-sets (*cittas*)' "[22] though these, in particular, the central component discernment, flow 'as the key feature of the subtle spirit (*gandhabba*) which exists in the intermediary period between rebirths',[23] they do not consist in a metaphysical or permanent Self, but are changing and conditioned states. The process of spiritual development is one of weakening these obscuring defilements of the mind-sets, 'by morality and meditative calming, and finally destroying them, by an insight which sees all that they latch on to as impermanent, *dukka* [suffering] and not-Self. The final destruction comes with the experience of "*nibbāna*" in which all the personality-factors "stop"'.[24] Such an enlightened person, termed Buddha or Arahat, has no focuses of attachment or 'I-identity', but retains discernment which transcends its normal limited state by abandoning all objects so as not to be dependent on anything at all.[25]

In this interpretation, amongst the physical and psychological personality-factors, one psychological factor, discernment, is especially emphasised: this is quite in tune with Western psychological approaches including that of Parfit. Moreover, in the state of nirvana, I-identity is extinguished or overcome, but the higher state of discernment remains: it can be said that the (Atomistic) Self-Identity dissolves, but a kind of psychological or mental factor still exists in Buddha or Arahat. According to Harvey, 'While this is still not-self, it is like a Self in many respects – permanent, blissful, not dependent on anything – though lacking the crucial aspect of I-ness'.[26] Nirvana is 'the Self-like goal which is attained when attachment to all not-Self phenomena ceases' , and, in this state, 'the empirical personality comes to be very strong: a "developed self". An Arahat is a "big person" precisely because the limiting I-delusion has been jettisoned'.[27]

Thus, in this description, the core of enlightenment is the transmutation of consciousness by its liberation from the state bound by Atomistic Self-Identity: even if the Buddha or Arahat does not *possess* an actual self, he/she is a non-atomistic person without an Atomistic Identity. Therefore, this picture harmonises with my account of non-atomistic or Holistic Person/Self. In fact, as Harvey himself acknowledges, his interpretation can be considered to be akin to some arguments which maintain the compatibility between the Buddhist doctrine of not-self and an idea of metaphysical, genuine, real, higher or greater self ('Self' or 'Real Self') seen in Hinduism: a number of modern Western and Indian writers including C.A.F. Rhys Davids, K. Bhattachaya, J. Pérez-Remon, I. B. Homer, and E. Conze have argued that 'in saying that many things are not-Self, early Buddhist sources implicitly, or even explicitly, asserted the existence of such a Self, beyond the realm of empirical personality'.[28] These interpretations contain ontological elements, but the direction is almost the opposite to the standard ontological interpretation of not-Self: the existence of a Real Self as the result of emancipation from the empirical self. In other words, not-self in Buddhism is regarded as the guideline for the conscious negation or extinction of empirical self which is ultimately an illusion, while self-negation is considered to lead to the realisation of a real Self, which is called *ātman* in Hinduism. Clearly, these exegeses also fit my theory quite well: the Buddhist concept 'not-self' signifies merely the denial of *Atomistic* self, and surmounting the Atomistic Identity/Self results in the actualisation of Holistic Identity/Self. There is no contradiction here between (temporally) 'atomistic' Buddhism and 'holistic' Hinduism.

Moreover, as Hamilton emphasised, these interpretations of not-self can be more closely linked with another important Buddhist doctrine, 'Dependent Origination' or 'Conditioned Arising' *(paṭiccasamuppāda),* than with the standard ontological interpretation mentioned first. This doctrine originally means the temporal causality or conditionality which relates causes/conditions to effects/consequences: in particular, spiritual ignorance causes suffering through various processes. The notion concerning temporal causality was later extended spatially or synchronically, and came to indicate that all things of whatever nature are dependently originated and, accordingly, nothing occurs independently or separately. It follows from this that 'it is erroneous, then, to attribute separate, independent self-hood onto anything, either subjectively or objectively'.[29] Thus, Hamilton suggests that 'the doctrine of *anattā* is not intended to be a denial of being as is implied in the English 'there is no self'. Rather, 'it is no different from the doctrine of *paṭiccasamuppāda* and is therefore simply intended to indicate *how* things are'.[30]

The doctrine of Dependent Origination describes, in its later form, the interdependency or interrelatedness of all things in this world; and, it is the most clearly holistic teaching in Buddhism: compared with the Hindu 'rigidly' version of holism concerning *ātman,* this is regarded as a 'roughly' version of Ontological Holism. Besides, according to Hamilton's interpretation, since all things are interdependent in this world, the point to note is that there is no *independent* self rather than no self: in this exegesis, the doctrine of not-self is also holistic rather than atomistic in any sense. Therefore, the doctrine of Dependent Origination is vitally important from a holistic perspective. It seems to me that, as the title of Collin's acclaimed book *Selfless Persons* exemplifies,

Western scholarship on Buddhism tends to overemphasise the doctrine of not-self in Theravāna Buddhism and unduly to disregard correspondingly that of Dependent Origination: this may result in distracting the attention of Western people from the holistic element in Buddhism.

In reality, from this perspective, the seemingly Temporally Atomistic conception of not-self turns out to be holistic. In this sense, Parfit's insight on the closeness between the temporally atomistic view and holistic view is appropriate – perhaps more appropriate than he himself imagined. The relation between Parfit's theory and Buddhism obviously depends on the interpretation of the former as well as that of latter. If Parfit's Reductionist View is regarded as non-ontological, it is perfectly in tune with Buddha's own teaching of not-self, and, therefore, it can be closely connected with the holistic idea of Dependent Origination; if the Reductionist view is ontological, it may not correspond accurately to Buddha's own utterance.

4. Later Buddhism

Nevertheless, even in the latter case, it does not necessarily follow that Parfit's theory is far from Buddhism in general: in the later developments of Buddhism after the life of Buddha himself, there are certainly ontological interpretations of not-self. As Collin's interpretation instances, this tendency was already conspicuous in Theravāda Buddhism. It, moreover, has become dominant in Mahāyāna or Northern/Eastern Buddhism (in Northeastern Asian countries such as China, Korea and Japan), since one of its central concepts, emptiness (*śūnyatā*) (of all things), bears both a more epistemological and a more ontological tone than not-self: though not-self, or 'empty self', can be interpreted psychologically or non-ontologically, it is difficult to attach such a non-ontological interpretation to the concepts of empty things or an empty world in general.

While the ontological interpretation of the Reductionist View has much in common with later Buddhist philosophies, even if not with Buddha's own teaching, nevertheless, most Buddhist philosophies could also be interpreted to be compatible with holism. To be sure, early schools on the *Abhidhamma*, for example, *Sarvāstivādins* (pan-realists), the *Sautrāntika* school and *Theravāda* argued for Ontological Atomism: all beings include five personality factors manifest only momentarily. Even some later forms of Buddhism have stressed the Temporally Atomistic Self: for example, (Japanese) Zen Buddhism emphasises the transcendence of thought as the principal key to enlightment, and directs disciples to concentrate upon momentary experiences, which are just 'here and now', in order to attain the state expressed by the term 'non-mindness or no-thought (*mu-nen* in Japanese)'.[31] Nonetheless, holistic elements can also be discerned in later Mahāyāna Buddhist philosophies (including Zen Buddhism).

To begin with, the first major school in Mahāyāna Buddhism in India, the Madhyamaka school founded by Nāgārjuna (c. AD 150-250) put forward the concept of 'emptiness' of everything, and 're-emphasised the Buddha's rejection of all speculative views'[32] by utilising apparently paradoxical philosophical reasoning: emptiness is 'neither a thing nor is it nothingness: rather, it refers to reality as incapable of ultimately being pinned down in concepts'.[33] This school interpreted Dependent Origination (Conditional Arising) 'as meaning that phenomena are not only mutually dependent for their "arising" in time, but are so in their very nature. Thus, they cannot really be spoken of as separate entities which interact. By "itself", a thing is nothing. It is what it is only in relation to other things, and they are what they are in relation to it and yet other things'.[34] Since the language-constructs *(prajñapa)* necessarily involve discriminating conceptualisation which abstracts the continuous flux of experience into various interrelated yet separate segments, even the talk of *dharmas* (truth or natural laws, which Buddha recognised) can convey merely conventional truth and is unable to express ultimate truth, which cannot be represented in its own nature by a language (the non-selfness or emptiness of *dharma).* Accordingly, no 'self-existent substance exists: the world is a web of fluxing, inter-dependent, baseless phenomena'[35] beyond any picture of truth depicted in any language. Since reality is ultimately inconceivable and inexpressible, it can only be indicated by some allusions such as 'thusness' or 'suchness'.

This school clearly contains a form of Ontological Holism: this is particularly implied in its new interpretation of Dependent Origination, namely, the spatial or synchronic extension of its original meaning mentioned above. The view of interdependency in the world reminds us of the Epistemological Holism of structuralism, which was inspired by structural linguistics. While the Madhyamaka school extended the Original Buddhist idea of not-self to empty self and world as a whole, structuralism has advocated a thought without a subject. The similarity between these is impressive, but the difference is that, while structuralism illuminates by means of holistic structural analysis hidden deep structures underneath our usual understanding of the world, the Madhyamaka school pointed to the unutterable ontological reality by designating the limitation of a language described as essentially atomistic in a manner more reminiscent of Wittgenstein's last proposition in *Tractus Logico-Philosophicus* [36] than of structural linguistics.[37] That is to say, the Madhyamaka school advocated the negative Ontological Holism of emptiness of all things by indicating the epistemological limits of language, which was regarded as essentially atomistic.

Next, another major philosophical school in Mahāyāna Buddhism in India is the Yogācāra school founded by Asanga (4 or 5 c.), whose 'teacher' is the mysterious Maitreya, and Asanga's half-brother Vasubandu. The Madhyamaka school adopted 'an analytical, dialectic approach to reality, emphasising *prajñā* (wisdom)'[38] of emptiness: Yogācāra literally means 'Practice of Yoga', and the school emphasised the development of consciousness through meditative concentration *(samādhi).* This school held a form of philosophical idealism: 'the perceived world is seen as "representation-only" (*vijñapti-mātra*) or "thought-only" (*citta-mātra*)'.[39] According to the Yogācāra school, beneath six forms of consciousness (eye-, ear-, nose-, tongue-, body-, and mind- consciousness) and *manas* (a subliminal consciousness), there is a deeper unconsciousness, *ālaya-rijñāna* (storehouse consciousness) where karmas are stored as 'seeds' of future karmic effects: 'this depth-aspect of *ālaya* is seen to be beyond the dualisms of subject and object, existence and non-existence, and is known as the *Dharma-dhātu,* the "Dharma-realm", or as "thusness", equivalent to emptiness and *Nirvāṇa.*'[40]

While the Madhyamaka school talks in terms of 'two levels of truth', namely, conventional truth and ultimate truth, the Yogācāra school puts forward three apparent 'natures' (*svabhāva's*). The first nature is 'the (mentally) constructed' or 'imaged' *(parikalpita),* which is 'structured by the subject/object discrimination',[41] and this is common appearance but illusory in reality; the second nature is the 'other-dependent' *(paratantra),* in which one thing is dependent on the other things, and this comprehension of mutual dependence and impermanence is on the level of relative reality, yet still not the highest level of reality because it retains the subject/object duality; the third and highest nature is the 'absolutely accomplished' (the *pariniṣpanna),* devoid of subject/object duality, and this brings the knowledge of emptiness and thusness, which are characterised, in contrast to the understanding in Madhyamaka school, by the emptiness of duality rather than the emptiness of existence.[42]

As regards holism, a double form of it can be discerned in this tradition. First, the second nature corresponds to the extended doctrine of Dependent Origination, so, this form of, (the 'roughly' version of) Ontological Holism is considered to embody the relative reality. Secondly, the third and highest nature corresponds to the transcendence of subject/object duality and the correlative collapse of subject, namely, the attainment of not-self or emptiness on the non-dual depth of *ālaya.* While, in the second nature, holistic interdependence is regarded as objective from the perspective of a subject, the third nature can be considered to represent a form of Onto-Epistemological Holism which incorporates both subjective and objective perspectives by the sublimation of the opposition between these: that is, whilst the former is classified as Objective and Ontological Holism, centred upon objective interdependency, the latter is a special form of Onto-Epistemological Holism beyond the subjective/objective dichotomy. Since the emptiness is considered to be that of the subject/object duality rather than that of existence, this is Onto-Epistemological Holism rather than simple Ontological Holism, on an epistemological and psychological plane of *ālaya.* Just as the Madhyamaka school indicated the inexpressibility of ontological truth, the Yogācāra school, at the highest level, concentrated upon facilitating epistemological transcendence through meditation, without attempting to explicate ontological reality. Thus, while the Madhyamaka school especially emphasised a negative form of Ontological Holism by indicating linguistic limitation, the Yogācāra school espoused a form of Ontological Holism at the intermediate level of the second nature, and an idealistic form of Onto-Epistemological Holism at the highest level.

To sum up, in both of the major schools of Mahāyāna Buddhism in India, some forms of holistic elements are distinctly discernible, especially in terms of the doctrine of Dependent Origination. Though there are various other schools or forms of Buddhism, the same applies in most of the schools. In particular, in the latest form, Tantra Buddhism (since 5th or 6th century AD), the world or universe as a whole is considered to be a manifestation of the Dharma-body, namely, the cosmic body of the one first and primeval Buddha, the *Adi-Buddha* (consisting of the 'Five *Tathagatas'* or 'Five *Jinas')* or *Mahavairocana/ Vajradhara:* [43] this is clearly a revival of the Hindu *brahman* or the 'adaption of Buddhism to Brahmanism',[44] and therefore, can be regarded as typical Ontological Pan Holism.[45] Thus, Parfit's insight (on the compatibility between Temporal Atomism and Holism) with the analogy of 'the curving horns of some bull' has proved to be right regarding most interpretations or forms of Buddhism including Original Buddhism, Theravāda Buddhism and Mahāyāna Buddhism.[46] Accordingly, from the holistic point of view, Parfit's Reductionist View together with some other Western theories on personal identity is compatible with, or can even be incorporated into, a form of holistic or synthetic theory. The construction of such a unified theory which includes a form of alliance or integration between the Reductionist View/Consequentionalism and Holism is a task that still lies ahead of a simple holistic theory proposed in the present paper.[47]

Notes to Appendix

1. This is quoted from Parfit's letter to myself in 11th May 1997, with his permission. Professor Parfit did not have time to participate in the conference, and his comments are based only on my drafts.

2. This is merely a standard explanation. For example, M. Monier-Williams, *Buddhism: In its Connection with Brāhmanisn and Hinduism, and in its Contrast with Christianity* (Munshiram Manoharlal Publishers Pvt Ltd, 1889, 1995), especially, pp. 3, 105; Gavin Flood, *An Introduction to Hinduism* (Cambridge, Cambridge University Press, 1996), pp.84-85.

3. Flood, ibid., pp. 229-230.

4. Ibid., p. 239.

5. Ibid., p. 243.

6. Ibid., p. 244.

7. Ibid., p. 246.

8 Steven Collins, *Selfless Persons: Imagery and thought in Theravāda Buddhism* (Cambridge, Cambridge University Press, 1982), p. l2.

9. Sue Hamilton, *Identity and Experience: The Constitution of the Human Being According to Early Buddhism* (London, Luzac Oriental, 1996), quoted from p.xviii. Peter Harvey, *An Introduction to Buddhism: Teachings, history and practices* (Cambridge, Cambridge University Press, 1990), pp. 49-50; Harvey, *The Selfless Mind: Personality, Consciousness and Nirvana in Early Buddhism* (Surrey, Curzon Press, 1995), p. 4.

10. Ibid.

11. Hamilton, op.cit., p.xi.

12. Eric T. Olson, *The Human Animal: Personal Identity Without Psychology* (New York, Oxford University Press, 1997), pp. 13, 16.

13. Ibid., p. 16.

14. Ibid., p. 20.

15. Parfit, *Reasons and Persons,* (Oxford, Clarendon Press, 1984), §102, p. 307; also see § 117.

16. Collins, op.cit., Ch. 6. See note 23 below.

17. Ibid.; Harvey, *The Selfless Mind,* op.cit., Ch. 4 and Ch. 14, especially, 14-2 and 14-10.

18. Hamilton, op.cit., p. 194.

19. Ibid.

20. Harvey, op.cit.

21. Ibid, pp. 7-8.

22. Ibid., p. 248.

23. Ibid., p.247. This argument by Harvey offers an important basis for affirming the Original Buddhist theory of rebirth: the dilemma with the doctrine of not-self has been so serious that some Japanese scholars have even denied the belief in rebirth in Original Buddhism. Once this untenable doubt dissolves, the idea of rebirth provides a manifest rationale for our concern for future generations from the Hindu/Buddhist point of view: a future person/personality-factors might 'be' myself/my personality-factors in rebirth. See note 93 on p. 198.

24. Harvey, op.cit., p. 249.

25. Ibid., p. 250.

26. Ibid., p. 246.

27. Ibid.

28. Ibid., p.8. In contrast, see Collins, op.cit., pp.7-12.

29. Hamilton, op.cit., in 'Short Glossary', *'anatta'* and *'paṭiccasamappāda',* quoted from p. 204. However, this explanation in the glossary does not seem to pay due attention to the original meaning of temporal causality or conditionality, which has often been linked with the notion of *karma* and rebirth.

30. Ibid., p. 195.

31. For example, Peter Harvey, *An Introduction to Buddhism,* op.cit., pp.270-279; see, Kido Inoue, 'Ever-Changing Life and Ever-Lasting Existence: The Eternal Path of Mankind Toward Tranquility of Mind', in *Thinking About Future Generations* (Institute for the Integrated Study of Future Generations, 1994), pp. 151-160.

32. Harvey, *An Introduction to Buddhism,* op.cit., p. 96.

33. Ibid, p. 99

34. Ibid., p. 98.

35. Ibid., p. 99

36. The question of the subject is very important in the interpretation of Wittgenstein's philosophy. For example, Jonathan Lear and Barry Stroud, 'The Disappearing "We"', in *The Aristotelian Society,* Supplementary vol. LVIII (1984), 220-258.

37. My neo-structuralism can be regarded as an attempt to integrate the two directions embodied in structuralism and the Madhyamaka school.

38. Harvey, op.cit., p. 105.

39. Ibid., p. 106.

40. Ibid., p. 108.

41. Ibid., pp. 110.

42. Ibid., pp. 110-111. In this school, the Original Buddhist doctrine of not-self was developed as follows; 'the full realisation of representation-only comes when the utter transcending of any "object" leads to the collapse of any notion of "subject", which is merely its dualistic contrast (...). Thus arises the experience of transcendent knowledge, which is an undifferentiated unity, beyond the subject/object duality and concepts of any kind, even "thought"'. Ibid., p. 112.

43. Edward Conze, *Buddhism: Its Essence and Development* (Munshiran Manoharlal Publishers Pvt Ltd, 1951/1994), pp. 188-191.

44. Monier-Williams, *Buddhism,* op.cit., p. 204.

45. On the other hand, some important parts of Original Buddhism such as the doctrine of not-self and suffering tend to fade in Tantric Buddhism.

46. As regards the understanding of Western scholarship on Buddhism, I am much indebted to conversations with Damien Keown, and I am also grateful for his kind help on this project: his books on Buddhist ethics are useful also for the theme of future generations. Damien Keown, *The Nature of Buddhist Ethics* (London, Macmillan, 1992); idem, *Buddhism and Bioethics* (London, Macmillan/New York, St. Martin's Press, 1995).

47. See my 'Synthetic Public Philosophy for Future Generations' (see note 38 on p.195), §15(2) 'Holistic Consequential Ethics'.

9

Political Identity and the Well-being of Future Generations

Takeshi Sasaki

This paper will discuss three items in response to the main theme. Firstly, it will be argued that the enormous changes in this century and their consequences have brought about unprecedented challenges to humans beings. Secondly, contemporary democratic politics will be shown to be fundamentally deficient in dealing with the interests of future generations. Thirdly, some possible measures to respond to this deficit will be discussed.

1. Society and self-identity in the 20th century

The 20th century has seen enormous changes in that the way of life of ordinary people has been fundamentally transformed and the historical continuity of their lives has come to an end on an unprecedented scale. While it was formerly convenient to characterise the 20th century as the century of political revolution and the world wars, it now seems to be more reasonable to say that this formulation has concentrated only on the most conspicuous phenomena of this century rather than on the real changes in social life and in political identity. The enormous technological and social changes originating in Western countries not only spelled the end of traditional society in these countries but also destabilised continuously the traditional social structure in non-Western countries. The globalisation of these changes has brought about the globalisation of the resulting problems in symmetrical as well as in asymmetrical ways. Human beings have great difficulty in coping with these transformations in various areas. Without checking these transformations the problems of future generations can not be discussed appropriately. It is necessary to recognise that this century has brought about enormous challenges and the problems have illustrated our vulnerability very transparently.

If we were to characterise social change in this century roughly, we should say that it was the systematic destruction of traditional societies by the rapid processes of industrialisation and modernisation. Since the 19th century, Western civilisation has steadily destabilised traditional society world-wide and contributed to bringing about a relatively homogeneous world and putting an end to the natural isolation of the traditional political geography. The declining of rural populations and the dramatic move of the peasantry to urban areas signalised the beginning of modernisation. Without this general trend toward comparatively global homogeneity neither the dramatic growth of nationalism nor the ideological politics of the Cold War could have been realised. The waves of democratisation belong to one of these trends. The Japanese case was an example of a relatively early and original response to the trends, but its basic structure began to change finally in the1950s.

Industrialisation and modernisation meant in fact the end of relatively stable, agricultural societies. The 20th century impressed people with the possibilities of both our everyday life and our social systems being fabricated in a different way. The growing weight of instrumental rationality changed dramatically the faces of our social life, and even our way of thinking can be manufactured as evidenced in indoctrination and 'brain washing'. Leaving the discussions of these moral and political consequences for Part 2, we have to consider the unprecedented impacts of science and technology in this century. The 20th century should be distinguished from the previous century by the fact that everyday life has depended upon highly developed technology resulting from scientific insights, rather than upon so-called common experiences. Since the mid-century our everyday life has been transformed by electronic equipment, and rapid economic growth has been made possible by technological development. The image of the mass consumer society has diffused from the USA to other countries, including developing countries. The revolution in transportation and communication technology has completed the demise of the old world consisting of innumerable isolated, heterogeneous societies. One of the most visible results of the social upheaval of this century is the population explosion. While modern health systems brought about a massive reduction in mortality and increase in longevity, the continuing high level of fertility resulted in rapid population growth on an unprecedented scale. The population explosion is believed to have occurred in moving from the old agrarian society to the new industrialised society and was one of the driving forces behind the political upheavals of European countries in the early 20th century. Population explosion should be described as a typical consequence of the modernisation process in this century. It is worth noting that even the greatest famine and systematic genocide could not prevent the explosion. The most serious aspect of population explosion is that it is taking place overwhelmingly in developing countries, in which the problem of malnutrition has become increasingly serious because of poor resources. The economic expansion of developing countries required to break their bottleneck situation is presumed to have negative effects upon the global environment and on nature. Technological responses such as biotechnology will not be available because they demand a high level of capital investment which cannot be easily found in developing countries. Moreover agricultural products traditionally grown in developing countries will be able to be produced in laboratories so that major export resources of developing countries will be radically reduced and their situation will possibly be worsened. What real alternatives are there for future generations in developing countries ? Are there any reasonable alternatives for them to be free from increasing famine, constant struggle for food and resources or civil war? For the time being neither aid from the North nor agricultural reform in the South can solve these problems.

Secondly, the danger to our natural environment has become serious and imminent as a result of rapid industrialisation and of technological dominance over nature. The danger has been described as the revenge of nature against human hybris. If there is something unique in today's situation it is that 'so many people have been inflicting damage on the world's ecosystem during the present Century that the system as a whole – not simply its various parts – may be in danger'.[1] The affluent society of the 20th century has heavily depended upon a rapidly growing consumption of energy resources, especially of fossil fuels. The pollution of the atmosphere has been caused by population growth as well as by the desire to industrialise and to improve living standards. We are now facing the greenhouse effect of global warming. Even though there are many uncertainties about global warming, it is clear that it will affect agriculture and land use, damaging mostly the industrialising countries.

Many programmes to control more serious environmental catastrophes have already been proposed, but serious conflicts of interests between industrialised and industrialising countries have provided us with many hurdles. On the one hand, the serious attempt by developing countries to industrialise is itself one of the main causes of environmental problems. On the other hand, industrialised countries have to cope with their disproportionate contribution to greenhouse gas emission, especially carbon dioxide. If both sides continue to criticise each other, no framework of collaboration will be achieved and future generations will have to face even more severe catastrophes.

These problems have shown that the net accounts of industrialisation and modernisation in this century have been very asymmetrical between different generations and different countries. While some people have enjoyed wonderful living standards without paying the costs, some people will have to pay for everything enjoyed by other people without enjoying any benefits. Ideological confrontation has uncovered this asymmetrical situation. The communication revolution has destroyed the isolation and self-containment of traditional societies and made this whole grotesque landscape clearly visible.

For most of the 20th century the state was not only the main promoter of modernisation and industrialisation, but also the controller of their results. The state in industrialised society realised successfully a compromise between the rich and the poor by taking advantage of the benefits of industrialisation. But the problems of population explosion as well as of environmental issues have thrown into relief the limit of the state as a problem solver, and finally the state itself has been forced to recognise that it cannot control the consequences of modernisation and industrialisation.

The limit has been more clearly revealed by globalisation of economic activities. The technological revolution has accelerated the mobility of goods, money, and human beings, so that the idea of national economy has lost its relevance. Some of the developing countries have benefited from the trends and realised economic growth under a flow of foreign investments. Especially in East Asia the trends have resulted in very remarkable changes in the face of their societies. But in other regions the economic growth has not been realised, and the transportation revolution has further encouraged migration from poor countries to the rich ones. The migration seems to be a natural response to a homogeneous, but terribly unequal world landscape. In fact there are rich countries with an ageing population on the one side and on the other side poor countries with a high proportion of young people. This demographic imbalance between the two kinds of countries is likely, in the context of the structured global market economy, to lead to migration being one of the most visible phenomena and most troublesome issues in the future.

The problems for future generations consist not only in the fact that the present generation has already enjoyed the fruits of modernisation and industrialisation, leaving the significant proportion of the costs to be paid by future generations but also in the reality that future generations may not be able to create any institutional framework – replacing the state – to cope with the consequences of these enormous changes. While the impacts of modernisation and industrialisation will increase continuously in the future, human beings may become dominated by the process of transition rather than being in control of it. When migration or anti-migration becomes a major social issue it is likely to become an impasse situation.

If we analyse the changes from the aspect of self-identity the metamorphosis of self-identity can be described as being as radical as the social changes. Industrialisation and modernisation have uprooted many people from their birth places as well as from their own family, and mobilised them as functional parts of the greater society. A kind of natural harmony between self and social environment has been replaced by functional-social identity and socialisation. The total war and the mobilisation system symbolised a new kind of self-identity. According to Hannah Arendt functional types of behaviour – not action and individuality – have dominated the social scene.[2] The artificiality of the new self-identity should be distinguished from the relatively static self-identity depending upon traditional, quasi-natural social institutions. The dominance of instrumental rationality has destroyed a well-structured stable social fabric and brought about a mass society consisting of de-structured floating selves. The affluent society – society of mass production and mass consumption – can be conceived as a necessary mechanism for realising a relatively harmonious situation among these selves. The big difference between the 1920s and the 1960s consists in whether this mechanism was viable or not. That means social stability can be realised by a well-functioning system rather than by the support of self-identity, and usually a good economic performance of the system can mobilise the stable support of these selves.

People in this century have not only been liberated from traditional social networks but are also not reluctant to attack the traditional social fabric represented by the family. In the industrialised countries the increase in divorce, in illegitimate births, in the single-parent household and the liberation of homosexuals has become a very common story since the 1960s. These phenomena have implied that a fundamental change has occurred in our self-identity, and the most basic mechanism for social co-operation has been seriously damaged by a series of liberations. According to Eric Hobsbawn, a rise of specific and powerful youth culture since the 1960s has indicated a profound change in the relations between the generations. A revolution in manners and customs was brought about by youth culture, and the enormous gap between the generations was accelerated very quickly. The weakening of the most long-lasting social arrangements has been conceived of as the triumph of the individual over society, but it has implied also an increase of individual isolation and the end of old value systems. There has been a growing tendency for self-identity to be reduced to expressions of an individual's personal preferences because the threads weaving humans into social textures have been broken. Hobsbawn finds the ideological expressions of the new self-identity 'in a variety of theories, from extreme free market liberalism to "postmodernism" and its like, which tried to side-step the problem of judgement and values altogether, or rather reduce them to the single denominator of the unrestricted freedom of the individual'.[3] The keen feeling of the loss of the old value systems 'was reflected in the rise of what came to be called "identity politics", generally ethnic/national or religious, and of militantly nostalgic movements to recover a hypothetical past age of unproblematic order and security'.[4]

This small sketch of self-identity should be understood in the context of the enormous social upheavals in this century. There are, of course, some differences among the cultural traditions in the world, but these differences or uniqueness will not be strong enough to counteract an enormous transformation of the basic social texture. Without overestimating the differences, the far-reaching impacts of metamorphosis of self-identity on the problems for future generations will be discussed in the next section.

2. Democracy and Poverty of Responsible Politics

In the previous section I have hinted that responsible politics for future generations will not be realised if we leave politics to follow its natural dynamics. This section analyses the real faces of the dynamics by investigating political tendencies in a more systematic way.

During the 20th century, waves of democratisation destroyed traditional, authoritarian, and totalitarian regimes one after another. We have experienced the last dramatic wave of this century, so far relatively peacefully. Nobody can disregard the importance of the systems of popular political participation which were established world-wide in the 20th century. The democratisation resulted in politicisation of former non-political social spheres and in the possibility of new, deepening solidarity among the members – potential as well as visible – of society. Thus, we need to consider whether the exercise of democratic power helps achieve the public interest of the community, particularly in terms of political responsibility for future generations.

First of all, democracy in this century clearly presupposed the existence of sovereign states which were essentially independent, autarchic, and isolated from each other. The institutional base of citizenship illustrates an exclusive character of the system, which can provide a solid base for solidarity among the members. The cardinal issue for their solidarity has been the relation between politics and economy. After World War II, it became a common political agenda in industrialised countries to solve the severe domestic conflict between the rich and the poor and to control violent class politics. The exceptionally prosperous era of consensus politics in the 1950s/60s embodied the achievement of solidarity in the 20th century democratic state. The state incorporated market mechanisms into itself in the interest of national economy and promoted a modernising strategy. Economic performance was conceived as being capable of being 'regulated' through public management of domestic demand. The state and government symbolised the central link of solidarity. The social security system and the welfare state which belong to one of the most conspicuous achievements in the era of consensus politics illustrated how deeply solidarity among the living members and among generations was mobilised and institutionalised.

But the golden age of consensus politics came to an end in most industrialised countries under a series of serious economic slumps and stagflation. The state lost power continuously against the mechanisms of the market and could not satisfy the high expectations of their citizens. The central link of the solidarity was eroded by a growing globalisation and the state was no longer able to control the process of industrialisation. The de facto alliance between the state and modernisation has been replaced by the dominance of globalisation – a metamorphosis of modernisation and industrialisation – over the state. The government has been paralysed between the rhetoric and the reality of interdependence, which is likely to lead to a new governability crisis. While the politicians and ministers still speaking the old rhetoric have been widely held in contempt by the people, the demagogue has a good opportunity to rise politically. Globalisation has continued to frustrate economic nationalists and the sectors damaged by the disinvestment of the multinational companies. As the national economy has become more and more disorganised, the solidarity and the social bonds previously uniting citizens has been weakened and the income gap between globally successful members and people belonging to the declining sectors has increased dramatically.[5] A number of social security systems have been damaged by the decline of the idea of national economy and the compromised agreement among members has begun to fragment substantially. In every country tensions between the rich/the poor and the old/the young have been rising, and the 'reform' of the social security system has been one of the most troublesome items on the the political agenda. The state in the 20th century replaced the traditional and natural system of solidarity with the public and official system, but neither of these can be maintained as before. The intergenerational trust and contract is losing its credibility. It seems natural for the decline of domestic solidarity to have a negative effect on attitudes toward international co-operation. The end of the Cold War weakened the political will of the industrialised countries to support the industrialising countries, so that the ODA has become one of the most unpopular items in national budget debates.

In the case of environmental issues, democratic government is hardly expected to be able to respond quickly and effectively to environmental damage. The failure of national democratic government in this field to realise global co-operation, for example, does not necessarily bring about its domestic delegitimation even though it will seriously damage environmental conditions for future generations. In other words democracy of this style cannot provide us with measures of sufficient power to cope with the serious consequences of modernisation and industrialisation.

As a result, increased democratisation within sovereign states can no longer be considered a political panacea even for present let alone future generations. As the 20th century comes to an end, the democratic political system of the 20th century has disclosed its limits in serving its members in a remarkable way. It is a wonderful formulation that 'the nation-state is becoming too small for the big problems of life, too big for small problems of life'.[6] This loss of relevancy should be disclosed more seriously in relation to the interests of future generations. Secondly we have to refer to the nearsightedness of democratic governance today. This phenomenon has resulted not only from the general supposition that elected officials are expected to pay attention to, and satisfy, the demands of their constituents, but also from a long and ideological tradition.

As to the first point, James G. March and Johan P. Olsen have formulated this very clearly:

> Democracy has difficulty seeing costs and benefits that are distant, either in time or in space, from the locus of political action. It responds to current and local pressure more easily than to future or distant ones The political necessities of immediate problems overwhelm the capabilities of political institutions to sustain a longer-term perspective. This is a direct consequence of the temporal distance, uncertainty, and diffuse-

> ness of the returns on investment in capability development Since long-run survival depends upon sustaining and augmenting capabilities, those tendencies to increase the utilisation of current capabilities and reduce investment in capabilities that might be needed in the future make democratic political process potentially self-destructive A democratic political system based on bargaining and exchange among self-interested citizens is poorly equipped to deal with exchanges between current citizens and future citizens.[7]

In order to examine the second point let me consider how future generations have been dealt with in traditional political theory. There is no doubt that pre-modern societies had a strong sense of intergenerational connection and solidarity on the level of family as well as of village, all of which was destabilised by the social upheavals in this century brought about by modernisation and industrialisation. If we survey the history of political theory, the issue of intergenerational solidarity is hardly discussed because it was automatically dealt with by non-political organisations rather than by formal political decision making. Traditionally, politics handled current, changing situations, while family and other social entities embodied the stability and continuity of society and generations. To deal with current issues for present generations can indirectly contribute to the welfare of future generations by assuring a continuing and stable social fabric.

After the ideology of progress became dominant, the activities of the living generation needed to be undertaken with the fortunes of future generations firmly in mind. At the same time, however, the ideology of progress forced political powers to reform traditional social bodies in order to realise a more rational society, thus eventually damaging the traditional fabric. When a philosophy of history such as the idea of progress was politicised and the presumed interests of future generations became a driving force in politics, solidarity across generations in time came to be replaced by political solidarity on an ideological base. The politicisation of social life in the 20th century produced a new type of political regime generally understood as totalitarian. Even the welfare state politicised some aspects of social life. What we have experienced in the last decade must make us question seriously whether human beings have the capability to design and fabricate a perfect future society which can realise the interests of future generations more perfectly. The ambitious pretension of living generations to act in the interest of future generations could actually bring about disaster for future generations.

My conclusion is that both modernisation/industrialisation and political rationalism have contributed to the weakening of the social fabric which has supported intergenerational solidarity naturally. This means that the traditional way of taking care of future generations cannot work as effectively as before and that what we are left with is simply the democratic mechanism of interest politics without ideology. As politics has become more and more involved with the everyday interests of constituents, democracy has meant a 'responsive' system which responds to, the living, breathing generation aggressively asserting their interests and claiming their rights. The social and ethical fragmentations have opened the way to a very short-sighted pork-barrel politics without limits.

The budget deficit can be interpreted as a symbol of egocentric demands and the now-nowism of the living generation, but the traditional limit of the deficit can be overcome by raising money through the global bond market for the time being as is shown in the case of the US in the 1980s and the 1990s. In the Japanese case, the government has borrowed huge amounts of money from post-office savings to pay off the budget deficit amounting to almost 5 trillion US dollars. At the same time, to borrow on the money market means de facto to absorb a great amount of money from resource-poor countries which could otherwise be mobilised to contribute to raising their living standards in various ways. Democracies with enormous levels of budget deficit will eventually be punished by the market, but presumably it will be future generations who will receive the brunt of the punishment. The growing instability of social security systems under the global economy has accelerated shortsighted political behaviour and poisoned intergenerational relations in industrialised countries. The enormously high financial demands of democratic systems in the industrialised countries have destroyed not only the principle of equity between the generations within one country but also the principle of equity between industrialised and industrialising countries. Even though modern democratic theory has been deeply committed to a kind of moral theory that everybody should be treated as an end to be respected rather than a manipulable means, its organisational base has been limited to visible, living people within a definite geographical territory. The tragic chasm between the universal idea of democratic system and its actual organisational base thus results in terrible consequences for people in other countries (whose interests are not usually counted in national decision making) as well as for future generations (whose interests and concerns are generally not taken into consideration).

Budget deficit matters have very often been discussed in terms of ideological confrontation between conservatives and social democrats. But if we consider the problem from this point of view, it can be discussed in different theoretical or psychological contexts. I doubt very much whether conservatives are seriously concerned about the next generation or people in other countries, but ironically they seem to contribute to the interests of those people neglected by interest group liberalism.

Generally speaking we have great difficulty in finding positive trends contributing to the interests of future generations. The developing countries will be continuously under even greater stress of overpopulation and poor resources and thus will possibly experience the breakdown of social and political systems. The immediate interests of the living generation naturally dominate politics and policy, so that people in poor developing countries cannot afford to pay attention to the interests of future generations. The resource-rich industrialised countries seem to have the capability to act effectively on behalf of future generations. But, as said before, most of them have been poisoned by the interest politics of the here and now and are exhausted from fighting against current domestic frustrations. Additionally, they will have to mobilise enormous resources to support the growing number of elderly people in the future and their economic growth will eventually be reduced. This may mean that rich countries will be unable to contribute extra resources to future generations.

In relation to many environmental problems, people have discussed how far the state, together with the state-system as a whole, has been viable in reality. Some have stressed the basic effectiveness of international co-operation and argued that environmental challenge has worked to reinforce the centrality of the state. Others have referred to the political and economic limits of the state and of the state-system which give us good grounds for scepticism. I have no intention of becoming involved with this issue here, but the state itself may be fundamentally a part of the problem as well as an important partner in coping with the problems.[8] This conflicting situation can only be resolved by reconsidering the political dynamism of the political entity. There is an urgent task for the political theorist to conceptualise a new means of creating future-oriented, more responsible democratic politics.

3. Some Proposals for Politics for Future Generations

There are usually three answers to the question of how we should establish structures of politics which will foster the interests of future generations. The first alternative is the state approach and the inter-state co-operation model. No doubt the state should be a strategically crucial actor, but its adequacy has been questioned in a number of discussions. Therefore it is clear that the state needs to be reformed in order to be viable in this function. The second alternative is the decentralisation-and-community approach, which stresses the importance of grassroots organisations. In spite of its various merits, however, its relevancies have been very much limited in space and in function. The third alternative concentrates on globalism in terms of a global civil society or a new sense of planetary consciousness. The global environmental movement has had a strong political influence and stirred up a sense of the common world good. If we formulate the second and the third alternatives according to Michael Walzer, the second maybe called the maximalist ('thick') approach and the third the minimalist ('thin'). The thin approach constitutes a necessary part of the problem solving, but should be supplemented by other institutional bases. My discussion will mainly concentrate on the state as a still cardinal actor – especially in Asia – and on the possibility of change toward a politics more friendly to future generations. But success in this reorientation cannot be achieved without serious trials on the other two fronts, so that the following arguments are not intended to exclude other institutional bases of discursive democracy.

Referring to discursive democracy I will clearly exclude the authoritarian state model originating from green politics. Generally speaking ecological politics can contribute to strengthening state power and to a call for tighter governmental controls. Some theorists in the 1970s insisted on the necessity of the interventionist, authoritarian state for the sake of human survival, so that the collision between democracy (as well as the market economy) and green politics has become a popular issue in political theory.[9] My argument presupposes democracy and the market economy and does not get involved with the collision issue. At the same time, it is out of question for me to accept the status quo of liberal democracy, which needs to be 'restructured' in order to be more friendly to future generations. The problem is how to 'restructure' it, because neither the 'piecemeal' nor the 'utopian' approach can be chosen as a persuasive alternative.[10] First of all, how can we reorient public policy from the short-term oriented to the long-term stance by restructuring our political identity?. This agenda results from my preceding consideration that contemporary politics has embodied an internal dynamics which has been easily dominated by the now-nowism of interest politics. Some industrialised countries are exhausted by the dynamics so that responsible politics for future generations seems to be out of sight. In this context the problem is how a more collaborative orientation for future generations can be realised especially among the better resourced countries. The most orthodox approach is to try to introduce a new public philosophy which can check the dominance of the strong claimants with weak claims in the political world. Future generations belong to the weakest claimants in contemporary politics even if the claims themselves are not necessarily weak. As long as we stick to the status quo politics of interest group pluralism, future generations will continue to be the weakest actor in the political scene. Our question is a classical one in political theory: is there any reasonable way to change politics from putting weak claimants at a disadvantage to militating against weak claims?

One of the typical answers to the question is to change the framework of our political discourse by referring to the idea of justice. John Rawls has greatly contributed to the solution of the difficult issue by his theory of justice, especially his theory of intergenerational justice. The criteria for justice between generations are chosen behind the veil of ignorance and in the original position. The parties do not know to which generation they belong, whether they are relatively wealthy or poor, whether their generation is wealthy or poor, agricultural or industrialised. But they have to guide their moral and ethical judgements both in temporal and intergenerational circumstances according to the principle of justice. Rawls said, 'The appropriate expectation in applying the difference principle is that of the long-term prospects of the least favoured extending over future generations. Each generation must not only preserve the gains of culture and civilisation, and maintain intact those just institutions that have been established'.[11] Rawls discusses the notion of the community of mankind and thinks of the community as extending over time.[12] At the same time it is not difficult to refer to a number of other arguments which regard future generations as an appropriate domain for issues of equity and fairness. There is an argument, for example, that future generations are members of our moral community and as members of the extended moral community, we should have obligations at the least to do no damage to the potential interests of future generations.[13]

According to Ernest Partridge, however, a part of moral psychology can form the base for intergenerational activities of human beings.[14] There are, he argues, many examples of the expression of moral instinct toward future generations: governments and schools illustrate the concern for the future which is a part of their moral psychology. This kind of argument of moral instinct provides us with a less philosophical, more empirical perspective with which to deal with intergenerational problems. It should not be overlooked, however, that some moral instincts have produced examples of institutions which jeopardise the interests of future generations. It is not my intention here to praise the Rawls theory of justice and to propagate a particular deontological orientation. These kinds of arguments, including Derek Parfit's 'a more impersonal ethic', should be described as a serious challenge to seek a conceptual base of new solidarity and community under a strong tradition of individualism. The confrontation between anthropocentric versus ecocentric perspectives in the field of ecological politics has illustrated another dimension of the same interest. My main interest in these arguments consists in how far they are able to restructure our political identity rather than establish which argument is more philosophically persuasive. If these arguments succeed in reorienting our way of political discussion, the theoretical difference between Rawls and Parfit, for example, will not be very important.

Other cultural traditions must have their own resources to be mobilised to contribute to the conceptualisation of similar ideas in their own way. But frankly speaking there seems to be no easy way for the non-Western tradition to respond to these theoretical challenges successfully. Simply to go back to tradition is not only unachievable but would also fail to provide satisfactory solutions to the questions because most of the traditions have already been devastated by the enormous changes in this century and the dynamics of short-term interest politics has been firmly established. Every non-Western culture can draw on some intellectual factors which can be useful in this context, but it seems that the same cultural tradition has already provided us with many counterproductive factors.

Secondly, the problem of institutions should be addressed. As argued in part 2, a competitive democratic political system makes the long-term interests of future generations vulnerable to the short-term interests of the current generation of political actors. In order to deal with those problems, it is a political imperative to establish some method by which future citizens may obtain political representation. The political interests of future generations must be given political voice by encouraging those current citizens who might speak for them. Of course, a number of people can speak for future generations de facto, but my main point is that a political system should appoint a definite spokesperson for future generations. It should create an agency with responsibility for defending the interests of the unborn.

This proposal starts from the recognition that the traditional way of dealing with the interests of future generations has lost relevancy in contemporary democracy. As I said in part 1, 20th century society has damaged the traditional social fabric which functioned as the institutional base of intergenerational continuity, for example, through the family. This has led to the erosion of natural institutionalised responsibility. At the same time, there has been a corresponding strong tendency toward glorification of the self and personal preferences, so that it is very difficult to expect the natural representation of future citizens. While the shortsighted interests of the living generation have dominated the political scene, democratic politics have systematically become more insensitive to the interests of future generations. Accordingly it seems to be necessary to strengthen the political position of future generations by promoting an artificial-political institutionalisation.

The first proposal for restructuring the political discourse by introducing a theory of justice and of moral community is opposed to the ideological glorification of the self. This position must be clearly articulated by an institution or organisation in order to be politically effective and meaningful. From this point of view we have to reconsider institutional mechanisms in democratic politics. In respect to the problems of future generations NGOs have already established a strong enough position to influence decision making of some public bodies on domestic as well as on global levels. Both their strong and weak points seem to result from their voluntary base. Because of being of voluntary associations they can take action very aggressively even against the state, but for the same reason are necessarily limited to a position representing non-official interests in society. What I would like to propose is to establish an official institution representing interests of future generations to counter balance the over emphasis on the short-term interests of current generations. People working for the institution would take on the role of acting as the trustees of future generations, rather than acting as a group of individuals. The problem is not whether we can find citizens totally devoted to the problems of future generations, but rather how we can arrange the institutional framework in such a way as to ensure that this specific function is discharged. Hayek has proposed two assemblies to deal with conflicts between short-term and long-term interests. One of these would be called a governmental assembly engaged with short-term demands and dominated by party politics just as contemporary parliament is. The other would be a legislative assembly consisting of people not committed to any political party who would focus more on the long-term interests of society.[15] Even though my basic interest is different from Hayek's, this kind of differentiation of representative functions seems to be suggestive. While traditionally this differentiation has been discussed in terms of the division of powers such as legislative/executive/judiciary or central/local, my proposal is that the division of representations between current and future generations should be newly introduced. The traditional differentiation should be supplemented by this new system of checks and balances, and public policy should be influenced indirectly by it. Just like other systems of checks and balances this new one also would be helpful in defending rights and interests.

Two issues are to be discussed in relation to this proposal. The first question is over who will choose the representative of future generations since the unborn cannot choose their representatives. As illustrated by Hayek there is no problem in the living generation choosing them as trustees of future generations provided that an effective framework is first established. The new division of functions is to be understood as a measure to correct the asymmetrical nearsightedness of the democratic process rather than to have the different interests of future generations represented directly in the political process. The main point is not who would choose the representatives but rather whether this reform of the political process would be achieved by establishing a trustee of the interests of future generations. In other words if the old political system is functioning fairly without provoking any serious intergenerational conflicts, the new division of function would not be necessary. The second question concerns the power and character of such trustees. I am not necessarily of the opinion that the trustees should form a large assembly such as Hayek's legislative assembly. A kind of ombudsman can function as the trustees. The main issue is not its size but its quality of power. It is possible to give this body of trustees power to exercise the veto or to intervene directly in the political process on behalf of future generations: its main function, however, would be to warn against decisions which might seriously damage the interests of future generations. The means of invoking these powers might be 'a climate of concern, guilt, or shame – the traditional way in which the weak have mobilised the strong in their defence'[16] rather than an exercise of power in a strict meaning. The trustees should mobilise the intergenerational moral instinct by appealing to the sense of shame and guilt and persuade the current generation to reconsider their decision-making. The new institution could restructure the market place by pushing a new type of public discourse. If we try to characterise their status more clearly, the old difference between censor and magistratus seems to be informative. While the magistratus exercises power in a strict meaning, especially enforcement, the censor is engaged in persuasion and its main sanction is to shame.[17] In fact the glorification of the self is to be described as an embodiment of shamelessness.

Here I have no intention to discuss particular policies and measures to be implemented for the interests of future generations.[18] My discussion concentrates on more basic issues. The democratisation of politics in the 20th century has solved the problem of participation, but the democratic regime has been enforced to face a number of serious issues which have been brought by industrialisation, modernisation and democratisation itself. What we can do is not to provide a comprehensive list of measures to be taken, but a necessary step to check unreasonable politics. In order to make the first move toward a more reasonable democracy, we have to start with keen recognition of its limitations and to fight against them continuously. The problems of politics for future generations provide us with an extremely good opportunity not only to review contemporary democratic politics but also to consider how it can be revitalised. If we incorporate the meanings of fundamental changes brought in this century into our political thinking, the problems to be coped with in this context might well be more challenging in the long-term than a number of wars and revolutions we have already faced in this century.

Notes

1. Paul Kennedy, *Preparing for the Twenty-First Century*, 1993, p.29.
2. Hannah Arendt, *The Human Condition,* 1958, p.322.
3. Eric Hobsbawn, *The Age of Extremes,* 1994, p.339.
4. Ibid., pp.341-2.
5. Robert Reich, *The Work of Nations,* 1991.
6. Daniel Bell, 'The World and the United States in 2013', *Deadalus,* vol.116, pp. 13-14.
7. James G. March/Johan P. Olsen, *Democratic Governance,* 1995, pp.98-9.
8. Andrew Hurrell, 'A Crisis of Ecological Viability? Global Environmental Change and the Nation State', in John Dunn (ed.), *Contemporary Crisis of the Nation State,* 1995.
9. For example, Brian Doherty/Marius de Geus(eds.), *Democracy, Rights and Citizenship,* 1996.
10. Marius de Geus, 'The Ecological Restructuring of the State', in ibid.
11. John Rawls, *A Theory of Justice,* 1971, p. 285.
12. Ibid., p. 523.

13. Martin P. Golding, 'Obligations to Future Generations', in: Ernest Partridge (ed.), *Responsibility to Future Generations,* 1981.

14. Ernest Partridge, 'Who Cares About The Future', in ibid.

15. Friedrich von Hayek, *New Studies in Philosophy, Politics, Economics, and History of Ideas,* 1985.

16. March/Olsen, op. cit., p. 99.

17. Jean Bodin, *Les six livres de la République,* 1983, pp. 849-50.

18. For example, Edith Brown Weiss, *In Fairness to Future Generations,* 1989.

10

Self-identity in a Postmodern Age

Takatoshi Imada

1. Drifting Identity

We are now living just before the turn of the century, at a time when advanced industrial society is undergoing revolutionary change. Globalisation due to the electronic media revolution and industrial activities which add high value are undermining the hitherto seemingly solid basis of society. We are forced to respond to an unprecedented reality and to define ourselves in various living environments. What is called the third information revolution, after the invention of language and printing technology, will result in a situation in which virtuality and reality are intermingled in every aspect of life. We have lost definite values to rely upon and are required to process meaningless information amid a flood of symbols which have lost all correspondence with entities. Under such circumstances, is it possible to establish a self-identity, or can identity itself exist?

Identity is linked with the concept of the sameness of self: ourselves as opposed to others, subjectivity, individuality and so on. What is common to these terms is the image of a unified self. In other words, identity has been used as a concept to show the way of existence of the self integrated through a certain standard of value. As Erikson put it, identity is our confidence in the process of ego development in the framework of a specific social reality, or is an answer to the question, 'Who am I?'[1]

According to conventional modern thinking, the concept of the self refers to a subject which has a personal and preserving identity. To be a human being is to have a self or an internal identity that remains unchanged throughout life. For many years, it has been considered a tragedy for both individuals and society as a whole to lack a unified self or a definite feeling of identity. However, such a viewpoint is now dubious for the following reasons:

1) If we have a fixed identity in a rapidly changing society, we will risk disaster or a lack of adaptability. Therefore, we need to have a flexible identity.

2) Since society is becoming increasingly heterogeneous in terms of sense of values and lifestyles, a limited identity will restrict people's social interaction and the development of individuals.

3) In addition, since a limited identity is a reflection of a lack of social experience, people should be encouraged to play a variety of roles.

Such a viewpoint suggests that the self is always situational. A self will not be unified completely or preserved forever. While having the cores of personality and identity, everyone has a set of selves for different roles and spectators. In previous discussions of the situational self, however, the self has been regarded as situational only in a limited sense, having rarely been seen as being formed or reformed according to the situation. A self is a unified and preserving entity in a sense, and is generally regarded as being maintained throughout life as a continuous chain of memories, and having a coherent identity.

In the present diverse and fluid situation, it is difficult for us to have a unified and definite identity. We cannot find a stable place to which we regress ourselves and are forced to live with a drifting identity. One of the causes of this situation is the coming of the consumer society, in which slogans to express individuality are for sale and we have been bombarded with ever-changing images of the self. The conventional self has been subjected to concentrated attack by images of the self offered to encourage consumption and has lost its substantial form. Most people have assimilated external identities into their apparently subjective selves and changed their own images.

As information media progress in the future, a hyper-reality that fits neither reality nor unreality in the conventional sense will repeatedly emerge and die off. When multifarious fragmented signs generated by virtual reality and hyper-media start to proliferate, it will become impossible to maintain a definite self. Self-identity will become fluid. People will be at the mercy of fragmented signs whose meanings are disorganised by the flood of information. We will hardly be able to survive, if we obstinately cling to the establishment of a subjective self.

This paper discusses the above problem regarding self-identity in a context of social transformation toward postmodernity. Although the appropriate term to describe the specific situation encountered in the present society is still controversial, here I use the term postmodernity to refer to characteristics which differ from those which are generally ascribed to modernity.

2. Fluctuation of Modernity

People have lost a stable place in which to anchor their consciousness and have to depend on a drifting identity. As the cause of this phenomenon, we can cite the shift of the social situation toward postmodernity. Traditional modern society sought human beings who did not ignore self evaluation and who made ceaseless efforts to attain their targets. People were able to construct self-identity by relying on this standard model. With the coming of postindustrial and information societies, however, 'grand narratives' such as emancipation, progress, enlightenment and universal truth lost reliability, and the baselessness and contingency of modern society were seen to cause identities to fluctuate.

One of the characteristics common to theories of postmodernity is insistence on the collapse of the *transparency of representation* or direct correspondence between representation and entity. Such scepticism causes decentralisation, multi-dimensionality and drifting not only of the self but of all identities as well, because identity which consists of creation and interpretation of representation becomes groundless, if it does not drop its anchor with a definite entity. When the representation is not a reflection of the entity, identity will be constructed independently of the entity. This is the essential problem of self-identity in the postmodern age.

What is modernity?

Before discussing postmodernity, we must define the modern age. What is modernity? What are its features? I define modernity abstractly as the process of establishing a society with *function primacy* that attaches importance to efficiency and rationality. The concept of function primacy means primarily orientation towards ensuring performance with control, or construction of a society with a *control-performance* scheme. According to this definition, it is possible to assess systematically most of the features of modernity such as technocracy (technology-ism) and industrialism, as well as the rationalisation process of the society.

There are a number of theories for defining modernity, such as those that regard it as the process of the penetration of technocracy; the rationalisation of society as symbolised by bureaucracy; the penetration of mechanised factory production and industrialisation where its effect pervades the society and culture; and democratisation to realise freedom and equality. Each of these definitions is correct, but none can be used to assess modernity systematically. Even when democratisation is regarded as the essence of the modern age, for example, it does not explain industrialisation, or vice versa.

Using the above abstract definition, however, we can comprehensively grasp modernity. Technocracy just means seeking efficiency and rationality. Bureaucracy means promoting the rationalisation of jobs and personnel affairs. Industrialisation means mass production with efficient factory labour and mechanical technologies. Although democracy is apparently beyond the definition, the idea of function includes the logic of democratisation. The functionalist idea implies the motto of universally adopting human resources and treating them according to performance (the principle of achievement), irrespective of family background, sex, race or other ascriptions. Establishing a society of function primacy, therefore, includes the principle of equal opportunity. Although democracy includes fundamental human rights, social rights and other principles that cannot be deduced directly from the functionalist idea, ensuring and protecting human rights is implied by it if we understand that they are indispensable for the functional operation of society and the rights are guaranteed for that purpose.

In fact, it is no exaggeration to say that what modern democracy has attained is a partial realisation of equal opportunity. Democracy in the modern age that aims at realising freedom and equality has often been subject to the function primacy, or has been recognised only to the extent that it does not compromise efficiency or rationality. This is because, once efficiency has fallen, causing economic stagnation, economic activities which reduce welfare or ignore human rights often prevail. In the modern age, democracy should have controlled industrialism, bureaucracy and technocracy and restrained runaway efficiency and rationality. However, the truth is that different 'isms' ran in different directions causing chaos beyond the control of the carter, democracy. In practice, therefore, the essence of modernity is to construct a society with function primacy that respects efficiency and rationality, whatever its ideal may be.

Consequently, the above definition of modernity covers the broadest range. This is in precise accord with the way that modernism is understood in architecture, where modernism is equivalent to functionalism. Modern architecture is equal to functionalist architecture, or an idea of thoroughly eliminating waste, play and decoration. The well-known propositions of modern architecture, 'Form (Structure) is subordinate to function' and 'Beauty (Meaning) is in function', precisely express the concept of function primacy.[2] In other words, the essence of modernity is to functionalise the social formation (structure) and culture (meaning).

Fading function primacy

Since the 1980s, the term *fluctuation* has been popular. Fluctuation in this context means undermining or compromising the basis of things, or a phenomenon that does not fit or cannot be treated using the established framework or mechanisms.[3] This popularity, which was largely caused by stalemated modernism, indicates that phenomena unsuited to the ideas of modernity are taking place everywhere. The term was not heard during rapid economic growth, when the same phenomena were called deviations, perturbations or protests. They were undesirable for sustaining orderly prosperity and, therefore, had to be controlled in order for the equilibrium to be maintained. In other words, there were definite standard models of people and society when the economy was growing rapidly. The same phenomena, however, are now called fluctuations. This means that conventional standard models no longer fit the situation. Furthermore, the standard models themselves are also fluctuating.

Modern society has pursued the realisation of an affluent society by trying to improve productivity, by valuing efficiency and rationality and creating growth-oriented control devices. We now have innumerable terms related to function, such as efficiency, rationalisation, management, control, plan, optimisation, productivity, equilibrium, growth, development and so on. People can think only by using their own vocabulary and ideas. Phenomena outside these frameworks are regarded as cumbersome or undesirable. In fact, phenomena that deviate from the functionalist idea have been degraded by being called perturbations, deviations, resistance or noise. They are merely the objects of control from the viewpoint of modernity.

However, the coming of an affluent society has caused people's values to diversify and their lifestyles to become personalised. Diversification and individuation represent a state in which behaviours and values cannot be decoded precisely using the predetermined standard models. A situation in which diversification and individuation are excessive incubates a fluctuating society. It also reflects the fact that people have become suspicious of social and personal values which indicate preference toward *function primacy.* Today, people tend to think that they cannot obtain true happiness merely by pursuing efficient and rational methods. Some people have become disillusioned with the rigorous efforts required. Most people are doubtful of the point of their efforts: whether they have intrinsic worth or promote enrichment of life. For that very reason, diversions, playing with difference and other postmodern phenomena have become fashionable.

Promoting social functions based on efficiency and rationality is not all that people do. Importantly, they also create new lifestyles and cultures by seeking and questioning the meaning of life. Conventional modern society, constructed mainly to pursue function, has lost momentum as it has failed to reveal respect for the need for meaning fulfilment.

Postmodern scenes

Postmodernisation is a movement to reinstate, from the viewpoint of existential life, the semantic space dismantled by modernity. The first common use of the term postmodern occurred in the fields of architecture and design, starting with criticism of the architectural modernism that pursued efficiency and rationality by eliminating as much unnecessary decoration and waste as possible. Postmodern architecture triggered a movement to adopt playful, symbolic expressions and free conceptions, as opposed to modern architecture which sought, to an extreme, to eliminate decoration and waste. Such a style spread beyond the boundaries of architecture to philosophy and cultural sciences.

Lyotard, who resembles the founder of a religion with respect to postmodernity in cultural sciences, insists that we are now in an age which declares the end of modern 'grand narratives'. He says that the present situation promotes mistrust of grand narratives, such as realising freedom and equality, aiming for revolution and emancipation, or seeking consensus and legitimacy.[4] Postmodernism denies efficient totalisation by systems and assimilation by consensus. It is based on the working of local and minor heterogeneity and the 'paralogy' (i.e., anti-logical imagination) of differing which is not mutually commensurated. In the background of postmodernism is mistrust of the ideals that have supported modern society, in particular the progressive thought of the enlightenment.

Regardless of whether the field is architecture, design, philosophy or the humanities, what is common to all forms of postmodern thought is that it incorporates criticism of modern functionalist reasoning. Modern society, which is extremely biased toward function, has colonised the search for the meaning of life which is an important human activity. It is true that modern society has effectively made use of people in terms of function. However, it could also be said that modern society has wastefully used people up in terms of meaning. The rise of postmodern thought indicates a recognition of the significance of symbolic meanings, uncontaminated by function.

In modern society, symbolic meaning, unrelated to function, is a subjectivistic, personal and floating phenomenon. It has been significant in art and literature, but has been regarded as of secondary importance for the operation of society and was relegated from the public field to private life. Since the coming of the affluent society, however, meaning has started to assert itself in relation to human existence. This is reflected in the tendency to respect self-actualisation, the value of life and personal decisions about lifestyle. These do not necessarily have correspondence with any entity, and are therefore related to the construction of identity by means of representation without transparency.

It may be an exaggeration to say that modernity has ignored the meaning of life, in particular the issue of representation which is not necessarily transparent. However, it is undeniable that modernity has at least functionalised this issue. A functionalised meaning is representation treated as a design to display utility, convenience and efficiency or as a symbol to maintain order. It is a meaning subordinate to function and not a logic specific to itself. It is nothing but a meaning 'colonialised' by function. One of the most important points in postmodernity is to insist that the aspect of symbolic meaning be recognised as a public factor as important as structure and function.

There are no alternatives for modern society but to cross the border of *function primacy* because it has pursued modernity to an extreme. Modern society succeeded in deconstructing medieval society, in which the idea of structure had primacy and which maintained patterns by rules, through introducing the functionalist concept in addition to structure. The main activity principle in medieval society was to process things according to predetermined stereotyped patterns. It was a society in which rules dominated people in the name of God. To break through these limits, modern society introduced functionalist ideas to improve performance by control. By doing so, modern civilisation invented a loop of structure and function as a device to construct a society. As fluctuations which do not fit the loop have started to occur frequently, however, new problems of the difference and meaning mechanism have arisen. The area of transfunctional and nonstructural symbolic meaning which surpasses function but is still at a nonstructural stage, has started to deviate from the modern stage of structure and function loop, and has caused postmodern fluctuations. This process is staging postmodern scenarios. At the moment, however, postmodernity features nothing but pastiche and schizoid tendencies. In postmodern scenarios, self-identity has changed to become a collage of sign-values of a variety of commodities offered by consumer capitalism and increasingly consists of fragile fragments that lack depth, entity and coherence.

It is easy to say that self-identity will fragment and disappear through the advance of the information society and consumerisation. However, such an expression is dependent on the modern idea that fluctuation can be viewed only with negative connotations, and does not reflect positively on postmodernity. Fluctuating identity does not necessarily mean collapse of identity. Postmodernity will not take shape unless it reflects a new type of identity.

3. Hyper-reality and Self-actualisation

The current advancement of information technology is intended to construct an institutional apparatus to enhance social control and efficiently transmit, accumulate and process symbols. Modern society has rationalised and improved the efficiency of processing materials and human resources. This thrust has now penetrated the realm of symbols mentioned in the first sentence. The resultant greater efficiency makes life easier in many ways. What used to consume time no longer does to such an extent. Options have increased for people. Through the videotex system, for example, people at home can shop and make reservations for hotels, transportation and theatres. People can transfer funds through banks any time from their homes, without being restricted by the business hours of banks.

Rising importance of the difference motive

With the advancement of information technology, modern society will complete an unprecedented high-level and soft control system. If not only materials and personnel but also symbols are contaminated by functional rationality, social integration will lose its power. However, people are not so simple as to unconditionally accept such rationalisation and control.

People nowadays, compared to those in the past, are less motivated by deficiency. For the functional mechanism to work effectively, people must be dominated by deficiency motives and stung with desires. Today, however, *difference motives* , such as self-actualisation and the authenticity and quality of life, related to symbolic meanings rather than functions,[5] are arising to add value to life.

Most of the need classifications offered during the postwar period assumed deficiency motives. Typical of these is the hierarchical model of needs presented by Maslow.[6] This theory holds that the satisfaction of needs shifts from basic to higher level needs, or that higher level needs will not become apparent until those of the lower levels are satisfied. Physiological needs to eat or sleep come first, followed by needs for safety, belongingness, and approval. At the top is the need for self-actualisation. Since the need for self-actualisation has the highest level according to this theory, deficiency motives do not work in seeking the next stage. If there is a higher level deficiency need, the functional mechanism is effective. But, as the need for self-actualisation is the highest level of human needs, deficiency motives become irrelevant. Although deficiency motives still exist, people are rather motivated by individualistic differences.

To seek differences is to realise a self different from the former self and/or others. The superficial embodiment of this is the coming of the consumer society in which people express their personal selves using the sign-values of commodities. Such a motivation does not perhaps go so far as a genuine seeking for self-actualisation, but nevertheless, the difference motive at least surpasses the deficiency motive. This suggests that people have become extremely sensitive to differences. Extreme sensitivity to differences means that symbolic meaning is held in greater esteem. A major act in pursuing and fulfilling meanings is to express one's self. For a meaning to emerge, moreover, a difference distinguishing it from other things must exist. Individuation and diversification are two terms which emphasise this difference. Under a difference motive, it is important to extract a variety of differences in one's self and interrelate them in order to express an individuality.

Modern society has continued to disorganise semantic space under the pressure of function primacy. With advances in information technology, an enormous volume of functional information to control materials and people will surge through society and will expand a blank world of lost meaning, where people feel like wanderers forcibly isolated not only from others but also from themselves. To recover the lost semantic space, therefore, people seek *another self* in pursuit of the meaning of life.[7]

Dominance of Simulacra

In the latter half of the 1970s, Baudrillard expressed the view that, today, all systems are fluctuating in uncertainty. Reality is absorbed by hyper-reality or codes and simulations. The principle of simulation is replacing the old principle of reality to control us. Compliance with purpose has disappeared. Models generate us. Ideologies no longer exist. What exist are *simulacra* alone, generated by an operation of simulations.[8] In an advanced information society, reality will be absorbed in the hyper-reality generated by codes and simulations. Information (representation) which does not directly correspond to the entity is a sort of bubble and smacks of fiction. Such an aspect of information is a simulacrum, a term for all representations with no correspondence to an entity.

In the world of simulacra, pseudo-reality consisting of representation without transparency is dominant. Distinctions between original and copy and between reality and unreality become vague. The essentially fictitious is taken as reality. In extreme cases, reality is recognised only in fiction. This hyper-reality piles up fictitious realities to create multiple layers. The space composed of symbolic signs abstracts usefulness and functionality, where insane recognition of reality flies around. Consequently, concrete realities such as 'what human beings should be' and 'what life should be' are replaced with a 'difference as image' unrelated to reality. Thus a movement is brought about to pursue a 'difference as sign' or an image of a human being which does not exist anywhere.

This paradoxical world of hyper-reality is filled with the experience of *ilinks* (dizziness or the whirl of the brain), a play typified by Caillois.[9] It is an eschatological aspect of contemporary controlled society. People existing there are no longer *Homo Sapiens* (intellectual animals) but *Homo Demens* (insane animals). To regard the Homo Demens image of the human being as unintelligent, incomprehensible or eventually controlled, as did Baudrillard, follows the viewpoint of modern rationalism. Baudrillard, who has an extremely nihilistic perception of contemporary society, is keen to describe its eschatological aspect. Nevertheless, the new space explored by high-tech media is indispensable for humanity's future and will be a frontier for next-generation industries. Nihilistic criticism of this fictitiousness does not yield fruit.

Even if the world of hyper-reality is paradoxical to modern intelligence, it will make another reality indispensable for human life in the twenty-first century. It is more important to question what human beings will become or how society will be constructed in the future. That the self-image in postmodern society will be distracted by simulacra, as Baudrillard suggests, is doubtful. It is certain, however, that at least the subjective self which has been problematic in modern society will fluctuate to form another image of self.

Another self

Simulacra with no distinction between reality and unreality will be formed to repeat infinite emergence and extinction. It will then become difficult to organise selves according to a specific value principle. Selves will no longer form distinctive shells.

As a case symbolising the image of the self in postmodern society, it is interesting to cite the story of a person who experienced virtual reality using a remote control robot. The robot, which precisely models the upper part of the human body, is designed to reproduce exactly the motions of the operator's neck, hands and arms. Its eyes are a three-dimensional camera. When its hands grip an item, the resistance is conveyed to the operator. An operator sitting three metres from the robot gripped a small bar and inserted it into a hole, tightened bolts, and picked up soft items and placed them in line. While playing in such a manner, the operator casually looked to his side and discovered a figure sitting in a chair and surrounded by a number of devices with cables hanging from its head and arms. It took several minutes for the operator to recognise that he himself was that figure. He said, 'I had transformed myself into the robot. The real myself seen by the robot's eyes was strange enough. Seeing my figure from the eyes of a robot or another myself gave a shock to my identity'. This is a story of a person who has become a robot in virtual reality and is shocked when he encounters himself in reality, or a story of a person who is surprised at experiencing *another self.* Schizophrenics sometimes say, 'I cannot look away from myself even for a moment. If I look away, I will be dissected into pieces. I am always tense. Otherwise, other people will enter me and I will be lost'. The story of the robot operator is similar to the loss of self experienced by schizophrenics. When we have a plurality of selves, we will live in a similar world.

If a virtual reality prevails, we may lose compatibility with the plurality of selves. Which is the real subject, the self who controls a plurality of selves, or the plurality of dissected selves? Whichever it is, the image of the self maintaining a firm subjectivity must dissipate. We may possibly believe that we are nothing but a figure circulating among a plurality of selves. The task of confirming the place to which we regress ourselves will become less important.

The characteristic image of the self in a society where *difference motives* are dominant is not the paranoid type but the schizoid type. To have the power of self-control is the condition for a paranoid type character not to become morbid, but the corresponding condition for a schizoid type character is not yet known. It may be the power of *self-editorship,* editing the chaotic state of fragmented differences and generating new meaning. The power of self-control must shift to the power of self-editorship. Without this shift, the result is paranoiac schizoid symptoms.

A typical example is 'PC kids'. It is not correct to refer to PC kids as autistic types. They are information citizens who experience *ilinks* by wandering from the display into the infinite world of the computer network. They do not expect efficiency from PC communications, but, on the contrary, unconsciously try to overturn the modern values of efficiency and convenience. Moreover, they have overturned meanings by dismantling the polarities of the framework of thought – such as fact and fiction, centre and periphery, intelligence and sensitivity, and work and play – established by modernity. Such behaviour is schizoid, but absorption into it is paranoiac.

In modern society, many people feel anxious about what they should do, unless they are given goals or tasks to attain or accomplish. There are no predetermined goals and tasks in the actions of meaning fulfilment. What exists there is only a process of creating new meaning through differing from orthodoxy or tradition. *Nomads* who repeat trial-and-error processes in unknown fields, or people of the schizoid type, are more suited to such circumstances than those of the paranoid type or efficient or diligent people. To be preoccupied in meaning fulfilment (the pursuit of truth, morality and beauty), however, means to be paranoiac. Therefore, people will not be able to thrive in the future unless they are double-minded people, paranoiac and schizoid at the same time. People will not be able to stick stubbornly to the establishment of a subjective self as before.

4. Self in Chaos

Self-identity will be chaotic until the modern self is dismantled and a new image of self is established. The chaotic self image may be perverse, distracting or morbid for conscientious people at the moment. Such confusion usually takes place in a period of transformation.

Perverse self-actualisation

Fetish adherence to materials in consumption affects communication, reversing the normal order of preference between object and language. What Ohira calls the *Monogatari* syndrome indicates this situation.[10] *Monogatari* is a Japanese word which normally means narratives. Since 'mono' means commodities or materials and 'gatari' means narrations, he uses Monogatari as a term to indicate the act of expressing selves through material commodities. The Monogatari syndrome is, therefore, related to the mental disease of people who seek self-actualisation by means of commodities.

Typical Monogatari patients cannot explain their acquaintances well. Once the subject has been directed to clothing, decorations or other personal effects, however, they suddenly become able to describe people vividly. They are fluent when material objects are available to mediate discourse. In associating with other people, they use consumer goods or treat people as consumer goods to avoid collisions of animated feelings. They confirm their identities by what they wear. They can express or personalise themselves only by means of material objects.

The Monogatari syndrome is a mental disease which appeared in Japan during the bubble economy when consumer society was at its peak. Unlike a society in which production is given priority, the consumer society expedites not so much the acquisition of low-priced, good-quality products as the expression of our selves using material objects as signs, or representing our selves with consumer goods. This situation of the consumer society is convenient to promptly diversify values, personalise lifestyles and actualise selves. When actual definitions of diversification and individuation have not been established, it is natural that people want to establish them quickly and easily. Thus, the belief that material objects, signs and meanings are equal generates a self-actualisation that relies on consumer goods.

Self-actualisation relying on consumer goods often causes disturbance in personal communications. One illustration of the Monogatari syndrome is the story of a 25-year-old man working for an electrical equipment manufacturing company, who visited a doctor with symptoms of neurotic diarrhoea. He could not understand what his problem was. The doctor asked him about his work and things in his life, but could not obtain definite answers. Once the topic changed to clothing, however, the Monogatari syndrome started. That business suits repress people's individuality was discussed. When his girlfriend came up in the conversation, he suddenly started a stream of Monogatari that was not understood except by experts in this field:

> 'I myself was deeply absorbed in fashion when I was a student, greatly affected by her. She was one of my classmates at senior high school. Her father was a manager in a trading company. She was certainly a daughter of a well-to-do family. She said, 'However fashionable you are, Poshboy cannot compete with Byblos'. It would have been allowed, if I had been a student. When I started to work for a company, I bought Armani suits, Coal Haan shoes and Nicole neckties. I had a Heuer watch, but I spent all my bonus pay to buy an Omega watch. I used an Ace attaché case for work and a Hunting World or Yoshida bag when I was off duty.'[11]

He might intend to express himself tactfully with plenty of brand names such as Byblos and Poshboy which sound like alien words to ordinary people. A consumer society features increased consumption of products that are not guaranteed to be useful; consumers consume these goods to integrate themselves with the image and meaning given by the commodities. In the case of people with Monogatari syndrome, however, sign-values have become separated from commodities and symbolise individual persons. They incarnate themselves or have a self in society only through the existence of symbolised signs. Only through this pseudo-meaning is there any ground for existence and self-actualisation. This may be acceptable, if people attain self-actualisation in this way. If they fall into mental disease instead, however, it is meaningless and futile.

The final destination of the information society is a world of hyper-reality where even human beings change to signs. This world will be dominated by self-purposed signs or *simulacra* which constitute a society every time the necessity arises. Absolute values or the guarantee of fundamental existence will not be present in this world. It will become increasingly difficult to apply dualistic norms such as superior or inferior, good or bad, or true or false.

Contemporary festival space

Self-actualisation has hitherto been seen in terms of bringing the subjective self close to the self expected by society, family, company and friends, in order to unify the self.[12] An age will possibly come, however, when people pursue *another self* in an area different from both the subjective self and the expected self. One phenomenon that predicts such a movement is the *Comics-market,* or what is normally called the *Comiket,* which is becoming increasingly popular among young people.

Comics are now one of the most powerful media in Japan.[13] In the world of comics are coterie magazines which parody original stories. Writers respectfully borrow characters from original stories and develop their own narratives. They extract favourite characters and elements from interesting animated cartoons and comics and generate new characters, relationships and plots. They gradually disorganise the original tales and lose their own stories as well.

Comikets are physical gatherings of people and materials for the exhibition, trading and direct sale of these coterie magazines. Comiket is not only a place for circulating such coterie magazines, but also a space where their contents are three-dimensional, or a space of hyper-reality. In this space, people, media and comics exist with identical weight.[14]

In Comiket, people do not use their real names but refer to one another with the names of characters in animated cartoons and comics or imaginary names which do not exist anywhere else. Many participants enjoy costume-play. Disguising themselves as characters in a cartoon or comic, they sell coterie magazines and act out specific performances. However, they do not pursue laughter or satire. For example, a person may hold a placard manifesting 'Sanrizuka's downright fight' in one hand, and a coterie magazine from the Peach Girl series in the other. Why does he appear to be making a protest? He is not appealing to others at all. He is expressing his self outside real space by erasing his subjective and expected self, and has transformed to something alien by connecting himself to the placard and coterie magazine. In Comiket space, there are individual figures which disorganise the meaning, composed of morality, common sense and manners that supports everyday life. However, this space is not chaotic. If it were chaotic, it could not have survived from 1975 until today. This space has succeeded in incorporating chaos as a type of order.

In Comiket, languages have been released from logic and have recovered their inherent poetic character. This space is exclusively composed of plays that have freed themselves from everyday life. Not only language but all categories of existence and signs are at play. All images are becoming a reality. From common and rationalistic viewpoints, perhaps nothing is more meaningless. However, such a view is not correct. Comiket space is meaningful, because it is meaningless. If signs are unified and controlled by the rules, semantic space will collapse. Meaning will never be unified. When it is unified, it will die. When languages and signs float without the entity, they recover the features of play and activate a semantic space.

In this way, Comiket exists as a hyper-reality where signs float without entities. Individual participants do not have an entity, either. Selves are created only in relation to floating signs. To acquire the evidence of existence, participants plunge a fragment of soul into the craziness and intoxication that envelope Comiket. This is a realisation of *another self* in the area which has eliminated the modern self.

The case of Comics-markets or the contemporary festival space is very specific and not universal. However, symptoms of a new order are always to be found in specific and extraordinary phenomena. I think

Comics-markets are displaying a power beyond the functionalist idea and predetermined routine structures. While modern selves are collapsing, a movement to pursue the ideal of another self is to be seen there.

5. Toward a Theory of Postmodern Identity

Modern society is already shifting towards postmodernity, while new requirements for self-identity are increasing among people. In Japan and other advanced countries, people have been released from material necessities to a large extent. Most things regarded as necessary are not held as such because of deficiency but rather have become the objects of selection. A typical case is, as discussed above, the coming of the consumer society which reacts to the cultural aspects of consumer goods, by regarding them as signs, differences and meanings.

From having to being

Self-identity in the postmodern age is not based on *Having,* but, rather, has become based on *Being.* Such a transformation cannot be coped with using the idea of function primacy, but requires that of meaning fulfilment. Function primacy is effective for pursuing material abundance, but the present functional mechanism will lose its validity in the postmodern situation where the production and distribution of information and cultural resources have become a major source of value and the phase of identity is shifting from possession to existence. This is because *Being* is related to a type of representation that does not necessarily reflect the entity and is concerned more with symbolic meanings, while *Having* can be described in terms of function. Regarding the context of information, the problem is that whereas functional information reduces uncertainty and thereby controls the entity, meaning information, on the other hand, constitutes existence as a representation without transparency.

In *Nomads of the Present,* Melucci, discussing a new social movement in postmaterial society, expressed the increasing requirements for new freedom as a change from the 'right to property' to the 'right to existence'.[15] In the background of social movements until the present have been requirements for economic rights and rights of citizenship.

Although we are still in such an age, a new horizon toward democracy is being exploited by appeals to meaningful existence (life) in the fields of birth, death, disease and coexistence with the environment, which together form the basis of human life.

Rationalisation and system control promoted in modern society have penetrated not only production and administration but also other areas which were formerly out of control. Emotional relations, sex, health, birth and death are all subject to control by medical or administrative organisations. In many cases, whether a person lives or dies depends on external factors beyond the individual's control. This can be seen in the moral issues surrounding cases of euthanasia, people being maintained by life-support machines, death due to overwork, troubles caused by the dosage and abuse of drugs, diseases related to pollution and troubles due to stress. The right to live is itself subject to control. Therefore, freedom of existence is an important subject.

New social movements include demands related to such problems. Most advocate environmental preservation, informed consent in medical treatment and opposition to nuclear power plants, but do not require sharing the gains of production. They do not rise up to demand distribution or redistribution of wealth. They are rarely routed through political parties or labour unions. Social movements appear at the citizen level centring on issues of existence and lifestyle.

Both the shift from the 'freedom to have' to the 'freedom to be' and from the 'right to equality' to the 'right to difference' are important factors that decisively determine what self-identity should be in the future. To guarantee the freedom to be, it is necessary, now more than ever, to recognise the 'signifying process' of individuals and groups and make it autonomous and free from outside pressure, because significant existence is to express the self as it is by confirming and affirming it with meanings. If this process becomes the object of control or management, the freedom of existence will not be guaranteed.

Expression of meanings requires a difference that distinguishes it from others. It is important to confirm and express an individuality by interrelating various differences. The modern functionalist idea enhances homogeneity and certainty by processing heterogeneity and uncertainties. It also encourages effective decision-making and actions toward goal-attainment and moreover tries to reduce differences as much as possible through standardisation. By doing so, however, it often entrusts confirmation of the meaning of existence to external society and makes it an object of control.

Meanings are sought in the relation of life or living with the world and generated through its articulation. Articulation brings some distinction into the vast and chaotic world. Through distinction, phenomena and objects are given a difference and sameness at the same time, and thus acquire meaning. In other words, meanings are the way the world should be, as experienced as a set of articulated phenomena and objects.

If the way of relation of life to the world is a meaning, there exists a power that relates oneself to the world. Namely, meanings are stuffed with the power of life. This is close to what the philosopher Nietzsche called *The Will to Power.* [16] To show the will to power, it is not sufficient only to describe society as a functional organisation from the viewpoint of adaptation to environments. Such an idea does not ensure the paramount activeness of human beings. Defining human beings according to their adaptability overlooks not only the essence of life and the will to power but also the power to give the world a new interpretation and determine new directions.[17] In short, the power of human beings cannot be expressed through adaptation to environments by means of functionalist ideas.

This reasoning can also be applied to the way self-identity should be. Today, society is highly differentiated into multiple functions diversifying the organisations to which people belong and upon which identity relies. Fragments of signs now devoid of meaning proliferate. Lifestyles are subject to the pressure of excessive choice. It is becoming difficult to state continuously and convincingly what we are. Under such circumstances, we will lose ourselves, if we have nothing but a flexible identity adapting ourselves to environmental changes.

As discussed above, in the postmodern situation where representations without transparency are dominant, we must actualise our selves by seeking *another self* through floating in society and editing the image of the self whenever necessary. However, the pastiche and schizoid character, specific to postmodernity, often leads to morbid phenomena of the fragmentation of identity and of homelessness. To continually confirm ourselves under drifting identities, we must maintain unification through fragmentation and coherence through change. To address such problems, the viewpoint of self-organisation of identity is most appropriate.

Self-organisation without a master plan

Self-organisation refers to a system which is able to reconstruct itself while interacting with the environment. The essence of self-organisation is to change itself relying on its own mechanism. What is important is that it can transform itself without being affected by the environment. Therefore, self-organisation is not environment-decisive or environment-adaptive, but self-decisive and self-adaptive. Such a nature is logically related to the problem of self-reference and sociologically related to the problem of self-reflexion. Moreover, self-organisation requires a cause for internal changes and seeks this in fluctuation. A fluctuation is a phenomenon that does not fit the existing framework or cannot be coped with by the existing conception. This is sociologically equivalent to deviation or differing from the orthodoxy.[18]

In contemporary complex society, it is not possible to seek the basis of identity in a specific model or collective body. Instead, it is necessary to have the internal ability to ceaselessly transform ourselves or the capability to redefine self-identity whenever necessary. This ability assumes self-reference or self-reflexiveness. The original discussion of this was included in Mead's theory of the self.[19] These ideas involve grasping the self-identity not as a coherent and preserved entity but as an ever-changing and flowing reflexive process. However, Mead used reflexiveness only as a keyword for mind and development of the self. In this sense, Mead's self-reflexion was subjectivistic and inevitably led to a discussion in which social norms and values were internalised in the self by individuals.[20] It is a socialisation of the self and an image of human beings adapted to society by the self. For self-organisation, it is not sufficient only to limit self-reflexion to the aspect of individuals adapting themselves to society.

The essence of the *narrative self* is to grasp the reflexive process as a more active process of self-formation. It can also be understood as a process in which a variety of personal events are organised into a unified story by a plot. From the viewpoint of narrative self, Giddens described self-identity as follows:

> Self-identity is not a distinctive trait, or even a collection of traits, possessed by the individual. *It is the self as reflexively understood by the person in terms of her or his biography.* Identity here still presumes continuity across time and space: but self-identity is such continuity as interpreted reflexively by the agent.[21]

According to Giddens, self-identity is a 'reflexive project of the self' consisting of biographical narratives which are subject to coherent and continuous revision. We agree that the narrative self makes it possible, by use of the plot, to bundle time as a historic feature and space as spread experience by systematically organising a variety of episodes in life. Under the present circumstances, however, it is doubtful if the plot of a story of life itself really exists. The narrative self has fallen into the 'dilemma that it must find a plot where it does not exist'.[22]

Self-identity is not programmed by a plot, but rather organises itself based on the episodes it has experienced in the developmental process. Although each episode in life has a meaning as an event, it is not organised in a narrative with a predetermined plot, but self-organises the narrative itself together with other episodes. In this sense, identity-formation is a self-organisation process without a master plan. This process assumes a paradoxical act of confirming the sameness by difference. In other words, the self is a self-referential process itself which continuously produces a new self (sameness) by generating and reacting to a nonself or the difference as a fluctuation inside itself. The self continues self-organisation by referring to its transformation during its life. A self as a definite, preserving and integrated entity does not exist. Yesterday's self can be today's nonself. Even if we admit that the sameness of the self exists at every moment, it is doubtful whether a self with continuity exists.

Mikami expressed this form of existence of the self as, 'I am I by not being I' and regarded this as the essence of the postmodern self.[23] 'Not being I' is a heterogeneous existence for 'the present I' or a fluctuation. This view of the self suggests that fluctuation generates a new self. Of course, most other selves generated as nonselves are controlled in order to maintain previous selves, or self-disorganisation comes true when the new selves destroy the unified previous selves. This is equivalent to the dilemma of unification versus fragmentation discussed in the context of self-identity in the past. The essence of the postmodern self is, however, to confirm itself through a nonself it has generated by a difference motive. Therefore, unification versus fragmentation is not a dilemma, but a factor indispensable to establishing self-identity.

The fluctuation (fragmentation) of identity is a source of a new order (unification). To realise self-organisation, however, the fragments as another self must maintain a relation with the previous self and form a new meaning. If fragmented selves remain meaningless in the dissipative state, this constitutes schizophrenia in the strict sense of the word. Self-organisation of identity is ceaselessly establishing a new self by generating other selves within self and editing them. In this sense, the postmodern self is a project of self-organisation of identity.

6. Conclusion

In this paper I have discussed the present state and prospect of self-identity from the viewpoint of the coming of postmodern age. Modern theory of 'self' has been assuming the existence of the unified and continuous self. In the contemporary age, however, such an idea is dubious.

A typical model of the self in modern society lies in integration of the subjective self and socially expected self to actualise a self. However, when representations without transparency such as *simuracla* and hyper-reality start to proliferate in society through the coming of consumer society and the advancement of information technology, the decentralisation and drifting of identity come out. One of the main characteristics of postmodernity lies in the fact that reality is constructed by representations which do not reflect the entity. When such a type of reality is dominant, the subjective self and the expected self which feature as the modern self lose their substantial meaning, and then people will pursue their self-actualisation and generate another self in the area which surpasses the self in a modern sense, by editing fragmented signs whose meanings are broken up by the flood of information.

Self-identity in an age of postmodernity is identity that has a high degree of freedom and a flowing character that guarantee unification through fragmentation and coherence through change. It should be formulated as a self-organising process without a master plan. The self is a process which continuously produces a new self by generating a nonself inside itself, or produces a self as nonself. This implies that self is nothing less than a paradoxical reproduction process of self =nonself. Namely, 'I really become I by not being I'.

Under the present conditions, it may well be that such a mode of identity seeking reflects perverse self-actualisation and distraction. These are disorders in an age of postmodern tendency, and self-identity will be chaotic until a new image of self is established. The important point, on which we must focus our attention, is not to regard these phenomena too easily as diseases of society.

The necessary condition of the self in a postmodern age is the editorship of differences which generates new meaning through editing fragmented and meaningless signs. This should be named the power of self-editorship, contrasting with the power of self-control required of the modern self. We should recognise that the nurturing of this power will bring people a new will to life, and in its turn the creation of a new culture.

Notes

1. Erik H. Erikson, *Childhood and Society,* (New York, Norton, 1950).

2. For function primacy, see Takatoshi Imada, *Konton no Chikara (The Power of Chaos),* (Tokyo, Kodan-sha,1994), pp. 91-93, and for the scheme of control-performance, see T. Imada, *Jikososiki-sei: Shakai-riron no Fukkatsu (Self-Organity: The Rivitalisation of Social Theory),* (Tokyo, Sobun-sha, 1986), pp. 238-241.

3. Takatoshi Imada, *Modan no Datsu-Kouchiku: Sangyo Shakai no Yukue (Deconstruction of the Modern: Future of Industrial Society),* (Tokyo, Chuo Koron-sha, 1987), p. 4.

4. Jean-François Lyotard, *La condition postmoderne,* (Paris, Minuit, 1979).

5. Takatoshi Imada, 1987, op.cit., pp. 30-33.

6. Abraham H. Maslow, *Motivation and Personality,* (New York, Harper & Row, 1954).

7. Takatoshi Imada, 1994, op. cit., pp. 151-156.

8. Jean Baudrillard, *L'echange symbolique et la mort,* (Paris, Gallimard, 1975), Introduction.

9. Roger Caillois, *Les jeux et les hommes,* (Paris, Gallimard, 1958/1967 éd.rev.).

10. Ken Ohira, *Yutakasa no Seishin Byori (Mental Disease in Affluent Life),* (Tokyo Iwanami Shoten, 1990)

11. Ibid., pp. 28-29.

12. According to the sociologist Mead, the self is composed of 'I' and 'Me'. 'I' can be called a subjective self and expresses what is often called subjectivity. In contrast, 'Me' is an expected self which has taken in others' eyes or social requests. In individual persons, 'I' and 'Me' interact to compose a self. This is a model to explain how society penetrates individuals, determines their behaviour and becomes a psychological part of the self.

Self-identity is integration of the subjective self and the expected self to actualise a self. This can be regarded as a typical model of self-identity in modern society. In a traditional society where the modern individual has not been established, the subjective self and the expected self are not distinguished from each other because the image of the self is not selected by the individual but is determined by his/her status in the community. The establishment of a modern subjective self has been emphasised in relation to individualism. This has separated two types of self (I/Me). However, the expected self in modern society was an ideal and hardly attainable image, such as that of heroes or the ideal images of people offered by society. The subjective self, therefore, could not help but approach the expected self for self-actualisation. Self-actualisation was an always-postponed process of becoming close to the expected self.

Cf. George H. Mead, *Mind, Self and Society: From the Standpoint of a Social Behaviorist,* (Chicago: University of Chicago Press.1934) and Takatoshi Imada, 1994, op.cit., pp. 150-152.

13. The market for comics in Japan is one billion volumes, or ten per person, each year. They were monopolised by boys and girls in the past, but have now been expanded to embrace middle-aged salaried workers.

14. The first *Comics-market* was held in December 1975, which reportedly was attended by 32 interest groups and about 600 people. Since then, the Comics-market has been held annually at different locations as the numbers of participants have increased. Six hundred interest groups and 9,000 people participated in the market of comics held in December 1988. *Comiket* 38, held August 17 and 18, 1990, was reportedly attended by 16,000 interest groups and 150,000 people.

15. Albert Melucci, *Nomads of the Present: Social Movements and Individual Needs in Contemporary Society,* (London, Hutchinson,1989), pp.177-179.

16. Friedrich Nietzsche, *The Will to Power,* (New York, Random House, 1967).

17. Friedich Nietzsche, *On the Genealogy of Morals,* (New York, Vintage Books,1969), chap.2, sec. 12.

18. We cannot grasp the essence of self-organisation, unless we focus on both fluctuation and self-reference. The self-referential mechanism which gives a positive meaning to fluctuations is important for self-organisation. At the same time, fluctuations are essential to prevent the self-referential mechanism from falling into a mere reproduction of system. A self-referential mechanism without fluctuations proves only that element networks to produce elements are continuously reproduced and maintained as a concrete unified entity, as seen in the discussion of autopoiesis. On this issue, see Takatoshi Imada, 1987, op. cit., pp.53-64 and 1994, op. cit., pp.104-108.

19. Cf. George H. Mead, 1934, op.cit.

20. Takatoshi Imada, 1987, op.cit., pp. 206-207.

21. Anthony Giddens, *Modernity and Self-Identity: Self and Society in the Late Modern Age,* (Stanford, Stanford University Press, 1991), p. 53.

22. Takeshi Mikami, *Posuto Kindai no Shakai-gaku (Sociology of Postmodernity),* (Kyoto, Sekai Shiso-sha, 1993), p. 75.

23. Ibid., p.124.

11

'Transindividuality' in Modern Korean Philosophies, and Some Implications for Future Generations

Yoon-Jae Chung

1. Introduction: 'transindividuality'

Human beings of this age are confronted with moral and ecological problems such as the human race has never known before. They are critical problems. Hedonism and materialism degrade humans into animal-like beings. Ecological imbalance and depletion of natural resources pose a crisis for human existence. The continuation of human civilisation depends upon whether we can find the right solution to these problems. This means that the pursuit of the right solutions should be attempted with sincere concern for the future of humankind. It is thus quite natural for contemporary political philosophers and theorists to demonstrate interest and concern for future generations.[1]

During the modern centuries of rationalism and industrialisation, the Ego has been predominantly taken to be an 'isolated centre' for everything else, as pictured in Cartesian philosophy. It sustained a presumptuous, inflated, arrogant, and atomistic attitude about man himself. Thus, Western modern man and woman have almost unconditional confidence in themselves and their power, i.e. in human reason, with respect to the matter of searching for truth and making an ideal world for people to inhabit. Truth lies within the boundary of human mental activity, and utopia is feasible within the design and management of rational beings. This is what the Western modern man imagined, and it is the core of Western Enlightenment.[2] Meanwhile, though the Ego which Rousseau discovered was a self 'so rich, substantial and transcendental', at the same time it embodied a profound arrogance that promoted self-righteousness, prohibited mutual understanding, and belied human diversity.[3]

However, it seems that the Western concept of the self, 'an arrogant and isolated centre', is not very useful for a new world order in which mutual co-operation and global interdependence among individuals and nations are indispensable for human survival and world peace. Political atomism defends the priority of the individual and his rights over society, and presents a purely instrumental view of society. It does not accept as unconditional a principle of belonging or obligation. But, if atomism means that man is self-sufficient alone, it is a very questionable thesis.[4] It has been argued that now is the time for us to change our attitude towards man: from an inflated, megalomaniac, and atomistic self-image to one that is modest, down-to-earth, and organic.[5]

From this critical approach to modern liberalism and its concept of man, the author considers that human transindividuality needs to be rediscovered for the well-being of present and future generations. Trans-individuality by definition refers to human qualities which demonstrate existential, temporal, or spatial interrelations beyond atomised isolation. In modern Western philosophies, human qualities of trans-individuality have been seriously neglected and it is possible that this, in itself, has been the main source of moral degeneration and ecological crisis in the Western world. It is therefore to non-Western philosophical traditions that we must turn for a substantiation of the concept of trans-individuality and hence a possible solution to our present moral and ecological crisis. Accordingly, this paper seeks to examine the human qualities of trans-individuality in three modern Korean philosophical works with a discussion of their theoretical implications. It will be argued that this human transindividuality introduces a more inclusive manner of thought which could radically alter the Western concept of self as an arrogant and isolated centre and thus could become the source of policy innovations for the well-being of future generations. In the Conclusion, some suggestions for future generations will be discussed.

2. Ch'oe Che-u's Self as Heaven (Hanulnim)

Ch'oe Che-u founded the Tonghak (Eastern Learning) in 1860. The Tonghak was an indigenous Korean religious philosophy which provided the ideology and organisation for the Peasant War of 1894.[6] Ch'oe was brought up with a Confucian education, reading not only the classical books of Confucius and Mencius, but also those of Lu Xiangshan and Wang Yangming. But his unfortunate social background as an illegitimate son, and the political corruption of the late Choson dynasty, made him seek spiritual salvation. He wandered around the country as a peddler, and during these wandering years he came across Buddhism, Taoism, and even Catholicism. But none of these could quench his thirst for the truth. Upon returning home, he studied religious and philosophical texts in earnest, even depriving himself of sleep, offering sincere prayers, meditating and contemplating for six years in order to found a new Way that would sustain the nation and save the oppressed people. One day suddenly he was inspired, and discovered the principles of the new Way.[7] Like many other founders of new religions, Ch'oe explained that he had arrived at spiritual enlightenment through a conversation with God in which he received God's revelations.[8]

Ch'oe named the new Way, 'Tonghak' (東學) or 'Heavenly Way', emphasising that it arose to confront Western teaching[9]. He propagated the Tonghak to 'sustain the nation and provide for the people (*poguk anmin*)' and 'save the oppressed people(*kwangje ch'angsaeng*)' by achieving a simultaneous breakthrough in the national and the feudal crises which the Korean people faced in the mid-l9th century. The Peasant War of 1894, initiated by the followers of Tonghak as well as the peasants, was a movement that concluded the numerous popular uprisings, demanding the end of the old system of a *yangban*-class society as well as the establishment of a new system clear of peasant oppression.[10]

There is no denying that Ch'oe tried to incorporate various doctrines borrowed from the established religions and philosophies, but it is apparent that he gave high priority to Confucianism. When he condemned the Korean Catholic converts, he said 'the simple people of our country have abandoned propriety (*ye*) and the five cardinal relationships (*oryun*) (of Confuicianism)'. For him, to protect Korea from Western imperialistic Christianity was to maintain Confucian virtues, particularly the five relationships of king to subject, father to son, husband to wife, aged to young, and friend to friend. A realisation of these relationships could come only from the Confucian style of self-cultivation (*sushim chonggi*).[11]

However, what attracts great attention is Ch'oe's new interpretation of the relationship between humanity and Heaven which is manifested in the very first sentence of *The Doctrine of the Mean*, one of the four main textbooks of Confucianism; that is to say, human nature is endowed by Heaven. He placed great emphasis on his interpretation that man and Heaven are one and the same. To see man and Heaven in unity, or the *innaech'on* (人乃天) thought which means *'Sarami Hanulnimida'* (Man is Heaven), is the most fundamental and significant idea of the whole Tonghak, and this led to his famous declaration of, the 'Awakening Period of Later Heaven' (*Huch'on Kaebyok Shidae*). If all people were considered to possess the same Heavenly nature as equal creatures, they should have been treated as Heavenly without discrimination during the Choson dynasty. But there was no Confucian scholar in the dynasty audacious enough to challenge the hierarchical interpretation of Confucian doctrine regarding the unity of man and Heaven.

It was Ch'oe who boldly declared, based upon his new conceptualisation of man as Heaven or God, that there should be no more discrimination between aristocrats and ordinary people(even slaves), or between men and women. His ideas are expressed in writings such as the Bible of Tonghak Doctrine (*Tonggyong Taejon*) and Hymns from Dragon Pool(*Yongdam Yusa*).[12] Yet, Ch'oe was arrested and executed in 1864 by the government authorities who declared Tonghak an evil way of thinking and made it illegal. The belief that 'Man is God', or the *innaechon* thought of Tonghak, needs to be analysed in detail.

First, the mind or spirit of man is a replica of that of God,[13] and thus Heaven does not dwell outside man but resides in the human mind or soul.[14] From this, the idea of attending God in humanity or 'Serving man constitutes service to God' was developed. Ch'oe Che-u preached that 'Man is God and God is Man'.[15] The idea of the equality of man and Heaven was well presented in the incantation that he recommended his followers to recite to reach the state of being united with God or Heaven. It reads 'serve God or the Heavenly Lord inside you and creation will be tranquil. If one remembers God throughout one's life, all will be realised'.[16] Ch'oe Si-hyong (1829-1898), the second patriarch of Tonghak who succeeded Ch'oe Che-u, taught that 'Man is God. Therefore serve men as you would serve God'.[17] He also taught that 'in the family, if a man should come, say that the Heavenly Lord has descended from heaven'.[18] Tonghak's emphasis on the immanence of God in the human soul is sometimes understood as an attempt to secularise Confucianism.[19]

Second, man is not God's possession, but God himself.[20] Tonghak emphasised the dignity of man, but its approach was different from other religions. All the religions of the world at the time, including Western doctrines, fixed God as a separate and absolute being that existed outside of man and preached that man should be ruled by God and should serve God as a servant of God. But Tonghak put him on an equal footing with God and established man as the most high and the most honoured being.[21] In The Doctrine of the Mean, the Heavenly nature is definitely described as being impersonal, whereas God or the Heavenly Lord in Tonghak philosophy is believed to be a more or less personal being.[22] As man is God himself, it follows that to serve man on earth is to serve God directly. This idea was expressed in a more sophisticated fashion in Ch'oe Che-u's teaching as follows: 'Do not believe in me at all, but in God. Do not say God is aloof because you serve him in your body (he resides in your body)'.[23]

Third, regardless of status and sex, every person can achieve by training and cultivation the ideal state of human existence, i.e. salvation or emancipation. To the Tonghak followers, it was advised that if a man serves his inner God well for three years, he can be a *chun-tzu* or *chisang sonin* (an earthly immortal being). In the past, *chun-tzu* as an ideal man of Confucianism or the earthly immortal being as an ultimate goal of religious Taoism had nothing to do with the religious lives of ordinary people (even less with those of slaves). These ultimate goals could have been reached only by a few members of the religious elite. But Ch'oe opened a new horizon for the religious populace by arguing that all men could search for the highest state of earthly immortal being with simple practice.[24] Regarding the method of serving God, he taught that 'the great Way consists of holding fast to sincerity and seriousness, and cultivating little by little.[25] In short, the Way is to serve God who is immanent in both men and women with sincerity, seriousness, and faith. It is said that this attitude represents the Neo-Confucian influences on Tonghak philosophy.[26]

Based upon this philosophical understanding of self, Ch'oe and his followers firmly believed that there should be no more discrimination between aristocrats and ordinary people because all men equally serve the same God immanent in their minds. However, Ch'oe's successful leadership as a revolutionary religious thinker does not lie merely in his theoretical assertion about the equality of all men, but also in his behaviour in putting this theory into action. He freed two of his female slaves to be his close relatives, making one his step-daughter and the other his daughter-in-law. Such an action had never been undertaken by any Confucian scholar during the entire 500 year history of the Choson dynasty. This event, breaking a long-held custom, can be seen symbolically to stand for egalitarianism; equality of all men and overcoming of sexual discrimination. This principle was more highly developed by Ch'oe Si-hyong, his successor, who advised his disciples to treat their daughters-in-law not merely as a daughter-in-law but as God. Apart from being engaged in the liberation movements of slaves and women, the *innaech'on* (Man is Heaven or God) thought had an important influence not only on the Peasant War of 1894 but also on later human liberation movements.[27]

The Tonghak and the Peasant War of 1894 are still important sources of ideas and images for the transformation of contemporary Korean politics and social structure, and the *innaech'on* thought is referred to frequently by most activists in social and political movements as well as by philosophers and social scientists in their search for intellectual and spiritual enlightenment. Some political philosophers suggest the essential ideas of Tonghak could be adopted as a political ideology for the Korea of the future, replacing the imported liberal democracy. It seems that the Tonghak and its *innaech'on* thought is popular among Korean intellectuals and activists, particularly because they understand that its philosophical projection of man as Heaven and the egalitarian principle would contribute to achieving the goal of true democracy in Korea in the future. In brief, in Tonghak, man and God were assumed to be related as identical and equal beings; man is directly united with God. Since each human individual is regarded as Heaven or

God and God dwells in each human being, Ch'oe's notion of self may be termed a 'divine' concept.

A theoretical emphasis on the human being's existential relationship with God seems to be a genuine starting-point for human dignity and mutual respect. In the modern West, liberal values were advocated because they were believed to be 'rational interpretations of the Christian God's requirements for men'.[28] But in modern liberalism, the Christian God has been replaced with the 'secular' concept of an underlying human nature.[29] Now it is argued that the loss of the transcendental anchor of modern democracy is the main reason for its lack of moral credibility and its political unsustainability. Western democracy is criticised for the relativisation of all moral norms, the crisis of authority, and the reduction of life to the pursuit of immediate material gain. It is emphasised that Western democracy must renew its own transcendental origins not only to survive but also to resolve the conflicts of cultures.[30] In this context, we can argue that Ch'oe's divine concept of self could provide the 'ailing' modern democracies with a transcendental justification of social and political virtues such as character,[31] self-respect, a sense of responsibility, humility, generosity, and love. Transindividuality in terms of the divine concept of self may encourage a more humanistic relationship of mutual respect and decency between 'heavenly equals'.[32]

3. An Chae-hong's Self as Cosmic Nucleus (Na)

An Chae-hong (1891-1965) was one of the most prominent political leaders in postwar Korea. As a boy, he demonstrated exceptional talent for understanding the major Chinese classics, and had resolved to become Korea's Ssu-ma Ch' ien, the great writer-historian of ancient China. He studied politics and economics at Waseda University in Japan. He was a well-known editorial writer and the president of the *Choson Ilbo,* a prestigious Korean newspaper, whose articles stirred the national spirit and anti-Japanese consciousness among the Koreans who longed for political independence and national autonomy. He was imprisoned nine times by the colonial authorities but remained one of the very few nationalists who persisted in resisting Japanese imperialism to the end of World War II. During the postwar years, his main concern was to produce a unified Korean government. As a leading figure engaged in the transitional politics of liberated Korea, he wrote several books and many articles on domestic and international issues, which distinguished him from his contemporaries. He founded the Korean Nationalist Party and attempted to establish a left-right coalition government to prevent the consolidation of national separation. He also worked for the American Military Government as Civil Administrator in charge of domestic Korean affairs. Against pro-Soviet communism and pro-American bourgeois democracy, he proposed a political doctrine of 'New Nationalism and New Democracy' or *Tasari Chuui* which is based upon indigenous Korean philosophical ideas, but he was not successful in making his 'dream' come true. He was kidnapped and taken to North Korea during the Korean War in 1950, and died there in 1965.[33]

An Chae-hong thought that the development of language was closely linked to the evolution of human perception and ideas, and thus, an interpretive understanding of languages would reveal the distinctive qualities of the human mind.[34] Thus, He expounded the Korean Political Philosophy (Choson Chongch'i Ch'olhak) through a unique interpretation of related pure Korean words. The concept of man is essential in his political philosophy which it is now believed could contribute to a theoretical reformulation of Korean nationalism into a universal and globally acceptable one. The content of *Tasari Chuui*[35] in terms of the concept of self can be summarised as follows.

First, human beings originate from emptiness (*pi*). An disagreed with the Cartesian foundation of Western idealism and materialism, and introduced a holistic philosophy of emptiness-seed-matter (*pi-ssi-mon*) which he considered to be the cosmological view that the ancient Korean people had discovered. By this he wanted to demonstrate that matter or material and mind or consciousness are not separate from, or contradictory to each other. According to his philosophical interpretation, emptiness is the creative source of all things in the universe. The *pi* is similar to the nothingness or non-being of the philosophy of Lao Tzu.[36] He suggested that the fact that many pure Korean words have *pi* as their linguistic basis reveals that the philosophy of emptiness has been embedded in Korean consciousness.[37]

On the other hand, An interpreted that the myriad creatures in the universe come from two visible fundamentals, the seed (*ssi*) and matter (*mon*); animate objects originate from the seed and inanimate objects are from matter. Human beings are born from the door of seed, the vulva (*ssi-ip*) of a mature woman (*assi*). All inanimate things originate from matter (*mon*), and dust is *monji* which means 'the residue of excrements of things'. Here, it may well be said that the Something in the philosophy of Lao Tzu was categorised into the seed (*ssi*) and matter (*mon*) as the two visible sources of all creatures in the universe.

With this interpretation, An Chae-hong attempted to demonstrate that the philosophy of emptiness penetrates into every level of experience of the Korean people – natural, human, divine, abstract, practical, visible or invisible. He considered that the holistic framework of emptiness-seed-matter philosophy is essentially the same as that of Hegel's philosophy of history which defines history as 'the integration of God, Nature, and Human Beings'. An's belief was that Korean political leaders, rooted as they were in Eastern modes of thought, would be able to avoid fragmentation inherent in Western political ideologies based upon the Cartesian worldview. He maintained that the revitalisation of this holistic philosophy could create an ideologically integrative environment which would promote the national goal of a healthy unified Korea.[38]

Second, Man is one of Three Fundamentals of the Universe. This idea originates from his interpretation of three pure Korean words, one (*hana*), two (*tul*), and three (*set*) which come first in counting numbers. These symbolically represent heaven, earth, and man, i.e., the three fundamentals which constitute the universe. One (*hana* or *han*) is also regarded as heaven (*hanul*). Thus, one means the Great or the Endless, usually equivalent to the Universe, and also represents a philosophical principle of 'One is Many'. Philosophically, one represents the Korean ideal of *Taedong Sahoe* (An Integrative Community). While *ha* in *hana* means everything in the universe, *na* means 'to bear' or 'I', from which it can be interpreted that Koreans traditionally consider that everything in the universe becomes meaningful or is recognised as an existing entity only when *na* or I assign a subjective value or meaning to it.

Two (*tul*) means the field or land[39] in which all creatures are filled and served. A similar idea was also implied by a phrase in the *I-Ching* which means 'the earth is full of creatures and materials, from which all beings get nutritions and grow'.[40] According to An's interpretation, three also means the seed, and all animate things including man evolve from seed or sperm. His interpretation was that the order of counting, one, two, three, implies a universal principle that heaven and earth would be meaningful only when they are utilised by man as the nucleus of the universe.

Third, I or man as individual (*na*) is the cosmic nucleus of others (*nam*), nation (*nara*), and the world (*nuri*). The three are spiritual extensions of I, and exist in a harmonious and integrative relationship. This idea is implied in the philosophical meaning of the pure Korean word, *net* which is four. He emphasised that this *net* and the pure Korean words for I, other, nation, and the world share the same linguistic root, beginning with the phonetic sign of 'n'. I am the actual subject who embodies and practices human ideas and ideals. I am the prior-state being whose rights and dignity cannot be arbitrarily infringed by the state. I exist in the universe before the institutionalisation of the state. Other (*nam*) is a spiritual extension of I or myself. I and other are closely akin. Other, like myself, exists in the universe only after a birth *(naum)*.[41] The nation is a spiritual cooperative based upon individuals and their desire for life and happiness, and all laws and institutions are the reflection of the free will of individuals as concrete constituents of nation. A nation forms, develops, and advances, realising the ideals of individuals, in which individuals could be truly free and happy. A mechanistic totalitarianism and an imperialistic state which does not value the freedom of individuals, and which infringes upon the universal principle of human well-being must be rejected. Accordingly, the individual must be free from the nation, and with the same logic, the nation must be free from other foreign nations.

Ideally, the nation is not a simple administrative instrument of political rule, but a spiritual entity. The individual is the fundamental basis of the nation, while the nation is an extension of the individual. Both are inseparable and united in oneness; individual is nation and *vice versa.* The idea of an inseparable relationship between individual and nation is rooted in traditional Korean philosophy which includes the orthodox principle that One is Many and the Great. Thus any political ideology, indigenous or imported, which devalues individuals as merely passive agents of the state is unacceptable. The Heavenly Way is the origin of the Fair Principle of the universe, and nation is the earthly embodiment of the Fair Principle for humankind. Therefore, the individual is the fundamental unit or cosmic nucleus of the universe. With his interpretative discussions of the concepts of *na, nam, nara,* and *nuri,* An Chae-hong attempted to demonstrate that the Korean nation cherishes healthy concepts of individual freedom, nationalism, cosmopolitanism and international peace as well as anti-imperialism and anti-totalitarianism. Through the concept of self as the cosmic nucleus or centre of the universe, he emphasised that human beings are endowed with fundamental rights and dignity and are not isolated but interdependently related to national and global contexts. In addition, he understood that fundamental rights and dignity are not sufficient conditions for a true democracy. He emphasised that human rights must go along with political obligations and the spirit of sacrifice for a healthy community life. It seems he thought that without character on the part of the individual, personal liberty would degenerate into mere animal licence.[42]

Fourth, individuals are to be governed by the democratic principles of *Tasari.* In his interpretation of number five (*tasot*), An Chae-hong understood that it represents the universal governing principle, *Tasari.* The pure Korean word *Tasari* means 'the fundamental principle that governs the universe', 'democracy', or 'governance or politics itself'.[43] He maintained that *Tasari* involves a pair of democratic principles which are inseparable in a healthy human polity. First, *Tasari* involves the principle of *manmin ch'ong'on* (萬民總言) which means 'since every individual is endowed with the fundamental right to express his or her opinion, everybody speaks out what they have in mind'. This is because the word *Tasari* originated from the word *ta sario* which means 'by allowing all the people to express their individual ideas'. On the other hand, *Tasari* has the principle of *manmin kongsaeng* (萬民共生) which means 'all the people should live together'. This is because *Tasari* also originated from *ta salinda* which means 'to let all the people lead their own lives safely'. It may well be said that the Korean democratic values of *manmin ch'ongon* and *manmin kongsaeng* correspond to those of liberty and equality in Western political philosophy. But, An Chae-hong explained that liberty and equality are reconciled [44] in *Tasari* as *means* and *goal* of political engineering; *manmin ch'ong'on* or liberty is the *means* of reflecting the people's ideas and voice in the political process, and *manmin kongsaeng* or equality as 'impartial'[45] well-being for all is the *goal* of politics.

According to An's analysis, in Korea the origin of *Tasari* can be traced in the time-honored principle of Well-Being for Humankind (*hongik in'gan*) which was proclaimed in the legend of Tan'gun's foundation of Ancient Korea. But he claimed that *Tasari* was an ideal form of Korean democracy that had never been practised fully in the history of Korea. He hoped that the ideal of *Tasari* would be revitalised into a modern popular form with the establishment of parliament in postwar Korea. He also believed that the ideological dependency involving the occupation by foreign powers and the short-sighted political factionalism could be overcome and that none of the privileged classes would monopolise social values and political opportunities in modern Korea. For him, parliament was the modern vehicle which would put into practice the *Tasari* ideals. He argued that 'the necessary prudent planning and persistent implementation of social reforms require knowledgeable, competent, and experienced leaders, who should be elected to form the parliament through a lawful process of popular voting'. He also anticipated that *Tasari* would be adopted as a political doctrine for a unified Korea.

In summary, An Chae-hong suggested that the concept of self as a cosmic nucleus is intrinsically related to the national and global contexts of human existence as well as to others. The individual is one of Three Fundamentals of the universe and endowed with basic human rights and dignity. The people as the collection of individuals is to be governed by the democratic principles of *Tasari.* It may be argued that An Chae-hong's concept of self as a cosmic nucleus was a typical example of the 'Cosmic-Together' philosophy which has recently been suggested as a critical alternative to Cartesian philosophy.[46] As An Chae-hong believed that human beings, nations, and the world belong to a unitary system of the cosmos under the universal principle of *Tasari,* his concept of self may be called 'cosmological'.

An Chae-hong's self or individual (*na*) is the cosmic nucleus which maintains a spiritual relationship with others, the nation and the world. It encourages a cosmopolitan worldview which, if adopted, would promote regional and global cooperation between individuals and nations towards world peace and justice. Past centuries have been the age of nation-states and nationalism. Cosmopolitanism was considered merely an idealistic worldview of the classical period. Its proponents were disdained as religious or over-passionate or were suspected of being Communist conspirators. But now in a global age, such cosmopolitan ideas are just common sense. Whether in theory or in practice, the issue of world government or some other institution for global governance is a significant part of contemporary political discussions for human survival or global peace and order.[47] The cosmological concept of self may expand human interrelations spatially, and it would be useful in dealing with the contemporary world disorders. It may be argued that while transindividuality in terms of the cosmological concept of self would undermine nationalism, it would also promote political initiatives for global cooperation and unity for the sake of human survival and peace.

4. Kim Ji-ha's Self as Life (*Saengmyong*)[48]

Poet Kim Ji-ha used to be a passionate front-line leader in the anti-government struggles of the 1960s and 1970s, but now is a typical participant-intellectual who actively propagates what is called 'life philosophy'. He does not describe himself as a philosopher; nonetheless, he has built a new outlook on society, the nation, the world, and the universe upon the key concept of life. He also has some concrete programmes to translate this new outlook into reality. Kim's concern is not with developing a metaphysical system but with renewing, in a fundamental way, human existence in society and on the earth, that is, vis-à-vis nature and the universe. Although he is no longer engaged in anti-government struggles, he is still involved in various kinds of movement committed to socio-political reform. As such, his ideas are meant to be of practical use, directly applicable to social reform.

From the latter half of 1991, after living in isolation for about four years to fight the illness he had contracted in prison, Kim began to speak and act. His lecture texts and articles were collected in a book entitled *From a Burning Thirst to the Sea of Life* (*T'anun mongmarum-eso saengmyong-ui pada-ro*). The book's title is suggestive of the dimensional shift Kim underwent. In 1982, he published a book of poems under the title *With a Burning Thirst* (*Tanun mongmarum-uro*). Here, the thirst was mainly for political democracy for which he had fought for so long and so resolutely as to risk his own life. Now this thirst is not so intense, though it has not disappeared. It is partly eclipsed by a will to sail the vast sea of life.

Kim says that he began to dwell upon the wonders of life when he noticed a tiny blade of grass growing in his dusty, lifeless prison cell. In formulating his ideas, Kim owes a great deal to the teachings of the Tonghak which he came across while in prison in the late 1970s. The key concept in Kim's ideas is life. Without a sophisticated definition of life or *saengmyong* (生命) in Korean, he is simply talking about the life that all human beings are given, and argues that today men are leading a lifestyle that has been greatly separated from the true order of life. This separation, in his view, is largely the result of the Cartesian dichotomy of mind and body and the Newtonian conception of a mechanical world. An examination of his books and articles reveals an outline of life philosophy as follows, from which his concept of self as life may be discerned.

First of all, following the line of many Oriental philosophies and religions, Kim believes that the human mind and body are not two different things, but are made up of a vital energy or force called *ki* (氣) in Korean. This ki is omnipresent in the universe. Everything in the universe, animate or inanimate, is made up of *ki*. This vital energy or force enables all things in the universe to communicate with each other. Kim argues that communication is possible not only between living animals but also between these and inanimate objects and even between inanimate objects themselves. Here, Kim is not entirely relying on Oriental philosophies. He relies on such eminent Western scientists as Ilya Prigogine, the 1977 winner of the Nobel Prize in chemistry, who alleged that water particles, when boiled, communicate with each other, exchanging information. This view that everything in the universe is made up of a vital energy called *ki* has affinity with Einstein's theory of relativity that states that mass can be turned into energy and *vice versa.* Einstein's mass-energy equation was a critique of the Newtonian conception that the world was composed of totally isolated and self-closed things.

Furthermore, based on the *ki* philosophy, Kim defines the life phenomenon particularly in terms of communication. Communicative ability is the proof of the existence of life, and everything in the universe has life in the sense that it can communicate. This definition leads him to regard even inanimate objects as having life. This broad and open view of life has direct implications for ecological campaigns. It is no wonder that Kim is one of the most serious and enthusiastic champions of ecological protection. He argues, however, that the term 'environment' should not be used as it implies human-centredness in man's relationship with nature. Protection is an even worse word. But he admits the practical use of the words as there are no better substitutes available at the moment.

Second, Kim defines man as an open system whose relationship with society is both continuous and discontinuous. It is discontinuous, as in the Hobbesian theory of struggle by all against all. But it is continuous, as human beings are after all social animals. He learned the fundamental grammar of the 'continuity-discontinuity' or 'yes-no' principle from the Tonghak. He believes this grammar is a more proper logical tool in understanding human affairs than the Hegelian or Marxian dialectic of thesis, antithesis, and synthesis. From this belief, he criticises the typical Western conception of society which views individuals as isolated, self-contained entities, as Newton describes the world of things mechanically. He feels that the Darwinian theory of the survival of the fittest, the Hobbesian argument of the struggle by all against all, and the Marxian theory of class struggle are offsprings of the Newtonian mechanical view of the world.

Western industrial civilisation, which is founded on this outlook, can by no means be said to be an appropriate civilisation for mankind. This civilisation, Kim argues, is nearing an end. There are many unmistakable signs that it is in crisis, not the least of which is, in Kim's eyes, the lack of any philosophy to cope with the ecological threat. Korean society, which is following in the footsteps of Western society, is also in crisis. He describes it as suffering from 'collective schizophrenia' which is caused by the multiplicity of pressures inherent in industrial society. The outcome of this schizophrenia is a sharp rise in violent crimes, a total collapse of social, political, and economic ethics, massive escape into religion and a sharp increase in the reliance on drugs in order to escape from reality.

Third, the life of human beings as well as that of non-human beings should be loved or respected. He obtained this message from the two founders of Tonghak, Ch'oe Che-u and Ch'oe Si-hyong whose basic teaching was that every human being is the embodiment of God and hence ought to be revered not only by others but by oneself. Self-respect starts from a sincere care for one's own body where God or Heaven dwells. Good nutrition based upon indigenous food is also emphasised because a man's body and the earth on which he lives are not different in nature. Tonghak also teaches that one should eat food with the same reverence as in ancestral rituals because eating is serving the God in one's body.

He preaches that a man cannot take a bowl of rice without feeling reverence when he comes to think of the process through which it comes to his table. A grain of rice is produced as the outcome of the collaborative efforts of many animate and inanimate objects. For Kim, the realisation of this process is the beginning of an awakening to the meaning of life and universal order and the moral value of love and respect in daily life. But today, few people feel reverence for the process involved in the production of a grain of rice. Kim thinks that this is one of the numerous indications of how far modern man has deviated from the true order of life. It is in this context that Kim calls attention to food and the way it is produced, cooked and eaten as the starting point of his environmental campaign and other socio-political reforms. Yet, he argues that the promoters of campaigns and reforms have first to discard some elements of the conventional philosophy they have learned and rearm themselves with a new world outlook based upon love and respect for life.

Fourth, Kim's philosophy of life, ultimately, is designed to change people's life style, by which he means the way people think, act, produce, consume, and communicate with each other. He envisions a change in diet as the beginning of a revolution in lifestyle which in turn will lead to the evolution of the present industrial civilisation. As one of the concrete programmes for this vision, Kim encourages organic farming which eliminates agricultural chemicals from the farm field. Organic farming, which makes farm produce more expensive to consumers, can take root, he argues, when the working class as a whole unites to purchase only chemical free agricultural products including rice. For the spread of a new vision and a new world outlook founded on the reverence for life or man as life, Kim calls for many reform-minded social groups to set up what he termed 'life schools' where respect for life is taught along with basic Oriental philosophies, new diets, meditation, and elementary medicinal knowledge.

He envisions a society consisting of small communities where important decisions concerning various aspects of life are made autonomously by their members. These small communities, however, would not be self-contained but related to each other through a loose network. They would be in a discontinuous but at the same time continuous relationship with the larger society. This conceptualisation of small communities as the basic social unit leads Kim to oppose any kind of centralisation, including government bureaucracy and large-scale production plants.[49] He urged workers to build their own communities in which they autonomously make decisions on production, and said workers can also help farmers build their own communities by purchasing organically cultivated farm products. He emphasised that reform-minded movements have to be directed to helping workers and farmers build such communities. Kim's vision of a new civilisation is aimed at transforming world civilisation, and he believes that the new vision founded on life philosophy would be able to accommodate the two different ideologies in Korea – the socialist *juche* ideology and capitalist liberal democracy.

Thus, Kim considers that all things in the universe are alive and communicate with each other as beings that possess the vital energy or force, *ki.* He was influenced by the Tonghak philosophy, and maintains that all human beings should be loved and respected by each other. In this way, those conventional life styles stemming from Cartesian dichotomy and the Newtonian conception of a mechanical world need to be transformed. He defines man as an open system whose relationship with society is both 'continuous and discontinuous, and suggests some concrete programmes for the practice of life philosophy. However, he is not totally against mechanisation and industrialisation. His argument is that mechanisation and industrialisation should be carried out in a more humane way, suiting the human condition. In Kim's worldview, all the universal lives and objects share the *ki* and communicate with each other. They are not self-contained, but related to each other through a loose network in the universal eco-system. Thus, where Ch'oe Che-u's concept of self could be termed 'divine', and An Chae-hong's 'cosmological', Kim's could be termed 'ecological'.

Kim Ji-ha's self as life (*saengmyong*) nourishes a new ecological movement as an innovative attempt to create a trans-individual civilisation in the coming centuries. For him, all animate and inanimate creatures share the omnipotent vital energy *(ki),* and communicate with each other. They should all be loved and respected by themselves and each other. Ecological wisdom from his Life Philosophy could play a vital role in the domestic and global decision-making processes for the protection of human lives and natural resources. Kim's ecological concept of self relates individuals even to inanimate objects as well as to animate lives in the universal Circle of Life. These ideas encourage small community movements, local autonomy, or organic farming as alternative life-styles for future generations. Transindividuality in terms of the ecological concept of self could enlighten modern civilisation stricken by materialism and industrialisation that have gone too far.

5. Conclusion: Implications and Suggestions

In the preceding chapters, three concepts of self in modern Korea have been examined along with their philosophical worldviews, and an assessment can be made of their contribution to our understanding of self and some conclusions can be drawn. First, the 'divine' self is directly related to God. This means that the individual is not just what is to be empirically observed but is the embodiment of the invisible God (*hanulnim*) as well. The divine concept of self is a philosophical source of decent equality. Second, the 'cosmological' self is spiritually connected to others, the nation and the world. The individual *(na)* is the actual subject who gives existential meaning to environmental objects, and is the cosmic nucleus which exists in harmony with other cosmic entities. Third, the 'ecological' self is an open system, sharing vital energy *(ki)* with all lives and things in the universe. All the universal beings communicate with each other, not being isolated but related to each other through a loose network in the universal ecosystem. In these models, interrelated worldviews, it may well be said that the concept of transindividuality has been substantiated, and it is anticipated that the concept could also be substantiated in the Western context. It can be argued that human transindividuality involves deity, cosmic unity, and life-sharing with all the universal beings. Now, with the concept of transindividuality what should or could be done for the well-being of future generations? Many ideas and options are possible, but just four suggestions will be discussed.

First, philosophers or moral theorists can no longer assume that human beings are no more than 'survival machines', instinctively driven by self-interest. Instead, one may posit that human beings as transindividuals are capable of overriding their egoistic nature and acting virtuously. Human societies are built on a far more complex basis than the primal urges of greed, lust, and fear, but as long as we sustain the conventional self-interest assumption, human society parallels the animal kingdom. This does not mean that the self-interest axiom should be instantly dismissed. Rather, advocates of the self-interest axiom need to acknowledge that virtuous or altruistic human behaviour is a superior form of enlightened, *long term* self-interest. Recently Matt Ridley criticised modern economics as having been founded on the assumption that human behaviour is driven by rational self-interest, and suggested a new economic model of the emotions in which human beings are assumed to behave altruistically, looking to their long term self-interest, rather than the short term.[50] The good Samaritan in the Bible, who took care of the wretched person whom the priest and the Levite had ignored,[51] should not be regarded as an angel, an ideal person who would not care for his own self-interest at all. Indeed, we often find and meet such good neighbours in our daily lives, and we may assume that all human beings are potentially good Samaritans; the good Samaritans possess transindividualities with which they would consider the well-being of present and future generations, living in a close relationship with God and his creatures. In this context, in the search for a new political economy for future generations, we may have to reassess the realism of Hobbes who had claimed that in its natural state the life of man is 'solitary, poor, nasty, brutish, and short', and place more emphasis on Adam Smith's *Theory of Moral Sentiments*,[52] the less well-known other half of *The Wealth of Nations.*

Second, in the light of transindividuality, politics would not be regarded merely as a 'power struggle' among members of the elite, but rather as a 'leadership process' between leaders and followers who share the same goals. Theoretically, the ruling elite is a positional concept, whereas leadership is a relational concept,[53] in accordance with the human transindividuality discussed above. While elitist politicians are assumed to compete and struggle for the attainment of social and political resources or power, leaders would take initiatives to solve problems for the general good. Leadership is a process of human interaction,[54] and partly a question of vision about the direction in which policy ought to be developed.[55] Political leaders are increasingly sought as moral guides through the uncertainties of the age.[56] In the contemporary global age, leadership in an interdependent world is highlighted.[57] Accordingly, politics can no longer remain a mere elitist power-game. Political leaders need to take creative and morally innovative initiatives for the benefit of the whole society. A political leader may come to be a problem-solver or caretaker for the society as a whole consisting of both the present and future generations.

Third, with the shift of emphasis away from egoism, society may encourage the multinational corporations to take on a more enlightened role including, for example, the supporting of intercultural programmes particularly for children and new generations. In the coming century, MNCs, far from being regarded as 'exploiters', may well be seen as post-modern vehicles for cosmopolitan peace and justice. Global corporations can utilise their transnational networks for the positive purpose of providing children and new generations with opportunities to experience a variety of cultures. Future generations need to be given access to world cultures when they are young and innocent of cultural or religious biases. Furthermore, some pioneering corporations could start a new project which may be called 'Our Sons and Daughters Program'(OSDP). The OSDP would emphasise that all children are 'ours' in the global family, and it would take human decency and harmony as its basic values to be taught for true peace and justice as well as for a healthy moral development of individuals. Along with economic aid to children in need, the OSDP would intensify concerns for future generations in terms of their self-actualisation as spiritual beings.

Finally, cosmopolitanism should be revitalised as a principle for future generations, and further functional institutions for a cosmopolitan management of world affairs need to be created. Globalisation should not mean merely a geographical expansion of the capitalist world market coupled with the logic of maximisation of economic interests and profits. Free and mass transactions of goods and personnel have to be accompanied by a moral enlightenment for global citizenship and safety. Cosmopolitanism should be rediscovered in both Eastern and Western traditions and should be reintroduced into social and political discourse. Cosmopolitanism need not refer merely to the multicultural life-styles of international travellers, but rather, embrace a compassionate 'family' attitude to all humankind. During the modern age of nationalism, such a cosmopolitan attitude or 'fraternity' was confined to the national level, but now in the global age, it is natural to expand it to the whole of mankind across the globe. Simultaneously, further functional institutions like the World Trade Organisation may have to be established. For instance, there will be an increasing need for such organisations as the World Environment Organization, the World Food Organization, and the World Children's Organization. Alternatively, the contemporary United Nations and its international organisations may have to be reformed in order for local and global problems to be tackled more effectively.

In summary, the analysis of three modern Korean philosophies has shown that individuals are not merely arrogant and isolated centres but can be seen as transindividuals who are intrinsically related to God, the cosmos, and all animate and inanimate objects in the universe. It is maintained that, if the concept of transindividuality become more widely accepted, Western rationalists would be stimulated into 'recharging' their conventional concept of self-interest to include human altruism through which long-term self-interest would be pursued. It is also argued that people aware of their transindividuality would support the return of cosmopolitanism and new postmodern types of governance across and within the national borders. Politics must not be allowed to remain an elitist power-game, but should be understood as a creative leadership process for the benefit of present and future generations.

Notes

1. Some philosophers and theorists have already demonstrated their concern about future generations. The English moral theorist, Derek Parfit, recently published a book in which one part out of four covers the issue of 'how we affect future generations', and he emphasises that 'this is the most important part of our moral theory, since the next few centuries will be the most important in human history'. For further references, see Derek Parfit, *Reasons and Persons* (Oxford, Clarendon Press, 1984), p. 351 and Part Four. Furthermore, the Institute for the Integrated Study of Future Generations (Japan) has published two books as part of a Future Generations Studies Series: Milton Moskowitz, ed., *Thinking about Future Generations* (1994, Series I); Tae-Chang Kim & Jim Dater, eds, *Creating a New History For Future Generations* (1994, Series II).

2. Myung Hyun Lee, 'Paradox of Techno Utopia', a paper presented at The International Philosophy Conference on 'Paths to Human Flourishing: Philosophical Perspectives', held by the Korean Philosophical Association, Seoul, August 19-20, 1992.

3. Robert C. Solomon, *Continental Philosophy Since 1750: The Rise and Fall of the Self* (Oxford, Oxford University Press, 1988), p. 1.

4. For a discussion of atomism or political atomism, see Charles Taylor, Atomism, in Shlomo Avineri and Avner de-Shalit, eds., *Communitarianism and Individualism* (Oxford, Oxford University Press, 1995), pp.29-32.

5. See Myung Hyun Lee, op. cit., pp. 3-4.

6. Shin Yong-ha, 'Conjunction of Tonghak and the Peasant War of 1894', *Korea Journal*, Vol.34, No.4 (Winter 1994), p. 59.

7. For the earlier experiences of Ch'oe Che-u in detail, see Ibid, pp. 60-63.

8. 'Podongmun (On Propagating Tonghak)', in *Tonggyong Taejon* (Bible of Tonghak Doctrine).

9. Ch'oesonsaeng Munjip Towon Kiso (Record of the Origin of Tonghak Learning), in *Tonghak Sasang Charyojip* (Source Book on Tonghak Thought)(Asea Munhwasa), Vol.1. p.171. Western Learning here refers to Catholicism.

10. Shin Yong-ha, op. cit., p.59.

11. Joon Sik Choi, 'The Concept of Peace in Korean Thoughts: A Study of the Concept Seen in the Thoughts of the Three New Religious Thinkers of Nineteenth Century Korea', *Korea Journal*, Vol .32, No.1 (Spring 1992) p11

12. Choi, op.cit. pp. 11-12;Lee Ki-baek *A New History of Korea* (Seoul, Ilchokak, 1984), pp. 258-259.

13. Lee, op. cit., p. 258.

14. Choi, op. cit., p. 12.

15. *Tonghaksa* (The History of Tonghak),p.5. Recited from Shin, op.cit., p.66.

16. Choi, op.cit, p.12.

17. *Ch'ondogyo Ch 'anggonsa,* chapter 2, pp.37-38. Recited from Shin,op.cit.,p.66.

18. *Tonghaksa,* p. 64.

19. Shin Il-ch'ol, 'Ch'oe Suun-ui Yoksa Uisik' (On Historical Consciousness of Suun), in Yi Hyon-hui , ed., *Tonghak Sasang-gwa Tonghak Hyonymyong* (Tonghak Thoughts and Tonghak Revolution) (Seoul, Chong-a Press, 1984), p.20.

20. Shin Yong-ha, op. cit., p. 66.

21. Ibid. But Shin's interpretation of 'all the religions' view of God' should be substantiated.

22. Choi, op.cit., p. 12.

23. Ch'oe Suun, 'Kyohun-ga'(A Song for Instruction), Chap.5. Recited from Choi, op. cit., p.12.

24. Choi, op. cit., p. 12.

25. Ch'oe Suun, 'Tosu-sa' (On Tao), Chap. 1. Recited from ibid.

26. In Neo-Confucianism especially sincerity and seriousness were considered the best methods of cultivating one's mind and nourishing one's nature (*sushim yangsong*). See ibid.

27. Ibid., p.14. For example, Pang Chong-hwan, an enthusiastic follower of Ch'oe Che-u, initiated a Child Protection Movement in the early 20th century for the first time in Korean history. Thanks to his efforts, a new Korean term for child (*orini*) which included connotations of respect was created, and a national holiday for children was also founded.

28. This view was discussed in detail in John Dunn, *Western Political Theory in the Face of the Future* (Cambridge, Cambridge University Press, 1993), pp.39-42.

29. Francis Fukuyama, 'Confucianism and Democracy', *Journal of Democracy,* Vol.6, No.2 (Summer 1995), pp. 29-30.

30. Vaclav Havel, 'Democracy's Forgotten Dimension', *Journal of Democracy,* Vol.6, No.2, p. 8.

31. It was J.S. Mill who argued that liberty is only vital to self-realisation and social progress when linked to character. For Mill the possession of character distinguished human beings from brutes. It entailed an overcoming of sin – usually defined as animal pleasure, and was the mark of one 'whose desires and impulses are his own'. See Richard Bellamy, *Liberalism and Modern Society* (Cambridge, Polity, 1992), p. 22.

32. This point is important, particularly when we agree with Ross Harrison who thinks that 'equality of respect has supported the goodness of the democratic machine'. Equality of respect is the source of the goodness of democracy. See Ross Harrison. op. cit. pp. 230-231.

33. For an analysis of An Chae-hong's life and thoughts, see Yoon-Jae Chung, *A Medical Approach to Political Leadership: An Chae-hong and a Healthy Korea.* Ph.D dissertation, University of Hawaii, Manoa, 1988.

34. For theoretical discussions of the relationship between language and politics, the following are useful: Noam Chomsky, *Language and Mind* (New York, Harcourt, Brace & World, 1972), p.3; Charles Taylor, 'Language and Human Nature', in Charles Taylor, *Human Agency and Language Philosophical Papers,* (Cambridge, Cambridge University Press, 1985).

35. An Chae-hong's ideas were formerly analysed by the author. Yoon-Jae Chung, 'Minse An Chae-hong-ui Chongch'i Sasang Yon'gu'(A Study of Political Thought of An Chae-hong), *Sahoe Kwahak-kwa Chongch'aek Yon'gu* (*Social Science and Policy Study*), A Journal of the Institute of Social Sciences, Seoul National University, Vol.3, No.3 (November 1982), pp. 167-199.

36. Presumably, it is considered that An was well informed of Lao Tzu's Tao Te Ching which includes such phrases as 'Something and Nothing produce each other' and 'The myriad creatures in the world are born from Something, and Something from Nothing'. The quotations are from *Lao Tzu: Tao Te Ching* (Penguin Books, 1963), translated with an introduction by D. C. Lau. pp. 58, 101.

37. Consider, for example, the words: *pirottada* (to be originated); *pilmi* (underlying cause of happenings); *pae* (belly); *paeda* (to bear); *pit*(light); *pul* (state), etc.

38. An Chae-hong, *Sinminjok Chuui-wa Sinminju Chuui* (New Nationalism and New Democracy) (Seoul, Minu-sa, 1945), pp. 20-22. Hereafter, the analyses are also based upon this booklet.

39. In Korean, the word for field is *tul*, very similar to *tul* (two).

40. See *I Ching:* The Classic Chinese Oracle of Change (Shaftesbury, Dorset, Element, 1996), Translated by Rudolf Ritsema and Stephen Karcher, pp. 103-113.

41. An did not discuss *nam* with *na, nara, nuri,* but the author considers that *nam* can be added to this part of discussion.

42. In this vein, An Chae-hong criticised Cho So-ang's *Samgyun Chuui* (Political Doctrine of Three Equal Rights), saying that though it represented a new political ideology, it neglected the moral character of political obligation and sacrifice which is indispensable for true democracy.

43. It may be noted that *tasrim* is another pure Korean word for politics or governance, and this also shares the same phonetic sign *'ta'* with *tasot* and *Tasari.* But it seems that *tasrim* is a man-centered concept while *Tasari* represents a universal principle which is believed to be operating as the Fair Principle in the cosmos.

44. For a useful discussion of the irreconcilable relations between liberty and equality in the Western context, see Glenn Tinder , *Political Thinking: The Perennial Questions,* Sixth edition (New York, Harper Collins, 1995), pp. 78-83.

45. Equality is at the heart of the democratic system, if not, perhaps, its final cause, and impartiality is the last offering as a fundamental basis of equality. Impartiality is one of democracy's best defences. See Ross Harrison, *Democracy* (London, Routledge, 1995), pp. 197, 230-231.

46. For the 'Cosmic-Together' philosophy, see Myung Hyun Lee, op. cit., pp. 5-7.

47. It is considered that the distinguished English philosopher and historian, Arnold Toynbee was the first scholar to suggest the idea of world government as a safeguard against nuclear war in the twentieth century. Karl W. Deutsch, a prominent American political scientist, also discussed the possibility of a vision of world government as one of the alternatives to nationalism. See Arnold J. Toynbee, *The Prospect of Western Civilisation* (New York, Columbia University Press, 1947) and *Civilisation on Trial* (New York,

Oxford University Press, 1948); Karl W. Deutsch, *Nationalism and Its Alternatives* (New York, Alfred A. Knopf, 1969).

48. It should be noted that this chapter on Kim Ji-ha is an abridged summary of an essay of Yu Kun-ha, 'Kim Ji-ha Writes about Life, Nature, Environment and the Universe', *Korea Journal*, Vol.32,No.1 (Spring 1992), pp. 100-105, by the author's choice and reconstruction.

49. So he is often invited by local communities or local social organisations to talk to about the importance of local autonomy and initiatives for a more humane life.

50. See Matt Ridley, *The Origins of Virtue* (London, Viking, 1996); a brief summary by the author is also available in *Prospect* (November, 1996), pp. 30-33. A review by Ferdinand Mount in *The Sunday Times* (15 December, 1996) is useful.

51. See *Luke,* 10:25-37. But it should be noted that through the parable of the good Samaritan Jesus wants the readers as well as the Jews to understand who is a true neighbour to the wretched: 'the law-abiding religious passers-by' or 'the ordinary caring individual'. Indeed, Jesus is talking about himself who has been sent by God as Saviour to us wretched human beings.

52. By applying the two moral concepts of 'impartial spectator' and 'self-command', Adam Smith forged a new moral basis for a society in which the creation of wealth through commercial activity would be both virtuous and an enhancement of civilisation. See J. M. Evensky, 'The Two Voices of Adam Smith: Moral Philosopher and Social Critic', in John C. Wood, ed. *Adam Smith: Critical Assessments,* 2nd Series, Vol. VI (London, Rout ledge, 1994), pp. 175-195; Donald Winch, 'Adam Smith: Scottish Moral Philosopher as Political Economist', *The Historical Journal,* 35,1(1992), pp. 91-113.

53. William A. Welsh, *Leaders and Elites* (New York, Holt, Rinehart and Winston, 1979), pp. 17-21.

54. Robert C. Tucker, *Politics as Leadership* (Columbia, University of Missourri Press, 1981), p.11.

55. Peter Clarke, *A Question of Leadership* (London, Penguin Books, 1992),p.3.

56. Graham Little, *Strong Leadership* (Oxford, Oxford University Press, 1988),p.2.

57. Ghita Ionescu, *Leadership in an Interdependent World* (London, Longman, 1991).

12

Cambridge, Future Generations and Self

Tae-Chang Kim

The Road to Cambridge is Paved with Good Encounters

The idea of an intercultural conversation on future generations and self has slowly but steadily grown through a confluence of encounters – conferences, people and books. As for the conferences three[1] have been most instrumental.

Encounters through Conferences

The first one was The Future Generations Forum held under the co-sponsorship of the Future Generations Programme, Foundation for International Studies, University of Malta and the Future Generations Alliance Foundation at Valletta, Malta (September 30 – October 1, 1994). The main theme was whether we need a guardian for the protection of the rights and interests of future generations and, if so, how that would be institutionalised within the United Nations framework as something similar to the office of High Commissioner on International Refugees. The idea was advocated theoretically by international legal experts and philosophers from Argentina, Australia, Canada, China, Hungary, India, Tunisia, UK and USA. It was the core of the message conveyed through the special speech made by the President of the Republic of Malta in person. It was at that time that the issue of the basic standpoint came to be discussed very seriously. While acknowledging the importance of creating and modifying institutions, we wanted to share with other participants the necessity of appealing to human conscience.

The second conference that I would like to talk about was the Boston Forum on Future Generations at the American Academy of Science (September 27-28, 1995). It was co-sponsored and organised by the Wright Center for Science Education of Tufts University. It was basically a series of discussions between distinguished scientists and philosophers selected by Eric J. Chaisson (astronomy professor and director of Wright Center) and representatives from Kyoto.

The theme of the conference was how science education today can contribute to the well being of future generations. Through presentations, discussions, questions and answers, what eventually became clear was, to sum up within the boundary of my interest, that today's Americans and presumably most human beings in the world, are seriously science-illiterate, anti-scientific and science hostile; that overall tendencies in contemporary society and education are becoming science-less and that every effort has to be made to build a science-friendly society in which higher science literacy can be enhanced through more science education. Although many other things were discussed there that seemed to me very worthy and encouraging, frankly speaking, I felt something really important was missing..

In my view, what we really need is not to try and have more science education but to return to the root of the scientific way of thinking itself and examine again right from the start as to whether current science education should continue along the same direction.

A science-less society may be very dangerous. But a scientistic society (infatuated with science and with a lost sense of aesthetic balance) could also be disastrous for the well-being of future generations.

The third was the Toronto Forum on Future-oriented Education co-sponsored by Ontario Institute for Studies in Education in Toronto (October 26 – 28,1996). It was to explore a future-oriented education for future generations through the co-creative process of intensive discussions between members of the World Futures Studies Federation selected by Allen Tough, professor of Future Studies, University of Toronto and participants from Kyoto and Beijing. What we learned from this conference was that while futures studies tend to look at the future from now forward, future generations thinking attempts to place now within the web of the interconnected past, present and future looking backward and forward. While acknowledging the importance of exploring alternative futures, our concern is to examine the human intentions, decisions and productions from the standpoint of our posterity as well as ancestors.

Encounters with People

Now let me talk about people, especially three people. The first person I would like to mention is a student at the University of Kiev, Ukraine, whom I met at my lecture made there in June 1995. He made a comment and it was something like this:

> Here in Ukraine, at least among young students, those people who talk about the future are considered to be either cheaters or robbers. Why? Because for the past seventy odd years, old regime leaders always talked about the future, all beautiful slogans and programmes. Do you know what our people eventually got ? It was nothing but a hellish economy and inhumane society. We were cheated and robbed of what we deserved to have under the excuse of building a better future.

It was quite a shock to me. Right at that time, one of the most frequently shown television commercials in Japan was a fascinating young lady smiling and telling the audience 'I like those people who talk about the future'. Right at that time I was member of the executive committee of The World Futures Studies Federation. I was in Kiev as President of the Institute for the Integrated Study of Future Generations. What I have learned from that experience is that thinking and talking about the future alone can be dangerous simply because the future is something that anybody can use for any purpose. The future has to be more *humanised*, *personalised* and *embodied*.

The second person to be mentioned is Bin Kimura whom I met at one of the Kyoto Forum meetings in 1995[2] where the main topic was Healing and Future Generations. One of the hottest debates was on the question of how to view life; as being or becoming. Though one of the most highly reputed philosophers of contemporary Japan was strongly advocating the view of life as being, I was strongly inclined to view life as becoming! Bin Kimura is one of the top psychiatrists, very well versed in both European and Japanese thought. After the debate, he came to me and said to me: 'Dr. Kim, Dr. Weizacker had the same view as you. Life is becoming'. Viktor von Weizacker is a world well-known German psychiatrist and philosopher who happened to be one of the most frequently referred to and quoted through the entire meeting. Kimura gave me a book written by Weizacker. I was awakened to the importance of viewing life as becoming and the multidimensional implications of this perspective. Through this encounter with this Japanese psychiatrist philosopher, I became aware of the underlying coherent way of addressing the issue of self in the intellectual heritages of the Kyoto School of Japanese thought. In the mainstream thinking of Kyoto School, self is viewed as field ('ba' = place or 'ma'= between-ness) though the concrete expressions vary. Self is not a 'thing' to be conceptualised. It should not be perceived as 'essence' or 'substance'. Self is rather an original ground where the other emerges first and only in contrast to the other, the ego consciousness takes place and interacts with the other.

On the basis of this awareness, I have also become able to develop and clarify a more interculturally significant comparative view of self and the world with regard to the epistemological and praxeological context of caring about the well-being of future generations. What has gradually emerged out of this process is that:

(1) The Confucian School of Chinese thought tends to view self as evolving through the ritual stages of human development at different levels of the basically ethical world (ego-body, family, country, and the entire world). Individual human beings are considered in terms of the relational on the basis of familial/ceremonial bond. The purpose of life is the cultivation of real self which should find a proper place in the world where basic ethical principles lie in the ritual observance of the Three Rules and Five Codes of Conduct prescribed by the teachings of Confucian classical texts. Intergenerational responsibilities are based on the sense of ritual-sharing community.

(2) The Han-Thinking tradition of Korean thought tends to view self as embodied life energy. The indigenous Korean word 'han' etymologically means 'one', 'big', 'many', 'different' and 'approximate'. Obviously it may be very difficult to try to describe

> something essential or substantive with this rather contradictorily polysemous word. This word itself is, in a sense, the epitome of Han Thinking. Han signifies a psychodynamic flow of life energy. Han has some similarity with the Taoist concept of 'Chi', or 'Ki' in Korean but 'han' is more directly related with human dimension. When 'han' is embodied and activated in a positive way it tends to work as constructive force like love, dedication, generosity, philanthropy, patriotism and so on. But if it happens to be activated in a negative direction, then it tends to work as destructive force like hatred, envy, jealousy, resentment, antagonism and so on. The purpose of life is to preserve and enhance life energy either in its human embodiment or that of family, society and the world. The world is perceived to be full of life energy – a vitalistic world. The core principle of human life and society lies in the preservation and empowerment of life energy. Individual human beings are thought of in terms of the personal placed in the context of genealogy and consanguinity considered to be the reservoir of life energy. Intergenerational responsibilities are based on the sense of continuity and extension of life energy through generations.

In comparison with the Confucian and the Han Thinking, the Kyoto School starts with the Zen Buddhist notion of the phenomenal world as the stage of co-arising and existential dimension as non-entity or non-self. The Kyoto School tends to view individual human beings in terms of the contextual placed in the situations where climatic and/or atmospheric dynamics exert the most important influence. Intergenerational responsibilities are based on the sense of this climatic and/or atmospheric influence.

The third person is Danah Zohar, an Oxford-based quantum physicist cum management consultant. I was first enlightened very much by her *The Quantum Self*[3] and *The Quantum Society*[4]. So I asked Japanese colleagues to invite her with Ian Marshall, her husband and London-based psychiatrist, to one of our Kyoto Forum meetings in 1996. Through formal discussions and informal talks at the Kyoto Forum and conversations held afterwards, I gradually came to feel that something is lacking in her basic formulation. The quantum self metaphor may be helpful in understanding some aspects of the concept of self. But the metaphor sounds like a schematic view of self as a 'thing'. Quantum self is not the human being, not the human body, or the human soul with which our living concern deals, but rather the scientific subject, the extreme abstraction of the world. This is almost always the case with attempting to explain human affairs in terms of the physical or the material, either Newtonian or Quantum.

Zohar made a thorough re-evaluation of Western intellectual history from a rather unique perspective. She especially made an extraordinary effort to shift the centre of gravity in our basic perceptual and behavioural paradigms from one she based on the Newtonian, atomistic, model of self and organisation to another based on a quantum physical outlook. Her competence and expertise are clearly shown by the way in which she makes complicated and difficult professional details relatively understandable and applicable to non-experts and non-professionals. What she tries to say is that the modern Western, Newtonian model takes only the particle aspect and has extended it to the extreme (individualism, egoism, competition, aggressiveness and many other related characteristics). She also says that the Newtonian model of organisation is mechanistic where people are just like cogs in a machine, mutually separated and disconnected, while relational dimensions are disregarded.

In contrast to the modern Western model, she looks at the Eastern model as taking only the wave aspect and extending it to the other extreme; collectivism, groupism, familiarism, conformity and other related tendencies.

Danah Zohar's favorite metaphor for the Western model consists of the billiard self and the big clockwork machine, and the one for the Eastern model is the wave-like self and the family network.

Her emphatic recommendation lies in a radical transformation for the West (specifically those executives and leaders in various sectors of the Western societies) to shift worldviews and mindsets toward the quantum model which alone can overcome the shortcomings and outdatedness of both the Western particle machine and the Eastern wave-only and family network-specific paradigms.

To me quantum self feels like a step backward from where I stand in terms of the view of self and the world made more explicit through the personal encounter with Bin Kimura. But, for the sake of fairness, I feel I have to make it clear that meeting this wonderful couple was the chance to see the possibility of a meaningful intercultural conversation on the issue of how to meaningfully view self. It was because I was interested in the concept of quantum vacuum (rather than the particle-wave relationship) that may have very much to do with the Taoist concept of nothingness or the Buddhist concept of emptiness or non-self. In spite of her painstaking efforts to convince me that the quantum model can be the synthesis of the Western atomistic (particle-like) and the Eastern (wave-like) models of self and society, I have never been able to share the view simply because I think it is her misunderstanding of the Eastern model, if there is such a thing as that, or simply her unfamiliarity with the deep meaning of concepts like nothingness, emptiness or non-self that makes her look for a synthesis rather than the common root of two different appearances on the surface.[5]

What is needed is not any attempt to put together and make one from above. What has to be done is returning and/or descending together to the original zero point (it can be a vacuum, emptiness, non-self or nothingness) and start to look at both/either particle side and/or wave side from there. A quantum model may be a very good paradigm, a step higher than the atomistic and/or the relational (as Zohar describes them) in the West. But the problem is that she overextended the quantum metaphor.

Encounters with Books

Now I want to talk about encounters with books. Their titles are legion. I would like to specifically mention three. While the Future Generations Alliance Foundation was sponsoring a series of international conferences on the issue of culture/civilisation and future generations in Seoul, Beijing, Taipei, and Ho Chi Minh in 1993, Washington D.C., Hong Kong Colombo, Chengdu, Boston, Kuala Lumpur, Bangkok, Gue Yang in 1994, one of the underlying questions was why people are generally inattentive and/or losing a sense of responsibility toward future generations and what sort of effective ways and means can be available for intergenerational concern. One of the many attempts to diagnose our realities was suggested by Christopher Lasch through *The Culture of Narcissism* and *The Minimal Self.* The two books seem to me to have offered an answer, which I was desperately exploring in the midst of growing frustration. Why are people careless about future generations? Why do men and women seem unmoved by our appeal, that it is now our responsibility to make the earth a safe and hospitable home for present and future generations?

Lasch was talking about the America of 1970.

> We are fast losing the sense of historical continuity, the sense of belonging to a succession of generations originating in the past and stretching into the future.[6]
>
> As a description of reality, it is not confined to the 1970's. I found the same reality almost everywhere I went.

Why? Because, Lasch said, our self has become the minimal or narcissistic self. What is the minimal or narcissistic self? Some characterisations are offered:

> In a time of troubles, everyday life becomes an exercise in survival. People take one day at a time. They seldom look back, lest they succumb to a debilitating 'nostalgia': and if they look ahead, it is to see how they can insure themselves against the disasters almost everybody expects.
>
> Under these conditions selfhood becomes a kind of luxury, out of place in an age of impending austerity. Selfhood implies a personal history, friends, family, a sense of place. Under siege, the self contracts to a defensive core, armed against diversity. Emotional equilibrium demands a minimal self, not the imperial self of yesteryear.[7]

> The minimal or narcissistic self, is above all, a self uncertain of its own outlines, longing either to remake the world in its own image or to merge into its environment in blissful union.[8]

> Narcissism signifies a loss of selfhood, not self-assertion. It refers to a self threatened with disintegration and by a sense of inner emptiness.[9]

> Selfhood is the painful awareness of the tension between our unlimited aspirations and our limited understanding, between our original intimations of immortality and our fallen state, between oneness and separation.[10]

> Narcissus drowns in his own reflection, never understanding that it is his

> own reflection. He mistakes his own image for someone else and seeks to embrace it without regard to his safety. The point of the story is not that Narcissus falls in love with himself, but since he fails to recognise his own reflection, that he lacks any conception of the difference between himself and his surroundings.[11]

Then what should we do? A 'society that fears it has no future is not likely to give much attention to the needs of the next generation'. Therefore this sense of no future has to be overcome. Because the 'belief that society has no future while it rests on a certain realism about the dangers ahead, also incorporates a narcissistic inability to identify with posterity or feel oneself as part of a historical stream'. Therefore the belief in a bright future has to be enhanced. The next step should be how to enlarge the contracted self under the stress of turbulence and unease and to empower the minimal self to hold the belief in the future.

And then *Modernity and Self-Identity* by Anthony Giddens. In early 1996, I was teaching at the University of Houston-Clear Lake. It was there that I read the book.

My interest in Giddens started with his idea of 'colonising the future'. To him, 'Colonising the future' is the inevitable choice of individuals and organisations in the high-modernity environment to secure ontological security. It is a means of seeking to stabilise outcomes in a situation of chance and risk.

> Modernity is a risk culture. I do not mean by this that social life is inherently more risky than it used to be; for most people in the developed societies that is not the case. Rather, the concept of risk becomes fundamental to the way both lay actors and technical specialists organise the social world. Under conditions of modernity, the future is continually drawn into the present by means of the reflexive organisation of knowledge environments. A territory, as it were, is carved out and colonised. Yet such colonisation by its nature cannot be complete:thinking in terms of risk is vital to assessing how far projects are likely to diverge from their anticipated outcomes.[12]

Giddens describes modern life in various ways from now forward and appropriating the future for the sake of the interests of the present generations. On one hand, as an intrinsic part of life-planning of individuals, and on the other hand as securing the collective futures of societies in general. In both cases, basic recognition is that the universe of future events is open to be shaped by human intervention though not unlimitedly, as far as possible, and its limitation is only regulated by risk assessment from the standpoint of presently existing people in a system basically geared to the domination of nature and the reflexive making of history.

Giddens also points out that morality is extrinsic in the colonisation of the future because moral principles run counter to the concept of risk and to the mobilising of dynamics of control necessary to stabilise outcomes.

My next point of interest lies in his observation of tradition, modernity and generational issues.

> ......tradition and the continuity of the generations are inherently tied to one another. Generational differences are essentially a mode of time-reckoning in pre-modern societies. A generation is a distinct kinship cohort or order which sets the individual's life within a sequence of collective transitions. In modern times, however, the concept of 'generation' increasingly makes sense only against the backdrop of standardised time......Temporal succession in this sense retains little of the resonance of collective processes of transition characteristic of earlier eras.
>
> In traditional contexts, the life-cycle carries strong connotations of renewal, since each generation in some substantial part rediscovers and relives modes of life of its forerunners. Renewal loses most of its meaning in the settings of high modernity where practices are repeated only so far as they are reflexively justifiable.[13]

Third point of interest is what Giddens calls 'self as a reflexive project'. According to Giddens, the 'late' or 'high' modern world is a 'runaway world' in the sense that not only is the pace of social change much faster than in any prior system, so also is its scope, and the profoundness with which it affects pre-existing social practices and mode of behaviour. And the self in high modernity appears:

> Modernity is essentially a post-traditional order. The transformation of time and space, coupled with the disembedding mechanisms, propel social life away from the hold of preestablished precepts or practices. This is the context of the thoroughgoing reflexivity...... The reflexivity of modernity has to be distinguished from the reflexive monitoring of action intrinsic to all human activity.[14]

> The modern world is a 'runaway world': not only is the pace of social change much faster than in any prior system, so also is its scope, and the profoundness with which it affects pre-existing social practices and modes of behaviour.[15]

Within this 'high' or 'late' modern context of reflexivity, self identity becomes a reflexively organised endeavour.

In the settings of what I call 'high' or 'late' modernity – our present-day-world – the self, like the broader institutional contexts in which it exists, has to be reflexively made.[16]

> In the post-traditional order of modernity, and against the backdrop of new forms of mediated experience, self-identity becomes a reflexively organised endeavour. The reflexive project of the self, which consists in the sustaining of coherent, yet continuously revised, biographical narratives, takes place in the context of multiple choice as filtered through abstract systems.[17]

> The self in high modernity is not a minimal self.[18]

> A self-identity has to be created and more or less continually recorded against the backdrop of shifting experiences of day-to-day life and fragmenting tendencies of modern institutions.[19]

Then Giddens describes where self becomes a reflexive project.

> The reflexivity of modernity extends into the core of the self. Put in another way, in the context of a post-traditional order, the self becomes a reflexive project....In the settings of modernity ....the altered self has to be explored and constructed as a part of a reflective process of connecting personal and social change.[20]

Then what is the reflexivity of modernity? Again Giddens' statement goes that:

> Modernity's reflexivity refers to the susceptibility of most aspects of social activity, and material relations with nature, to chronic revision in the light of new information or knowledge.[21]

Then, appraising key aspects of modernity's development, he says that:

> Besides its institutional reflexivity, modern social life is characterised by profound processes of the re-organisation of time and space, coupled to the expansion of disembedding mechanisms – mechanisms which prise

> social relations free from the hold of specific locales, recombining them across wide time space distances.[22]

And institutional reflexivity is defined as:

> the regularised use of knowledge about circumstances of social life as a constitutive element in its organisation and transformation.[23]

I found an aspect of his view in a different context.

> To be a 'person' is not just a reflective actor, but to have a concept of a person (as applied both to the self and others).[24]
>
> The self, of course, is embodied.[25]

After reading through Modernity and Self-Identity I felt the following things. Firstly, his view of self is a cognitive self, trying to conceptualise itself to match the rapidly changing life world. It is not the Promethean (volitional) self to make the world in his/her image. Nor is it the Narcissistic (emotional) self to merge into the world in blissful union. It is the Protean (agilely metamorphosing) self. I understood him in this context when he stated that the self in high modernity is not a minimal self. His self is more of a knower or a thinker than an actor or a maker.

Secondly, his self is something to be created. He does not think that self persists over time as something just given. His self is rather something that is routinely created and sustained in the reflexive activities. So his view of self is basically present-focused, without being connected with either the past or extended into the future.

Thirdly, his view of self, on one hand, is Human in the sense that he doubts the existence of self as substance, and on the other hand, Lockean in the sense that he does not deny the existence of self, reflexively understood by the person. Anthony Giddens reminds me of John Locke, in many different places. Locke has defined a person as: 'a thinking intelligent being, that has reason and reflection, and can consider itself as self, the same thinking thing, in different times and places'.[26] His self may be, in a sense, a typical European self and, at the same time, while Lasch's self represents some aspects of American self.

Fourthly, his view of the future is looked at mainly in terms of the extension of the security of the present generation by colonising the future. The wellbeing of future generations is not the matter of concern.

After having been enlightened through reading of Lasch and Giddens, two problems remained to linger in my mind thereafter: (1) Are their views of self too reactive, rather than proactive? (2) What is the more pragmatic concept of self, with which we are more proactive and not just reactive to socio-cultural milieu?

As the third encounter with books, I would like to refer to *Metaphors of Interrelatedness* by Linda E. Olds, professor of psychology at Linfield College in McMinnville, Oregon, and *Metaphors of Identity* by Thomas K. Fitzgerald, professor at the University of North Carolina, Greensboro.

Metaphors of Interrelatedness starts with this observation:

> Perhaps the most powerful legacy of the twentieth century for science and philosophy has been the steadily accumulating challenge to the possibility of 'objective' knowledge, uncoloured by assumptions or interpretations. The core implication is that there can be no such thing as neutral fact or finding....[27]

And on the basis of viewing knowledge as approximation, Olds continues to expound:

> If knowledge is approximate, there may indeed be alternate ways to conceptualise and approach the nature of what is to be known. Within the freedoms of imagination opened up by this inability and the limits posed by the interface of theory and experimentation lies the terrain where metaphor and model become the tools of science and inquiry. Theorists are the architects and synthesisers in the process of inquiry, and metaphor becomes an aid to creative theorising and hypothesis construction.[28]

She then emphasises:

> We arrive at the importance of metaphor, model and analogy as tools for grasping and suggesting connections between new and as yet unrealised aspects of reality in the search for theoretical understandings. Metaphor involves the use of images or concepts from one field of discourse or experience to describe some other field of experience in such a way as to suggest certain parallels, commonalities or useful paradoxical connections between the two areas. In their root sense, metaphors transfer or carry meaning across ('phor' from 'pherein') and beyond ('meta') from

> one context to another. Metaphors are 'meaning transports' which extend our level of understanding by comparison, or some might argue by smuggling extra dimensions into an analysis. In either case they enrich the field of potential comprehension.[29]

She also has this to say:

> The power of metaphor resides in its capacity to hold in interactive tension both similarities and differences between two compared objects or events, the two poles of the metaphor.[30]

After telling us why the metaphorical approach is effective and useful she provided a rather detailed inventory of attempted metaphors of different kinds such as self as rational ego, self as identity, self as active process, self as wholeness and finally concluded with systems metaphors for self. She especially made clear that self is a viewpoint or a perspective and not a thing.[31] What she seems to be trying to say is that self does not need to have a viewpoint or a perspective, but is itself a constantly self-organising viewpoint. Self is a perspective from which I see 'me' as only one level of hierarchy, connected to all.[32]

Metaphors of Interrelatedness has given me a clue to exploring a new dimension. It is the merit, power and value of metaphorical thinking with regard to the discourse of self and future generations, from a cross cultural perspective.

Next, *Metaphors of Identity.* This book is an extensive yet intensive multidisciplinary work on the meanings of culture, identity, communication, attempting to clarify the concept and role of self in the communication process and surveying cultural and biological research on self, individuality, personality and mind-body questions.

The author's view of metaphor is:

> Metaphor, the essence of which is the conceptualisation of one thing in terms of another, has always played an extensive role in the dialogues surrounding discussions of identity.[33]

He then points out that:

> Metaphors of identity in the culture-communications dialogue have evolved from the older, more static images of 'person in society', as the

> mirror of social reality, to the more action oriented dramaturgical metaphors, suggesting role competence and 'on-stage' activity; finally, to more contemporary metaphors that – rightly or wrongly – imply that we humans are in total control of our lives, and hence are potentially constructing, creating or transforming identities as situations vary.[34]

After acknowledging that the modern Western meaning of self is that of conscious individuation, that is, the subject as self-defining and self-sufficient, the author does not neglect to observe… 'some concept of the self is undoubtedly found in all cultures, but self must be treated both individually and socially; and there will always be some tension between self and other'.[35]

He also says that:

> All individuals and groups must deal with both public and private displays of self. Cultures simply vary in the amount of emphasis given these expressions.[36]

Finally in concluding, the author is very cautionary.

> How effectively have cultural and social meanings been communicated through image-metaphors in the culture-communication dialogue? Guiding metaphors are ubiquitous in scientific descriptions of identity, the academic metaphor for self-in-context. In order to judge the aptness of metaphor in this dialogue, then these figures of speech had to be assessed in reference to specific contexts. Metaphorical ambiguity was seen to be heightened in cross-cultural comparison. Metaphoric descriptions, subject to subtle ideological manipulations, remain problematic in scientific discourse. When judging the elegance of research models, the effectiveness of their guiding metaphors must be carefully evaluated.[37]

Metaphors of Identity has awakened us to the potential that good metaphor images can have in our intercultural communication efforts. But Fitzgerald has also cautioned us that we have to be very careful about the hidden dimension of ideological manipulation and/or scientific/realistic inappropriateness.

What we have learned so far can roughly be summarised in the following tables:

Approach	Human Approach (Future Generations, Kyoto)	Institutional Approach (Future Generations, Malta)
Strategy	'Back-to-the Origin' strategy (Future Generations, Kyoto)	'More of what we have in better shape' strategy (Wright Center, Boston)
Perspective	Looking at Now from both past and future backward and forward (Future Generations, Kyoto)	Looking at Future from Now forward (Alternative Futures, Hawaii)

Table 1. Basic Standpoints Compared

Danah Zohar	Quantum Physical View	Self as Particle Self as Wave
Christopher Lasch	Psychocultural View	Narcissistic Self Promethean Self
Anthony Giddens	Sociological View	Reflexive Self
Linda E. Olds	Metaphorical View	Self as Thing Self as Perspective
Thomas K. Friterald	Metaphorical View	Self as Person in Society Self as Identity Transformer
Kyoto School	Action Philosophical View	Self as Betweenness Where Ego and the other emerge and interact

Table 2. Selected View of Self Compared

Why Cambridge?

For the past several years of the international activities of The Future Generations Alliance Foundation and my own within and without the organisational framework, the UK has somehow been an out-of-the-way country. And it was when I began to frequently travel to some English and Irish cities to give lectures (Oxford, London, Cambridge, Sheffield, Manchester, Leeds, Dublin and a few others) that my serious and concrete interests started to materialise. While I was associated with Oxford Brookes University my major concern was whether a joint programme on future generations could be developed with some of our well-meaning friends at the undergraduate/postgraduate level.

While the effort was underway, I came to know about the philosophy of John Macmurray through *The Personal World: John Macmurray on Self and Society* selected and introduced by Philip Conford. There I discovered a British philosopher who died not so long ago (1976) whom I did not know before at all. But according to Mr. Tony Blair's foreword, he was modern in the sense that he confronted what will be the critical political question of the twenty-first century:the relationship between individual and society. This British political leader (whom I did not know but has since become Prime Minister of the UK) appraises his philosophy as 'more accessible, better written and above all far more relevant than most of what I and many others studied as hallowed texts at University'. I felt somewhat ashamed of my ignorance and tried to grasp what is so relevant.

So I read his *The Self as Agent*, *Persons in Relations* and *Reason and Emotion*. I found it really surprising. It was for reasons similar to those described by Mr. Blair in *The Personal World*. My surprise was because nowhere else have I ever been able to find anything more formatively congenial. Here are some quotations from Macmurray:

> (1) We should note….the essential fact that life is a process of development. We take the living creature at one moment, and consider it as it is at that moment. In fact life never is at any moment. It is always becoming. We often talk as if the material of which a living body is composed were preserved throughout its life. Yet life is essentially, so far as it is material, a process of metabolism. It consists of getting rid of the material of which the body is composed, and replacing it continuously by new material, not exactly but with variations. The matter of the living body is not preserved. It is a continual process of dissolution and replacement. The form is preserved, but again not exactly, but with variations.[38]

> (2) The self must be conceived, not theoretically as subject, but practically, as agent. Secondly, human behaviour is comprehensible only in terms of a dynamic social reference; the isolated, purely individual self

> is a fiction. In philosophy this means....that the unity of the personal cannot be thought of as the form of an individual self, but only though the mutuality of personal relationship. In face of both difficulties a radical modification of our philosophical tradition is demanded.
>
> The first requires us to substitute for the self as subject, which is the starting point of modern philosophy, the Self as agent; and to make this substitution is to reject the traditional distinction between the subjective and the objective. The second compels us to abandon the traditional individualism or egocentricity of our philosophy.[39]
>
> (3) Our conclusion was not merely that a self is an agent; but that the self has its being only in its agency, and that its reflective activities are but negative aspects of this agency. The self as 'the mind', which is the self as non-agent, is a nonentity. It follows from this that so long as we maintain, whether consciously or unconsciously, the traditional standpoint, no account of the personal is logically possible. The Self must then be conceived either as a substance or as an organism, while in reality it is a person.[40]
>
> (4) In reflection we isolate ourselves from dynamic relations with the Other; we withdraw into ourselves, adopting the attitude of spectators, not of participants.[41]
>
> (5) The idea of an isolated agent is self-contradictory. Any agent is necessarily in relation to the Other. Apart from this essential relation he does not exist.[42]

There are many other statements which, in a nutshell, emphasise that self as thinker should be replaced by self as actor; that the isolated self has to be changed into the self in relation; and the self should be conceived not in terms of the material nor the organic but definitely the personal. Through internally dialogical encounter with John Macmurray's philosophy my attention to contemporary British thinking began to be rejuvenated after having forgotten for a while the adolescent inclination toward Hobbes, Locke, Bacon, Smith, Smiles, Newton, Shakespeare, Keats, Wordsworth, Byron, Handel and many others.

While indulging myself in Macmurray's philosophy, I was also pleased to be able to meet two of my very promising younger colleagues when I visited Cambridge. They are Masaya Kobayashi, political philosophy professor of Chiba University, Japan and Chung Yoon-Jae, Korean political thought professor of The Academy of Korean Studies, Korea. I have expectations that both will make potentially great contributions to the academic communities of the two countries. We met and had talks on future generations and self. Kobayashi proposed the possibility and significance of holding a seminar on this issue with several deeply involved scholars on Cambridge Campus. Thus the idea of the Cambridge Forum on Future Generations started in concrete terms. In spite of his very busy research schedule Kobayashi did all the time-consuming logistical arrangements at every stage of organising the meeting. Chung also made contributions in many less conspicuous ways.

In addition to the sincere co-operation, there were two intellectual motivations. Number one, Isaac Newton, Number two, Ludwig Wittgenstein. I have never been able to think of one without thinking of the other. And both are closely related with Cambridge. What about Newton in connection with a forum on future generations and self?

Since meeting and talking with Danah Zohar and quite a number of thinkers who tend to view Newton as a source of the outdated model and/or worldview to be radically transformed, I have always felt something different and want to re-illuminate the real value of Newton. To me Newton is the essence of the modern West in the real sense of the word. To me Newton is living everywhere around and within us. To those whose main enterprise is to create something new out of nothing (ex nihilo) anything old has to be destroyed or denied, and Newton can be a good target to make that something look new. But to those whose ultimate purpose is to generate something new anything old has to be maintained through the process and incorporated into the product. I have long been of the opinion that the act of generating is as much needed today as the act of creating in spite of the fact that creativity has more often been talked about in many spheres of our life.

In Newton's universe, there is no room for uncertainty. All that happens in the world, according to Newton, has a specific cause and gives rise to a definite effect, and the future of any part of the system cannot in principle allow any unpredictability.

Newton was thus able to develop a complete mathematical formulation of the mechanistic view of science. Newton provided humanity with more reliable foundation for science and philosophy. Newton pictured the world as a perfect machine. Newton's God is a Great Mathematician and man is a small mathematician eager to fathom the mysteries of God's mind.

Newton is the highest peak of abstract thinking. Abstract means 'removed' or 'extracted', or 'taken out'. Abstract thinking is pure thought with emotion or will removed. It is mathematical thinking and mechanical thinking. Electronic communications, information, cybernetics, artificial intelligence, cyberspace networking – all these are progenies of Newton. If the world is devoid of everything other than Kant's pure reason, or Descartes' mathematical reason, then it becomes a big machine-clock, calculator or computer. The worldview that we have inherited from Newtonian physics continues to have a profound effect on our whole lives. It is still our most important window on reality, permeating our attitudes and values, influencing the way government, business, societies, families and relationships are managed.

If we take the thinking self of Descartes, Locke, Bacon, Russell and Giddens and carry it to the extreme abstraction, I can presumably find there Newton's mathematical self.

If someone says that all philosophies after Plato are footnotes to Plato, then we can say that all science and philosophy are the footnotes to Newton. Cambridge has an unceasing attraction to me on account of Newton. Having said this, I should immediately add that my special interest in Newton is as complement of Wittgenstein. It is only through understanding the significance of Newton that you can see the significance of Wittgenstein.

What is so significant about Wittgenstein? To me at least, there are three aspects.

Firstly, because of what is referred to as his '180 degree turn'. It is the total rejection of the 'metaphysical stance' in which the human knowing subject confronts the world object. What does giving up the metaphysical stance mean? It is a destructive task, tearing down the 2000-year-old 'inner façade' of metaphysically produced assumptions about the subject's relation to itself. He was out to destroy the Cartesian 'inner world of knowledge', the strange duplication by which we not only experience, feel and think but also seem to know what we experience, feel and think, as well as the very processes which seem to be involved in all of this.

As one of Wittgenstein's scholars said:

> Wittgenstein's greatest achievement was that he overturned the assumption of two millennia of the Western thought that an 'inner world' of the subject has to be constructed on (and can be justified by) the model of the metaphysicalised objective world.[43]

Secondly, because of his abandonment of the conception of the metaphysically private self. The metaphysically private self is a 'myth that the independence of the self somehow depends upon its having a metaphysical underpinning or validation'.[44] The attempt to ground both self and object in the allegedly logical principle of self-identity, like the Kantian thing-in-itself-ness ('Ding an sich') or the Hegelian in-itself-ness ('an sich') lies at the very heart of the rationalistic – epistemological duality – construct which created the pyramid of Western metaphysics. Wittgenstein tried to undo the Western way of thinking that locks us into the absolutely private self. His denial of the metaphysically private self was established on the basis of his discovery after a thorough investigation into language that an absolutely private language is a mirage. The real significance of this aspect can be well understood only when it is clearly seen that to reject the metaphysically private self, not to assume any metaphysical ground or foundation for its logical validity or psychological security, is actually to pave the way for a new, genuine, open and generative self. If I use Wittgenstein's favourite metaphor, the metaphysically private self is 'the fly in the fly-bottle' (prison) and a newly opened self is the fly out of the fly-bottle (choice).

Thirdly, because of what Henry Finch called the kenotic spirit of Wittgenstein which is the spirit of emptying and identitylessness. It is the very opposite of the metaphysical idea of self-identity. He denies the concept of self-identity in Tractatus.

> To say of one thing that it is identical with itself is to say nothing at all.[45]

> There is no such thing as the subject that thinks or entertains.[46]

Then what does identitylessness mean? Henry Finch raises the question anybody would ask at this point. Here is his answer:

> Mainly non-attachment, as this was understood by philosophers from Meister Eckhart to Heidegger. And this means non-identification with, not to be identified with family, tribe, nation, class, people, profession, gender and of course, above all, with possessions, including knowledge, ego and self. This is the principle that unites religion (in which it is called skepticism), Buddhism and Christianity (which both require giving up ego and self) Sufism and Taoism, Tolstoi and Dostoyevsky. Attachment is severed at the root when the ego disappears. And ego is not in a small part vanity.[47]

Wittgenstein's self is a self opened through total abandonment of the absolutely fixated identity. His self is against the average modern self that is wordless, being locked away in false subjectivity and privacy. By dropping the private self entirely, together with the inner world and mental processes, Wittgensteinian self is an inwardly opened self through the emptying out of the 'inner world' as the main locus of the most valuable kind of experience. From the perspective of my own concern with our society's criminal indifference to the needs of future generations Wittgensteinian self is a new source of encouragement .

Now what potential intercultural significance can we find specifically at Cambridge? Where can we find the relevance of linking Newton, Macmurray and Wittgenstein with a Future Generations Forum between Cambridge scholars and Northeast Asian scholars? To me they represent the interculturally meaningful aspects of the Western view of self, which may match most symbolically the three different, yet mutually interconnected flows of viewing self in the Northeast Asian cultural heritages. Northeast Asian views are summarised in the following chart, which is tentatively attempted to show an intercultural correspondence between issues or concerns in the East and West. In this way I came to feel that Cambridge was able to provide an ideal intellectual climate.

What about conversation then? Conversation is basically dialogical. It is different from the predominantly monological lectures, speeches, or paper presentation focused seminars. It is supposed to be a co-creative process of lively two-way communications. I wanted to see what would eventually emerge if Newtonian, Macmurrayian and Wittgensteinian themes, either explicitly or implicitly, directly or indirectly, meet as compared with the Chinese, Korean, and Japanese cultural construals.

Cambridge/UK	**Kyoto/North East Asia**
Newtonian Metaphor	*Confucian Metaphor* (Chinese)
• Atomistic Self in Mechanical World	• Ritual Self in Ethical World
• Human being as the Individual based on Egocentric Identity	• Human beings as Relational based on Familial/Ceremonial Bond
• Seeking Self-interest	• Aiming at Cultivation of Related Self
Intergenerational Responsibilities based on contract of Reciprocity and /or Utility	Intergenerational Responsibilities based on Five Fundamental Codes of Conduct
Macmurrayian Metaphor	*Han-Thinking Metaphor* (Korean)
• Self as Agent in Personal World	• Self as Embodied Life Energy ('Han' or 'Ki')
• The Individual in Action based on Mutuality of the Personal	• The Personal based on Genealogy/Consanguinity
• Aiming at Communal Action	• Aiming at Enhancing Life-Energy
Intergenerational Responsibilities based on Ethics of Friendship	Intergenerational Responsibilities based on Ethics of Empowerment
Wittgensteinian Metaphor	*Kyoto School Metaphor* (Japanese)
• Identityless Self in Foundationless World	• Self as Field ('Ba' or 'Ma') Co-arising World
• The Individual Inwardly Opened through Abandoning Metaphysicalised Identity	• The Contextual based on Climatic/Atmospheric Dynamics
• Aiming at Non-Attachment	• Aiming at prevention of Turbulence
Intergenerational Responsibilities basedon Ethics of Emptying and Identitylessness	Intergenerational Responsibilities based on Ethics of Non-Self

Table 3. Tentatively attempted 'Interculturally Significant Conversational Theme Pairing' between Cambridge and Kyoto

At Cambridge and After.

While at the Cambridge Forum on Future Generations and Self, I was expecting to learn from participants from the Cambridge side what they intended to contribute to caring about the well being of future generations.

What I was able to learn was that there were basically three different and yet mutually connected lines of thinking.

1) that we have to take the position that future generations are our neighbours temporally distant. And as we have responsibilities toward remote neighbours (spatially distant) we are required also to be responsible to future generations;

2) that even if we follow what is called typical Western atomistic, rational and utilitarian model of self it is possible to make a positive argument in favour of the well being of future generations; and,

3) that there is very little theoretical ground for validating our caring about the well being of future generations.

I was happy to learn that a group of Cambridge scholars have been addressing the issue of future generations for some time under the initiative and leadership of Peter Laslett. There are of course a lot of other scholars and practitioners in different parts of the world who are concerned and engaged in this issue. But a continuing and committed group of scholars is still rare though futures-named associations are many. To think about the future is one thing and to care about the well being of future generations is quite another. Thinking about the future is primarily epistemological.

Caring about future generations is, par excellence, re-examining our ethos, values, action, decision, lifestyles and many other issues faced by the present generation.

What I felt after discussions with Peter Laslett and his colleagues was that though there was a difference between our centres of gravity we shared similar problematiques. While they were interested (it sounded to me so) in how to theoretically validate and/or legitimise their concern and attitude toward future generations on existing philosophical grounds, my colleagues and myself tried to generate a new view of self and society through conversing, which may contribute more to empowering people to be motivated to care about future generations.

There are three things I wish we could have done but that we have not yet been able to do.

Firstly, I wanted very much to have an intercultural discussion whether we need a theoretically formulated ground in order to take responsibility for what must be done.

I would not myself take the position that we should wait until a verifiable theory can be established to take a responsible stance. Today's world needs our immediate choice and decision. It sounds very unresponsive to try to save theoretical coherence by sacrificing axiological imperative. That kind of stance reminds me of one of the episodes concerning what happened in Vietnam. I heard this from one of my Vietnamese friends when I went and gave a lecture at the University of Hanoi in 1994. When the French Navy tried to invade Vietnam and was just about to attack, a high ranking official, trying to find a theoretical clarification, returned to the library and struggled with esoteric classics, thus postponing urgently needed practical actions. If you cannot find appropriate theoretical grounds, then you cannot find the meaning and/or validity of taking responsible care about what desperately needs it. Is it really so? I wanted this and other related fundamental questions to be raised and discussed.

These questions are not to know the answer but to facilitate the conversation interculturally. How interculturally?

Because at the conference was Kido Inoue, a well known Mahayana Buddhism Zen Master, whose deep rooted view has been that what is urgently needed is to be wholly liberated from the spell of metaphysically enslaved, theoretically enclaved and narrowly closed self.

Because at the conference was Katsuhiko Yazaki, a businessman-philosopher and the sponsor of this Forum, whose ultimate goal is to go beyond the boundary of egoism, economism, scientism, nowism and nationalism. And I was also there with all the questions I had with Christopher Lasch, Danah Zohar, Nobel Prize winning scientists, Newton, Locke, Hobbes, Descartes, Giddens and Wittgenstein. It would certainly have been a stimulating conversation, had it actually taken place.

Secondly, I wish we could have discussed the issue Takeshi Sasaki had in mind.

Democracy, especially in its contemporary representative form of democracy, voting mass and public opinion, electoral system, political party structure and platforms, tends to be influenced, manipulated and directed on the basis of short term narrow interests, and so consideration of future generations is very difficult to come by.

Now the democratic system itself has many enemies around for various reasons. Future Generations can be one of them. If caring about future generations needs longer term perspectives, bigger forward-looking mindsets, broader interest calculus, more future conscious political parties, it will be that the democratic system in its current operation may have to be radically reformed or some other alternative derived. This is a dangerous threat to democracy. For this reason and due to many other discontents, future generations can be a formidable enemy to democracy. Is it not so? What do you think? What can be done about it? With John Dunn and Ross Harrison, it would have been a fascinating conversation!

Thirdly, I wanted to see lively discussions concerning what caring about future generations actually means in the contemporary socio-cultural environment regardless of how it is defined; either as that of 'high' or 'late' modernity or postmodernity.

Finally before concluding, I would like to mention a new idea which occurred to me as a result of an internal dialogue before, during and immediately after the Cambridge Forum on Future Generations and Self. It is the idea of intergenerationally responsible self (culture and society). It is an agenda or project to be explored theoretically. It is an objective for education. It is an issue for political debates. I want to make it a public topic.

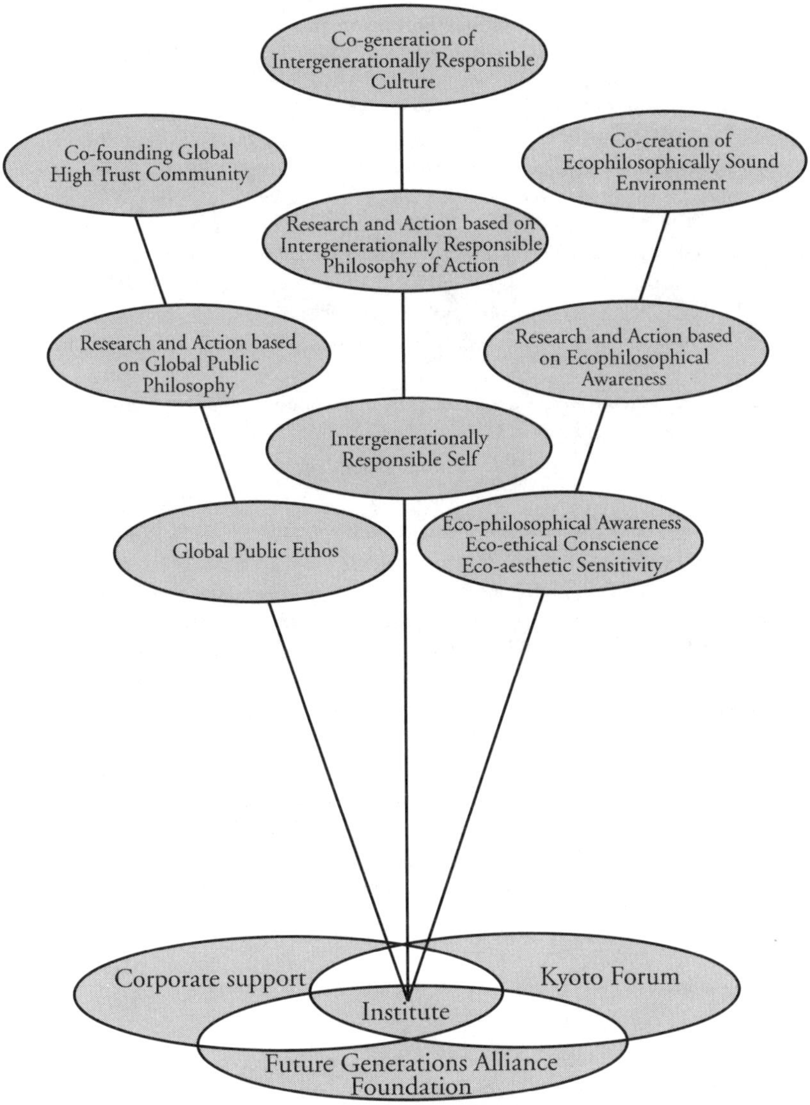

Three axes of Generation: 2001 Project Promotion Chart
Institute for the Integrated Study of Future Generations (1998–2001)

Notes

1. The Future Generations Alliance Foundation has sponsored or co-sponsored what we call International Future Generations Forums in thirty-two different places – Seoul (October 11, 1993), Beijing (November 15-16, 1993), Ho Chi Minh City (December 27-28, 1993), Washington D.C. (January 18 1994), Hong Kong (February 22-23, 1994) Taipei (February 25, 1994), Colombo (March 22, 1994), Cheng Du (April2-3, 1994), Toronto (May 16-17, 1994), Boston (May 19-20, 1994), Sydney (July 16-17, 1994), Kuala Lumpur (August 4-5, 1994), Bangkok (August 29-30, 1994), Beijing (September 15-16, 1994), Gue Yang (September 27-28, 1994), Valetta (September 30-October 1, 1994), Jakarta (October 27-28, 1994) Stellenbosch (March 13-15, 1995), Pretoria (March 17-18, 1995) Islamabad (April 13-15, 1995), Izmir (April 19, 1995), Istanbul (April 18, 1995), Beijing (May 15-17, 1995), Kiev (June 1-3, 1995), Hamilton (June 19-21, 1995) Valetta (September 16-18, 1995), Reykjavik (September 21-22, 1995) Boston (September 27-28, 1995) Toronto (October 26-28, 1996) and Houston (March 7-9, 1996).

2. The Future Generations Alliance Foundation has sponsored Kyoto Forum meetings 54 times at Kyoto International Conference Hall since 1992.

3. Danah Zohar, *The Quantum Self*(New York, William Morrow Quill; London, Harper Collins, 1990).

4. Danah Zohar, and Ian Marshall, *The Quantum Society* (New York, William Morrow Quill; London, Harper Collins, 1994).

5. Incidentally when right after her acceptance of an invitation she told me she was reassured in her way of looking at the Eastern model through reading Fei Xiaoting's *From The Soil*, I suggested that she had better not hastily try to generalise anything concerning what she calls the Eastern model based solely on the book. What he may have pictured as a Chinese model is sure to turn out to be a tiny tip of the iceberg in the very diverse and complex intellectual heritages of the Northeast Asia. She was unable to digest what I meant: It is demonstrated in her most recent book, *Rewriting The Corporate Brain.*

6. Christopher Lasch, *The Culture of Narcissism; American Life in an Age of Diminishing Expectations* (New York, W.W. Norton & Company, 1979) p. 5.

7. Christopher Lasch, *The Minimal Self: Psychic Survival in Troubled Times* (New York, W.W. Norton & Company, 1984) p. 15.

8. Ibid., p. 19.

9. Ibid., p. 57.

10. Ibid., p. 20.

11. Ibid., p. 184.

12. Anthony Giddens, *Modernity and Self Identity: Self and Society in the Late Modern Age* (Cambridge, Polity Press, 1991) pp. 3-4.

13. Ibid., p.145.

14. Ibid., p.146.

15. Ibid., p. 20.

16. Ibid., p.3.
17. Ibid., p.5.
18. Ibid., p.181.
19. Ibid., p.p. 186.
20. Ibid., p. 32.
21. Ibid., p. 20.
22. Ibid., p. 2.
23. Ibid., p. 20.
24. Ibid., p. 53.
25. Ibid., p. 56.
26. John Perry 'The Problem of Personal Identity' in John Perry, ed., *Personal Identity, 3-32* (Berkeley, University of California Press, 1975) p. 12.
27. Linda E. Olds, *Metaphors of Interrelatedness: Towards a Systems Theory of Psychology* (Albany, State University of New York Press, 1992) p. 7.
28. Ibid., p. 19.
29. Ibid., p. 24.
30. Loc. Cit.
31. Ibid., p. 91.
32. Ibid., p. 92.
33. Thomas K. Fitzgerald, *Metaphors of Identity: A Culture Communications Dialogue* (Albany, State University of New York Press, 1993) Page 10.
34. Ibid., p. 11.
35. Ibid., p. 44.
36. Loc. Cit.
37. Ibid., p. 223.
38. Philip Conford Select. & Intro. *The Personal World: Foreword by the Rt Hon. Tony Blair MP* (Edinburgh, Floris Books, 1996) p. 61.
39. John Macmurray, *The Self as Agent* (London, Faber & Faber, 1970) page 38.
40. John Macmurray, *Person in Relation* (London, Faber & Faber, 1970) page 15.
41. Ibid., p. 16.
42. Ibid., p. 24.
43. Henry L. Finch, *Wittgenstein* (Rockport, Massachusetts, Element, 1995).
44. Ibid., p. 86.
45. *Tractatus Logico-philosophicus* translated by D.F. Pears and B. F. McGuinness with an Introduction by Bertrand Russell (London, Routledge & Kegan Paul, 1961) 5.5303
46. Ibid., 5.631.
47. Finch, *Wittgenstein*, pp. 138–139.